BE A MASTER® OF MAXIMUM HEALING

HOW TO LEAD A HEALTHY LIFE WITHOUT LIMITS

Dr. Theodoros Kousouli

A Personal Empowerment Book

Kousouli Enterprises
Los Angeles, CA

Copyright © 2017 by Theodoros Kousouli D.C., CHt.

All rights reserved. No part of this book may be reproduced or utilized in any form or by any means, electronic or mechanical including photocopying, recording, or by any information storage and retrieval system, without permission in writing from the author and publisher, except for the inclusion of brief quotations in a review with proper credit cited.

The BE A MASTER® BOOK SERIES (http://www.BEAMASTER.com) trademarked brand and work is Copyright of Dr. Theodoros Kousouli.

The KOUSOULI® mark and the Kousouli® Method 4R Intervention health system are registered trademarks of Theodoros D. Kousouli D.C., CHt. and Kousouli Enterprises.

Heartfelt gratitude to the following for their contributions:
Editor: Essence Chandler
Co-Editor: Latasha Doyle
Research & data assistance: Arindam Chaudhury, PhD
Cover and internal photography: Matthew A. Cooke
Freehand sketch illustrations: Eric Vasquez
Layout coordinator: Gustavo Martinez

ISBN: 978-0997328561   Softcover
ISBN: 978-0997328578   Epub
ISBN: 978-0997328585   Kindle

Library of Congress Control Number: 2016943713

Kousouli Enterprises
P.O. Box 360494
Los Angeles, CA 90036

Printed in the United States of America

CONTENTS

Forewords xi

Disclaimers xv

Acknowledgements xvii

Chapter 1: My Story 1

Chapter 2: The Curse of Ignorance 11
    2.1 The U.S. Healthcare System 11
    2.2 Why Consider Chiropractic Healthcare Services? 12
    2.3 How does US Healthcare Compare to the Rest of the World? 14
    2.4 Concerns with Conventional Care 21
    2.5 The Pharmaceutical Company-Politician Connection 21
    2.6 What are the Disadvantages of Chiropractic Healthcare Services? 22

Chapter 3: Follow the Money 25
    3.1 Who is Playing Who for the Fool? 25
    3.2 Pharmaceutical Companies - All for Profit Making 26
    3.3 Prescription Drug Enacted Deaths 27
    3.4 The Socio-Political Link that Subserves Pharmaceutical Success 31
    3.5 AMA: Doing all the Wrong Things as the Country's Pioneering Medical
        Organization 33
    3.6 Damage Done by the AMA? 34

Chapter 4: Marginalizing Truth as a Fringe Element 35
    4.1 How has Alternative Medicine Been Treated by the Medical Industry? 35
    4.2 AMA and its Long Standing Discrimination Against Alternative Health
        Practices, Especially Chiropractic 36
    4.3 Is Medical Licensing Killing the Novelty of the Medical Profession? 38
    4.4 Cost of Care – Conventional Medicine Compared to Alternative Medicine . . . 41

Chapter 5: Insider's Club Secrets - Don't Believe the Hype! 47
    5.1 Is Your Fashion Right for you and Your Health? 47
    5.2 Toxic Mouths – Mercury Containing Dental Fillings 48
    5.3 How can Chiropractic Help Plastic Surgery or Dental Patients? 49

    5.4 Getting Vaccinated? Think Twice 50
    5.5 AIDS: Another Perspective 52
    5.6 Psychiatric Disorders and Mass Corruption 54
    5.7 Posture and Back Pain – Does Your Spine Have Personality?........... 55
    5.8 Chiropractic Myths – Busted! 56
    5.9 Usefulness of Chiropractic in Gentle Pregnancy and Baby Care 57
    5.10 Chiropractic Success in Infertility Cases 57
    5.11 Secret of Muscle Testing and Applied Kinesiology (AK).............. 58
    5.12 Chiropractic and Stroke: Propaganda Against the Chiropractor 60
    5.13 Secrets of Those Neck and Back 'Popping' and 'Cracking' Sounds 60
    5.14 Can Someone Get Too Many Adjustments? 61
    5.15 The Great Straight or Mixer Debate 62
    5.16 How Many Chiropractic Techniques are There? Which is Best? 63
    5.17 Subluxation and Neurological Compression Syndrome 63
    5.18 Is There any Specific Technique I Should be Looking for in a Chiropractor?.. 69
    5.19 How Does Your Life Change After Your First Chiropractic Adjustment? 71
    5.20 Toxins Around the House That Cause Dis-ease and Slow Death 74

Chapter 6: The Body's Natural Healing Capacity 81
    6.1 Holistic Medicine - The Mother of All Treatment Regimens 81
    6.2 The Serendipitous Birth of Chiropractic Care....................... 83
    6.3 Ayurveda... 83
    6.4 Aromatherapy 85
    6.5 Color Therapy (Chromotherapy or Color Breathing) 85
    6.6 Moxabustion Therapy.. 86
    6.7 Magnetic Healing 86
    6.8 Cupping Therapy.. 86
    6.9 Applied Kinesiology (AK) 87
    6.10 Acupuncture... 87
    6.11 Yoga.. 88
    6.12 Chi Gong 88
    6.13 Ancient Medicine in a Modern World................................ 89
    6.14 Prescription Drugs Interfere With our Body's Natural Metabolism ... 90
    6.15 Big Pharma Tries to Block Your Access to Healing Herbs and Vitamins 90
    6.16 Prescription Drugs and Bankruptcy................................. 91
    6.17 Why Isn't Natural Healing Preferred Instead of Prescription Drugs

 and Surgical Procedures in the United States?.. 91

Chapter 7: The Kousouli® Method of Healing 93
 7.1 The Mind in the Dis-ease Process... 93
 7.2 Entering Healing - Retracing Your Recovery Pathway......................... 94
 7.3 How do Negative Emotions Create Unhealthy Patterns?..................... 95
 7.4 The 4R Kousouli® Method Intervention System................................. 96
 7.5 The Kousouli® Method and Acidosis 104
 7.6.1 The Kousouli® Method and Detoxification................................... 106
 7.6.2 The Kousouli® Method and Chelation Therapy............................. 108
 7.6.3 The Kousouli® Method and Arthritis 109
 7.6.4 The Kousouli® Method and Depression 109
 7.6.5 The Kousouli® Method and Scar Tissue Removal 109

Chapter 8: The Kousouli® Method Spinal Stretches (KSS™) 111
 8.1 Rejuvenate the Body, Empower the Mind, and Free the Soul.............. 111
 8.2 Ergonomic Do's and Don'ts for the Home and Office 121
 8.3 Sleeping Incorrectly Can Make You Look and Feel Older Than You Are..... 123
 8.4 How Are Your Organs Affected by Bad Posture?............................. 126
 8.5 Staying the Course With Chiropractic Relief and Corrective Care Plans..... 128
 8.6 Corrective Care for Chronic Pain.. 130
 8.7 Stress... 131
 8.8 Healthy Stress-Free Lifestyle Approach 132
 8.9 Biofeedback 132
 8.10 Energy Management.. 133

Chapter 9: Healing of the Emotional Subconscious and Unconscious Mind......135
 9.1 The Chakras 135
 9.2 The Importance of Color 137
 9.3 Epigenetic Changes in Healing 140
 9.4 The Placebo Effect in Healing 141
 9.5 Hypnotherapy 142

Chapter 10: Nutrition/Diet, Rest, and Exercise - Keys to Success 145
 10.1 Nutrition... 147
 10.2 Myths and Truths of Genetic Engineering.................................... 148
 10.3 Know Your Greens 150
 10.4 Take Advantage of Light to Enlighten Your Life............................ 153

    10.5 Should You Avoid the High Protein Diet? 154
    10.6 Healthy Plant and Meat Protein 154
    10.7 Milk Does a Body What? 155
    10.8 Dining at Fast Food Restaurants – Should you Re-consider? 156
    10.9 Carbonated and Diet Sodas – Great Alternative Uses 156
    10.10 Be a Mindful Eater 157
    10.11 Eating According to You 158
    10.12 Antioxidants, Diets, and Degenerative Diseases 159
    10.13 Supplements and Vitamins 163
    10.14 Foods and Supplements That Reduce Inflammation for Faster Healing ... 164
    10.15 Supplements for Sleep 165
    10.16 More Water Please 165
    10.17 Exercise 167

Chapter 11: Natural Ways to Heal 169
    11.1 Time to Take Charge of Your Health 169
    11.2 Don't Forget Your Recommended Daily Vitamins and Minerals 170
    11.3 Your Holistic Reference Guide – Take Control of your Health! 172

Chapter 12: Conclusion 215
    12.1 Setting Yourself Up For Success 216
    12.2 Start Making Changes 217
    12.3 Keep an Open Mind, Use Common Sense and Do Your Own Research 217

About the Author 219

References 221

Be a Master® of Maximum Healing

Life Changing Products · Books · Seminars · Empowerment Audios · Get on the Newsletter!

Connect with Dr. Kousouli, www.DrKousouli.com and on all Social Media Platforms

@DrKousouli #DrKousouli #KousouliMethod

You Will Also Enjoy Dr. Kousouli's Other Published Works Available Now from Major Retailers:

BE A MASTER® OF PSYCHIC ENERGY
Your Key to Truly Mastering Your Personal Power
- Uncover and Amplify Your Hidden Psychic Abilities to Change Your Life!

BE A MASTER® OF SEX ENERGY
Hypnotize Your Partner for Love and Great Sex
- Build a Stronger Bond with Your Lover(s) Using Subconscious Science!

BE A MASTER® OF SUCCESS
Dr.Kousouli's 33 Master Secrets to Achieving Your Dreams
- Solid Success Principles You can Apply Right Now to Empower Your Life!

BE A MASTER® OF SELF IMAGE
Dr.Kousouli's 33 Master Secrets to Living Healthier, Happier and Hotter
- Simple Holistic Tips & Tricks for More Weight Loss and Body Benefit to You!

BE A MASTER® OF SELF LOVE
Dr.Kousouli's 33 Master Secrets to Loving Your Extraordinary Life
- Overcome Bullying, Abuse, Depression and Build Massive Self-Esteem & Self-Love!

BE A MASTER® OF YOUR REALITY
Authentically Manifest Your Desires
- Use the Law of Attraction to Radically Transform Your Life!

If you would like to share your story of how Dr. Kousouli's books, audios or seminars have impacted your life for the better, we would love to hear from you! (Messages are screened by staff and forwarded when appropriate.)

For A Free Gift from Dr. Theo Kousouli visit www.FreeGiftFromDrTheo.com

This book is dedicated to the souls seeking wellness cooperation rather than competition, love instead of fear, affirmation of life instead of diseased self-doubt; and to all who further the promise of hope in humanity.

❖❖❖

"The superior doctor prevents sickness;
The mediocre doctor attends to impending sickness;
The inferior doctor treats actual sickness."

~ Chinese Proverb

Foreword

By Robert Kotler MD, FACS

The challenges today's patients have with respect to getting personalized, competent, and dedicated medical care have become enormous. The decline in the medical profession's healthcare delivery begins with the evolution of MD training in the United States.

American medical education was unsurpassed until medical schools morphed to gigantic 'medical centers,' or better said, medical factories. In some cities like Pittsburgh and Cleveland, university medical centers became the largest industry in the city, replacing manufacturing. Teaching medical students, residents, and fellows became secondary to dispensing medical care to large numbers of people in a profitable industrial production- line manner. The 'full time' MD-employees of such centers were not specifically hired to teach students, interns, residents, and fellows. Many did not necessarily have the temperament, interest, nor talent to teach. Many were hired because they were good at snaring research grant dollars or fundraising, or who - through the medical centers' publicists - would be promoted to the public to generate patient traffic. Thus the nature of faculty changed.

The corps of volunteer teachers, traditionally from the front lines of medical practice, who could impart the 'art' of medical practice, e.g. taking care of patients, not medical customers on a conveyer belt, were no longer valued by the medical centers and thus were no longer visible role models whom the students could emulate.

Today, young MDs, burdened with enormous financial debt, seek a 'job,' usually with a big medical center. Irregular and limited hours, no practice management responsibility, and so forth. Attractive to them because they just work their shift and don't have to think much beyond that. Shifts do work in industrial production, but not in Medicine, where individualized attention and competent decisive action is needed. The 'hand off,' or transfer of care to the patient, once or twice a day is not conducive to the minute-by-minute observation and treatment of disease.

At every level of medical service, one needs to understand the benefits or hazards of proposed treatments. For today, medical centers often first look to economics as a guide to medical services, hiring only the doctors who will do what they are told, rather than what is needed to be done.

Ultimately, every one of us becomes a patient. There is value in the search, sift, and sort for the scarce doctors who understand that, "The secret of the care of the patient, is caring for the patient."

Dr. Theo Kousouli is one of those doctors who has helped awaken mass awareness of the realities of today's healthcare and provides savvy 'insider information' that every patient should value and digest.

Today, you need a shepherd to navigate through the healthcare delivery system. With Dr. Theo Kousouli, you have a great one.

Robert Kotler MD, FACS
Inventor, Teacher, Author & Cosmetic Surgeon

Dr. Kotler is a Beverly Hills super-specialist in rhinoplasty and facial surgical and non-surgical cosmetic surgery. With over 4,500 nasal procedures and 37 years in practice, he has been featured as a guest on Oprah, DR 90210, and written in a plethora of journals, newspaper, and magazine articles. His two category best-seller books 'The Essential Cosmetic Surgery Companion' and 'Secrets of a Beverly Hills Cosmetic Surgeon' are a must have for any patient considering highlighting their natural beauty. For more information visit www.robertkotlermd.com

Foreword

By Peter Lamas

"Though we travel the world over to find the beautiful, we must carry it with us or we find it not."
~ Ralph Waldo Emerson

Every culture has its own definition of beauty. Although the image of beauty is not always perceived the same, the struggle to fit into what society deems beautiful IS. There are millions of face creams, shampoos, lipsticks and other beauty products sitting on the shelves of your beauty counter; all claiming to help make you more beautiful. But at what cost?! Harsh chemicals that can irritate or damage your hair and skin are high prices to pay! Many of today's beauty product ingredients are so toxic that they are considered carcinogenic (cancer-causing).

As a professional in the beauty industry for over 30 years, I have been privileged to work with some of the most beautiful people in highly prestigious salons, and on the most glamorous runways. During these times, I witnessed the damage that harmful chemicals and a toxic environment can have on a person's health. The infamous Jacqueline Kennedy Onassis, a very prominent client of mine, was diagnosed with non-Hodgkin's lymphoma. When doctors publicly stated her hair dye may have contributed to the development of this disease, I was devastated to discover that the very thing I'd applied to Mrs. Onassis' hair, with the intention of enhancing beauty, was the same thing that was slowly affecting her health. Mrs. Onassis' situation is only one of a multitude of cases that motivated me to find better ways to achieve healthier beauty. After years of studying and searching for effective ingredients that could help enhance a person's features *naturally*, I formulated my own line of skincare and hair care products using exotic herbs, potent extracts and certified organic ingredients. With hopes of setting a new standard for my peers in the beauty industry, I prioritized producing products that are paraben-free, petrochemical-free, sulfate-free, and began using natural ingredients as much as possible. It was imperative I stayed true to my belief in the Healthy Living Philosophy.

True healthy living encompasses an entire lifestyle. From what you eat, to the products you use on your hair, to the nail polish you put on your feet; each has an effect on your entire body. I am thrilled to have found a practitioner, Dr. Theodoros Kousouli, who has treated me with miraculous outcomes, and is as committed to sharing the Healthy Living Philosophy as I am.

Dr. Kousouli uses his unique holistic "whole person" approach, called the Kousouli® Method, which takes the nervous system into accountability, which gets to the root of illness to find the proper solution. As a long-time friend and patient of Dr. Kousouli, I am truly grateful to have been touched by his healing hands.

The information you are about to read will give you the knowledge you need to help cleanse your body of toxins and live a healthier, more beautiful existence! I hope it inspires you to take the steps to change your life for the better.

Peter Lamas
Founder of the Peter Lamas brand & author of '*Dying to be Beautiful*'

PETER LAMAS is recognized in the United States and internationally as an innovator in natural and organic beauty. He's often featured in leading beauty and fashion media, and is a favorite among beauty experts and celebrities. PETER LAMAS products can be found in various retail locations worldwide. For more information visit www.peterlamas.com.

DISCLAIMER

In a land where being politically correct seems more 'right' than standing for the 'truth,' or more desired than expressing an honest opinion, it's sad that I must digress and add the following legal disclaimer to remind you, the reader, that *you must think for yourself*.

This book is a collection of experiences and research that form my thoughts, opinions, and conclusions as a board certified Doctor of Chiropractic (D.C.) and Hypnotherapist (CHt); not a Doctor of Medicine (M.D.). The content herein is controversial as it presents an alternate view to the status quo. There are establishments who may disagree with certain contents of this book, and would have preferred that this information never found your eyes. However, this book is not intended for them; it was written for the countless individuals yearning for better health and well-being amongst a society that has lost its way.

The writings in this book are based on my personal research, experience, interpretations and beliefs. Your personal beliefs will affect your ability to review this material, as you will put it through your own filters. I intend to guide you in developing your own ability to use your personal energy in a healthy manner, and this book is a guide for you to grow, but is not by any means the final word on the subject.

I encourage you, the reader, to research, analyze and develop your own opinions on the subject matters discussed. As a holistic health care provider, I express the truth as I have come to know it. It is my duty to aid in the growth of my beloved patients, family, and friends with this love so they too may reach the heights of what their Creator made possible for them to be.

Theodoros Kousouli D.C., CHt.

LEGAL DISCLAIMER

This publication is for informational purposes only. The material presented herein denotes the views of the author as of the date of press. The material and ideas provided herein are believed to be truthful and complete, based on the author's best judgment and experience, formed from the available data at the time of publication. Because of the speed by which conditions and information change, the author reserves the right to amend and update his opinions at any time based upon the new data and circumstances. While every effort has been made to provide complete, accurate, current, and reliable information within this publication, no warranties of any kind are expressed or implied. The publisher, author, and all associated parties involved with this publication assume no responsibility for errors, inaccuracies, oversights or conflicting interpretation of the content herein. The author and publisher do not accept any responsibility for any liabilities resulting from the use of this information. Readers acknowledge that the author is not engaging in rendering guarantees of income or outcome of any kind in connection with using any methods, techniques, or information stated or implied. Any perceived results of the material's use can vary greatly per case and individual circumstance. Mention of any persons or companies in this book does not imply that they endorse this book, its content, or the author, and similarly the author does not endorse them. Any supposed slights of specific establishments, corporations, organizations, peoples, or persons are unintended.

You should consult your own chiropractor, acupuncturist, herbalist, naturopath, hypnotherapist or other holistic doctor(s) in combination with sound medical advice. Readers are cautioned to first consult with proper health professionals about their individual circumstances on any matter relating to their health and personal well-being prior to taking any course of action. The author is not a licensed medical doctor or psychiatrist and the ***information provided in this book should not be construed as personal, medical, or psychiatric advice or instruction.*** All readers or users of the information herein, who fail to consult proper health experts, assume the risk of any and all injuries.

The contents of this book and the information herein have not been evaluated or approved by the Food and Drug Administration for the treatment or cure of any disease, disorder, syndrome, or ailment mentioned herein.

Acknowledgements

"As we express our gratitude, we must never forget that the highest appreciation is not to utter words, but to live by them."
~ John Fitzgerald Kennedy

Foremost, I would like to recognize and applaud the countless pioneers, past and present, in the holistic and natural health care movement who risk everything for the sake of healing mankind. I would need encyclopedias that wrap around the equator to mention every inspiring name, and tell your stories of humanitarianism and self-sacrifice, to which no book can do justice. I am thankful to my parents for giving me life and showing me what a man should be for his community. Much gratitude goes out to my younger siblings Nicholas and Chrisa, whom I love more than they will ever know. My appreciation also to my remarkable friends, Peter Lamas, Oleg Romanoff, Angela Pond, Dr. Halland Chen, Essence Chandler and Elina Loukas who have lent an ear to hear me out, advice to ponder another perspective, and presented emotional support that would make the strongest mountains jealous. To my mentors, Dr. Michael Kostas, Dr. Hari Bhajan Singh Khalsa, Dr. Scott Lewis, and Dr. Scott Brown who continue to serve the masses unconditionally with love and humility; I'm grateful for the priceless value of the healing, wisdom, and technical knowledge you've bestowed upon me. For the proactive lifesaving medical community's miraculous advancements in science, and superb training of surgeons like Dr. Clark Hargrove III, who replaced my failing aortic valve and allowed me more time on this earth to do what I was meant to do – my largest humble *thank you*. Thankful for the peaceful teachings of Dan Millman and inspirational giant Bob Proctor, who continue to remind me to serve compassionately and to always speak deep from within my soul. To my wonderful patients who entrust me with their spirit, which animates their existence, I am grateful and honored to be part of your world. And lastly, but definitely not least, I thank the almighty Creator of all things visible and invisible, small and great, explainable and unexplainable. I stand in awe of your pure magnificence as you lead me through your playground day by day.

This list deserves to be far longer than it reads. If I have forgotten your name in these writings of ink, kindly forgive me, and know that I am in gratitude to you from the depths of my heart.

Chapter 1:
My Story

"Adversity is not bad – it's inconvenient, uncomfortable and sometimes painful – but it's the most powerful catalyst for positive change and growth."
~ Jim Whitt

Incidental Blessings

I grew up in a Greek American Eastern Orthodox home, in a very traditional setting consisting of the now rare 'nuclear' family, with my wonderful two younger siblings, who are fraternal twins. My father, a strict ex-merchant marine for the Greek Navy, became a restaurant owner when he immigrated to the U.S. in the 70's, whereas my mother was a traditional stay-at-home mom who took care of three highly energetic kids. We lived in Deptford NJ, a quiet middle-income suburban town barely on the map. My father always provided the practical good work ethic, food, clothing and roof over our heads. My mother provided the tough love and religious laws needed to live a structured life within society. When we went to Greece every other summer, we would always visit a summer camp for teens to get out of busy Athens. Getting a little mountain air is what mother thought would be best, since it allowed us American children to make some Greek friends at the camp, and enjoy our summer a little more.

Boys will be boys, and we played games of 'Chicken' as we wrestled in the pool to see who would be victorious. That's where two people would hoist a person on their shoulders, and see who could knock the other pair down first. In a round that did not go our way, my partner on my shoulders lost the wrestling match and as he fell, his legs took my head and neck with him. There was a violent turn to the right, and I felt an immediate sharp searing pain deep in my neck and chest. It felt as if someone lodged a dagger deep into me. My left arm felt limp as I gave all my effort to move it, and I was suddenly having difficulty breathing. There were no positions I could move to escape the pain, and even swallowing was a difficult task. My heart and lungs slowed down, labored in their function, as if someone hit the slow motion button. It was frightening to feel that way; so vulnerable, fragile, as if I could die at any moment. At the same time, any head movement felt as if hot liquid tar was running down my neck, back, and chest even at the slightest quiver of motion. After I was pulled out of the pool, I calmed down. My condition stabilized slightly, but could hardly be called 'improved' during our remaining time in Greece, until we headed back to the States to get proper care. My mother would do all she could to comfort me and tell me it will get better, although even she felt helpless to offer thoughts on how. My father, being ex-military, told me to bear the pain, and even teased me about it; telling me to just tough it out like a Spartan. It could've been easy for anyone to give such advice, since I looked perfectly normal on the outside, but I felt like I was dying slowly on the inside. My mother's voice of reason pressured my father to take me to our family medical doctor. My father routinely looked at the overall expenses and costs of a medical visit rather than its benefits, but after weighing the options of not having to hear me whine anymore from the pain, he reluctantly took me to get checked. The medical doctor took my medical history, x-rays, did a small evaluation and then brushed it off as a strain sprain of the neck. I merely received a prescription for painkillers from the M.D., and he told us it would soon go away.

A little ice, pain pills, and rest, then my problems would be a thing of the past, right?! Wrong! Two weeks later I felt the same pain without any relief. On the follow up visit, the doctor suggested an MRI, with the possibility of surgery if nothing else worked. They were not the options that any of us even wanted to entertain, and my father cringed at the $2,000+ costs for an MRI back then, so we waited it out to see if my pain would at least lessen in severity by the next week. When the 'kink' in my neck didn't improve much, I slowly managed to drive myself to a massage therapist for a treatment. With clenched teeth, I held back screams of pain as the masseuse pushed on my neck trying to relieve the knot. Next, I found myself in a physical therapist's office that was also unable to get their treatment in properly; hindered by all the moaning and pain, as I felt worsening irritation with every movement. After many sleepless nights and many tears shed, one day I passed by a local chiropractor's office in town. The office was busy and there were many cars outside, but from the things my father had said about chiropractors I was afraid to even try walking through the door. He felt they were not to be trusted, with their 'pseudo-science' back and neck popping wrestling maneuvers. He said we would just be wasting more money. Of course, as with most things misunderstood, my father spoke about what he heard from rumors and mass media, not from what he'd experienced with a chiropractor for himself. Yet, thoughts of voodoo, chanting, lotions, and potions ran through my mind when I heard the word chiropractor, thanks to my father, and also my own naïve understanding and lack of research at that time.

I figured since nothing else had worked to cure my arm, chest pain, and semi-paralysis, maybe some voodoo magic would bring me relief! I was ready to try anything! Somehow I convinced my father to take me to the chiropractor. I remember that day clearly, as I lied down on the table staring at the light on the ceiling, waiting to be seen next. I was motionless and hopeful, but mostly fearful. When the doctor came into the room he looked nothing like the witchdoctor I had envisioned in my mind, but was a very professional, youthful, energetic gentleman in his early 40's who seemed very confident that he could help my condition with what he saw on my x-rays. I'd went to specialists within the medical field who looked much more knowledgeable and were also much older than this guy, but he was telling me he was sure he could fix me up?! He continued telling me how he was going to help get me back to normal. I relaxed the best I could, but my doubt turned to fear again as he took hold of my head, felt my neck muscles and pushed to feel my bone alignment that he'd viewed on the x-rays. He instructed me to breathe and I found my thoughts wandering as I closed my eyes. "God please don't let him further paralyze or kill me," I remember saying to myself. Others had tried to move my neck and nothing good came out of it other than more pain and moaning.

Then, just as I ended my pleading thoughts, in one fast effortless swoop of his hands and tilt of my neck, I heard an audible noise and a current of power surged into my body. I started to gasp at what felt like ten thousand waterfalls overtaking me in a rush of relief. I had such a moment of peaceful serenity from the sudden release of pain that I was now in tears, laying on my back in this voodoo witchdoctor's room, totally amazed at what had just taken place within a fraction of a second. My arm started to tingle and re-animate as my heart and lungs were going back to full speed and regulating. A great deal of the pain lifted, and I was speechless and in awe of every feeling that I was feeling! My life force was coming back; it was once again flowing through me and being expressed with vitality! Still speechless and with my mouth wide open, I sat up and started moving again. What a miracle! I remember wiping back tears as I asked the doctor, "What happened!? What did you do to me? What did you do differently that no one else could do? What are you? You cured me!! I can't understand why I didn't come here first!" I had so many questions. He said, "I removed the interference (subluxation) from your neck, and your brain was able to reconnect again to your body through your nervous system, allowing the full expression of your life to flow again." With total amazement, wonder, respect and gratitude I uttered the words that began everything I am today: "I want to do this for others, just like you did it for me. I want to free people like you freed me!" Soon after I registered for school to learn the healing manual therapeutic art and science that is called **chiropractic** (Greek "Chiro," meaning "hand"; "Praktikos," meaning "done by/practiced by").

When I told my father how life changing the experience was and that I wanted to now be a chiropractor myself, my father could not understand how much I valued the work I had seen with my own eyes and experienced firsthand. He even feared the shame that my decision to go into chiropractic might bring upon the family. His limited knowledge of what chiropractic healing really was (and is) overrode what this science and art could do, as the public did not recognize it as widely then as it does today.

Fast Forward to Age 28: Valuable Lessons in Health - Round 2

October 5, 2005. I will never forget that day. I remember it vividly, as anyone in my position would. *"You have about eight months to live if we don't get your aortic valve replaced. Your heart will give out and then you'll internally bleed to death."*

It does not sink in - at first - when you're told that you might die soon.

Time speeds up, as if racing you to see if you can catch up.

Life was stressful with relationships, board exams, and mounting bills. After passing out at my desk twice within a week for no reason, I got concerned and started getting full blood work, a physical, EKG's, and echocardiograms to find out why I was blacking out for no reason. Up until then, when I felt any chest pains, I had the typical macho tough guy mentality: Stick it out as long as possible and deny everything, even if it kills you. Thank God common sense prevailed as I worried that I might black out while driving, so I submitted to more tests and follow up visits. It was just like the movies - I would be fully alert and then all of a sudden it was if someone turned the lights out; only this time there was no beautiful vision or premonition seen like in my teens. How ironic that my mother had always told me I was special because I had a big heart; *literally, I did!* The cardiologist called it cardiomegaly: a condition of an enlarged heart caused by the stress of pumping blood out to the body. My aortic valve was malformed since birth with two cusps (bicuspid) instead of the normal three (tricuspid). Instead of pumping blood away from my heart towards my head and neck, where it should have travelled, my aortic valve's two leaflets had become overstressed, and were leaking blood (regurgitating) backwards towards the heart. As a result, I blacked out because of the lack of oxygen and nutrients to my brain.

Terror once again gripped me as my mind remembered the swimming pool accident years earlier. My fears worsened as I inherently wondered if the heart murmur that I was diagnosed with as a child had suddenly suffered enough stress. Now that innocent little heart murmur I was born with, that gave me three heartbeats instead of two, was about to go on permanent strike. I was still too young for my heart to be taking a final lap around the track, when I had not done all the things in life I wanted to do yet. You can say that my "lack of" life started to flash before my eyes, as I began to see my uncertain future, and all of the things I'd said I would get to later. "Later" was suddenly sooner than anyone could have expected - Especially to 28 year old me!

As I stared at the clock wishing the second hand would not move so fast, I began to resent myself for not traveling more, wasting away days, not saying "I love you" more to my family, and not spending enough quality time with friends. As my lack of life became crystal clear, I wasn't happy with what I saw.

I was at my cardiologist's office for my final appointment, before scheduling my surgery, and I argued with the doctor. "But there has to be another way to fix it without having to be on Coumadin for the rest of my life. That's like a death sentence!" I raged on: "It's like rat poison. That stuff is a slow death. In addition, I have to monitor my blood levels every day? No…no way. Not me. How can this be modern medicine? Hasn't something more progressive been invented by now?"

I was upset that the only options I had were a metal valve that needed Coumadin (blood thinners to keep the metal joints of the valve from clotting with possibilities of stroke), or an animal valve that might eventually fail and then need to be replaced with another surgery in the future. I had two not-so-fabulous choices, but was grateful that I still had choices that could keep me alive. I chose the natural cow-bovine valve, knowing it would only be a matter of time that I might be going through the same fate again in the future, when the valve degenerated. However, unlike the metal valve's need for blood thinners, with a natural cow's valve I would at least have a chance at a more normal life.

I was snarling at the doctor for not having better solutions, and felt angry with God that I was in this position. I felt there had to be another way. The cardiologist tried to calm me down, stoically touching my shoulder, but his forehead was wrinkled with worry.

After many exhausting nights of deep thought, I finally made peace with the fact I had to go through with the surgery. Before I knew it, the surgery date came and I was prepped and put into my requisite gown. I kissed my family goodbye and watched them disappear into the waiting room, as my mortality was becoming clearer by the second. *"I might never see them again,"* I thought to myself as I was wheeled down the cold hospital hallway to the operating room for what seemed like forever. I quietly started to pray. In desperation and mounting anger I was beginning to lose my faith, but like most folks facing possible death, I decided to make a deal with God.

Up to this point in my life, I realized that I'd lived too selfishly and egotistically. I took too much for granted - my family, my friends, my time, my purpose - my whole life. What a waste it would be to let this life go without making something more of the gifts and talents I'd been given. I remember praying, *"God If you want me to come back – And yes I do want to come back - I will dedicate my time to serving you through helping others. Let me know you are with me when I ask, and when people ask for help, let me be able to give it to them through your grace. But please, if you want me to open my eyes and come back to continue this life, please make it easier for me so that I don't have to struggle like I used to. God, I want to feel love. I want to know what love is - real Love. If you agree to all this, then I want to live and fulfill the highest purpose you have for me here."* With those last words in my mind, I saw the anesthesiologist's hand place the mask over my face as I dropped into rest. I had finally let go and surrendered myself, as I allowed my soul much needed inner peace.

The surgery was rough; the surgeon had to open me up again a second time after they believed they were done - I bled internally and they raced to re-stabilize me. My folks in the waiting room were very worried, and my mother went into super-prayer mode. The surgeon's second attempt, although completed later than planned, was a success. As I came in and out of consciousness, I could see things coming into focus. I was on machines, unable to breathe for myself, and in a strange bed with tubes everywhere. I saw what looked like a white lab coat come into focus. Then I saw a doctor or technician in front of me doing his routine business. I made noises of distress and finally caught his attention; he turned to me, saw I was awake, flipped a few switches, and I was able to breathe again. I frantically took many deep breaths, and I was out again - back to a deep sleep. It was such a freaky moment. It was what I now remember as my second chance – my rebirth in the Intensive Care Unit.

Post ICU, nurses used me as a human pincushion as they jabbed both my arms for blood every few hours. They missed my highly visible veins several times, to the point that I angrily yelled at the staff for no more blood withdrawals. I would listen to the small talk of nurses as they came into my room during their routine checks, and I could tell who truly had their heart in their work and who was there just to pass the shift. The unappetizing processed meals including wheat, milk, and cheese products given to patients were too unhealthy for recovery or proper body nutrition. The television helped stimulate our brains, but they had it on negative news castings. I would get myself out of the bed and take walks around the hospital since there was no rehab program that encouraged body movement or stretching there. As I passed others' rooms in the hallway and peeked in,

I would witness people in agony, and with a stoic trance of desperation evident in their eyes, and some would stare at me while lying motionless in their hospital beds. I had an eerie feeling that it didn't matter to the staff If I got better or if they kept me there as long as possible; there was no actual push or healthy incentive to get better soon after surgery - just their job to monitor me. I started realizing how hospitals were a big business; with many holding cells of the sick for their profit making. Post-surgery, the majority of my real healing was to happen outside those walls, not within them. As I came to the conclusion that only I could get myself back to 100% from here, I asked to be released as soon as possible and decided to take recovery further into my own hands.

In subsequent visits, the cardiologist told me that full recovery would take 4-6 months. I was impatient and wanted to get on with my new life; there was too much to do. I always knew from my hypnosis and mind-body studies how powerful suggestions were, and that the mind can speed up my recovery. I went into meditation every chance I got while in the hospital and after being released. I must have meditated for 14 hours a day. I would envision cells healthy, my heart repairing itself, and reinforcing tissues around the new valve. I would see myself in the gym, running, in the pool swimming, jumping rope, etc., seeing myself as normal, healthy, and free. I was alive, my heart was beating, and amazed at what I'd just experienced. A cow's valve is now functioning as my own heart valve! I was extremely grateful for my surgeon's knowledge and skill.

Back home, I enjoyed my mom's fine Greek cooking, took my vitamins, supplements, herbs, drank plenty of fluids, watched many funny movies, and only discussed positive things with positive people. I neglected to take my pain meds though; I didn't like how they slowed down my digestive system, giving me horrid constipation and unbearable pain in my abdomen. I focused on the benefits of not taking the pills because I knew from my chiropractic studies how painkillers and other drug neurotoxins can affect the nervous system - prohibiting healing instead of aiding it. With constant meditation, my mind quickly dealt with the pain as if I had taken the painkillers anyway. When I gained the strength to get around, I immediately scheduled a treatment with the same "voodoo" chiropractor who had healed me from semi-paralysis years earlier. The trauma of the operation and bad positioning in the hospital bed had my neck and body misaligned. Now that the surgeon did his amazing job of replacing the valve, it was my job to give my body what it needed to recover the wounds. I knew when the chiropractor properly adjusted my neck it would take away all internal neurological stress, and I would start to heal much quicker, as my body's energy would focus completely on the heart again. Since the neck is the pathway to the rest of the body (especially the chest, heart and lungs), this would open vital pathways and my brain could begin fixing and sending proper nutrients to their respective places for repair without hindrance. The combo of good nutrition, meditation, rest, visualization, self-hypnosis, a loving environment, and chiropractic care allowed me to super heal completely in about 45 days post-surgery! I remember finishing a bench-press set upon returning to the gym in awe and gratitude to God that I was able to get back to life so quickly after such a major surgery. The steps I took post-op helped heal my heart so that I could quickly resume living with purpose!

When I gained some power to move and get around, I immediately scheduled a treatment with the same 'voodoo' chiropractor who had recuperated me from semi-paralysis years earlier. The trauma of the operation and bad positioning in the hospital bed had my neck and body misaligned. Now that the surgeon did his amazing job of replacing the valve, it was my job to give my body what it needed to recover the wounds. I knew when the chiropractor properly adjusted my neck it would take away all internal neurological stress, and I would start to heal much quicker as my body's energy would focus completely on the heart. Since the neck is the pathway to the rest of the body (especially the chest, heart and lungs) this would open pathways and my brain could begin fixing and sending proper nutrients to their respective places for repair without hindrance. The combo of good nutrition, meditation, visualization, a loving environment and chiropractic care allowed me to super heal completely in about 45 days post-surgery! I remember finishing a bench-press set upon returning to the gym in awe and gratitude to God that I was able to get back to life so quickly after such a major surgery. The steps I took post-op helped heal my heart so that I could resume 'living' with purpose!

My personal experiences, clinical successes and research in various Eastern healing arts, has led me to the development of my method of healing, the Kousouli® Method, which I've taught to help thousands of patients achieve phenomenal results in my private practice, and now I'm sharing with you and millions of people all over the world.

As the gold standard, both alternative and complementary medicine have been utilized since the time of Hippocrates; who believed that the body ought to be treated as a whole and not just a sequence of parts. The use of herbs was the tool of the old school and 'original' medicine man. When industry started to standardize healing, there was a sad turn of events. The age-old application of what was inexpensive and provided results; herbs, rituals, prayer, and other natural healing therapies, was shoved into the territory of voodoo witchcraft and religious superstition. However, in the past 25 years, alternative medicine has seen a revival due to overwhelming personal patient testimonies and a fight for saving what really works.

There continues to be a noteworthy debate about the proper blend of private and public funding of health care, and who among the public or private providers deserves to receive the people's hard earned money. Patients often get overwhelmed when searching for health in an intimidating system of hospitals, medical facilities, HMOs, PPOs, psychiatrists, surgeons, pharmacists, etc. Should those in preventive and health restoration services get higher reimbursements or should it go to those who profit from monitoring and controlling the diseases that keep people sick?

There are two main points to adequate healthcare, (i) total efficiency, and (ii) its associated cost, which must be fully calculated before proclaiming success. Usually, these arguments split either along ethical lines or corporate stakeholder interests. With over 40 million people in the U.S. without health insurance, why does the insurance company-politician union boldly proclaim that U.S. healthcare is the best in the world?! I will leave you the reader to make this decision after looking at some obvious statistics.

Thank you for allowing me to present you with this vital information. It is my pleasure to help bring clarity to how you or your loved ones can begin to holistically move your life away from pain and discomfort to reach a new level of awareness, and consciousness; possibly even vibrate at a level you never experienced before. You can live your life with more passion and zest. It begins with proper care of your spinal column, our bodies' antennae. It's the direct link of nerve impulses to and from your body, which allows the expression of your life to manifest in this physical plane that we call our world. Enjoy your exploration!

Chapter 2:
The Curse of Ignorance

"Health is a state of complete physical, mental and social well-being, and not merely the absence of disease or infirmity."
~ World Health Organization, 1948

The goal of this book is to set the main issues of health controversy before you clearly, alongside the credible advantages of a chiropractic regimen. In turn, I will provide a framework for you and your family that will assist with maintaining proper daily health, and a strong foundation to ensure a longer, happier, and more productive life. Moreover, since the central theme is to spread knowledge so that we are capable of making more informed healthcare related decisions, this whole book is delivered in an educational format, with understandably simple (yet objective) terms. My comments and assertions in this book are not only for my beloved patients, but also directed to those who sincerely care and practice their wellness craft/modality as a calling to service, and not as a burden or just a means of making money.

2.1 The U.S. Healthcare System

"I don't need to see a chiropractor, I feel great." That's one of the most dangerous statements anyone with a spine could make. When I hear someone say this, it tells me about the lack of proper health education in this country. It shows the total negligence of our educational system and the failure of all 'health' programs in America, from kindergarten through college, to properly educate its citizens about the true master control system of the body - the nervous system. The individual making the above statement has ignorantly or fearfully focused on the superficial, without giving due notice to the core workings of body structure. Just as a cavity may lead to a root canal or high blood pressure to a heart attack, not understanding our spinal health as a society will keep us focused on symptoms rather than the cause of our dis-ease.

So many dynamics affect healthcare costs, amongst which 'toxic lifestyles' tops the list. Toxic lifestyles include the lack of awareness of healthy habits, work-related stress, lack of exercise, and insufficient intake of required vitamins/minerals through whole foods. The only way of stopping this downward spiral of health in a world looking for 'symptom relief," especially in America, and amongst a rapidly aging population, will require understanding and using the natural healing mechanism that is encrypted within your body by your Creator.

The health care system in the United States is a conglomerate of private and public sector providers. Most of the primary care physicians in the U.S. are in the private, for-profit sector, and belong to group practices. For-profit ownership is the most prevalent form of ownership in the hospital industry, and the majority of nursing homes are organized on a for-profit basis. Between out-of-pocket payments, individual health insurance coverage, employment-based health insurance, and government financing, people are able to finance the care of their health somewhat affordably. The U.S. has a multi-payer system for reimbursement of health care providers, and includes third-party payers, such as federal and state government, as well as private health insurance companies.

With so much money to be made in the healthcare system, many people are wondering if they are really getting the care they need. This is why chiropractic care can be such a benefit to the masses.

2.2 Why Consider Chiropractic Healthcare Services?

There are several reasons to choose chiropractic healthcare services for your wellness and healing regimen. Consider:

- The overall ineffectiveness of current medical treatment for chronic health conditions and proper maintenance of health.
- The unacceptable status quo within physician-patient relationships.
- Insurance companies with too much 3rd party control.
- The increased requirement of individualized personal care, and the need for patient responsibility; teaching awareness of their participation.
- The non-invasive mechanism of chiropractic treatment without concordant side effects.
- Long-term holistic care and peace of mind, with a focus on preventive care.
- Realizing chiropractic regimens are improving health by observation and improvement of your overall lifestyle, which is hardly existent in current treatment modules.
- Expenses associated with conventional treatments are currently too high.
- Chiropractic holds the highest percentage of satisfaction of healthcare outlets by consumers.

- Safer and less expensive for many common ailments, compared to lengthy traditional allopathic primary care maintenance.

Now that chiropractic healthcare services are being utilized at an increasing rate, even by the elderly, and 38.3% of adults in the United States are utilizing alternative medicine (according to the National Health Interview Survey in 2007), it is becoming common to combine conventional medication and alternative medicine. The synchronization of conventional and alternative healing methods are becoming the norm under this new Health Care Bill (the Affordable Care Act) and integrated medicine is playing more centralized role in overall health care affairs within the United States.

In a Dutch study comparing the improvements and sustainability of those improvements obtained from chiropractic and physical therapies for back and neck complaints, it was openly observed that remission of symptoms and longevity of such remissions are significantly better with chiropractic care; both in the short term and the long run. Similar conclusions were made when effects of chiropractic care between 1930 and 1981 were analyzed. Additionally, this later study also showed that the quantum of patient satisfaction with the positive outcomes also was higher for chiropractic care. In fact, a retrospective study analysis conducted during the early 1990s encompassing 395,641 patients clearly showed the huge difference in healthcare costs between medical and chiropractic approaches. This served as a revelation for many insurance companies who would not pay for chiropractic care until that point.

The choice of a healthcare modality also dictates the burden of cost associated with a particular disease. In a retrospective study conducted in Australia covering 1,996 cases of work-related mechanical lower back pain, the number of compensation days off for the chiropractic patients (6.26 days) were four-fold less than medical patients (25.56 days). More importantly, the average cost of payment for medical management ($1569) was also four times higher than chiropractic management ($392). In another study, the number of compensated days off for medical care management was ten folds higher than for patients with chiropractic management.

Cost is always one of the prime considerations before patients decide on a management modality or a treatment regimen. Way back in 1991, the State of Virginia's Corporation Commission's Bureau of Insurance reported that chiropractic practitioners helped patients afford the lowest median cost per visit for different management strategies and treatment regimens.

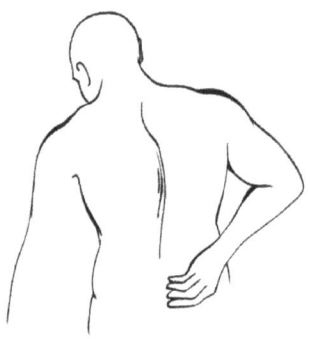

The other major concern in embracing a new treatment regimen is the safety of the procedure, or protocol. A 50 year review of chiropractic management showed a mere 103 cases of complications (which is approximately the number seen with medical management per month). A study conducted by the Ontario Ministry of Health in 1993 categorically showed that chiropractic management is in fact much safer than medical management of low-back pain. This amounts to a complication rate of only 1 in 500,000 treatments!

The intent to increase effective chiropractic management is prevailing among the masses for over two decades now. In 1990 itself, 388 million Americans paid visit to medical physicians, and 425 million Americans rested their faith with chiropractors. This was a study published in *The New England Journal of Medicine*, so the medical physicians cannot scream about facts being distorted or presented wrong! A national survey conducted by the Gallup Organization suggested that the success rate with chiropractic management is a mind boggling 90%! Yet, two decades after such a revelation and chiropractic management is still majorly maintained as an 'alternative therapy' and barely enjoying the recognition it deserves due to its all-around effectiveness. It is time to realize that chiropractors serve as primary-care providers and gatekeepers to the medical management system. Under all circumstances and in a free world, it should be entirely the patients' choice that should decide whether they are subjected to one treatment, or the other, for dis-ease management protocol.

2.3 How does US Healthcare Compare to the Rest of the World?

Universal or public healthcare is defined as a government regulated healthcare system that ensures that all citizens of the country have access to medical services, which are funded by the tax revenues generated. U.K., Denmark, Finland, France, Germany, Canada, Iceland, Ireland, Israel, Italy, Japan, Luxembourg, Netherlands, and New Zealand are a few countries that champion the public healthcare system. The benefits of a universal healthcare system are (i) free or nominal cost for healthcare for people (everyone covered, without exception), (ii) unemployment or pre-existing conditions do not exclude free treatment options, and (iii) has a reign-in on the pharmaceutical companies preventing them from over charging for prescription medications. The downside of the universal healthcare system are (i) high tax rates and less frequent tax cuts as tax revenue is feeder of the system, (ii) increased wait times, and (iii) decreased options of doctors and treatment options.

Private sector healthcare, on the other hand, is a system where healthcare costs are paid for by private insurances or private funds (in case of no insurance coverage). Employers often provide total or partial insurance coverage, which also means unemployed people do not have insurance coverage unless they have the money to buy insurance. Private healthcare is a profit-oriented industry. America is the only industrialized country in the developed world with a predominant private healthcare system. The benefits are (i) faster treatment, and (ii) wider treatment choices, as would be expected from a money whirling policy. The downside of such a system is more tangible and includes (i) huge number of un-insured citizens and hence lack of access to healthcare benefits (losing a job might translate into losing health care coverage), (ii) pre-existing conditions might exclude one from coverage or will need higher premium, (iii) high and hidden premiums, (iv) pharmaceutical companies plan their move of overcharging for drugs, and (v) given the profit intentions, the insurance buying public ends up paying continuously increasing insurance premiums.

Having fewer patient choices, basic 'quality of care issues' overlooked, and giving pharmaceutical companies increased regulatory control in major health care decisions contributed to the heightened health care crisis. A successful healthcare system will concentrate less on evading costs, and more on delivering valuable care. In order to succeed in significant cost control, both American payers and providers must focus more on new technology and the prevention of disease. The U.S. healthcare system is still very much a work in progress, and there are struggles between two sides: making money and helping people. The two are entirely separate in the American healthcare system.

While there are tons of 'healthcare reforms' that have occurred, such as the Affordable Care Act (commonly referred to as Obama Care), they are only small changes to a broken system – not a reversal. However, some of the positives of these reforms are preventing health insurers from denying children healthcare, banning of lifetime caps on the quantity of insurance someone can get, and tax credits for smaller companies covering 50% of employee premiums.

Below, I will present statistics on the current nature of healthcare in the U.S. and ask you to judge the current situation for yourself, and the vital need for alternatives in the current circumstances.

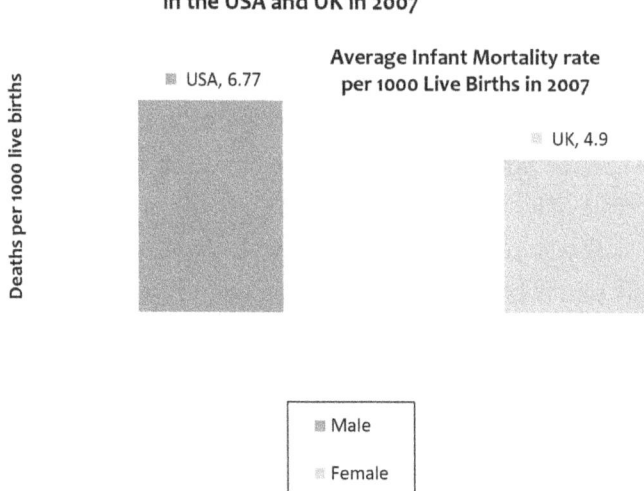

Infant Mortality

The rates of infant mortality are significantly higher in the USA compared to the UK, and is possibly a reflection of the large number of uninsured people in the US healthcare system.

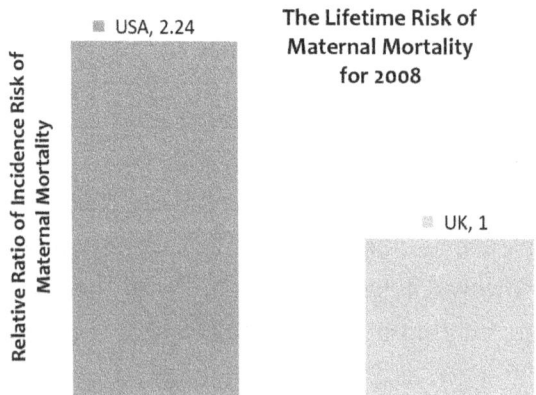

Maternal Mortality

In 2008 women had a higher chance of death during or shortly after pregnancy in the USA. In essence, this means that women in America were 2.24 times more prone to experience maternal mortality than in the UK.

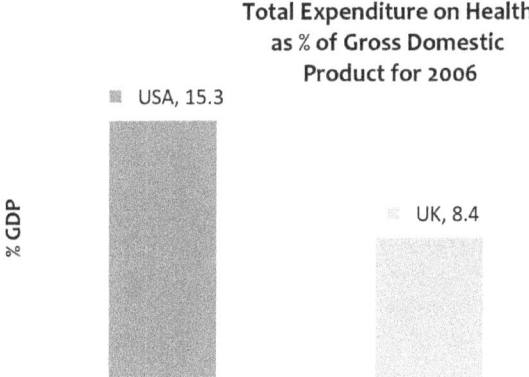

Total Expenditure on Health as a Percentage of GDP

In 2006 the USA's total expenditure on healthcare as a percentage of Gross Domestic Product (GDP) was 15.3% as compared to 8.4% in the UK. This shows that the USA spent a significantly greater amount of GDP on healthcare and would be expected to excel in all quality indicators of the healthcare system. However, as the data collected shows this isn't the case. Therefore spending in the US is not being allocated efficiently or correctly. It can possibly be argued that the extra money must be redirected either to excessive health insurance or drug company profits.

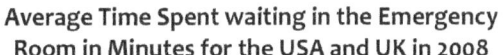
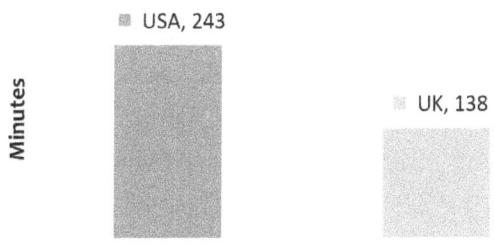

Emergency Room Wait Times

The data for 2008 shows there is a longer average wait time in the emergency room in the USA (243 minutes) than the UK (138 minutes). This finding is counterintuitive since higher healthcare spending would apparently suggest improved resourcefulness of medical facilities. It also contradicts the belief that a greater public healthcare system will lead to an increase in emergency room wait times. The UK has a much larger public healthcare sector, yet it has a comparatively shorter emergency room wait time.

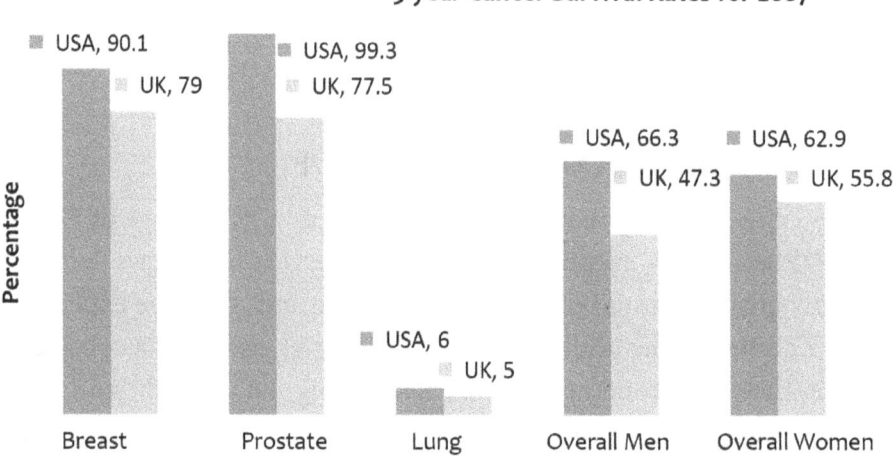

Cancer Survival Rates

It could be concluded that the 5 year cancer survival rate showed a marked difference between USA and UK, with the better outcome in USA, perhaps due to greater and more aggressive screening leading to early detection. Catching the cancer early means a better 5-year survival rate, but doesn't necessarily mean better overall treatment. A possible indicator of this is the lung cancer survival rate, where both the USA and UK have a very similar low survival rate. This is because lung cancer is an extremely aggressive form of cancer, with most patients dying within the first year of diagnosis. In this case early detection makes no difference. A clear picture emerges once we consider the 10 year survival rates of cancer, where the results were very similar between those observed in UK (77.0%) and USA (76.0%).

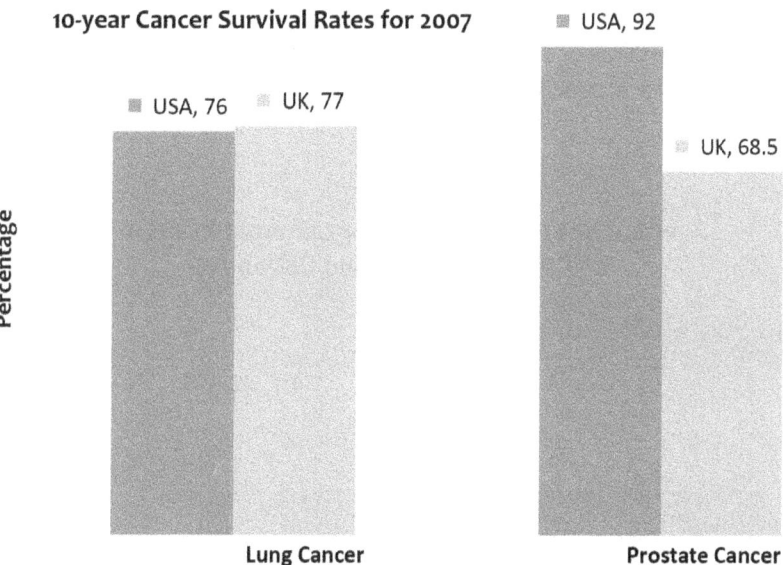

10-year Survival Rates of Cancer

A counter assertion is the significant difference in the 10 year survival rate of prostate cancer in the USA (92.0%) and the UK (68.5%). The later will suggest that early detection has nothing to do with the treatment of prostate cancer; instead the USA appears to have a better capacity to treat prostate cancer than the UK does. Taken together, the above results show that the USA healthcare system detects cancers earlier than the UK systems and is either on par or slightly better than the cancer treatment in the UK.

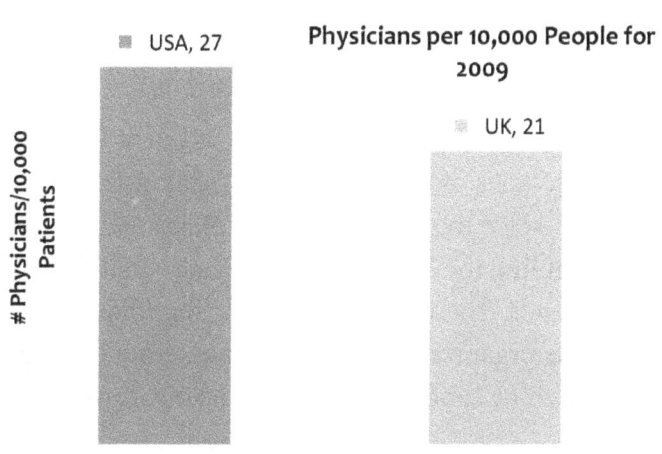

Physicians-Patient Ratio

Since the overall population size of USA is larger than UK, the "physicians per 10,000 people" yardstick provides a more relevant understanding of the overall quality of the healthcare system.

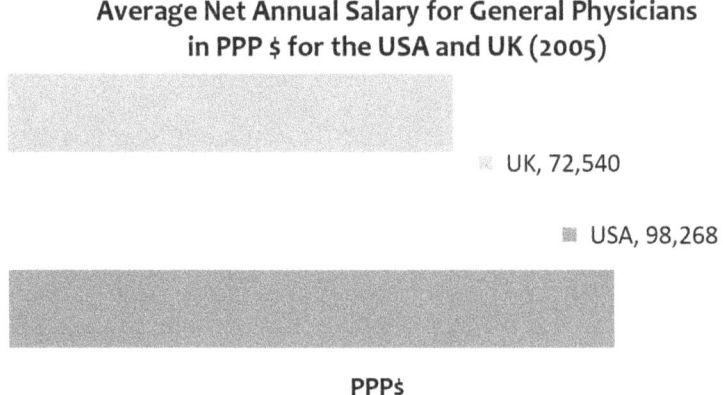

Average Job Salary of Physicians

Data shows that the average net salary (post taxes) in 2005 for a General Physician is higher in the USA ($98,268) than the UK ($72,540). The relatively lower physician wage for the UK is expected, since it is a government-run system, and it is also burdensome for many physicians when faced with the prospect of a greater public healthcare system. With a higher wage paid in the US, it would be expected that the US healthcare system would produce a significantly better healthcare system. However, the results from the data prove this not to be the case. It is plausible that the high wages paid to the physicians contribute to the overall increased healthcare management cost in the USA.

These numbers should tell you something: more money is spent for fewer results! One must ponder that over four decades of scientific study, "walk-a-thons," marathons, and fundraising efforts have yet to solve the cancer crisis. It makes us feel like we're doing a good deed to participate in funding the "push for a cure" cause, but the numbers indicate the money isn't make a difference. These companies and "Big Pharma" keep the majority of the money tangled in the organization's business marketing and operational costs. Before you donate to a research or fundraising cause, make sure you know where your money is going.

2.4 Concerns With Conventional Care

Our healthcare system takes up 17.1% of America's Gross Domestic Product (GDP), which is equal to the total GDP of the United Kingdom - the world's sixth largest economy! A recent study claimed that the U.S. is the highest healthcare spending nation in the world, due to higher prices for prescription drugs, higher doctor salaries, and hospital stays being more expensive, with higher administrative costs. The study reported that the USA spent $7,290 per head on healthcare in 2007, whereas the U.K spent $2,900 per head. The high spending did not equate to better life expectancy or infant mortality rates. America has a lower life expectancy than the U.K. and a higher infant mortality rate (6.4 per 1,000 compared to 5.0 per 1,000 for the UK). The study concluded that private healthcare burdened the consumer with years of premiums, and President Obama's healthcare plan fell short, as it was still very much based on the old private healthcare system. Future presidents and their administrations will undoubtedly have to tackle the fallout of both older, and newly established policies.

And yet, only 40% of physicians refer clients to chiropractic due to weak excuses, like lack of evidence on effectiveness. The general attitude is that chiropractic and alternative care do not have as effective method as conventional care. Conventional care also has 'practicing regulations' that determine cost for chiropractic services, making it financially unattainable without insurance support. But just think for a second, and you will see: all of the aforementioned points apply more to the allopathic (conventional) community! Is it not the reason why they obtain protective insurance for millions of dollars each year? Their methods are not as effective as they wish them to be; they're just not willing to admit it.

2.5 The Pharmaceutical Company-Politician Connection

Some of today's biggest pharmaceutical companies started during the period of 1900-1960. Federal laws came into force very early to distinguish prescription and non-prescription drugs as the pharmaceutical companies redirected their focus on increasing profits. The market for prescription drugs within the U.S was $300 Billion in 2010. In fact, prescription drugs account for 10% of $2.7 Trillion dollars of healthcare spending. The pharmaceutical industry evolved due to systematic political manipulations, and the enactment of industrial modernization in a rapidly changing world economic scenario. During the 1970's, most countries adopted a legislation allowing for strong patents to cover both the specific products and the process of the manufacturer. This totally revolutionized the pharmaceutical industry and started the era of profit-only intentions in every aspect within it. Things came to such a point, that the Hatch-Waxman Act in 1984, also known as the Drug Price Competition and Patent Term Restoration Act, was enacted to at least allow generic drugs into the market. Even this was fraught with problems, as patents were then still allowed for 20 years. By this time a company would come up with yet another drug for marketing and maximizing profits! It's difficult to conceive the reason why we still have nearly 100 marketed drugs for hypertension alone! Now instead of using the information that came about with the completion of the human genome, the pharmaceutical companies are tapping into the field of personalized medicine, which is about to become the next biggest funds puller in the history of The Pharmaceutical Industry. Discussion is already being initiated about implementing a bio-similar legislation, which will allow companies greater leverage in determining the price of various medical treatments and regimens.

2.6 What are the Disadvantages of Chiropractic Healthcare Services?

Conventional medications have huge safety concerns that are only effective for a relatively small portion of treated patients, yet it's ironic that contentions and doubts arise around the safety and efficacy of most types of alternative medicine, from the archaic minded Pharmaceutical companies and physicians that consider them non-scientific. However it's actually surprising that so many conventional medications are still in widespread use given their detriment to society. The "partnerships" of academic medicine, pharmaceutical, and technology companies are really a corporate control of public health. A good example is the "randomized, double-blind, controlled study," the results of which are subject to investigator bias, mainly to benefit the funding agency of the medical modality. For instance: If a new product is investigated by the company that makes it, it works 100% of the time. When the same new product is investigated by a non-aligned third party, it works 50% of the time. Of course, I am not suggesting that you should adopt chiropractic care in the absence of convincing information about safety and efficacy. You will discover plenty of substantial evidence within this book that will ultimately help you to make informed decisions about your healthcare choices.

In fact chiropractors have educational hours in anatomy, and understand the interconnectedness of body functions as much, or more than, their medical counterparts. They apply more emphasis on bringing back natural health from an "inside out" approach; unblocking the inborn health so it can express itself outwards. Traditional medical thinking uses chemicals from the "outside in" philosophy; believing that when the body is diseased, we need to put foreign chemicals into the body to return to full health.

Adam Smith is quoted wisely discerning that: "*Society may subsist, though not in the most comfortable state, without beneficence; but the prevalence of injustice must utterly destroy it. The wise and virtuous man is at all times willing that his own private interest should be sacrificed to the public interest*".

So my question to you is this: Are you ready to try out my method of natural healing, which in essence endorses the rationale of social and natural solidarity, and will lead to opportunity and liberty to make your own correct choices; which in turn will ensure a better overall quality of life?

If you declare YES! Read on…

Chapter 3:
Follow the Money

"No one should approach the temple of science with the soul of a money changer."
~ Thomas Browne

3.1 Who is Playing Who for the Fool?

Let us now discuss the case of Vioxx, the painkiller marketed by Merck to highlight the gross negligence inherent in the FDA system for current drug approval, administration, and regulation of the Big Pharma.

Merck spent millions of dollars promoting Vioxx when it first hit the market as 'the greatest painkiller of all time.' Merck had a plethora of studies supporting the success of Vioxx that highlighted its *apparent* efficacy and safety. What was never shared, however, were the findings in studies that have shown Vioxx can cause cardiovascular disorders. Also, it was later revealed that Merck paid huge sums to doctors and scientists to buy their authorships and publish their studies. Reports started coming in of deaths from heart attacks in patients who were taking Vioxx. Merck readily denied any connection between the two, and the FDA declared that Vioxx was safe until the time when the number of fatal cases left absolutely no doubt, even in the minds of an illiterate person, as to the cause of the death. The count was 60,000 and upwards- more than the number of US Army personnel that died in the Vietnam War! But Vioxx was on the market long enough to allow Merck to generate huge revenues that even paying a few hundred million dollars in class action lawsuits did not put a dent in. Fosamax, Avandia, and Gardasil are three other Merck products which are under the radar right now.

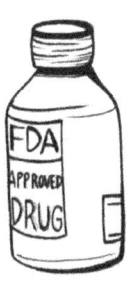

Have you ever seen any of these prescription drugs being advertised on the different television channels? They talk about all the benefits and relative comparisons, and then in the last fifteen or thirty seconds, quickly run through all the side effects while showing paid actors smiling and dancing around merrily as if nothing is wrong. First: the side effects are hardly understood given at the pace in which they are mentioned, and second: in almost all cases, death or fatality is a side effect! I believe it is time we ask ourselves an important question, rather than finding problems in current operation systems: *"Even though we have the independence to choose and make better choices available to us, why do we always fall for something that is harmful to us and mankind, both in the short and long run?"*

3.2 Pharmaceutical Companies - All for Profit Making

Neither normal market dynamics nor economic recession seems to hit the pharmaceutical industry. In 1980, Fortune Magazine considered it the most profitable business, and 35+ years later it still maintains that position. The pertinent question is whether the comprehensive and incredible success of the pharmaceutical industry is built on a foundation of honesty, integrity, and an urge to cure disease, or whether it is based on a model of innovative ways to continually fooling the masses?

The United States government developed a system based on a Canadian style of drug purchasing, which put a cap on sale prices in order to curb the profit levels of pharmaceutical companies - the measures of which were merely a minor setback to the profit-making pharmaceutical market. Health Maintenance Organizations (HMOs) unsuccessfully attempted to redefine the regulation of prescription drug prices by contending for the wide distribution of generic medications. The pharmaceutical companies quickly took uprising biotech companies under their wings to maintain a formidable profit making alliance.

Dr. Herbert Ley, perhaps the only FDA Commissioner with his conscience intact, made a revelation. *"The thing that bugs me is that people think the FDA is protecting them. It isn't. What the FDA is doing and what the public thinks it's doing are as different as night and day."* He was referring to the role the pharmaceutical companies played in the policy decisions and implementation within the FDA. No doubt, the FDA ensured that none of its future Commissioner's would follow the path of honesty that Dr. Ley did.

A serious yet ridiculous reflection on the actual functioning of the FDA came when two national surveys were published in 2011. 82% of the general public sincerely believed that the FDA would take all actions to keep medicines safe and effective. Interestingly, 2/3 of the FDA's employees, who were also part of the survey, had a completely opposite notion!

Some steps that pharmaceutical companies often resort to for maximizing their profits are of course not in the best interest of the patients. These steps include:

1. Use of synthetic chemicals to treat disease condition.
2. Manipulate clinical trial results in order to gain approval for their product.
3. Give away incentives to doctors and FDA officials to gain increased market access for

their product. Pfizer admitted paying 4,500 medical doctors and other medical professionals a sum of $20 million during the later half of 2009 to advertise its products. In the same period, it spent $15.3 million for clinical trials. This is counterintuitive – spending less on the actual 'research' to study safety and efficacy of a drug compared to what is spent on marketing the pharmaceutical products.

4. Gain advertisement mechanisms to communicate with patients by playing on their emotions through television, radio, newspapers, and false Internet marketing; displaying drug information instead of cure information. Buyer beware: many websites for helping people find cures are 'dummy sites' set up by marketing firms hired by pharmaceutical companies.
5. Influence policy makers to get legislation and market dynamics that will suit their product and kill competition.
6. Do everything to get inclusion approval in the American Psychiatric Association's DSM-IV (the standard reference guide for psychiatric disorders), which in turn increases their market share by attracting more prescription amounts.
7. In cases where lawsuits are filed, they'll opt for out-of-court settlements using a fraction of their massive profit margins, thus never having to admit guilt on record.

3.3 Prescription Drug Enacted Deaths

An astonishing statistic for you: the fourth leading cause of mortality in the US is prescription drugs! A great read on this topic is Stephen Fried's book, *Better Pills: Inside the Hazardous World of Legal Drugs*. The story documents how his wife suffered detrimental neurological side effects after consuming a drug called Floxin, usually prescribed in urinary tract infections. Fried candidly outlines the major side effects of prescription drugs, fatality topping the charts, closely followed by manic changes in personality and well-being, and the need for more prescription drugs to take care of the side effects.

Some other interesting statistics of prescription drugs 'racketeering' in the US:

➢ It is a multi-billion dollar industry – the only one that did not feel the pinch of economic recession.
➢ The annual price increase on prescription drugs is higher than the market inflation rate, suggesting that prescription drugs have its own monopolized market dynamics, fully utilizing its 'promised' benefits.
➢ Cost of treatment, or 'prescription drug side-effect,' also runs as a multi-billion dollar industry, with $76-$136 billion annual turnover.
➢ On average, you'll spend $292 to buy the drug and another $306 for taking care of

the adverse effects – a unique hand-in-glove business strategy! A glorious example is sendenafil sulfate, or VIAGRA, marketed by Pfizer. Given its potency and deleterious cross-reactions with other nitroglycerine compounds, the drug caused a lot of fatality and detrimental side effects.

Prozac as a Case Study for FDA's Ineffectiveness

Eli Lilly and Co. launched the psychiatric drug 'Prozac' with huge promises as a 'miracle drug,' and the drug soon became the prescription-of-choice for millions of doctors across the globe. The major adverse effects of the drugs were convulsions, delirium, hallucinations, aggressive behavior, hostile personality traits, self-mutilation, psychosis, suicidal tendencies and the list can go on and on. Interestingly, the FDA received 28,623 such reports and chose NOT to do anything about it! 1,734 deaths were reported after using Prozac, which was topped with another 1,885 suicide attempts – clearly something was wrong. Research shows that clinical trials prior to FDA approval resulted in 27 deaths, yet Prozac made the cut for FDA approval to market the product! Eli Lilly Co. later blamed oversight in failing to report that psychotic disorders were a usual norm in all their pre-clinical and clinical testing. Eli Lilly is one of the most promiscuous funders for the Pharmaceutical Manufacturers Association, and later did everything to sweep all the adverse results under the carpet. Subsequent investigations pointed to the FDA's role in getting the drug approved, although a placebo used during pre-launch testing had a similar effect on depression, just like Prozac. Unfortunately, the drug was not shelved; instead FDA statisticians suggested alternative forms of data analyses that skewed the data to make it look favorable for Prozac. Here's a prime example of medical malpractice at its ruthless best. For Prozac users, the following side effects were reported by The Physician's Desk Reference Family Guide to Prescription Drugs: heart attack, kidney disorders, coma, pneumonia, inability to control bowel movements, hepatitis, bronchitis, duodenal ulcers, gallstones, eye bleeding, deafness, stomach ulcer, impotence, convulsions, spitting and vomiting blood, cataracts, urinary tract disorders, breast cysts, breast pain, pelvic pain, migraine, painful sexual intercourse for women, headache, hair loss. The rational question is: Does Prozac actually cure *anything*? Why is a drug that cures nothing and causes all of this mayhem still on the market?!

An almost similar outcome was seen in case of Celebrex, a non-steroidal anti-inflammatory drug (NSAID). Celebrex caused cardiac diseases with 2.5 folds propensity than other available NSAIDs, and still the FDA gave approval for it to be marketed. The same can be said of the launch of Lipitor to cure hypercholesterolemia, even though scientists at Yale University proved that high cholesterol prolongs life. Then there are other similar issues with drugs like Advair, used to treat asthma. After releasing the inhaler in 2005, it was found that it actually *increased* the severity of a patient's asthma, and resulted in nearly 5,000 deaths from asthma attacks by 2007. Sounds like a great drug, right?

Antibiotics are second on the list of drugs used across the globe. However, it is estimated that wrong dose, duration, and choice of drug are seen in a ridiculously high 40-50% of the all antibiotic prescriptions given out by physicians. The overwhelming amount of information available to consumers on the misuse and abuse of antibiotics in medicine alone is enough to question  what's going wrong and why these chemical issues aren't being fixed. If safety and efficacy are not part of the FDA's considerations for approving a drug for marketing, then what are the actual considerations? The answer has to be MONEY.

What About Statin Drugs and all This Cholesterol Hype?

There is a lot of confusion around cholesterol, and that is not by mistake. Big Pharma loves the profits it's bringing in from people unable to make sense of their cholesterol levels, so don't expect any clarity coming from that industry anytime soon. Statins are powerful anti-inflammatory and immune suppressors with no connection to helping heart patients' health. I believe statin drugs are useless, and only exist to extract money from patients who are buying into the lies. The pharmaceutical companies have taken something normal and made everyone think their cholesterol is way out of control, creating hypochondriacs out of the entire nation.

Cholesterol is needed for every cell structure, to repair intestinal lining, rebuild arteries, and for brain and nerve activity. It's a vital component for making sex hormones, as well. It's part of proper physiological function to have cholesterol in your body; you need it to live. Low-Density Lipoproteins (LDL) are the transporters of cholesterol from the liver to the arteries in the body. Since they deposit cholesterol to the arteries, they got a bad rap and have been termed 'bad cholesterol' while the opposite, High-Density lipoproteins (HDL's) transport unneeded cholesterol from the cells and back to the liver from the blood stream, so they have been termed 'good cholesterol.' What the medical field neglects to mention is that, in reality, *both* are necessary and vital for a healthy life! High LDL cholesterol is less desired and naturally will happen if one consumes too much of the wrong foods. This will overburden the liver's ability to remove cholesterol from the body back to the liver, thus showing high LDL levels in the blood. This is where it gets tricky.

High cholesterol is a symptom, not the actual cause of heart disease. When arteries weaken, the body naturally starts the repair process by increasing cholesterol. This is mostly because collagen production is impaired. Collagen is the building material of blood vessel walls. This can be hindered by low levels of vitamin B6, copper, Lysine, and other necessary nutrition that is unavailable when the body is malnourished. Lack of proper nutrients for building healthy artery walls contributes to over deposition of cholesterol in the arteries. Over time this can lead to clogging blood flow and cause heart attacks or strokes.

Cholesterol is a sterol, 80% of which is made by the body and 20% taken from the diet. So if we take in more or less cholesterol, our body will produce as much needed to overcome any lack, or lower any overproduction. Our bodies are always regulating our HDL and LDL cholesterol levels. When the LDL particles of cholesterol, the 'bad' cholesterol, mix with excess blood sugar and insulin, it causes thickened artery walls and higher blood pressure, and excess fluid retention in the body. It accelerates the oxidation of LDLs, mixed with homogenized fat from dairy products, and then with the introduction of fluoride from our water systems, you get severe damage to the lining of the arteries. Small nicks are formed in the lining of the arteries, causing pockets where cholesterol can form plaque in the blood vessels leading to atherosclerosis and heart disease over time.

So, is taking statin drugs that artificially lower the LDL count the answer? No –it is excessive ingestion of sugar and glycemic foods such as all sugars, starches, and carbohydrates. People need to understand that statin drugs are extremely dangerous when taken - especially long term. Some of the problems associated with use include: muscle-wasting, chronic muscle pain, fibromyalgia, mental disorders, loss of memory, brain fog, and signs of dementia or Alzheimer's. Statins interfere with sex hormone production and the functioning of your endocrine system, thus inhibiting your cholesterol, not helping it.

Will taking these drugs do anything to stop this rollercoaster of madness? No. Will proper dietary consumption of the proper foods, proper patient education, and removal of toxins from an already weakened body help the patient?

Always! Americans get so caught up in their 'cholesterol number' that they do not acknowledge the real issue: their diet. Foods such as cereal fiber and almonds, non-GMO tofu, soy protein, as well as plant sterols could possibly lower total cholesterol, especially LDL levels.

Food manufacturers looking to cut costs and maximize shelf life of their baked goods and packaged products use artificial fake ingredients made in labs and then put them into the foods as 'preservatives' for 'maintaining freshness.' They also remove the fat but skyrocket up the starch and sugar content, causing low nutrient high sugar foods. You can see this trick evident everywhere at your local supermarkets. It says 'No or Low Fat' but when you read the label, the sugar content is through the roof! I recommend that you look into chelation therapy, as well as removing homogenized milk from your diet, and fluoride from your water. Sound nutritional science is the answer here. Patients taking medication for cholesterol regulation should inquire from their functional medicine doctors about prescription niacin of up to 3,000mg/day. There is now hard evidence that high levels of niacin lowers total cholesterol and LDL counts, while lowering triglycerides and raising high-density cholesterol. See Chapter 11 also for holistic solutions to high cholesterol and atherosclerosis.

3.4 The Socio-Political Link that Subserves Pharmaceutical Success

In 1790 an 'act to promote the progress of useful arts' was passed, and began the foundations of what today is infamously known as The Intellectual Property Rights and Patent System. It was a federal government initiative to provide financial rewards for outstanding innovation (mostly for pharmaceutical products). Patents were used to derive profits from products that differed slightly from another patented product by even the thinnest of margins. However, what exactly was patentable wasn't very apparent in this law. As a result, Thomas Jefferson passed a modified version of the patent law, which eventually proved to be a gold mine for the pharmaceutical companies. The only real improvement to the system was its stark contrast to the German model, where medicinal drugs were not even patentable. The new patent procedure ensured that application fees were minimal and allowed for the widespread patenting of conventional medicines. Jefferson's democratization of the new patent procedure also permitted an unfortunate skyrocketing of pharmaceutical industry profit margins. A rapid recovery of investments for pharmaceutical companies encouraged more to jump on the innovation 'opportunity train.' Once aboard this perpetually derailing train away from wellness, more financial resources were put towards advertising and marketing, rather than towards basic research.

This resulted in marketing pharmaceutical products neither thorough nor adequate research, which significantly compromised the quality of products distributed by pharmaceutical companies in their effort to maximize profit and have enough financial reserves for more marketing. Any innovative medication that would actually help control or curb various human disorders and/or diseases rarely cooperated with the co-dependent nature of the profit making paradigm. Instead of utilizing more natural ingredients supplied by our plentiful Earth, fillers were used 'to lower costs without compromising the overall manufacturing output.' The U.S. Navy decided to manufacture its own drugs, a fact which highlights the complete lack of faith in the quality of the products dished out by the pharmaceutical companies. Following the reaction of the U.S. Navy, Massachusetts officials discovered that 37% of all imported drugs were contaminated.

When Dr. Harvey Wiley was appointed the chief chemist at the Bureau of Chemistry in 1883, and the campaign to remove all adulterated products (not just those manufactured abroad) became intense, and things began to change somewhat. Wiley's team found that both food and drugs were routinely diluted: peas, beans, and soap were mixed in with chocolate, chalk, and other things, while clay was added to flour, and even lice carcasses were found in brown sugar. These discoveries helped persuade 10 states to pass laws regulating food and drugs, and set the stage for the 1906 Food and Drug Act.

Still, in February of 1937, a medicine manufactured by Massengill & Company of Tennessee killed 107 people (the majority of whom were children). They died *because* they consumed an unsafe medicine which had been artificially sweetened in order to be more appealing to children. Unfortunately, the company used diethylene glycol in order to create a liquid version of this sweeter sulfa drug which, per the law, they properly included on the bottle's list of ingredients. Unfortunately, neither they, nor their consumers, realized that diethylene glycol was poisonous. The public outcry over the deaths of so many children became increasingly heated when they learned that the unstructured regulatory environment limited prosecution for this crime. 'Misbranding' was the most severe penalty the FDA could pursue as a charge for this crime, which carried a penalty of $26,000; roughly $250 per child.

A well-known case, which further proved the indiscretions in the pharmaceutical industry, was the tetracycline case. Tetracycline prices had increased over time, and in matching amounts among companies, while the manufacturing costs to produce tetracycline had fallen. In every part of the 'fair' bidding process, the numerous manufacturing companies were only within $0.004 of each other's costs - even as prices increased! A rival Italian manufacturer even offered a price less than 1/3rd of the identical U.S. cost. Even though the pharmaceutical firms claimed price-fixing was much too challenging for them to pull off, Congressman Holfield responded, *"It has been suggested that a price-fixing conspiracy in polio vaccine is unlikely because voluntary price reductions were made. Actually, the fact that identical price reductions were made by all companies at the same time tends to prove rather than disprove the existence of a conspiracy."*

This contrasts with the studies of science and technology, which contend that organizations almost universally resist potential paradigm shifts. So Thomas Samuels Kuhn, one of the most influential philosophers of science in the twentieth century, in 1970 that new scientific discoveries were met with disdain and indifference, and occasionally even failing to displace existing dogmas despite their superior explanatory power. Later in 1986 and 1990, Michael L Tushman and Philips Anderson, both astute science administrators, found that firms in multiple industries rejected technological advances even if they offered gains in efficiency. Instead, they found that firms capitalized on the uncertainty that accompanied new developments; to suggest that the technologies would be costly, have dangerous unintended consequences, or fail to meet expectations.

The relationship between the FDA (Food and Drug Administration), AMA (American Medical Association), and the pharmaceutical companies has been very aptly summarized by one of their own, Dr. J.W. Hodge, M.D., as:

"The medical monopoly or medical trust, euphemistically called the American Medical Association, is not merely the meanest monopoly ever organized, but the most arrogant, dangerous and despotic organization which ever managed a free people in this or any other age. Any and all methods of healing the sick by means of safe, simple and natural remedies are sure to be assailed and denounced by the arrogant leaders of the AMA doctors' trust as fakes, frauds and humbugs. Every practitioner of the healing art who does not ally himself with the medical trust is denounced as a 'dangerous quack' and impostor by the predatory trust doctors. Every sanitarian who attempts to restore the sick to a state of health by natural means without resort to the knife or poisonous drugs, disease imparting serums, deadly toxins or vaccines, is at once pounced upon by these medical tyrants and fanatics, bitterly denounced, vilified and persecuted to the fullest extent."

3.5 AMA: Doing all the Wrong Things as the Country's Pioneering Medical Organization

The American Medical Association's (AMA) website claims the mission of the organization to be *"an essential part of the professional life of every physician and an essential force for progress in improving the nation's health."* So the most apparent question raised by the public is: *Why would the AMA ever accept advertising money from the tobacco industry and even put their advertisements within their Journal of the American Medical Association* (JAMA)? How unbelievably counterintuitive to their own mission statement! More money motivated 'ethics' surfacing as it behooves their profit making, possibly? Dr. Gary Null wrote in his book *Death by Medicine,* "Even the AMA was complicit in suppressing results of tobacco research. In 1964, the Surgeon General's report condemned smoking; however the AMA refused to endorse it."

A national estimate showed that only 25-30% of physicians in the USA are members of the AMA. Interestingly, almost half of these registered members are medical students and residents who primarily register to be eligible for member associated discounts. Given the aforementioned logistics, it is rational to question the relevance and validity of AMA. However, AMA exercises immense regulations on Congressional decisions, partly because of its spending prowess.

3.6 Damage Done by the AMA?

Where the AMA has caused the greatest damage to America lies elsewhere though, its long standing canvassing of fee-for-service medicine has ensured that the general public ends up paying a ton for specialist services and sky-high diagnostic tests and procedures. That has also resulted in a shortage of primary care physicians in the country, as everyone wants to align themselves with where the money is. Given their sheer lack of enthusiasm in embracing anything innovative that can potentially jeopardize their status quo, the AMA in fact assumes the role of an obstacle for any patient-oriented development. That is partially the reason for the Kaiser model (where preventive medicine is given more focus in comparison to treatment post-illness) and why it has not been universalized across the country, even though it has been highly successful in preventing illness among patients in places where it has been tried.

The two key areas that the AMA needs to improve are (i) accepting general public option as a way and basis for socialized medicine, which will ensure universal healthcare implementation, and (ii) stop encouraging defensive medicine practices by physicians. According to an article published in the New England Journal of Medicine, a high percentage of diagnostic tests are normally asked for by the physicians out of fear of being sued, and that it might contribute to 1% of GDP spending. Cumulative implementation of both the aforementioned reforms will ensure a patient-relief oriented healthcare system where physicians from different practices (allopathic, chiropractic, etc.) can work in unison in alleviating disease from society (which was thought to be the ultimate goal of medical practice), and at the same time, not balloon up as a huge burden to the economy as it is today. Allowing a person to die by not offering treatment or treatment at a high cost is almost the equivalent of killing a person, or asking a 1-day-old baby to prepare his/her own food.

Chapter 4:
Marginalizing Truth as a Fringe Element

"The longer I live the less confidence I have in drugs and the greater is my confidence in the regulation and administration of diet and regimen."
~ John Redman Coxe

4.1 How has Alternative Medicine Been Treated by the Medical Industry?

The AMA used the Flexner Report of 1915 to inappropriately brand holistic therapists: "The chiropractics, the mechano therapists, and several others...are unconscionable quacks... The public prosecutor and grand jury are the proper agencies for dealing with them." The AMA even prosecuted 1,500 chiropractors within the next three decades with charges of pursuing quackery. Even charities and churches were vilified by the AMA for providing free medical advice and care to the poor. The AMA used its bullying tactics to incorporate legislation that could impose jail terms and hefty fines for offering treatments without getting a patient's financial status.

The very fact that chiropractic science has been branded as alternative medicine is ridiculous at best. Time is proving that what traditional medicine classifies as 'Alternative Medicine' is in reality 'ADVANCED MEDICINE.' The 'Quackwatch' website is run by a retired psychiatrist and additional medical doctors for the promotion of a narrowly defined, yet evidence based, focus on healthcare. It is a glowing example of medicine's dogmatic reaction to patient explorations of health services. But the trends for an end to the exclusivity of traditional medicine were taking shape early on. In the 1930's nurses were not even allowed to take a blood pressure, yet today in many states, nurse practitioners are considered competent to write prescriptions.

The implications of greater involvement by policy makers in the affairs of professions and the changing communication structures are profound. Still, there are increasing influence and arm-twisting activities enforced by policy makers in order to save the pharmaceutical industry and marginalize alternative medicine. In other words: The old pharmaco-medical status quo knows its weaknesses, and it's doing all it can to survive by any and all means necessary- including attacking those who threaten its existence rather than cooperate for the best intentions of patient well-being.

It is this set of occupations (i.e., chiropractic, naturopathy, acupuncture, etc.) that traditional medicine has designated as alternative, "quacks," or snake oil salesmen before the public at large. Marginal professions, such as chiropractic, have been historically "blacklisted" both within the ranks of the medical profession and in public campaigns attempting to eradicate them altogether. These are the professions that are referred to today as "Complementary and Alternative Medicine" or "CAM" disciplines.

For decades, the chiropractic profession has gained increasing prestige, and even dominated the complementary alternative medicine (CAM) practices in the United States, while withstanding the pressures presented against it by traditional medicine. However, there are some authorities who don't prefer to see chiropractic utilized in the widespread treatment of patient ills, despite its popularity, or being the proxy in contrast to conventional medicine modalities.

4.2 AMA and its Long Standing Discrimination Against Alternative Health Practices, Especially Chiropractic

Before its inception in 1847, traditional medicine was considered a novel profession, inclusive of formally trained physicians and personnel who would use herbal remedies and other natural alternatives. The AMA initiated and subsequently implemented licensing methodologies which has resulted in the current persona of medical professionals as scientifically-oriented, white-coat laden, 'super-professional gods.' But every award of AMA's history is outspoken about the fact that it is no more than an organization that goes to any length to uphold its own hollow and self-centered interests.

The AMA, through its bully tactics, was successful in marginalizing healthcare providers like chiropractors, osteopaths and nurse midwives. The reason behind this was the sole aim of AMA to tightly regulate the supply chain of physicians for the nation, and to advance its monopolistic marketing strategies. Ridiculously, the AMA even discriminated against black physicians for as long as can be remembered until they came out and apologized for their insinuating behavior in 2010. Even physicians seemingly had enough of the AMA, and a new parallel association called the Doctors of America has now been established. It will be interesting to see how the latter will pan out its path of redemption.

In the book, *When Healing Becomes A Crime*, author Kenny Ausubel mentions:

> "For over 12 years and with the full knowledge and support of their executive officers, the AMA paid the salaries and expenses for a team of more than a dozen medical doctors, lawyers and support staff for the expressed purpose of conspiring (overtly and covertly) with others in medicine to first contain, and eventually, destroy the profession of chiropractic in the United States and elsewhere."

Circumstantial evidence strongly supports his view. Doctors of Chiropractic Chester Wilk, Michael Pedigo, Patricia Arthur, and James Bryden were all awarded a landmark anti-trust lawsuit verdict against the AMA by the U.S. Court of Appeals 7th circuit. The court ruled that the Sherman Act was "conducting an illegal boycott in restraint of the trade directed at chiropractors generally, and at the four plaintiffs in particular."

The facts would be incomplete without mentioning Dr. Morris Fishbein, the editor of the Journal of the American Medical Association (JAMA) between 1924 and 1949. He was instrumental in a big way in ear marking services and products that would be approved by the AMA, based on huge payoffs he personally received. Dr. Fishbein was uniquely placed to carry this out, as being the editor allowed him to regulate and filter information about products and services that would reach the public. That is also the reason why innovative and holistic cure methods, with their integrity intact but with a small budget, never found their way into JAMA. Fishbein suppressed the information of Dr. Royal Raymond Rife's 'Beam Ray' that was believed to cure cancer, as Richard Gerber (author of *Vibrational Medicine*) mentions, "Sadly, the research was suppressed by medical authorities under the covert direction of Morris Fishbein… who sought to buy into and control the use of the Rife Beam Ray. Fishbein was spurned by Dr. Royal Rife when he attempted to buy into his company. In response, Fishbein decided that if he could not control the therapy, he would suppress it." Rife used resonance to destroy pathogens, and found that each pathogen vibrates at a different frequency. If the resonance of any disease organism is identified correctly, it could be used to break the pathogen apart similar to a singer who shatters a wineglass with the correct tone. Rife named this the (MOR) Mortal Oscillatory Rate. Rife was a genius microscopist who had identified a virus that he believed caused cancer. Using his techniques, he created 400 tumors in a row and then successfully cured the cancer in all 400 experimental animals! So it seems the cure for cancer may have been around as early as 1934, though continued research was suppressed. Albeit, Dr. Fishbein was later convicted and sentenced for racketeering charges, but he did this for 25 years without any interference by the AMA.

Nothing changed six decades later in 1998, when the New York Times reported that Sunbeam Corporation, manufacturer of blood pressure monitors, was paid $9.9 million by the AMA to avoid litigation. The reason was the AMA retracted their involvement in a multi-million-dollar endorsement deal, where they would approve their instruments post-testing testing. Afterwards, it was discovered the deal was all 'only on paper,' since the AMA did not have the infrastructure or any actual strategy to test the devices. AMA, in a press release, mentioned they were "now fully focused on its historic mission to serve America's patients and the quality of American medicine," basically acknowledging that until then all it was involved in money making schemes at the public's expense.

The AMA seems it just does not want to improve. Even today, its activities are directly against its mission statement. It still is accepting huge advertising money from pharmaceutical companies to advertise different drugs in their publication, JAMA. They are also still supporting the use of antidepressants in children, even after all the research convincingly shows that they give rise to unmanageable proportions of violent behavior and suicidal tendencies.

Let us ask ourselves today: Why is it considered malpractice if a chiropractor, acupuncturist, naturopath, or other holistic doctor fails to refer someone to a medical doctor, but a medical doctor can recommend immediate toxic or harmful medical intervention without exploring holistic methods first? There are countless medical doctors who should be referring to and working together with holistic doctors, like chiropractors, for conservative spinal care before the more radical choice of drugging the body or surgically cutting out body parts. Today, a medical practitioner can still get away with charging the patient thousands of dollars for surgery, and can give toxic, ineffective drugs without too much repercussion. In many cases the lives of patients affected by the drugs or unnecessary surgery has been highly intrusive or fatal. Isn't this the ultimate malpractice? Many treatments could have been much less costly and far more effective, had they first given the patient the choice of chiropractic. However, the tables are slowly turning to the medical profession giving its own testimony, explaining why it didn't refer patients to a holistic provider first, and instead performed expensive, unnecessary and out-dated methods.

4.3 Is Medical Licensing Killing the Novelty of the Medical Profession?

"If we want to see medicine change, we have to change how doctors are educated."
~ Bernie Siegel, MD.

The Medical Practices Act, first initiated way back in 1806, allowed legal protection to registered practitioners. In the 19th century, patients had all the powers to choose the kind of healthcare services they wanted to opt for. Additionally, they had a wide variety to choose from: oriental medicine, naturopathy, hydrotherapy, homeopathy, herbalism, midwifery, allopathic or a combination of any they wished. In fact, chiropractic, naturopathy, and osteopathy assumed more importance than allopathic means until the end of the 19th century.

When the AMA came into being, one of its foremost goals was to monopolize and turn healthcare services into a healthcare industry through control of disease rather than cure. The AMA initiated a 'quack hunt,' which was essentially a hunt for competition. New standards were defined by the AMA and a Code of Medical Ethics was put in place. The Code of Medical Ethics prevented physicians to even give free medical services. 42 states followed suit and enacted the revocation provisions, whereby the license of a physician can be revoked if found consulting with a 'non-regular' physician. Interestingly, only 2 out of 42 states had 'incompetence' as a provision of revocation, showing utter ignorance for healthcare standards right from their inception. The only basis for classification of regular and non-regular health practices was the presence or absence of a formal training regimen. But the AMA never made any attempts to formally institutionalize the training regimen for the so-called 'non-regular' physicians, and slowly they turned the 'non-regular' into 'unscientific,' and finally to 'quackery.'

Professor Lori B. Andrews at Chicago-Kent College of Law suitably defines the inadequacies of the classification system adapted by the AMA:

> "Licensing has served to channel the development of healthcare services by granting an exclusive privilege and high status to practitioners relying on a particular approach to healthcare; a disease-oriented intrusive approach rather than a preventive approach... By granting a monopoly to a particular approach to healthcare, the licensing laws may serve to assure an ineffective healthcare system."

Nobel Prize-winner and economist, Dr. Milton Friedman, made an honest assessment of the benefit of such divisive licensure procedure when he observed, "I am persuaded that licensure has reduced both the quantity and quality of medical practice... It has reduced the opportunities for people to become physicians, it has forced the public to pay more for less satisfactory service, and it has retarded technological development... I conclude that licensure should be eliminated as a requirement for the practice of medicine."

Part of the reason for the AMA's desire to safeguard its own base stemmed from the outstanding success of homeopathic physicians in the early part of the 20th century. An analysis showed that homeopaths did seven times more business than the allopaths. On top of that, the following statistics helps you understand why the AMA was worried about other forms of healing taking hold:

(i) Homeopathic physicians lost only 3% of their patients compared to 60% by allopathic physicians during the 1849 cholera.

(ii) During 1878's yellow fever epidemic, homeopaths saved three times more patients than conventional physicians did.

The story of William H. Holcombe further outlines the statements above. Dr. Holcombe had observed in his diary that conventional physicians "were blind men, striking in the dark at the disease or the patient; lucky if they killed the malady of the man." Bloodletting was one of the most prominent treatment methodologies during his time. Once, while visiting a sick child he wanted to perform the procedure, but the parents refused bloodletting, and Dr. Holcombe failed to convince them. He was certain that the kid would not survive the night, yet he returned the following day only to find the child completely cured overnight by homeopathic intervention. Dr. Holcombe mentioned "after having blistered, bled, and drugged my patients for twenty-seven years, I determined to find some more humane mode." As expected, the AMA charged him with violating medical ethics because he blatantly accepted the failure of his professional methods.

Daniel David Palmer (D.D. Palmer), the founder of chiropractic, was the first chiropractor to be jailed for practicing medicine without a license in 1906, after refusing to pay the $350 fine he was given by the Scott County Grand Jury. He was sentenced to 105 days in prison and served for 23 days, before he paid the fine to get out of the prison. Dr. Herbert Ross Reaver, noted as the profession's most jailed chiropractor (12 times), spent a large part of his life behind prison walls. Dr. Reaver was subjected to constant harassment and hostility from the medical establishment. Ironically, each time he was jailed, inmates, guards, and guard supervisors would ask for chiropractic treatments. Each time Dr. Reaver served a jail term, his practice grew. Dr. Charles C. Lemly, an ex-pharmacist and co-owner of a chiropractic sanatorium, holds the infamous record of the maximum number of arrests (66) in relation to chiropractic practice. In fact, more than 15,000 chiropractors were jailed or tried for the so-called 'illegal practice of medicine' before the legalization of chiropractic.

In 1990, the American Chiropractic Association (ACA), the Council on Chiropractic Education (CCE), the Consortium for Chiropractic Research, and the National Chiropractic Mutual Insurance Company, in collaboration with the Foundation for Chiropractic Education and Research (FCER), established a panel of experts under the scope of the RAND Corporation. The panel openly ruled that 94% of spinal manipulations are conducted by chiropractors and it is an appropriate treatment for certain different forms of low-back pain. Still, the AMA was silent.

4.4 Cost of Care – Conventional Medicine Compared to Alternative Medicine

"It's so much less expensive to pay for a lifestyle-change program than it is to pay for bypass surgery, angioplasty, or a lifetime of cholesterol-lowering drugs."
~ Dean Ornish, MD.

Through persuasions of former Senator Harkin and Congressman Bedell, and with the backing of the National Institutes of Health (NIH), Congress allocated four million dollars to create an Office of Alternative Medicine. Other recognized representatives and practitioners met several times in Washington D.C. before recommending the overall design of this office. However, this doesn't account for the amount of money spent by companies and lobbyists to attract more 'sick-care' support from the government. We're talking millions and millions (if not billions) to be made by Big Pharma- $4 million is a drop in the bucket comparatively.

These issues became even more prominent after the 'China Study' was completed in collaboration with Cornell University. Below are some glaring examples why Alternative Medicine should be given due respect.

Atherosclerosis

Hardening of the arteries, atherosclerosis, is conventionally treated with an projected cost of $30 billion in medications and surgical procedures; i.e. balloon angioplasty, coronary artery bypass, femoral artery bypass, amputation, and carotid artery bypass. Alternate therapy of chelation therapy comprises of an intravenous drug mixture of EDTA, and improves the flow of arterial blood; it's an alternative to angioplasty and bypass surgery. The quantity of prescription medications that a patient receives can be significantly reduced with chelation therapy and the need for surgery is usually cut by 50%! Depending on the nature of the condition and its severity, the typical cost for a chelation treatment regimen is about $3,000. Compare that to the $30,000 price tag on a coronary artery bypass, all its side effects, and post-surgical medications.

Many nutrients are often of value in the treatment of angina and congestive heart failure; large amounts of leafy greens that are rich in chlorophyll, such as barley or wheatgrass, should be included in their dietary modifications. Nutritional support includes magnesium, niacin (B3), carnitine, folic acid, potassium, selenium, copper, chromium, grape seed extract, Chinese red yeast rice extract, Vitamins E, C, B6, B12, Coenzyme Q10, Alpha-Lipoic acid, Alpha-Linolenic Acid, and L-Arginine. (If you take prescription blood-thinners, consult your doctor before taking supplemental vitamin E.) Patients should also avoid consuming homogenized cow's milk, animal fats, and fluoridated products.

Additionally, chiropractic treatments of the occiput, cervical 1, and cervical 2 to thoracic 5 spinal levels, has shown positive effects in removing stress and lowering blood pressure, as these areas innervate the associated regions of the heart. It's challenging to estimate, but if all patients were offered alternative therapy, it would likely result in a savings of approximately $9 billion annually.

Heart Attack

Heart attacks, or acute myocardial infarctions, are conventionally treated with fibrinolytics; 'clot bursting' drugs, such as TPA (tissue plasminogen activators), or streptokinase, which cost $2,300 and $280 respectively per dose. Roughly $500 million to $1 billion is spent every year on these conventional heart attack medicines, which could all be saved if doctors switched to magnesium for alternate therapy. Intravenous magnesium costs only about $5 per dose and lessens the fatality rate from acute myocardial infarction, equal to or greater than fibrinolytic drugs do - with fewer side effects. Dietary modification includes green food supplements rich in chlorophyll. For example: barley grass or wheatgrass contains magnesium that is easily assimilated. Nutritional therapy includes vitamin C, vitamin E, (If you take prescription blood-thinners, consult your doctor before taking supplemental vitamin E), vitamins B6 and B12, magnesium, chromium, folic acid, potassium, selenium, copper, grape seed extract, Chinese red yeast rice extract, Alpha-Lipoic acid, Alpha- Linolenic Acid, L-Arginine, Coenzyme Q10.

In addition to other conventional therapies, diet and lifestyle modifications, patients should add chiropractic support and treatment of the occiput, cervical 1, cervical 2 to thoracic 5 spinal levels (particularly levels c1 and thoracic 1 to 3), as these areas innervate the heart, its valves, and coronary arteries.

Peptic Ulcer

An estimated $2 billion is spent treating peptic ulcers conventionally with over-the-counter antacids and medications; i.e. Prilosec, Carafate, Zantac, Pepcid, and Tagamet. In alternate therapy, deglycyrrhizinated licorice root extract (DGL) is one-third the cost, and yet equally effective with fewer side effects than conventional medicines in the healing of peptic ulcers, and preventing recurrences. Additionally, diet modification and chiropractic treatment of the thoracic 5 to thoracic 10 spinal levels, particularly thoracic 7, has shown positive effects in chiropractic therapy, as this area innervates the associated region. Comparatively about $1.33 billion, would be saved utilizing alternative treatments for peptic ulcers.

Enlarged Prostate

The average cost to treat prostatic hypertrophy patients with conventional therapy is an estimated $2 billion annually for surgery, medications, and Proscar treatments (Estimating 400,000 operations at $5,000 each with hospital expenses and surgical fees, and an approximate $1,080,000 for medications when 2,000,000 men receive treatments at $540 per person annually). In alternate therapy, 320 mg/day of Seronoa Repens (saw palmetto berry) is regularly used in Europe to treat an enlarged prostate, and research studies have proven its effectiveness in as quickly as one month's time, with reports of fewer side effects than Proscar treatments. The annual cost of this alternative therapy is an average of $150, which means an estimated savings of $2.78 billion annually; $2 billion saved by reducing conventional surgical procedures, and $780 million can be saved by consuming Seronoa repens as an alternative to Proscar. Additionally, heavy metal detoxification, diet modification, and chiropractic treatment of the lumbar 1 to sacral 1 spinal levels, particularly lumbar 4, has shown positive effects in chiropractic therapy as this area innervates the associated region.

Osteoarthritis (OA) aka Arthritis or (DJD) Degenerative Joint Disease

DJD is a mechanical irritation of the joint, usually due to unbalanced motion and pressure. The joint responds to the imbalance and stressed motion by forming new bone growth (spurs) on the edges of the vertebral bone to build support. Treating joint arthritis, or degenerative joint diseases such as osteoarthritis conventionally, with non-steroidal anti-inflammatory drugs has an estimated annual cost of $2-4 billion. In alternate therapy, a low-cost B-vitamin called niacinamide improves osteoarthritis at least 50% of the time for patients and it's been found to be especially effective against knee osteoarthritis. Although monitoring of liver function tests are recommended occasionally afterwards, side effects are minimal or non-existent. Nutritional therapy should include the removal of starches, sodas, coffee, and acidic foods. Avoidance of allergenic foods and a dark leafy green based alkaline diet are favorable dietary modifications.

A chiropractic checkup and treatment of the spinal levels or joints of the affected area(s) are very helpful in removing pain, increasing function, limiting further DJD, and preventing it in normal joints. Chiropractic management is excellent in maintaining and restoring spinal joint function when in conjunction with exercise, sunlight, hydration, and proper nutrition for healthy bone growth. Utilizing alternative treatments would save patients from fewer complications of conventional medications prescribed, and the cost of the drugs themselves, which would be an estimated savings of at least $1 billion annually.

Ear Infections

The conventional therapy for recurring ear infections costs an estimated $650 million in medications like antibiotics, and surgical tubes ($1500 per procedure), which are placed in the ears of children when infections persist. In alternate therapy, the identification and removal of an individual's allergenic foods from their diet eliminates recurrent ear infections and the necessity for tubes in three-fourths of cases.

Chiropractic care is possibly the best conjunctive therapy when suffering from an ear infection. Chiropractic does not treat ear infections directly, though doctors of chiropractic have noticed a profound effect on ears and hearing when upper spinal structure is improved. The first chiropractic patient, Harvey Lillard, was deaf and a spinal adjustment restored his hearing. Reestablishing normal nerve supply through proper alignment with chiropractic has helped many head, ear, eye, nose and throat issues resolve naturally. Particular levels of focus are the cranial bones - notably frontal, sphenoid, ethmoid, temporal, parietal, and occipital bones, as well as the cervical vertebrae. It is essential that anyone with an ear infection consider a chiropractic spinal checkup along with nutritional support. Alternative treatments reduce the occurrence of ear infections by 75%, which would save at least an estimated $487.5 million annually!

And now, for your reading pleasure, here are a few potential side effects from common antibiotics that we give to our children nationwide for ear infections:

Side effects of antibiotic use may include:

Pain or tenderness at the injection site, including redness, blistering, peeling or loosened skin inside or outside the mouth. Vomiting, nausea, stomach pain, and vaginal discharge or itching with yeast infection of the mouth or vagina. Swollen, black, "hairy" tongue or thrush, white patches in the mouth and throat, difficulty breathing, and closing of the throat, hives, swelling of the face, tongue, lips, and/or throat, with watery or bloody diarrhea that is severe or lasts longer than 3 days, clay-colored stools, dark urine, nosebleed, unusual bruising or bleeding, mucus or blood in the stool, or having lessened or complete inability to urinate, agitation, confusion, unusual thoughts or behavior, chills, fever, body aches, loss of appetite, headache, flu symptoms, seizures, black-out or convulsions, jaundice (yellowing of the eyes or skin), swollen joints, unusual tiredness, insomnia, nervousness, gas or heartburn.

Asthma

Conventional therapy to treat asthma comes with an estimated yearly price tag of about $10 billion dollars when you include hospitalizations, doctors' visits, medications prescribed, and various breathing devices. The identification and removal of an individual's allergenic foods from diet is an alternative approach that in time yields substantial improvement in 75% of asthmatic children and a third of adults. Nutritional supplements like vitamin C, vitamin B6, and magnesium often reduce the incidence and harshness of asthma symptoms, and for some patients chiropractic treatment completely diminishes asthma by restoring healthy nervous system functions that affect the respiratory system. Correcting the spinal misalignments has a very positive effect on the asthma sufferers, as well as relaxes them, thus lowering cortisol levels - according to Dr. Ray Hayek of Australia who conducted trials on the effectiveness of chiropractic treatment for asthma. Therefore, chiropractic therapy, used in conjunction with other alternative therapies or mild conventional medical therapy seems far more prudent and advantageous for the patient's overall wellness. At least $3 billion would be saved per year in terms of fewer doctors' visits, emergency room visits, and hospitalizations if alternative therapy was a priority.

See *Chapter 11: Natural Ways to Heal* for more holistic solutions to dis-ease.

Think about it…

What would happen if chiropractors and sound whole food nutrition were utilized in rehabilitation programs in every hospital across America? Chiropractic is excellent for helping patients post-surgery and can help boost patients' immune systems so that they can recover quickly from illness by taking stress off the body systems. Our healthcare 'crisis' would be a thing of the past if we routinely included holistic therapies, in conjunction to usual medical care; however, that would be opposing big interest groups' primary goal of profit-making, and the hospitals would complain that they are not getting a full house of customers (*read as 'patients'*) at over two thousand dollars (and up) per night.

"I believe that a lot of hospitals will go bankrupt. My hope is that they will be resurrected as healing centers . . . where people go for a week or so and learn how to eat, exercise, and use their minds to access their own healing power. This kind of treatment would be paid for by insurance."
~ Andrew Weil, MD.

If you're ready to avoid the hospital and the 'sick-care' system all together, it's time to look at what we've been told all along, and maybe seek new insights into our daily behaviors.

Chapter 5:
Insider Secrets - Don't Believe the Hype!

"Disease is somatic; the suffering from it, psychic."
~ Martin H. Fischer

This chapter provides fact-based evidence, dispelling some of the common myths and falsehoods associated with current healthcare strategies and treatment protocols.

5.1 Is Your Fashion Right for you and Your Health?

In today's world, your look often defines the audience or groups that you get into and your stature among your peer group. Often, there is a mad rush to obtain whatever new fashion accessories are hitting the stands every week. But it is extremely important to take a step back and carefully choose your accessories, because they are central in defining your comfort levels as far as correct body posture is concerned. Some fashion choices can age you quickly; in the case of wearing the wrong makeup ingredients or the overuse of high heels. Both speed up aging and make you look older beyond your years, while others keep you young and vibrant (wearing organic botanical oils for fragrance instead of lab made chemicals or wearing open colorful colors that accentuate your youthful spirit).

Some cardinal points for consideration while deciding on your accessories: Choose the right shoe! High heels are not recommended, but if you just cannot stay away from them, then you should always carry a flat wedge or low platform pair to change into immediately when you feel any discomfort. Remember, if you are not comfortable while trying on the shoe at the store, then chances are you will never be comfortable while walking in them.

1. It is highly recommended to choose shoes that will support your body weight, structure, and posture. Even though designer spikes might let you make a fashion statement, please keep in mind they will be highly detrimental to your spinal alignment, symmetrical hip movement and foot comfort while walking. Fashion designers usually have one goal in mind: design and sell as many shoes as possible by appealing to popular sex culture. The goal is not health and sometimes, sadly, not even comfort.

2. As a matter of habit, stretch your legs during breaks to ensure that your hamstring muscles are not atrophied (wasting) from not being used. This is especially true for those who do a majority of their work in a sitting position.
3. While choosing apparel, go for the comfort-fitting ones prior to style. If you are obsessed with tight fittings, they should still be pliable to you when performing your daily work. Choose shoes with padded insoles, or add gel inserts with arches when possible.
4. The bag or purse you carry around needs to have a wide and adjustable strap. It is recommended that you carry it across both shoulders, which will ensure equal distribution of weight of the bag across your body, rather than affecting your center of gravity when you carry the bag on either shoulder. If your strap is not big enough, or you dislike carrying it across your body, frequently change sides. Travel light; if you are always carrying that 'stuff' that you can do without - take those items out of your bag right now. If it is an item you do not use daily, consider leaving it at home or in your car.
5. There are several small adjustments to your lifestyle that you can do at every step to decrease the overall stress on your body. One secret for males that saves their lower back is keeping the wallet in the front-pocket so that the pelvis sits smoothly even on the seat, versus wearing it in the rear pockets. Having a one to two inch thick wallet in the back pocket when sitting down on it rocks the pelvis to one side; causing low back and pelvic tension. This is one of the biggest reasons for low back and sciatic pains in males that can easily be remedied.

5.2 Toxic Mouths – Mercury Containing Dental Fillings

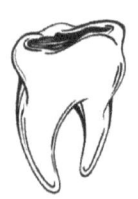

It took Charles Brown at the National Counsel for Consumers for Dental Choice, and the Moms Against Mercury (MAM) nearly a decade of numerous lawsuits to finally force the FDA to acknowledge the fundamental truth. Mercury used in dental cream and fillings is toxic to human beings. The number of people put at risk by the continual refusal of the American Dental Association (ADA) and the FDA to acknowledge this basic fact is countless. But even after all this, the FDA website does not classify mercury as toxic; it merely says that "Dental amalgams contain mercury, which may have neurotoxic effects on the nervous system of developing children and fetuses." In their FAQ section, is the question "Should pregnant women and young children use or avoid amalgam fillings?" Their answer: "The recent advisory panel believed that there was not enough information to answer this question." What!? Not enough information? This is legal bureaucracy at its best, and maybe the FDA is waiting for a nationwide class action lawsuit to classify mercury as toxic in dental fillings.

5.3 How can Chiropractic Help Plastic Surgery or Dental Patients?

A common question that I get from both male and female patients in the 'Hollywood' industry is: "Do you think I should get plastic surgery?" This seems an unlikely question, as I am not a plastic surgeon, though patients will often consult me prior to and after seeing their plastic surgeon. I am their consultant on posture and structural well-being, which dictates how others see and perceive them. Aggressive chiropractic care plans that focus on posture correction can indeed help you look more attractive and confident by improving incorrect posture pattern. Knee, hip, shoulder, neck and head alignment, when reprogrammed, have the ability to make you look more attractive. Patients should understand how their surgery can affect their health globally. The patient that undergoes plastic surgery, such as breast enlargement, should know that their center of gravity will be affected, and the way they walk and carry their body will be evident to onlookers. If their spine is not ready to accept the changes, then their post-surgery experience will be an unpleasant surprise as the pains magnify, and spinal degeneration or deformity increases. The new weight of the implants, even if minimal, will place new stress forces on the body, and the patient eventually expresses a rounding forward of the shoulders, caving in of the chest, limited chest expansion, tight pectorals, tightening of the neck, shoulders and upper back musculature; any or all of which will make them look and feel years older! This is especially true if the patient already suffers from kyphosis, a forward leaning disfigurement of the neck (cervical) or thoracic spine (upper back hump) prior to their surgery. Add to this the fact women love wearing their high heels that radically change the ankle, hip, and foot mechanics, and then multiply this all by each step the patient takes. Now, you have a recipe for disaster. It would be far wiser for anyone looking to alter their body to consult with their chiropractor (i) a few weeks to months *prior to surgery* to evaluate spinal stress, ranges of motion, and ready the body for the coming changes, and (ii) *post-surgery* to monitor changes, ensure proper weight transformation, assess body posture and movement, ranges of motion, gait stability, and overall progress.

For men, it's mostly a question regarding rhinoplasty and dental work. Patients usually ask if the jaw or neck alignment will be affected when the surgeon operates on the nose and how the facial and cranial bones will be changed if the operation is rough. The frontal, parietal, temporal, occipital, sphenoid and ethmoid bone positioning, as well as the cranial nerves, are immensely related to one's well-being where vision, hearing, smell and taste are concerned. It is not uncommon for patients to present with headaches or eye, ear, nose and throat disturbances post-dental or facial surgery caused by the surgical trauma itself or because of the malposition of the head and neck during the procedure. Patients having any dental or facial cosmetic procedures should always consult not only with their plastic surgeon and dentist, but also their chiropractor prior to and after the procedure for a neurological spinal checkup. Chiropractors can help patients be sure everything is healing and functioning both symmetrically and optimally.

Surgical alterations of the body are not a natural process, but in some cases they are needed. The intrusion can cause short-circuiting of our neural pathways to and from other areas of our being. Chiropractic treatment opens the vital healing flow from the brain to the body by removing the stress on the nervous system, thus dramatically cutting down healing time, and creating a win-win situation both for the patient and the plastic surgeon's office when dealing with patient post-surgical complaints.

5.4 Getting Vaccinated? Think Twice

Vaccines have been historically declared as magical and required preventive measures for many infectious diseases. This idea is as baffling as anything can possibly be. There are government mandated national immunization programs across the globe. Schools and colleges in the U.S. forcibly require completed vaccination records for admission. How about all the flu vaccines you take every season without even thinking for a second what you or your children are actually being injected with?

The biggest problem with vaccination is effectiveness, and the lack of appropriate answers from the authorities that strongly proclaim and recommend their usage. Vaccines can actually be fatal and can contribute to disease, which perhaps under normal circumstances would never have occurred.

Strategic public relations advertising campaigns have deeply ingrained that 'vaccinations' and 'immunizations' are the same thing – which is nothing more than a word association game, unsupported by any evidence whatsoever. However, checking any medical dictionary will tell you how different they are. Vaccination can only provide immunization in cases where the child gets exposed to the microorganism causing the disease. Vaccines are essentially exposing people to the microbes/diseases, thus forcing the body to build immunity. The only thing it does is perhaps decreases the time of developing immunity post-infection. Even if you do not vaccinate a child, he will still develop immunity after getting exposed to that microorganism, even though it may take longer. But is it worth taking injections of attenuated microorganisms that will make you sick?

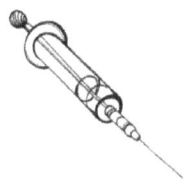

Also note that most vaccines have adjuvants, which may contain formaldehyde - a proven carcinogenic agent. Even formaldehyde and aluminum are used to attenuate the microorganisms during the vaccine manufacturing process. So you are basically getting shots of a carcinogenic liquid and a metal that causes neurotoxicity, which can push you towards catastrophic diseases like Alzheimers. The thimerosal that is added to vaccines to preserve them contains mercury, an element known to cause potent neuro-degeneration. To top it all off, no one has actually proven, with conviction, the exact mechanism of vaccine action.

The author of *Dispelling Vaccination Myths*, Alan Phillips, comments: "natural immunity is a complex phenomenon involving many organs and systems; it cannot be fully replicated by the artificial stimulation of antibody production." The biggest gauntlet that the supporters of mass vaccination/immunization programs play is in the eradication of certain infectious diseases in the USA post-mass vaccination. Even though the European Union did not adapt a similar strategy, these diseases were wiped out also in Europe. So either our vaccination strategy has a 'trans-continental effect' or the assumption that extermination of infectious diseases was due to mass vaccination is profoundly mistaken.

'Sudden Infant Death Syndrome,' (SIDS) is referenced in a 1999 letter to Congress by Viera Scheibner, PhD.:

> "Immunizations, including those practiced on babies, not only did not prevent any infectious diseases; they caused more suffering and more deaths than has any other human activity in the entire history of medical intervention. It will be decades before the mopping-up after of the disasters caused by childhood vaccination will be completed. All vaccinations should cease forthwith, and all victims of their side effects should be appropriately compensated."

Scheibner reviewed over 30,000 pages of published research in medical journals on vaccines, and her findings have been verified by many physicians and research scientists.

"*Public policy regarding vaccines is fundamentally flawed...permeated by conflicts of interest. It is based on poor scientific studies that are too small, too short and too limited,*" says Jane Orient, M.D., Executive Director of the Association of American Physicians and Surgeons.

"Hundreds of published medical studies document vaccine failure and adverse effects; several dozen books have been written expounding on these, and related information condemning vaccines. Yet, amazingly, most pediatricians and parents are completely unaware of these findings," says Alan Phillips, an independent investigator and writer on vaccine risks and alternatives.

We are essentially guinea pigs or lab mice, and whenever a vaccine mishap happens, we get financial compensation to help us keep our mouth shut. In fact, the Federal Government's National Vaccine Injury Compensation Program (NVICP) since 1986 has payed out $1.2 billion. Add to that 10,000 babies dying each year in the U.S. due to Sudden Infant Death Syndrome (SIDS) that is believed to be linked to vaccination. Incidence of diseases like asthma, allergies, and inflammation has steadily increased in 1980 from 6.7 million to 17.3+ million cases currently, making medical professionals believe that it could be a result of the over-vaccination trend.

Robert Mendelsohn, M.D., Professor of Medicine at University of Illinois Medical School, said, "There is a growing suspicion that immunization against relatively harmless childhood diseases (measles, mumps, chicken pox, etc.) may be responsible for the dramatic increase in autoimmune diseases since mass inoculations were introduced." Hence, as parents you should question the need, safety, and efficacy of vaccination for your children. Have you read the toxic ingredient list?

5.5 AIDS: Another Perspective

There are now a plethora of noteworthy scientists, misdiagnosed and 'spontaneously' cured patients, and esteemed expert doctors who believe the global AIDS epidemic is, in fact, a fraudulent massive PR marketing strategy. It's believed that the main objective is to brainwash the public into accepting a disease and its prescribed drug cocktail, in turn spiking pharmaceutical revenues while robbing people of their dignity, health, money, and making them life-long dependents of the AZT drug.

Perhaps this all seems a bit far-fetched? All is still not well within the scientific community on current HIV/AIDS data. Dr. Joe Sonnabend, physician and co-founder of amfAR (The Foundation for AIDS Research), left the organization when his PR firm sent out false claims that said straight men could catch and die from heterosexual AIDS. He then came out to expose the false press releases and fundraising ploys of the organization as told in the documentary film *House of Numbers,* saying, "It was a total fraud and scam… it was a fundraising ploy…It resulted in a Life magazine cover." In order to get more attention and money, at the expense of their ethics and moral fiber, their PR firm changed the magazine cover to read "Now no one is safe from AIDS" which was reworded from the original concept, "The new faces of AIDS." Publication of the cover on Life magazine sent heterosexual men into mass paranoia, panic, and caused chaos worldwide. To this day, misinformation that no one is safe from AIDS still exists. Interestingly enough, there is no definitive test for HIV or AIDS- both the Elisa and Western blot tests continuously misdiagnose patients with false positives. In different countries, patients get different diagnoses depending on the tests being used. Depending on the country and a plethora of error factors, you could be positive in Africa and negative in Norway, or negative in Italy and positive in the United States.

Dr. Leonard Horowitz, an independent researcher and Harvard graduate in public health, wrote an eye-opening book, *Emerging Viruses: AIDS & Ebola: Nature, Accident or Intentional?* He presented the theory of HIV/AIDS as being a man-made product of a Cold War biological/germ warfare program around the late 60's early 70's, and backed this theory with top-notch research. He says that those most probably responsible for the HIV/AIDS outbreak were the very same persons who were offering the treatment.

Many experts agree that the HIV/AIDS epidemic was deliberately created to target African Americans and homosexual men. In Africa, an AIDS diagnosis is an invisible boogeyman, which can cover anything from TB to the common cold depending on misdiagnosis. The unsanitary conditions in many villages undoubtedly cause a variety of diseases, but the media spinners label everything AIDS. Distinguishing between diseases is a difficult task because of the lack of funding, medical testing, and equipment available to Africa's poor inhabitants.

Retrovirology is the branch of virology that studies single-stranded RNA-containing viruses. Retrovirology began around 1908, and grew larger scientific interest in the 50's. On April 23, 1984, Dr. Robert Gallo, an American biomedical researcher, was declared, "the doctor who found the cause of AIDS" by Margaret Heckler, who was the Secretary of the Department of Health and Human Services at that time. Oddly enough, right after this announcement, Dr. Gallo filed for a U.S. patent on an HIV test kit, and Margaret Heckler awarded the AZT drug contract to Burroughs-Wellcome Pharmaceutical Company - before any scientific cross-examining efforts on the claims could be done. The drug now costs about $6,400 a year; dropped from the $10,000 price tag in 1989 because of desperate patient outcry. It is believed by some authorities that this experimental drug, AZT, was shelved at the National Institutes of Health (NIH) since the 1960's, due to its past failure as a cancer cure, and because it was considered too toxic. The makers may have been looking for hosts to retry testing and this could have been the opportunity to cash in. As the lies grew, the money from fear-mongering campaigns and empathetic supporters worldwide started pouring in. Everyone involved seemed to be way over their heads, so they rode out the ride.

As things currently stand, there is no current data that proves the existence of HIV/AIDS as it's marketed, and it is not an absolute science, and misdiagnosis of patients happens constantly. The discussion on HIV/AIDS is incomplete without discussing the dedicated work of Dr. Robert Willner, who authored the book *Deadly Deception*. To prove there were lies being told, he injected himself with the blood of Pedro Tocino, a HIV positive hemophiliac LIVE on Spanish national television in 1993 and it was televised across Europe! He never became HIV positive. He repeated the act many times and even in front of American media outlets such as ABC and NBC, but it was never televised in the United States. Search his name on the internet and see the video for yourself - Incredible!

HIV/AIDS is a multifactorial autoimmune dis-ease, which means that an infected person has developed an antibody to a virus that the 'official' medical community has no known treatment for. However, being HIV positive is not a death sentence as once told to us by those marketing misinformation. Undoubtedly, we need more honest and definitive disclosure about the start, development and cure for this disease or syndrome. However, many within the holistic medical community are very aware that there many non-toxic 'alternative' treatment protocols available to patients; alkalization methods, laser therapy, nutrition and lifestyle counseling, naturopathic and homeopathic medicine, ozonation, blood electrification devices, frequency generators, etc. These have shown promise in patients eliminating the HIV virus from the body and blood. For those patients who have done the research and found their own truth, removing HIV/AIDS from the body may be a possibility.

5.6 Psychiatric Disorders and Mass Corruption

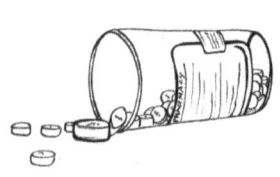

The AMA outlines strict guidelines for terming a condition as a disease (or what constitutes the curing of that disease). There is a prerequisite for the existence of recurrent symptoms, and a mechanistic understanding of the symptoms is also warranted. Mental disease does not satisfy the criteria, yet is still classified as a disease, and reaps huge insurance pay offs for treatment. There are no solid pathological tests to diagnose a mental condition. Some cardinal lapses in the mental health industry will further highlight the rampant situation.

(i) The annual loss from healthcare fraud in the USA is $100 billion. 40% of this is attributed to the mental health industry alone.

(ii)   US Medicaid and Medicare insurance fraud in New York between 1955 and 1977 reveals that psychiatry is always consistently at the top of the ladder.
(iii) Patients are kept in the hospital and primary care facilities until they run out of their insurance coverage.
(iv)   All the aforementioned is the same across the globe, with similar reports in Germany, Australia and Canada.

Mark Schiller, the president of the American Association of Physicians Surgeons, remarked in 2003, "I have frequently seen psychiatrists diagnose patients with a range of psychiatric diagnoses that aren't justified to obtain reimbursements."

The Diagnostic & Statistical Manual of Mental Disorders is the guidelines that psychiatrists go by; voting new mental disorders into existence, then immediately releasing these new 'diseases' to the public. There are absolutely no biological tests to prove there is a chemical imbalance to diagnose someone with a mental disorder like bipolar disorder or depression. Medications given to people are chemically toxic and alter the brain, causing the imbalance. Psychiatrists admit that they can't cure any of their patients, and they also admit that there are no medical tests that can prove a mental illness prior to giving a diagnosis like bipolar disorder – yet they still do. Insurance in the US pays out $69 *billion* in mental health costs yearly. It's simply time to start asking better questions and taking swifter action. Psychiatric drug sales, internationally, have passed $75 billion per year, even with warnings that they can cause suicide, psychosis, heart attacks, violence, and sudden death.

"I want to undermine people's blind faith in the medical establishment in order to restore their faith in themselves, in the remarkable healing powers they possess... We often act as though health comes from the doctor or the drugstore or the hospital. We approach our physicians with a mixture of terror and worship. We view them as experts... rather than as collaborators, supports, and resources
~John Robbins..."

5.7 Posture and Back Pain – Does Your Spine Have Personality?

A published Canadian study (Guimond and Massrieh, 2012) looked at the personality of the individual and how their posture reflected how they looked. In the study, it was stated that:

"...Complications with posture and back pain are projected to become a widespread medical and socio-economic issue across the globe; with more than 70% of the population predicted to be engrossed in the problem. Every year up to 45% of the population between the ages of 35 and 55 years get affected by acute back pain; with 2 to 7% of this cohort exacerbating to chronic back pain. It has been estimated that 1 in 25 people will change his or her work because of lower back pain or will retire due to disability stemming from low back pain… It is estimated that $16 billion is spent annually in the U.S.A. alone for the treatment of musculoskeletal pain. In the United States, 6-8% of the adult population has been found to have back pain at any given time. The prevalence rises after age 25 to a peak in the 55- to 64-year range, with a falling prevalence after age 65…"

Studies like the one above help prove there is a definite need for chiropractic spinal care not just in youth, but also throughout our life and into old age. Interestingly enough, the study also noted that there was a correlation between flat back and sway-back postures in those with shy personalities. On the other hand, a matching relationship was noted between ideal and kyphosis-lordosis posture and extraverted personalities. So your spinal health and posture may just be able to portray parts of your personality by showing your level of confidence.

5.8 Chiropractic Myths – Busted!

1. **Myth: Chiropractic care can slacken your spine** – Fact: What people overlook is that adjustments are rendered in the "locked up" areas that need more movement, which allows the spine to resume proper function. If the spine is locked up in a segment without care, the areas around that motionless segment will form hyper movement to compensate for the lack of motion.
2. **Myth: You can be your own chiropractic provider** – Fact: Chiropractic interventions are performed by very well-informed/trained practitioners, and performing them without proper knowledge would be like trying to fix your laptop computer wiring without having any knowledge of computer circuitry. To adjust a patient properly, and get healing effects, the spine should be in the most possible relaxed anti-weight bearing state; not engaging the insertion and origin of the associated musculature (e.g. lying down and relaxed). Even chiropractors have other chiropractors adjust them, as they cannot self-adjust correctly their own spines.
3. **Myth: Chiropractic care can cure all disease** – Fact: This statement is actually a misnomer. Potentially, chiropractic management is capable of addressing most health issues with much success, but it comes with an addendum of correct application for correct treatment goals. Patients must stick to a regimen of proper nutrition, correct lifestyle, and follow recommended treatment regimens. Chiropractic removes neu-

rological interference allowing the body to do what it was designed to do naturally – stay healthy. If the spinal energy block being removed is associated with the specific symptoms or a specific dis-ease process the patient is afflicted with, then positive results will usually show in time as the adjustments are administered. The body, when unobstructed, cures the dis-ease; the doctor is just the guide.
4. **Myth: Chiropractic care is dangerous, especially for children** – Fact: Numerous studies, as detailed in different chapters in this book, have proven, beyond any reasonable doubt, that chiropractic management is absolutely safe for patients with a complications rate of 1 in 500,000. Even children can be given safe and gentle chiropractic management.

5.9 Usefulness of Chiropractic in Gentle Pregnancy and Baby Care

It has been observed that pregnant women receiving chiropractic care tend to have a shorter labour and comparatively less discomfort than women who did not have such care. In fact, trained chiropractors can help expectant moms to have an easier and hassle-free pregnancy experience. Pregnancy and spinal health are related because the mother's center of gravity is continually shifting because of the growth and movement of the fetus, causing compounded changes in spinal stress. Four factors that cause lower back pain in pregnant women are (I) rapid growth of the fetus, (II) persistent hormonal changes, (III) stress on the pelvic region, and (IV) the lack of connective ligaments to sufficiently withstand all the physiological transformation. Chiropractic care will not only relieve some of the discomfort but also normalize neuronal function, which is subservient to general health maintenance also.

I strongly recommend (I) moderate exercise protocol, (II) appropriate dietary adjustments, (III) regular chiropractic care and (IV) absolute cessation of drinking and smoking habits prior to and through post-pregnancy in order to have a carefree and enjoyable pregnancy experience. This is an important consideration in developing a sound and healthy environment for embryonic development. It is of note that regular dynamic changes, along with physical and emotional stress effects, make pregnancy highly responsive to chiropractic care through the Kousouli® Method.

5.10 Chiropractic Success in Infertility Cases

We know that the nervous system is the master communication system to all the body systems. Chiropractors are nervous system specialists who concentrate their whole career in reducing interference in the nervous system so that your body functions the way it was designed to. It is good to know this is especially true for the reproductive system. Creating new life is one of the miraculous gifts that a woman can experience. Under the direction of the brain and nervous system, the ovaries and uterus receive their commands for their function. Infertility issues can sometimes be solved by realignment of low back and pelvic regions, L2 to L5, rendering proper neuronal supply to the region that will harbor the fetus. This dislocation of energy can originate from many factors of the woman's history prior to trying to conceive (i.e. being rear-ended in a car accident and never seeing a chiropractor for proper recovery of spinal trauma, or suppressed emotional trauma concerning her ability to provide as a mother). If this is the case, then the reproductive system will have a difficult time getting commands from the master computer, the brain. Add to that the high emotional stress to conceive, possible poor diet or lifestyle habits, and we can see slim chances for a successful conception. When a mother- to-be keeps her spine in proper alignment, the nervous system clear of interference, has proper nutritional counseling, exercises correctly and detoxifies her lifestyle, we see higher percentages for success in bringing new life into the world. Using chiropractic spinal corrective procedures, in conjunction with medical procedures such as IVF, can greatly enhance a couple's success at becoming parents.

5.11 Secret of Muscle Testing and Applied Kinesiology (AK)

What is the muscle testing I see chiropractors use in their treatments?

It's beautiful to see a new patient gain proper understanding about what chiropractic does for their lifestyle. The look on their face is like that of a child opening a gift, or an adult finding out they just won the lottery. It's rewarding when knowledge 'clicks.' Applied Kinesiology helps teach patients about how powerful their body can be when allowing proper nerve flow through the body with chiropractic care.

One of the common questions patients ask me when performing an AK muscle strength test is: "Dr. Kousouli, why does my arm get weaker or stronger depending on how I bend my neck, and why can't I hold it up no matter how hard I try?" Then I'll usually get a funny comment about the process looking like magic or wizardry. Some first time patients even insist on trying it again and again in hopes that maybe they were just 'caught off guard' or 'weren't ready' for the test, but after being repeated the result is still the same. Once the patient receives the adjustment, however, the arm strength shows the patient can effortlessly hold their arm in position. However, if no adjustment is delivered, there is neurological stress present and the arm fails.

George J. Goodheart, a chiropractor, discovered Applied Kinesiology (AK) in 1964 and began instructing other chiropractors. He tested muscle groups and found they were weak or strong depending on the stimulus. Kinesiology means the science of movement. He added the term 'applied' because his version was not the workings of standard kinesiology. AK is incorporated now as a chiropractic diagnostic and treatment modality, utilizing manual muscle-strength testing, which provides feedback on how the body is functioning.

Your body is an electromagnetic field of innate (inborn) intelligence. Chinese medicine claims the body is 'all electric' within its meridians, and states that all matter has some type of electromagnetic charge around it. Transference of these electromagnetic charges could affect each of us in a positive or negative way, depending on the nature of the object. The CNS, or central nervous system, quickly responds to any substance that causes blockage of an energy pathway if it recognizes that material to be toxic or harmful. The brain mobilizes the body's defenses which turn up as pain signals, weakness, or allergic reactions. When these unsuitable electrical charges (of food, drink, air, fabrics, solids, liquids, beauty and body products, emotional memory, etc.) come within the body field, there is a conflict, causing repulsion. This repulsion of disharmony creates obstruction of the meridians, or energy channel, a 'shorting' of the circuit. If it is an incompatible charge, the strong indicator muscle will go weak, causing the indicator arm to fall or ratchet down when tested.

Everything is energy vibrating at different speeds. If someone walks into a crowded elevator, everyone feels the energy in that space change. If we add another person in the space who is in a good mood, the energy will be significantly different than if the person is in a bad mood. You can immediately 'feel' the difference in energy shift. You have noticed this also in events where someone so energetic walks in that they are named 'the life of the party,' or in awkward situations where the tension in the room is so thick, you could cut it with a knife. These 'feelings' are being felt by your body's magnetic field (some call it the aura), and the receptors are accommodating to the stimulus around your environment. You will feel stronger or weaker depending on the makeup of the energy you come into contact with.

This phenomenon involves physiological and metaphysical properties at play, and without the above explanation, it can indeed look strange or paranormal when experiencing the test. Applied kinesiology is usually accompanied by static and motion spinal palpation, skin temperature changes, objective and subjective findings, orthopedic and neurological tests, leg length inequality tests, in addition to other diagnostic tools (X-ray, CT and MRI) available to the chiropractor for determining care.

5.12 Chiropractic and Stroke: Propaganda Against the Chiropractor

People against the chiropractic movement have put out fear mongering claims that chiropractic neck adjustments are not safe and might cause stroke within 24 hours of chiropractic manipulation. A Stanford study reported that incidence rate as 1 in 1 million adjustments, which fades in comparison to similar disorders resulting from pharmaceutical drug usage. How many die each year from prescription drugs? Over 100,000! That's about 272 people a day! Also, that's not counting the wrong drug given due to mistakes; that's the number of normal usage of prescribed drugs as directed! What is not understood is that cervical subluxation does not cause strokes - a blood clot does - which would have caused a stroke regardless of the chiropractic manipulation. The clot is there because the person may have a toxic lifestyle, or illness that caused the clot, which is the real issue. If proper health precautions are taken there is no issue. Antagonists of chiropractic claim adjustments can cause a tear in the artery walls of the neck. The correctly trained chiropractor adjusts the neck with a motion limiting excess rotation as to not harm the patient's intervertebral arteries. Strokes can occur also at the beauty parlor which is the case when the client puts their head back in an extended position for a long period of time. Also cab drivers or others who rotate the neck to look back while driving have been known to have strokes. There is no way to know which patients are prone to having a stroke, though it seems the most 'at-risk' patient is female between their 20's to 40's, takes birth control, has high blood pressure, chronic headaches, and usually takes aspirin or blood thinners. So the reality is that strokes can happen anywhere, and to those with compromised circulatory systems, though some 'authorities' have decided to point the finger exclusively at chiropractors. Responding to this published study, Dr. Louis Sportelli, acting as the spokesperson for American Chiropractic Association commented: "I'm glad the Stanford group's intent was to be cautious in bringing alarm to this issue; however, they have done just the opposite."

5.13 Secrets of Those Neck and Back 'Popping' and 'Cracking' Sounds

The sounds by themselves are not a part of the healing nature of the treatment, although they usually accompany the treatments. The joints of the spine are named synovial joints and contain synovial fluid. Synovial fluid lubricates and nourishes the health of the joint so it can maneuver and glide properly. When a chiropractic adjustment (specific high velocity low amplitude thrust) is delivered in treatment, a sound many refer to as a 'pop' or 'crack' may be heard. The sound is actually called a cavitation audible and is the release of gas from the joint capsule. The byproduct gasses - oxygen, nitrogen, and carbon dioxide - are found as small pockets of air bubbles in the tissue surrounding the capsule. Because associated chemical endorphins are released along with the capsule pressure, patients usually feel a light euphoric high. A good analogy would be the release of built up gas in a soda bottle when the cap is opened. Once the pressure is released, the sound doesn't occur any more. Likewise, once the joint is adjusted, the sound does not reoccur. Although the joint may move again, or be 'adjusted,' the sound won't return until more pressure builds inside the capsule from gas accumulation with blood flow after a period of time. Likewise, the phenomenon of a closed soda bottle will not make any sounds if you recap the bottle a second, third, or fourth time; unless you give the gas time to accumulate (24 hours or so). As time passes between patient treatments, (usually more than 24 hours); the joints misalign, capsule pressure is raised, and the sound is heard during an adjustment again.

Furthermore, it is important to disband the idea that there is always 'cracking of bones' or 'popping of joints' when patients receive chiropractic treatment. This wording incorrectly infers that there is breaking or grinding of spinal structures when the complete opposite of that is occurring. Chiropractic-specific spinal application alleviates associated tissue pressures of spinal misalignment, helps return proper mechanical and physiological joint function, and improves local circulation/lymph flow that facilitates the body's healing of the spinal level in question. It is important to note that the sound is not an indication of correct movement; only gas release. There can be a chiropractic adjustment performed and no sounds occur - just as you can remove the soda cap and get no air release.

Only chiropractors are correctly trained to detect, analyze, and remove vertebral subluxations. Therefore, if any other doctors, masseuses, physical therapists, best friends, or your barber/hair dresser tells you they are able to manipulate your spine (especially your neck) to get the cheap thrill of a pop or crack, say: "No thank you!" and see a qualified chiropractor who is trained correctly. Your spine is much too important to risk whiplash or worse!

5.14 Can Someone get too Many Adjustments?

The number of adjustments patients receive varies greatly and is based on the patient's specific condition, situation, and goals. If the condition is new or chronic, the age of the patient, the patient's ability to receive full treatment and whether pain is in multiple sites or confined in one area, all factor in. Chiropractors are experts at finding incorrectly moving joints and adding motion where needed. Chiropractors deliver relief to the problematic spinal areas with quick, gentle, safe, and specific hand and instrument thrusts called **adjustments**. Adjustments correct spinal misalignments and nerve interference called **sub-lux-ation** over time, which in most cases leads to complete alleviation of medical symptoms.

Directing the treatment against the cause (nerve interference) rather than the effects (disease symptoms) helps to completely dismantle the disease process. Here is where chiropractic triumphs over the medical philosophy that we are sick and we need outside intervention, surgery, or drugs to be healthy. By focusing on the cause, or faulty wiring, the connection between brain and organ is reestablished through the nervous system and the body starts to heal again.

If, however, the forces continually applied to a spine are not correct (referred to as gross manipulations) by untrained individuals, the ligaments may start to become too loose; a condition called 'hyper-mobility' where too much movement can occur.

When people forcefully twist or move their head, necks, or spines in a desperate effort to relieve pressure, they whiplash themselves and rip small tears in the surrounding tissues. Scar tissue at the area builds up causing joint stiffness or a condition called 'hypo-mobility' (too little movement) resulting in chronic neck problems. If you are feeling the need to continually 'pop or crack your neck' as laymen state, then that is a sure sign you need to have your spine correctly re-aligned and checked for degeneration by a qualified doctor of chiropractic.

5.15 The Great Straight or Mixer Debate

Early chiropractors were split on how to practice their profession. Some doctors believed in practicing their profession exactly the way it was originally developed by its founder, D.D. Palmer; using only the hands to address the spinal subluxation. These chiropractors considered themselves the originals and on the straight path, thus earning the name 'straights.' Other chiropractors sided with the 'mixers' who believed in using modalities such as ice or heat in conjunction with hand treatment. Today, chiropractic schooling, training, hands on experience, technique, and skill level varies greatly across the world. Within the chiropractic profession there are two main schools of thought primarily represented by the American Chiropractic Association (ACA) founded in 1922, and the International Chiropractic Association (ICA). Both associations have their own agenda, and set standards for care within the chiropractic profession. The ICA is the oldest chiropractic association, founded by B.J Palmer in 1938 in Davenport, Iowa. The ICA guards the "by hands only" treatment approach, and opposes the ACA's thoughts on full scope chiropractic.

Both associations claim to keep true to the philosophy of chiropractic. Both promise to advance chiropractic throughout the world as a distinct health profession through its unique philosophy, science, and art, to improve and promote the chiropractic profession and the services for the benefit of patients.

The largest disagreement between the ACA and ICA is one of unity. In 1988 the ACA voted in favor of a merger, while the ICA denied. The ICA members are very loyal to the original Palmer family traditions of how chiropractic should be and distrusts the sincerity and actions of the ACA, feeling that they allow the profession's future to be open to divide and conquer by the medical and pharmaceutical establishments.

5.16 How Many Chiropractic Techniques are There? Which is Best?

Chiropractic institutions train their doctors in many techniques and with a variety of philosophy and specializations prior to opening a practice – just like in the medical profession. What works for one patient may not for another. Currently, there are about 55 established chiropractic adjustments that are part of about 20+ different technique-sets available to chiropractors, and most will choose several to help their patients with. The most used chiropractic interventions in the US are Diversified, Gonstead, Cox/Flexion-Distraction, Activator, Thompson, Sacro-Occipital, and Nimmo/Receptor Tonus. This was found following a survey conducted among 5000 chiropractors by the National Board of Chiropractic Examiners in 1993. The fact that there are so many different methodologies is proof of its diversity and preparedness to competently tackle dis-ease conditions of the human frame.

5.17 Subluxation and Neurological Compression Syndrome

Some doctors describe the subluxation process as neurological compression syndrome. The word subluxation is still used by the majority of chiropractors and is defined as less than a break; a misalignment. Subluxation occurs when one or more of the bones of your spine (the vertebrae) move out of proper position and creates pressure, inflaming spinal nerves and surrounding structures. The nerves malfunction and interfere with signals traveling over those nerves. Symptoms, like headaches, cramps, etc., will then occur. These issues may be coming from your spine!

A good analogy would be if you were stepping on a garden hose; where the hose represents the spinal cord and the water represents the nerve flow of energy or information. Removing the pressure on the hose allows water to again flow from the source to the garden. In the case of our bodies, nerves flow, and vital health instruction flows from the brain back to the deprived cells, tissues, and organs. The noxious stimulus would be the foot, causing the kink on the hose. It is believed that most dis-ease conditions are a cumulative outcome of 'nerve interference,' which refers to an impediment to the normal physiological functions of the central and peripheral nervous system. Nerve interference disrupts motor functions by affecting effector organs, such as muscles and glands and the information flow from the peripheral to the central nervous system. Think of how many dis-eases could be a result of limited or no nerve flow!

There are two classes of subluxation: structural and facilitated. Structural subluxation is a segmental distortion associated with a breakdown of the inter-vertebral structure inside the foramen. It's usually caused by local physical distress, making it inadaptable to normal spinal cord tension patterns. Facilitated subluxation correlates to an inability to recover from chemical, emotional, or mental stress, in addition to possible mechanical spinal cord tension. Subluxations are a form of multi-layered deficit.

Kinesiopathology (KINESIO-patho-logy) is a vertebral subluxation involved in changes in joint mobility. Myopathology (MYO-patho-logy) involves decrease in muscle mass and tone, and is often connected to dysfunction. Pathophysiology (PATHO-physio-logy) is related to oxygen supply, blood flow, quantity and composition of tissue fluids and denotes disease. Histopathology (HISTO-patho-logy) is the tissue structure, including degeneration of cartilages, disc atrophy and rupture, and in the formation of osteophytes related to disease. Neuropathophysiology (NEURO-patho-physio-logy) is related to each of the above, either as cause or effect, and results neural malfunction.

How Does This Affect You?

NORMAL SPINAL JOINT

Your nervous system controls and coordinates all the functions of your body – that's how! If parts of the body are hampered, signal messages traveling over nerves improperly will not be communicated, in turn compromising function. Hence, sub-lux-ations are referred to as SILENT KILLERS. They start off slow and small and manifest as debilitating issues later in the life. The figures in this section clearly show (a normal spinal joint up to stage 4 degeneration) the drastic effect on the spine during progressive stages of degeneration over time.

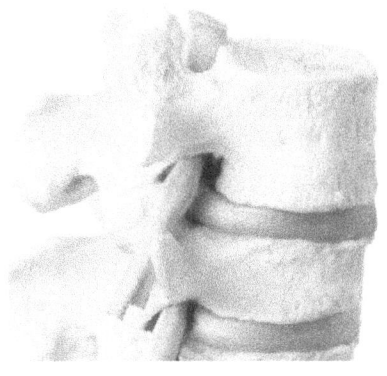
STAGE ONE DEGENERATION

Medical practitioners usually define subluxation as a joint misalignment that is an order of magnitude less than a gross dislocation or luxation (break); they don't take it into account any more than that, though. Chiropractors are a step ahead in including misaligned joints, improperly moving joints, or temporal positioning and movement problems into the definition of subluxation. Therefore, the medical definition and the chiropractic definition of subluxation is very different. Chiropractic management is focused on causing manual *adjustments* to reduce the vertebral subluxation, which ultimately eliminates the root cause of the dis-ease: the nerve interference. The methodology used to achieve this also serves as the basis of classifying chiropractors as *straight* or *mixer* as previously discussed. Whereas, a *straight* chiropractor uses the hands-on adjustment technique alone, and a *mixer* uses a combination of nutritional inputs, exercise regimens, physiotherapy, or other supportive care.

Patients who are under chiropractic treatment are usually well aware of their precise level of functioning, and will often be capable of identifying what part of their body is malfunctioning in a particular condition, e.g. whether their spine is subluxated. However, this is entirely impossible for other patients who are not well informed of their body's level of functioning. They usually don't take any action to get better and slowly start sliding into more dis-ease over time.

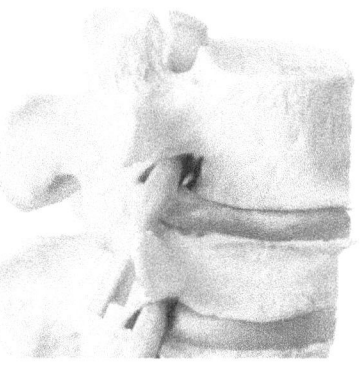
STAGE TWO DEGENERATION

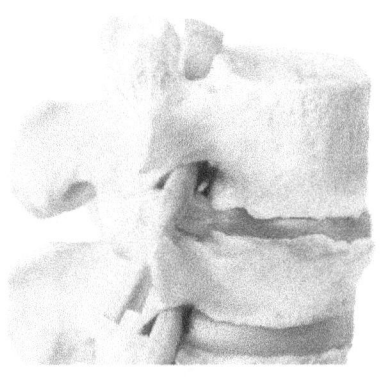
STAGE THREE DEGENERATION

Some symptoms that may be tell-tale signs that you are suffering from subluxation and need to visit a chiropractor are low back pain, neck pain, headaches, migraines, shoulder problems, postural abnormalities, fatigue, breathing issues, disc injuries, nerve root irritation, sports injuries, stress related disorders, digestive complaints, hyperactivity in children, hormonal disturbances, allergies, and skin complaints that don't go away or reoccur.

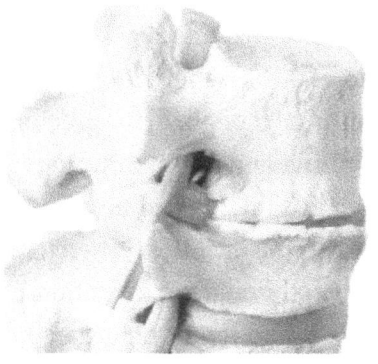

STAGE FOUR DEGENERATION

The purpose of reducing a vertebral subluxation is to remove nervous system interference associated with that condition. It is believed that, all else being equal, a nervous system unimpaired by subluxation freely directs the body's innate abilities to maintain an optimum state of adaptability, including spinal integrity. This state, in turn, contributes to the overall health and well-being of the individual.

Let's analyze the different problems we face during cervical subluxation by breaking down the example below. On the left is the original cause, cervical subluxation (an improperly functioning spinal joint affecting neural function), that ends as symptoms within a diagnosis that the medical community usually prescribes drugs for (treating only surface symptoms).

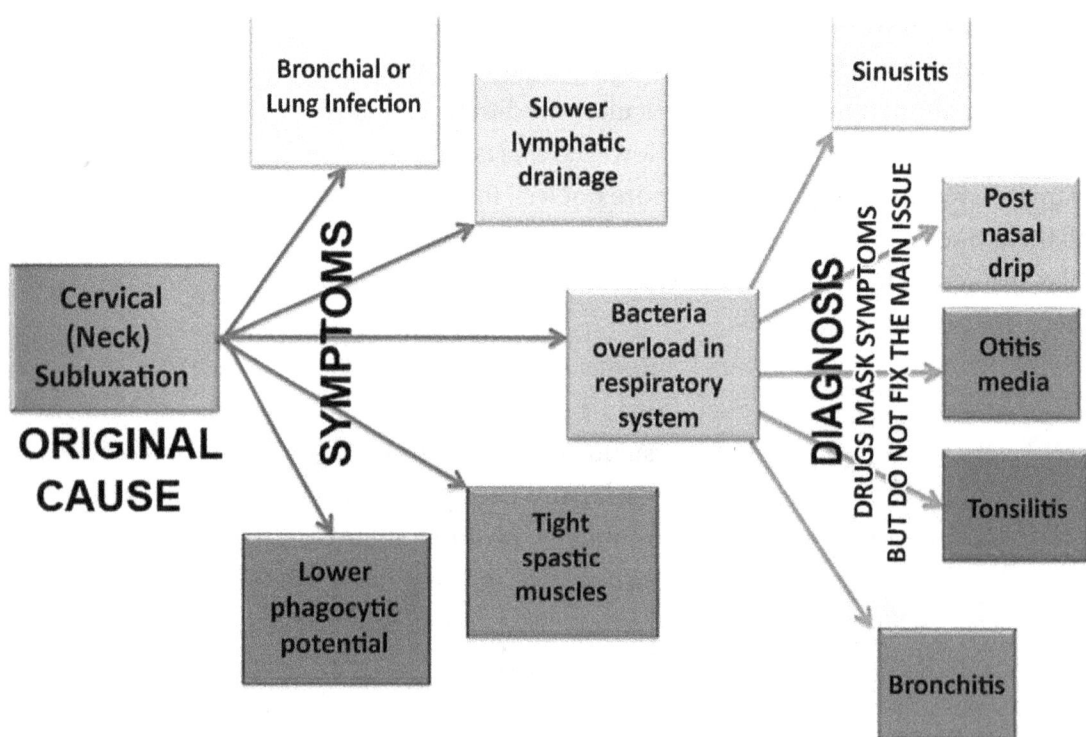

The best option for the patient is a combination of addressing the cause through chiropractic care, while also minimizing discomfort by addressing their symptoms medicinally as the subluxation heals. Simply adding chemicals to mask symptoms does nothing to address the original cause or fix the problem long term.

Let's take a look at how the spine can be affected globally by subluxation. The table on the next page highlights the different vertebrae present in your body, and the different parts of the body that the neurology directly connect to. The symptomatic presentation occurs when one or more of these connections are disrupted by subluxation.

Vertebrae	Parts of Body	Possible Symptom
C1	Intracranial Blood Vessels; Eyes	Headaches, Migraines
C2	Lacrimal Gland, Parotid Gland	Dizziness, Sinus Problems
C3	Scalp, Base of Skull, Neck	Allergies, Ear Infections
C4		Ringing in the Ears, Head Colds, Fatigue, Vision Problems
C5	Neck Muscles, Shoulders	Runny Nose, Sore Throat
C6	Elbows, Arms, Wrists, Hands	Stiff Neck, Cough, Croupe,
C7	Fingers, Esophagus, Heart, Lungs, Chest	Arm Pain, Hand and Finger Numbness or Tingling, Asthma, Heart Conditions, High Blood Pressure, Immune System Dysfunction
T1	Esophagus, Heart, Lungs	
T2	Chest, Larynx, Trachea	Wrist Pain, Hand and Finger
T3	Arms	Numbness or Pain, Middle Back Pain
T4		Congestion
		Bronchitis, Difficulty Breathing
T5	Gallbladder, Liver, Diaphragm	Asthma, High Blood Pressure
T6	Stomach, Pancreas, Spleen	Heart Conditions, Bronchitis
T7	Kidneys. Small Intestine	Pneumonia, Gall Bladder
T8	Appendix, Adrenals, Middle	Conditions, Jaundice, Liver
T9	Back	Conditions, Stomach Problems, Indigestion Heartburn, Gas
T10		Bloating, Ulcers, Gastritis
T11	Small Intestines, Colon	Digestive Problems, Kidney
T12	Uterus, Buttocks	Problems
L1	Large Intestine, Kidneys,	Constipation, Colitis, Diarrhea
L2	Buttocks, Groin,	Gas, Abdominal Pain
L3	Reproductive Organs, Bladder	Irritable Bowel, Bladder
L4	Colon, Thighs, Knees. Legs	Problems, Urinary Conditions
L5	Feet, Lower Back	Menstrual problems, Low Back Pain, Pain or Numbness in Legs
Sacrum	Buttocks, Reproductive Organs, Bladders, Prostate Gland	Constipation. Diarrhea, Bladder Problems. Menstrual Problems
Coccyx	Legs, Ankles, Feet, Toes	Low Back Pain, Pain or Numbness in Legs

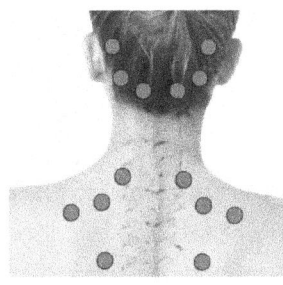

Subluxations also cause neurological short-circuiting in the muscular system, which is commonly experienced as spastic tough nodules with pain upon pressure (called trigger points). These points can be found anywhere along the spine from the neck down to the pelvis, but can occur anywhere muscle/nerve flow is interrupted. When nerve flow from subluxation is inhibited to muscles, the muscle cells cannot get the proper instruction to remove waste efficiently, so toxins will back up and cause local pain in the area. Often the area will need help in the form of deep tissue cross friction myofascial release to break down stagnation and help the toxins move along for cleansing through the lymph system. Remember, no matter how much one gets massages in these areas, until the neurological component of the problem is addressed first, there will always be pain from dysfunction.

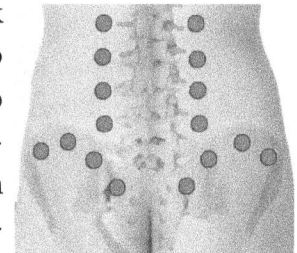

5.18 Is There any Specific Technique I Should be Looking for in a Chiropractor?

Chiropractors have replaced the general medical family practice of the 80's and 90's, with specialization in various techniques that better handle the maintenance of a family's health when there is not a medical emergency. All chiropractic techniques produce results for anyone deciding to utilize the skills of a qualified specialist. The patient would be better served to focus on a doctor's reputation, philosophy, and work ethic, rather than shop a doctor by technique.

There are some practitioners of chiropractic that have done the proper academic procedures but have not had the required hands-on training for properly removing nervous interference. Chiropractic is a very physical, hands-on therapy. It is possible that a practitioner may decide to choose one low force technique and apply that to every patient they encounter, and get some low level results. It is also just as possible to graduate from a chiropractic school not having the full clinical training in a specific part of the body, such as the neck or pelvis. This is not because the schools or professors are inadequate. They are more than qualified and offer much opportunity to students so that they may grow as healers.

This scenario is fully the result of the particular student's attitude or insecurities about their abilities as a chiropractor to deliver an accurate specific adjustment. It's a skill – and art – that, if not well perfected in the clinical years, may prove daunting for some when they start their practice. When those practitioners get into practice, they may continually apply other modalities like ice, heat, traction, massage, and not fully address the spine while still claiming to provide chiropractic care. But this is not correct. The spine must be addressed each and every visit if you are truly seeing a doctor of chiropractic.

Some chiropractic school interns may focus just on one area of the spine and neglect to master the others pre-practice. For instance, it is possible for some students to adopt a superiority complex from one specific instructor or having only one technique they practice early in their training, dismissing all other techniques. Although that specific technique they practice and learned may work, it may not be specific enough for certain conditions, resulting in receiving a subpar experience with that particular doctor, when other doctors of chiropractic are using many variations of techniques that can deliver better results. Just as medical doctors vary in their choice of techniques, attitudes, confidence, and skills, so do chiropractors. With chiropractors, though, an ability to deliver the full physical adjustment is paramount.

I recommend patients look for these basic ten characteristics in finding a great Doctor of Chiropractic:

I. Practices passionately and compassionately. Shares their personal story of how they were also helped by chiropractic or why they decided to practice.

II. Enjoys teaching and takes the time to explain how the body works.

III. Is in touch with current technological advances in the profession.

IV. Does not bad mouth or steal patients from other practitioners.

V. Offers house calls if patient cannot come to office (i.e. hospital or bedridden)

VI. Maintains the hands-on chiropractic adjustment as the key office therapy.

VII. Is educated in many techniques and attends continued education seminars.

VIII. Leader in the community and does public service events outside the office.

IX. Helps patients afford care despite insurance or third party payments.

X. Receives regular spinal care by a fellow chiropractor. If not, or hesitates to tell you who adjusts them - leave the office immediately. They are not practicing what they preach.

5.19 How Does Your Life Change After Your First Chiropractic Adjustment?

Everyone's experience is uniquely different. Depending on what has been previously 'turned off' in your body will determine what you may feel as your adjustment turns it back 'on' again. Think of a house with a blown fuse. Once the fuse box is adjusted and the electric flow is reconnected, the lights come back on. Once adjusted, your body's cells, tissues, and organs will all start to again receive full input from the main computer - your brain. The first adjustment usually starts to bring feelings of positional realignment of your head and neck, and you may notice that you can take a deeper breath! You may feel taller and experience an overall feeling of weight being moved off of your shoulders. Many patients report having better vision, a feeling of floating or being lighter on their feet, or claim they are so relaxed that they could sleep like a baby. The subsequent weeks of care will bring awareness to the positive changes, such as the release of tension and pain from your body, and the pleasure of reconnecting to a more centered and grounded you. After the spinal realignment, your neuronal signals are flowing with much less impediment and are now capable of dissipating energy to the dis-eased organ sites. Until now, the energy was not dissipated, or was slower and stagnant due to the subluxation and tissue congestion. It almost feels like a re-birth after your first chiropractic visit. Your spine feels freedom, expressing more integrity and stability, in turn lifting your mood to a happier you. This phenomenon is termed *Spinal Awakening*; your first step to a successful and longer lasting healing.

What's Next?

You already have this feeling of elation by starting on the path of healing and recovery. If you have chosen corrective therapy, you go through multiple rounds of spinal realignment, and your healing process hits the ground running. Persistent care of your spine will help you remain injury-free, increase your emotional well-being, make you more aware of your surroundings, and help your body's signal synchronicity between the different organs. The spine and nervous system have their own memory; once stresses are removed, they both utilize the past experiences to train and adapt themselves better to any such future nuisances.

What's Going On? The Retracing Process

After your first adjustment your body will be accessing information from your neural information super highway at such an alarmingly quick rate that it will start to demand much more energy from your reserves to do its many jobs. Life-sustaining tasks such as balancing hormone levels, blood pressure regulation, oxygen uptake by the brain, and liver and kidney waste removal management are just a few of the millions. After your adjustment, your body has to take time to "housekeep," and to begin regulating all of the systems that weren't working well before. Soreness or tenderness is normal after an adjustment and will occur as waste products in the body accumulate in muscles and get taken to the blood stream, filtered by the kidneys, liver and transferred to the appropriate evacuation channels. Buffering acids and neutralizing toxins before they are transported to your bloodstream is also an enormous task that could be overwhelming to your recovered system, which can cause extreme fatigue. Be sure to keep open communication with your doctor so that you are correctly monitored for any changes.

Did you ever do years of hard-core partying and drugs? Were you eating lead paint chips and playing with mercury thermometers as a child? Do you currently (or have in the past) eaten lots of junk food or taken prescription medications? Do you have any daily alcohol, smoking, caffeine, artificial flavour, or sugar consumption habits? All unprocessed foreign chemicals are stored in the body and when the nervous system gets woken up, it's clean up time - and **you will feel it**!

Compare the process with going to the gym to lose weight or tone up after you haven't been to the gym in a long time. You're feeling ok - but know you can feel much better and you are going to the gym for exactly that reason: to feel better and get in shape. You know it's going to take (I) Time and travel to the gym, (II) Dedication - physical effort and sweat, and (III) Monetary investment - gym membership. There is always a price when you want something better. If you go to the gym, you will get a great workout, and in 24 hours to 48 hours what happens? Soreness - lots of it. Why? Lactic acid and waste products that are not needed are being moved from your body and you FEEL it! Though you KNOW you're getting more fit and this is a 'good' sore. What happens if you keep going to the gym without losing your dedication? You lose weight and tone up and there is no more soreness! If you don't go, you fall right back into your old flabby routine with no change, wasted time and money. It's the same with chiropractic. There are certain commitments you need to make to get the most out of it: (I) Time - you go to the clinic to get treatment, (II) Dedication -initial discomfort as your body adapts to the changes – soreness, and (III) Money investment - clinic membership or fee for service. Remember, there's always a price to pay for going towards something better. Decide you're worth it - and pay that price.

Relaxing After Your First Adjustment

After your first chiropractic spinal adjustment, you should take it easy and plan on relaxing the rest of the day. Drink plenty of water and keep your body hydrated to help with toxin removal. Follow your doctor's instructions and be sure to soak your body in a soothing relaxing lavender epsom salt bath before you turn in for the night. Get to bed early so you can have your body maximize its repair time. Do not cheat yourself by drinking alcohol, coffee, eating junk food, etc. You want to start cleaning out the body and allowing only the highest quality foods and liquids in. You wouldn't put clean water in a dirty glass would you? So choose to now be on the path of health and treat your body as a holy temple. You deserve it!

You may feel some soreness as ligaments, muscles, and tendons start to stretch or shorten. Remember, not everyone feels the initial soreness. If you don't feel it right away, that's okay; it's unique for everyone depending on where they are with their recovery. If the doctor gave you stretching exercises, supplements, or other instructions, be sure to follow instructions and contact the doctor if you need clarification or help with anything. Maintaining clear communication between you and your doctor is important.

After each adjustment, the areas worked on are less stressed and there is improvement in tissue and body function. A common misconception is that the spinal bones are all 'aligned' after one or two adjustments. Depending on your lifestyle, age, and toxic load, it takes months to years to improve global spinal posture; it can take months to years to get bad posture in the first place! The recovery depends greatly on your dedication to your care plan, along with being aware of your day-to-day routine. My responsibility as a chiropractor is educating the public in order to bring a greater degree of understanding of the spine and nervous system to you, so that your healing process is on the fast track. Most chiropractic treatment is focused on pain removal and function enhancement. Talk to your doctor of chiropractic about longer-term postural enhancement and what you can do to help make that a reality for you. Many posture tips and exercises are mentioned here in this book.

Usually, your initial frequency of treatment will be higher at the start of the program, as there is more work for the doctor to do. A typical schedule of chiropractic care may be three treatments a week for a month, which drops to twice a week for eight weeks, and then once a week for four to six weeks. Depending on your progress, your doctor may advise a biweekly maintenance or monthly wellness treatment program to maintain the positive changes made. Each treatment builds on the previous one, so it's important to stick with the program of care for optimal results. Re-examinations are usually done every twelfth treatment or thirty days to assess your progress. During your first re-examination, you may be asked to answer an assessment questionnaire, and future frequency may revolve around your degree of improvement during the first month of care. The health of your spine and how the doctor feels you are progressing are the main considerations for your subsequent visits; finances should not be the reason for determining if you can continue caring for your health. Talk with your doctor so an affordable payment plan can be worked out to keep your spine and nervous system progressing to optimum levels. It's the system that controls everything in your life. What is more important than this?

5.20 Toxins Around the House That Cause Dis-ease and Slow Death

Many experts from around the world support the idea that life on Earth is susceptible to electromagnetic phenomena. Electrically active ions, specifically heavy metal ions, interfere with the body's flow of electromagnetic energy, causing the dis-ease process to unfold. They can also increase free radical production exponentially. Dr. J. Higgensen, responsible for Research on Cancer for the World Health Organization in Geneva, Switzerland said, "90% of all chronic and severe illnesses could be avoided if we were able to remove the 600 most dangerous toxins." Holistic practitioners are well aware of the overwhelming impact of heavy metal distress on a patient's mental, emotional, and physical health and wellness. Most health professionals and scientists used to think that heavy metal toxins had to be taken seriously as a threat only when a patient showed specific poison symptomatology. Science now understands that the health and well-being affected by heavy metals is much more serious than previously thought. It has become increasingly difficult for medical doctors to precisely determine which pharmaceutical product is proper for a particular dis-ease case because the incidence of heavy metal ions causes more symptoms for the patient by the mal-absorption phenomena.

Heavy metals are toxic trace metals that are can't be metabolized by our body. Toxic heavy metals like mercury, lead, cadmium, arsenic, or nickel have no place inside us and cause major health problems. When mercury is in the body's tissues, it prevents the entry of essential minerals such as Mg, Zn, Fe, Ca, and Cu. In fact, it is fair to also say that the effectiveness of antioxidant therapy is considerably lowered in the presence of heavy metals. This is why it is important to determine first the case of heavy metals and the degree of involvement in ill patients.

To some extent, our fit body can bind, or chelate, free heavy metal atoms, neutralizing their electromagnetic charge and eliminate them. If this system is unable to function because toxins have overloaded the body, the amount of free radicals will quickly compile. This is most noted when the body has a lack of good nutrition and antioxidants at the point of attack. In this case, taking large amounts of supplements will not remove the toxic load and may be counterproductive until the heavy metal toxins themselves are addressed.

Current detection methods, such as hair and blood testing are not able to reveal these connections perfectly since the actual biological sample usually gets destroyed during the analysis attempt. These procedures are hence unable to discriminate between atoms bound to organic complexes and metal ions. A sheep study conducted at the University of Calgary in Canada (the sheep had mercury fillings placed in the mouth) clearly showed that very little mercury is found in urine and blood, but the highest rate is localized to the kidneys. Nevertheless, blood and hair testing can still be helpful when combined with the patient history, exam, and other lab tests to determine possible toxic metal exposure and contamination.

Some other common symptoms initiated by the displacement of heavy metals, minerals, or vitamin deficiencies are:

Vitamin A: dry eye, night blindness, macular degeneration, photophobia, acne.

Vitamin B: itchy, flaky, patchy or dry skin, dandruff, tongue and lip cracking.

Vitamin C: eczema, gum disease, cataracts, bruising easily, wrinkles, skin aging.

Copper: anemia, thyroid dysfunction, poor digestion, scoliosis.

Iodine: thyroid dysfunction.

Iron: anemia.

Magnesium: irregular heartbeat, gingival recession, osteoporosis, glaucoma, eyelid tics, etc.

Zinc: Anorexia nervosa, PMS, decreased libido, loss of taste, decreased immunity.

Our day-to-day living has toxic concerns hidden under the technology of 'convenience.' Imagine the small doses daily that eventually add up, and from out of nowhere someone can get diagnosed with a seriously fatal disease process, such as cancer. To these people it's sudden, even though the cause for what has manifested has been taking years, and sometimes decades, of compounded toxicity. When the body's natural detoxing mechanisms are overpowered and drained, the body's next defense is to accumulate and carry toxicity away from major organs into the surrounding tissues. Toxicity builds and the body area then decays. Most, if not all health problems, are from one of two things: Not ENOUGH of a nutrient or substance the body needs, or TOO MUCH of what the body doesn't need.

Let's take a look at commonly used personal items that could be harmful to you over the long term, even in small doses:

Toothpaste should contain no fluoride. Fluoride is a toxin! Fluoride paralyzes enzymes in your body and then sets the stage for global body dysfunction as it disrupts iodine flows and affects thyroid function. Contrary to popular belief, it does not cause less tooth decay, but it does cause white spotting in the teeth (fluorosis), and can even lead to osteosarcoma in young males. Replace all future use of toothpaste with a natural non-fluoride brand without lauryl sulfates or propylene glycol. Remember that your dental health has a huge connection to intestinal, body, and spinal health; as the nerves in your mouth are very much in close proximity to your neck and brain neurology.

Colognes and perfumes should be botanical oils, not commercial store brands made in a lab. Chemicals unnatural to the body are absorbed by your skin and filtered by the lymph system. Overuse and accumulation of some of these chemicals will lead to breast, skin and organ cancers – especially if exposed to radiation over time (tanning beds or the sun).

Shampoos and conditioners should be from certified organic botanical ingredients, not brand commercial names with cancer causing chemicals made in a lab. Absolutely no parabens, laurel sulfates, or synthetic colors/dyes! An excellent choice I personally recommend is: Chinese Herbal Shampoo and Conditioner by the Peter Lamas brand.

Shower filters remove chlorine from city water and should be changed often to help keep your hair and skin smooth and soft. Chlorine is a toxin! Filters are a solution to the 'hard water' problem during showering. It is important to know that when your pores are open (even when your body is heated or steamed) they are very absorbent of any chemicals soaking into your body. Chloride-free water for both drinking and showering is critical to good health.

Reverse osmosis filtration systems help water stay healthy for human consumption, and remove the fluoride and chlorine in the tap water.

Tap water contaminants sometimes can be just as bad as those in bottled water. However, bottled water has no true regulations. Reverse osmosis is the purest way to clean water for human consumption.

Throw out your microwave and purchase a heat convection or infrared oven; microwaving food has been linked with many types of cancers. Never drink microwaved water or juices in plastic, as this has been linked to throat and thyroid problems. Plastic leaks into water when it's radiated or heated, and you drink it. Plastics are estrogen mimickers because synthetic estrogens occur in plastic when heated, causing precocious puberty, where many young women develop early.

Gum is now poisonous. Do not chew gum that has aspartames. Gum makers left natural gums because they wanted to say their gum did not cause cavities or tooth decay - but instead the artificial chemicals now give us much more to worry about than just bad teeth: cancer. Check labels for "Phenylketonurics – Contains Phenylalanine." Another common poisonous artificial sweetener, saccharin, is proven to cause cancer of the uterus, bladder, skin, ovaries and other organs in animal studies. In humans, bladder cancer occurrence is high with the use of saccharin; which is disguised in gum, tabletop sweeteners, and no-sugar added foods. Other chemicals linked to cancer in gum are BHT, propylgallate, acesulfame K, Red 40 Lake, Blue 1 Lake, maltitol and the list goes on. Seek out natural gum without these ingredients; they do exist.

Detergents - What are you washing your clothes with? Commercial detergents have chemicals that may clean clothing, but also clog the skin and lymph system. Make sure you are using a biodegradable, dye-free non-toxic detergent, or research ways to make your own from natural soaps. Chemical detergents are notorious for causing all types of skin ailments, itching, color changes, and even cancers when exposure is long-term.

All garage chemicals, car polishes, and **wash solvents** are highly toxic. Also, lawn fertilizers and pesticides act as estrogen mimickers and cause both breast and prostate cancer; be sure not to handle them without adequate skin protection.

That new rug smell is highly toxic with factory chemicals leaking into the air; gets onto the skin and in the lungs, causing allergies developed over time.

Flame retarding chemicals in mattresses and pillows are highly toxic thanks to a law put into effect by the Consumer Products Safety Commission (CPSC). They add antimony, boric acid and other cancer causing chemicals to the outer lining of the mattress. Toxic chemicals in the surface of new mattresses meet the new law, but I feel the risks of the new law outweigh the benefits. This will expose us all to sleeping in toxic chemicals for the rest of our lives. You can still get a non-toxic mattress *by prescription only*.

Teflon anti-stick cookware may be highly toxic. In 2009, scientific advisers to the Environmental Protection Agency recommended that a chemical used in manufacturing Teflon, perfluorooctanoic acid (PFOA), and other coated and stain-resistant/non-stick products, should be considered a 'likely carcinogen' and avoided!

Some toxic food items that you should keep at a distance:

Toxic Ingredient	Why should you avoid It?
Artificial Colors	Proven to cause allergic reactions, asthma, skin rashes, fatigue, hyperactivity and headaches.
Artificial Flavorings	Shown to cause dermatitis, eczema, allergic reactions, hyperactivity and asthma; may also impede normal enzyme and thyroid gland function.
Artificial Sweeteners	Proven to negatively impact metabolism and cause hallucinations, dizziness, headaches, and even cancer.
Benzoate Preservatives	Results in dermatitis, hyperactivity, asthma, angioedema, rhinitis, hives, and estrogen imbalance.
Brominated Vegetable Oil (BVO)	Toxic substance found in sodas that competes with iodine leading to thyroid problems and iodine deficiency. Causes hypercholesterolemia, increased triglycerides and may also lead to organ damage.
High Fructose Corn Syrup	Because it is not metabolized by the liver, it tells our body to convert fructose to fat, thus contributing to obesity. It is especially high risk in Type-II diabetes, high risk for stroke and coronary heart disease.
Monosodium Glutamate (MSG)	Appetite stimulant hidden in many foods that causes headaches, edema, dizziness, wheezing, weakness, and heart rate changes. When taken together with Aspartame (found in sodas) the combined neurotoxins attack the body causing anything from fatigue and brain fog to IBS and Fibromyalgia symptoms.
Olestra	Competes with inhibition of nutrients and causes many gastrointestinal disorders.
Shortening, Hydrogenated and Partially Hydrogenated Oils	High amount of trans fat will increase bad / LDL cholesterol and decrease the good cholesterol / HDL, resulting in atherosclerosis and coronary heart diseases.

How Toxic Am I? Self-Check

About 150 years ago, many of our current toxins were non-existent because they were never synthetically made in a lab. Toxins in our current environment find their way into our bodies and have a hard time being filtered out, and accumulate over the years. The goal of this exercise is to show you how living a normal life still results in massive exposure to hidden toxins in common use products.

Do a self-check and see if you may be toxic. Go down the list and check off **Yes** if the statement is true about you, or **No** if it's not. Add the Yes answers at the end.

> Yes___No___ I use or have used finger nail polish.

> Yes___No___ I drive in heavy traffic to or from work.

> Yes___No___ I drive in a car at least three days a week.

> Yes___No___ I have swam or swim in chlorinated pools.

> Yes___No___ I use makeup or other cosmetics.

> Yes___No___ I use body lotions, moisturizers and/or sunscreens on my skin.

> Yes___No___ I have used plastic containers or Styrofoam to heat my food with in a microwave.

> Yes___No___ I drink from the home or building main line/ tap without filtering it.

> Yes___No___ I use mosquito, cockroach, or other pest sprays or liquids in my house.

> Yes___No___ I use cleaning products to scrub the tub, kitchen, oven, etc.

> Yes___No___ I shower or bathe without using a chlorine filter.

> Yes___No___ I have taken or am currently on antibiotics.

> Yes___No___ I wear perfumes, colognes, or aftershave.

> Yes___No___ I use standard commercial liquid soap when I wash the dishes.

> Yes___No___ I use commercial grade detergent for washing my clothes.

> Yes___No___ I use toothpaste with fluoride in it.

> Yes___No___ I had or now have an occupation that exposes me to chemicals daily (ex. mechanic)

> Yes___No___ I had or now have an occupation that exposes me to radiation daily (ex. X-ray tech)

> Yes___No___ I eat in restaurants at least twice a week and am unsure how food was prepared.

> Yes___No___ I eat fast food at least three to five times a month.

> Yes___No___ I eat shellfish.

> Yes___No___ I eat sushi or other raw meat (rare/medium rare).

> Yes___No___ I eat pork products.

> Yes___No___ I eat products produced by large publicly traded companies (pre-made TV dinners)

> Yes___No___ I buy brand name food products that are advertised on television.

> Yes___No___ I have been vaccinated or do get vaccinated often.

> Yes___No___ I have taken aspirin, ibuprofen, or any other over the counter pain medication.

> Yes___No___ I use artificial sweeteners instead of organic cane sugar.

> Yes___No___ I drink **DIE**T sodas and usually eat 'diet' products.

> Yes___No___ I have fewer than two large bowel movements per day.

> Yes___No___ I have taken or currently take over the counter non-prescription drugs.

> Yes___No___ I use non-stick pans when I cook.

> Yes___No___ I live within 75 miles of a manufacturing plant.

> Yes___No___ I live within 75 miles of an agricultural area for produce.

> Yes___No___ I live within 75 miles of a livestock, cattle, chicken or other animal ranch.

> Yes___No___ I often use brand name deodorants and antiperspirants.

> Yes___No___ I have used prescription drugs in the last 4 years.

> Yes___No___ I do not drink at least 8- 10 glasses of pure filtered water every day.

> Yes___No___ I drink bottled water (unregulated).

> Yes___No___ I have never had a colonic or enema.

> Yes___No___ I live, work, or sleep near high power electric lines.

> Yes___No___ I sit in front of a computer monitor or television most of the day.

> Yes___No___ I use a cellular phone without any electromagnetic frequency chaos protection.

> Yes___No___ I use a wireless laptop computer or other wireless handheld devices.

> Yes___No___ I use wireless telephones and cell phones often.

> Yes___No___ I smoke or drink alcohol often.

If you answered YES to even 20% - 40% of the questions then you may be toxic; consider consulting a holistic doctor qualified with helping individuals rebalance their body system(s). Take note that some toxic experiences in life carry more weight than others. For instance if you ate lead paint chips as a child or played with a broken mercury thermometer, you are immediately considered highly toxic, and shouldn't worry so much about drinking bottled water.

Chapter 6:
The Body's Natural Healing Capacity

"The introduction of homeopathy forced the old school doctor to stir around and learn something of a rational nature about his business."
~ Mark Twain

Nature has its own healing process that was used exclusively until the last century, when managing sickness was transformed into merely treating symptoms of a disease. In turn, profit making became more important than integrity, humanity, and healing. It was globally accepted that medical freedom is one of the basic rights of an individual, and perhaps it should have been encrypted into the constitutions of all countries. As colonial physician Dr. Benjamin Rush declared in 1787, "The Constitution of this Republic should make special provision for medical freedom. To restrict the art of healing to one class will constitute the Bastille of medical science. All such laws are un-American and despotic." Unfortunately, it never was formulated into the Constitution or the Bill of Rights, and we are seeing the fallout of the omission. Dr. Rush was right in predicting, "Unless we put medical freedom into the Constitution, the time will come when medicine will organize into an undercover dictatorship and force people who wish doctors and treatment of their own choice to submit to only what the dictating outfit offers."

It can be reasonably argued that Traditional Chinese Medicine, based solely on natural healing resources, was based on strong scientific grounds, as compared to Westernized medicine as we know it today. While Traditional Chinese Medicine derived its expertise from 6,000 years of hands-on experience, Westernized medicine started its journey into exploration only in the latter half of the 19th century. In fact, it was initiated because of the perceived threat from alternative forms of therapy.

6.1 Holistic Medicine - The Mother of All Treatment Regimens

"The ability to heal is an innate part of every human being and everything in nature. When we align with that power, approximately 90 percent of what we currently call healthcare will not be necessary."
~ Christiane Northrup, MD.

Before looking at the various alternative treatments for chronic disease, it is important to take a moment to understand the origins of holistic treatments. Many natural treatments are rooted in ancient medical systems dating back thousands of years. The first known incidence of manipulative therapy dates back to 2700 B.C., within a Kung Fu document used in China. In addition to China, there are four other areas of ancient medicine that are particularly noteworthy: Egypt, Babylon, Greece, and India.

- *Egypt:* Ancient Egypt has been well known for its systematic, well-documented medicine practice. An Egyptian priest by the name of Imhotep was known as the Egyptian father of medicine, and he is recognized as the first physician by several historical sources.  The reason that there is so much value in the history of ancient Egyptian medical practices is because this civilization created specific processes for diagnosis and treatment, using a system which is reflected in modern medical practices today. They used very specific documentation as new information was discovered, keeping track of the information for future reference and treatments. Records were maintained relating to disease symptoms and conditions, treatment processes, and prognosis. Popular treatments in ancient Egyptian medical practices centered on herbal remedies, energy treatments, as well as surgical processes. Medical practitioners found quite a bit of success using these natural approaches, which is important, because these ancient practices can be combined with additional modern knowledge to create even more effective treatments today.

- *Babylon:* Like the ancient Egyptians, the Babylonians also followed a process of structured medical practices. Their medical system focused on diagnosis and prognosis first, in addition to physical examinations. Treatments were commonly implemented in the form of prescriptions, as well as therapy. Babylonian physicians actually had a "diagnostic handbook" which they referred to in order to document symptoms and conditions that occurred in their patients. Diagnosis, prognosis, and treatments were recorded for future reference. Some of their diagnostic notes, as well as treatment plans, have been found inscribed on tablets that detail the medical practices that they followed.

- *Ancient Greece:* Similar to the healthcare systems of China and India, Greek Medicine is a traditional healing system. Socrates (469-399 BC) knew the importance of spinal health and advised, "If you would seek health, look first to the spine." Hippocrates, the Father of Medicine (460-370 BC), described manipulative procedures in his monumental work known as the Corpus Hippocrateum. He wrote, "Get knowledge of the spine, for this is the requisite for many diseases." The history and development of Greek medicine was the cornerstone for the evolution of modern medicine, the explicit study of which helps us realize the true potential and roots of medicine itself.

6.2 The Serendipitous Birth of Chiropractic Care

It all started in 1895 by a teacher and magnetic healer, Dr. Daniel David Palmer. Dr. Palmer's focus was always to understand the mechanism by which a disease was caused, as he strongly believed understanding the mechanism is the only way to completely cure a disease. In the same building where he worked, a janitor, Harvey Lillard, had post-traumatic auditory problems after a workplace injury. Dr. Palmer expressed his interest in examining the spine of Harvey, and when he complied with the request, Dr. Palmer found a lump in Harvey's neck, which by his own admission seemed to be an alignment problem that was perhaps "pinching" the nerves connecting to Harvey's ears. He performed the first crude chiropractic technique of adjusting the vertebrae with calculated thrust. It was a success! Harvey Lillard recovered his auditory senses after a series of treatments by Dr. Palmer. His sound knowledge of human anatomy and physiology helped in diagnosing the actual cause of the disease, and hence the cure came naturally. This event marked the birth of what is considered our modern day chiropractic.

6.3 Ayurveda

Ayurveda is a holistic system of medicine that dates back several thousand years, originating in India. Ancient Egyptians followed Ayurvedic practices as early as the 4th century B.C., and it is suspected that they learned the techniques through the sea trade with India. Additionally, Ayurveda had a great influence on ancient Chinese medicine, and historians estimate that the Chinese began implementing these techniques between 1 AD and 1000 AD. This system of medicine focuses on treating and managing health, but also focuses on preventing illness. Many of the treatments focus on homeopathic methods such as herbs, food, oils, and lifestyle changes. The word Ayurveda actually means "the science of life."

The study of Ayurveda focuses on a mind-body-soul healing process, focusing on a comprehensive healthcare approach (total healing), instead of simply treating individual symptoms. When an overall approach is taken, complete balance can be achieved, which results in self-realization in all aspects of life. It is believed that an imbalance in mind, body, and spirit can cause physical ailments, so Ayurveda focuses on overall alignment, which allows the physical manifestations (symptoms) to heal. In order to achieve this balance, it is necessary to create physical purification, as well as spiritual and mental well-being.

Traditional Ayurvedic care uses multiple facets of healing practices, including: diet, yoga, herbs, acupuncture, aromatherapy, lifestyle, meditation, surgery, massage, bodywork, etc. Historical Ayurvedic texts actually describe the research that was completed thousands of years ago. These classical texts document the surgical and clinical information, detailing research and results for numerous ailments and diseases.

Ayurvedic science focuses on "Five Great Elements," and these elements are:

- Fire (agni or tej)
- Earth (prithvi)
- Air (vayu)
- Ether or Space (akash)
- Water (jal)

Each of these elements is an integral part of our daily living, and we must have all five elements in balance in our life for maximum health. For example, our bodies are nourished from the food of the earth (Earth); we are made up of 70% water (Water) and it is a necessary part of life; heat and energy (Fire) are necessary to sustain internal chemical reactions and metabolic functions, as well as regulating body temperature; our cells need oxygen (Air) to function and this oxygen keeps the biological functions running properly; and the playing field of space (Space) allows the other four elements to interact and work together to keep the system running smoothly.

This is a very brief and non-comprehensive explanation of the five elements of Ayurveda. If you study more about the topic you will learn that these five elements play a strong role in many aspects of life. They affect bodily functions, personality, attitudes, and physical qualities. This practice diagnoses symptoms through the process of looking at a patient's habits as they relate to daily life, as well as things like diet, perspiration, eyes, lips, face, nail beds, pulse, tongue, etc.

Ayurveda should be used in conjunction with other treatments in order to achieve quick healing. Additionally, a good Ayurvedic practice focuses on disease prevention instead of symptom treatments. A treatment process called "Yogasanas" works two-fold: First, to maintain good psychological conditions and healthy blood circulation; and second, to focus on body strength in order to keep essential body parts healthy (liver, stomach, heart, intestine, bones, muscle, etc.). Another important aspect of Ayurveda is the process of following a diet that supports the 'dosha type' of each person - the emotional and physical tendencies within the body and mind. Identifying a person's dosha type can speed up the healing process by catering the treatment plan to their dosha type. This can help to strengthen the immune system in order to provide a natural form of healing and disease prevention. The medical system of Ayurveda puts a strong emphasis on the fact that a person's mental state plays a big part in physical health, and dis-ease and illnesses can be a direct result of one's mental state.

6.4 Aromatherapy

Variously termed as aromatic medicine, holistic aromatherapy, or conventional aromatherapy, aromatherapy uses oily herbal extracts to alter mood or to improve individuals' health and appearance. The uses are varied – from relieving stress to unlocking emotions from past experience and enhancement of autoimmunity. Herbal sources that are used for the oil extracts are flowers, fruits, leaves, roots, and grasses. Administration methodologies include massage, sniffing, adding to bathwater, and ingestion. Aromatherapy restores balance and harmony through interplay with the temporospatial and spiritual dimensions of an individual.

6.5 Color Therapy (Chromotherapy or Color Breathing)

This type of therapy involves prayer, visualization, meditation, and affirmations, where you imagine breathing one or several colors associated with disease, pain, cosmetic problems, artistic benefits, intellectual benefits, material benefits, and spiritual attunement. You imagine being surrounded by a preferred color and breathe deeply, and imagine the color filling the lungs and then traveling through the body or to the particular area that has been affected by a particular dis-ease. It is also advisable to wear certain colors depending on a person's auric field or energy vibration to affect a higher mood or health state. Aromatherapy, as well as color therapy, has not been given the proper recognition in the West, though widely recognized in Eastern healing methodologies. Color is linked to one of the languages of the soul, influencing our moods and emotions, and it can help us understand the energy flowing through our body (aura). This will be discussed with greater detail in Chapter 9.

6.6 Moxabustion Therapy

Moxabustion is a therapy believed to have been started in the upper parts of China near Mongolia. This therapy is usually used in conjunction with acupuncture. It is achieved through the burning of moxas - dried leaves from the wormwood tree (*Artemisia chinensis*) *or* the common mugwort (*Artemisia vulgaris*). Accupoints stimulate the movement of energy (chi). The moxa is normally rolled into what looks like a cigar stick or in smaller pieces attached to the end of acupuncture needles. Those who have used the technique report positive effects for back pain, anxiety, headaches, migraines, muscle stiffness, tendonitis, digestive disorders, arthritis, menstrual cramps, irregular periods, and even infertility.

6.7 Magnetic Healing

Magnets have been around since ancient times and are still widely used to treat pain and dis-ease. The theory is that a magnet's north pole causes contraction and its south pole dissipates energy. Biomagnetic therapy tries to move chi (energy), and re-balance the magnetic bio-potential of the body improving the function of the involved body systems. Magnets can be inserted in everything from gloves and t-shirts to mattresses and shoes. Some patients claim miraculous healings from sleeping on magnetic mattress pads. It is believed that our body's natural magnetic frequency is knocked out by daily use of cell phones, televisions, computers, etc., and re-energized back to normal after using magnet therapy. Some of the claimed success of magnetic healing are: removing joint pain, blood pressure regulation, kidney, liver and thyroid problems resolved, no more fatigue, skin diseases vanishing, and there have even been many cases where tumors simply dissolve after being exposed to the correct magnetics.

6.8 Cupping Therapy

One of the most amazing and simple healing therapies is the art of cupping (called 'Vendooza' in Greek). Cupping therapy uses simple suction to provide its therapeutic effects. Cupping has been recorded in use as early as 281–341 AD by the famous Taoist herbalist and alchemist, Ge Hong. Further used in Egypt dating back 3,400+ years, it was also represented in Egyptian hieroglyphics. In ancient Greece, the Physician Hippocrates used cups for a wide range of disorders. In China, cupping therapy has been researched prominently and today is even part of their most valued TCM hospital therapies. The practice first started out with hollowed out animal bones, bamboo, and seashells, but is now done with plastic or glass cups. With glass cups, a flame is placed under the cup's opening to heat the air and create a vacuum; then the cup is quickly applied to the painful or sore area to be treated. The suction creates a pulling of the skin into the cup, which brings in nutrients by improving circulation in the area. This helps the lymph system push out stagnant energy, thus encouraging local tissue repair. A red bruise or mark may result, which lasts about 7 to 10 days and then fades. Sometimes therapists will cut or prick the skin before they apply the suction cup, drawing blood out of the affected area and into the cup. Cutting practice is more common in the Eastern traditional cultures and not seen as much in the US, as scarring could occur.

6.9 Applied Kinesiology (AK)

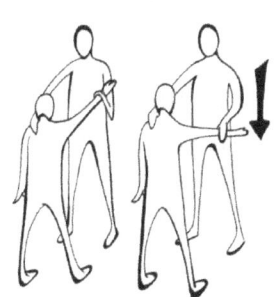

Applied Kinesiology has become a dynamic movement in healthcare in its relatively short existence. AK is a non-invasive system of evaluating body function, chemical, structural, and mental aspects of health. It was further developed by chiropractor George J. Goodheart Jr. in 1964, by diagnosis using manual muscle testing in addition to other standard methods of diagnosis. Muscles share 'energy pathways' with our organs and every disease is related to a blocked muscle, or nerve pathway. Testing muscles for tonicity and relative strength helps practitioners detect specific dysfunctions. Applied kinesiology encompasses clinical nutrition, craniosacral therapy, dietary management, homeopathy, meridian or *Ching Lo* therapy, acupressure, acupuncture, and reflexology.

6.10 Acupuncture

Utilizing acupuncture for medical treatment originated in China thousands of years ago. Eventually, it spread to Korea, Japan, and throughout other areas in Asia. Even today, healthcare systems in these countries commonly recognize acupuncture as an effective treatment for numerous diseases and conditions.

Acupuncture is often used to treat pain symptoms, as it can effectively reduce the amount of pain an individual experiences. But, there are also other health benefits that can be gained besides simple pain relief.

The process of acupuncture involves placing tiny needles on specific points in order to clear blocked energy in the body. Acupuncture is able to unblock and redirect the energy for positive healing results. Researchers at the University of California-Irvine discovered that acupuncture could activate the endorphin system, which can reduce blood pressure and can be especially effective in reducing the risk of heart disease. When used for heart disease, the acupuncture treatment reduces sympathetic nervous system activity, which is the system responsible for regulating blood pressure and heart beat. When a person is experiencing elevated blood pressure, abnormally high heart rates, or, in the extreme, congestive heart failure, it is often a result of the sympathetic nerves overreacting, which causes unnecessary stress on the heart. Additionally, the use of acupuncture has been found to help people with chronic heart disease recover more quickly, as compared to patients treated solely with pharmaceutical medications.

Acupuncture can lower blood pressure in a patient who is experiencing hypertension. On the other hand, an acupuncture treatment on a patient with hypotension may produce the opposite effect because the blood pressure may be elevated in this case. This regulating action can be found in other health conditions as well, such as lowering/increasing gastric secretions, depending on the health condition of the patient. It has been found that acupuncture rarely worsens the condition, because it usually works to balance out the health areas that are abnormally functioning.

6.11 Yoga

A study completed at the Yale University School of Medicine found that yoga reduces heart disease risk. Practicing yoga at least 3 x per week can reduce a person's pulse and blood pressure. This research study involved a group of individuals that participated in a 6 week yoga/meditation program, and found that blood vessel function improved in all participants. Healthy individuals experienced an average of 17% increase in blood vessel function, and heart disease patients experienced as high as a 70% improvement in their blood vessel function.

Other research studies have found that regular yoga practice can positively impact overall cholesterol levels, including LDL and triglyceride levels. Hypertension can also improve, as well as body mass, and a decrease in body mass can decrease the risk of heart disease.

6.12 Chi Gong

Chi Gong is a traditional form of Chinese medicine that focuses on aligning the 12 main meridian channels in order to allow proper flow of energy and increase awareness of

spiritual and mental health. Chi travels through these main meridian channels, which are linked to major organs in the body. In this practice, it is understood that energy flow needs to be uninhibited.

Chi Gong training focuses on meditation, static and dynamic movements, and activities with external items:

- Dynamic training typically uses martial arts movements that are choreographed for mental and physical discipline.
- Static training focuses on holding a specific pose, similar to yoga.
- Meditative training uses breath awareness and visualization.
- External training items include things such as massages and herbal treatments.

Chi Gong can be used in both dis-ease prevention as well as dis-ease treatment. It has been found to improve many chronic conditions, including chronic heart dis-ease. Chi Gong practice strengthens a person's immune system and enhances self-healing capabilities, thus improving the person's ability to prevent and heal from disease.

There are four major application areas within the topic of Chi Gong:

- **Healing Chi Gong:** Also known as medical Chi Gong, it is a form of preventative Chinese medicine. This practice helps a person manage their reaction to stress in order to prevent the physical side effects that occur when a person internalizes stress.
- **External Chi Healing:** In External Chi Healing, the healer funnels healing energy through his or her own body into the body of the patient. This healing treatment becomes more effective over time, as the healer practices meditations and exercises that raise the energy field sensitivity.
- **Spiritual Chi Gong:** Spiritual focus commonly increases a person's inner harmony and self-awareness, giving a strong foundation for a whole-body approach to healing.
- **Sports/Martial Arts Chi Gong:** Using Chi Gong techniques in sports and martial arts can improve an individual's performance by improving various aspects of athleticism. Some of the areas that can be improved are: accuracy, strength, flexibility, speed, stamina, and balance.

6.13 Ancient Medicine in a Modern World

These ancient medical traditions are important to our modern day medical treatments because ancient knowledge can be combined with modern-day knowledge to create some of the most effective preventions and treatments of disease. These ancient medical practices from Egypt, Greece, Babylon, as well as China and India, have been proven to be effective in treating and preventing many diseases. The advantage to using alternative treatments lies in the fact that these treatments focus on whole body healing. Ancient medical information helps us to understand that the body is a system of energy, and it needs to be treated as such.

6.14 Prescription Drugs Interfere With our Body's Natural Metabolism

Consider this: When you are prescribed a cholesterol-lowering drug, essentially the liver is forced to make less cholesterol. Have we not learned that pressuring or forcing an issue never brings the desired outcome? Instead, a methodology is needed to appropriately train the body to adapt a useful mode for it, rather than playing around with the body's metabolism.

The AMA outright condemns the chiropractic trend of prescribing vitamins and balanced nutrition to patients, even though it calls for fortified food products in its own backyard! The AMA will not even entertain the notion that vitamins may cure disease, even though it's been proven scientifically and without question in the alternative medicine arena. Alternative medicine has proven that that vitamin C remedies scurvy of the gums and L-Lysine helps suppress the herpes virus into non-expression. According to the AMA, however, there are no cures for many diseases. They are right if you do things according to their methodology; there is merely control and maintenance of disease.

6.15 Big Pharma Tries to Block Your Access to Healing Herbs and Vitamins

Under the constant 'inspiration' of the pharmaceutical companies, the FDA is trying at every chance it gets to classify all vitamins, minerals, and health supplements as 'drugs.' Why in the world would anyone even think this would be a good idea? If they succeed, not only will their profits grow to even more mind-bending numbers, but their power to say who stays healthy and who doesn't becomes reality. Actor Mel Gibson has been very proactive against this when a vitamin ban became a threat in the past. You can watch his activist video against the FDA vitamin ban on Google videos or YouTube under search words "Mel Gibson FDA vitamin ban" or "Mel Gibson Codex Alimentarius." It was apparently a spoof video on the subject, but shows the issue of the raids that the FDA has conducted on physicians' offices, raw food supermarkets, and health stores for simply selling whole raw foods or harmless vitamins. You the consumer are still protected by the

Dietary Supplement Health and Education Act (DSHEA), but must remain proactive to ensure that the Act stays active. It will be utterly ridiculous to require prescriptions for vitamins and mineral supplements.

6.16 Prescription Drugs and Bankruptcy

A national estimate puts heightened healthcare expenditure as one of the prime causes for almost half of all nationwide bankruptcies. Both high insurance cost and pharmaceutical costs are to be equally blamed for such an outcome. Companies are finding it extremely difficult to stay competitive and still offer health insurance to their employees. As a result, many companies are going offshore in an effort to reduce cost, causing wide spread unemployment in the country.

The elderly, who are the ones most hit in the pockets by healthcare costs, are steadily turning towards chiropractic care. The older generation is increasingly becoming informed about the killer side effects of prescription medicines being given to them to alleviate their chronic pain conditions related to inflammation or joint pain. Prescription drugs can cause dementia, debilitating skin rashes, significantly lower sexual urges, and can ultimately be fatal. It can be rationally said that traditional medicine has outlived its shelf life and it is high time for America to adopt more natural ways of healing.

6.17 Why Isn't Natural Healing Preferred Instead of Prescription Drugs and Surgical Procedures in the United States?

Nature's healing methods have long-standing evidence of proper functionality and minimal to zero side effects. Traditional medicine considers evidence only when it is published in one of their flagship journals, where what is published is strictly regulated to align with the pre-set conditions by an uncountable number of controlling bodies. As a result, only profit-driven pharmaceutical products and services are shown to have any proven benefits.

Is a new drug or surgical procedure always examined at least a few hundred times and honestly reported on its side effects prior to being acceptable for human patients? Of course not. The real data comes years (and many deaths) later because the public is the guinea pig. Medicine celebrates after performing the first liver, kidney, or face transplant, so the first drugs or procedures obviously can't be prior-tested unless done so on laboratory animals.

Unnecessary elective surgical removal procedures, such as cholecystectomies and gastric bypass surgeries, are two examples of outright malpractice that conventional medicine continues doing. If you are removing part of the digestive system and terming it as a weight loss technique, then perhaps in the future a patient will come in with chronic muscle pain in the leg, and he or she will be advised to undergo an amputation of that leg as the cure. Think of that! Instead of removing the organ or tissue if diseased, there should be adequate attempt to naturally heal and save its function first, rather than surgery resulting in losing the organ forever!

The reason why more and more people are switching to alternative medicine forms is simply because they produce results in a reasonable time frame, at a lesser cost, and without any of the side effects associated with conventional medicine. The next several decades will surely see a much wider acceptance of chiropractic therapy, healing touch, anti-cancer food, vitamin supplementation, hypnotherapy, Chinese herbal medicine, acupuncture, Reiki energy healing, and other holistic methods.

Chapter 7:
The Kousouli®Method of Healing

*"On earth there is nothing great but man, and in man
there is nothing great but mind."*
~ Favorinus of Arelate

The mind is vast, with unknown realms of electromagnetic energy guided by the principles of thermodynamics. It has been proven that your mind and body are like super recorders, remembering every move you make - from the numerous falls you had as a child to the sports, work, and auto injuries of today. It all adds up. Your spinal cord has been stressed by many forces both in your childhood and now, which causes communication loss between your brain and vital organs, tissues, and cells. When this occurs, there is lack of proper nerve flow from the brain, causing malfunction, premature aging, and dis-ease. Your current health condition is reminiscent of the choices you made for your body throughout all your years leading to today.

7.1 The Mind in the Dis-ease Process

The mind is not just in the brain, it is everywhere- in every cell, tissue, and organ of our creation. Every mental state is identical to a corresponding physical state. Mental terms or 'thought energies' and physical terms of 'body health' are different descriptions of the matching states, showing how our body, mind, and health conditions are all interconnected and deeply rooted in each other. The mind is a highly differentiated functional cluster which achieves high integration in a few milliseconds; acting as the driver for all brain activities.

Physical strain, chemical imbalances, emotional issues, environmental toxins, and the everyday stresses of life are impacting you even as you are reading this right now. The real danger lies with those who they think they are 'okay' and mask a headache by taking medications, or for those who let a chest pain continue, which places them at higher risk. The most complicated health concerns hit suddenly when the container 'body' can no longer hold the stress. This may end up in an emergency situation costing you countless dollars, aggravation, lost time, severe pain, and may even be fatal. So take control of your choices - and your life - while you can.

It is widely believed by laypeople that chiropractors are simply back pain doctors who cure neck and back pain by 'cracking or popping the back.' Unfortunately, most people are ignorant about the real process and the effects that spinal misalignment and nerve interference have on our overall health. Many chiropractors, like myself, have experienced extraordinary success over the years in helping patients beat a multitude of health problems. Most people don't discern that (in combination with using proper exercise, lifting procedures, better eating habits and drinking plenty of fluids) the spine requires a specific patient-tailored plan of periodic spinal adjustments for encouraging alignment. Generally speaking, when the spine is aligned properly, innate energy flows freely throughout the entire body so that various body functions remain normal. In a misaligned spine, nerve interference occurs along the spinal path and normal body functions are disrupted. The sad thing is many nerve related problems mimic severe medical conditions and patients never know it. They repeatedly get misdiagnosed by their doctors who can't find out what is going wrong, and consume over-the-counter drugs and prescription pills to cover their symptoms, never realizing that the real cause could be spinal in nature. A misaligned spine that is not coordinating the necessary instruction from the brain to its corresponding organ(s) or tissue(s) can create dis-ease.

Without spinal adjustments, multiple site misalignments that lead to dis-ease develop in approximately nine out of ten people. Many in today's conventional medicine circles are unaware of the massive research available and, ironically, uninformed that much of the research presented has come from their own colleagues in the medical profession. So many of these poorly informed medical doctors are quick to tell their patients: "There's no research on chiropractic, it's all theory, or it's never been proven." The fact is, chiropractic is strong enough to hold up against the biggest scientific sceptics.

7.2 Entering Healing - Retracing Your Recovery Pathway

Life is a circle of events and lies somewhere between 2 points: the health state and the current dis-ease condition. One important way to ensure a healthy revitalization is being able to retrace the pathway of illness all the way to the beginning, when things started to go awry. Retracing essentially allows restoration of all the phases through which you progressed to the current dis-ease state. Examine these three factors when retracing to health:

1. **Time element:** Time is of paramount importance in detailing your recovery path. If you had symptoms that were prevalent for a long time (chronic) the recovery will take some time to retrace the path to health. The rule of thumb is that acute (new)

diseases take less time to recover, whereas chronic conditions take longer time to heal.

2. **Extent of Involvement:** Some injuries might involve and encompass more extensive tissue damage than others; the more widespread the damage is, the longer the process of healing will be. It must be added, though, that no matter what dis-ease condition it is, it always has subservient damaged tissue in the cells that are malfunctioning. Consider a cut or wound: it takes time to recover to a ' normal state' and in some tougher cases, if the damage is too much it leaves a scar behind.

3. **The Dis-ease Production Phase:** To remedy a disease, it is first imperative to know the dis-ease process, otherwise the symptoms are only alleviated and the dis-ease *per se* is never cured - only temporarily concealed. Tissue requires three things to maintain health: (I) appropriate quantities of oxygen, and (II) quantitative and (III) qualitative amounts of nervous-system-mediated vital energy. In fact, tissue oxygenation is also directly regulated by the nerve supply to the tissue. On the flip side, oxygenation is also required for the nerve tissue to function properly. When a vertebral misalignment happens it causes partial closure of the entry-exit site through the spine, causing a deficiency of vital energy transfer to different parts of the body, causing dis-ease over time. Depending on the numbers of fibers affected by the misalignment, different areas of the body can be affected and will remain as such until the misalignment is treated.

7.3 How do Negative Emotions Create Unhealthy Patterns?

Our lower frequency emotions of fear, anger, and grief, can all have a long lasting negative effect on our well-being. When these emotions stay with us for a long time, they get encrypted into our subconscious system, so much so that it jumps into action when we feel a certain way, or undergo a certain stress (i.e. relationship breakups, death of a loved one, boss yells at us, etc.).

If we happen to be in a destabilized state when heightened states of emotional distress happen due to chemical stress, physical trauma, poor nourishment, or other low frequency emotions, they may lodge deep and take much longer to resolve (or never resolve). Then, years later, we encounter a comparable issue, state, or condition, and the deep-rooted previous emotive reaction kicks in and tries to save the day from any proposed danger or threat. The past event and the present-day situation is connected intimately, without your conscious knowledge. Remember that the emotional reality you hold as 'truth' can radically affect your health.

Parts of our body can hold or express emotional energy too. This is the reason for sweaty palms or cold body extremities before a presentation or an exam. Many emotions plague the bodies of chronic worriers, and these people can end up with stomach ulcers!

I have developed a technique named Kousouli Neural Emotive Reconditioning or KNER® for short, which is part of a larger healing process; the Kousouli® Method 4R Intervention System. My unique technique utilizes visual imagery, hypnosis, deep diaphragmatic breathing, colour therapy, spinal adjustments, and positive verbal declarations. The therapy identifies and neutralizes negatively stimulated emotional belief or vibratory frequency running wild in the subconscious, chakras, and body organs. It closes energy leaks that are producing unpleasant results in the patient's life so that the loop can be reconditioned positively.

KNER® therapy helps conclude if the present physical and energy bodies are stressed with certain restrictive beliefs associated with current unsettled issues, or previously experienced events. The practitioner helps the patient form an emotional picture of the original initiating event for the negative situation by flashback via hypnosis. The body of the patient assumes a similar emotional state very similar to the way it reacted during the event or previous trauma, and the patient is asked to contact the specific body area or chakra storing the emotion, which would have been identified through the practitioner's prior analysis. As the patient inhales or exhales, the practitioner stimulates the associated energy points with their hands or spinal tool while simultaneously instructing the patient with specific imagery cues and verbal declarations.

When applied effectively, the patient's nervous system releases the lingering stress entity through the spine and energy body. It is not unusual to sometimes find the patient go into an extreme dumping of repressed feelings during the session expressed as heavy tearing, heat, rage or laughter. Success varies per individual patient lifestyle variables; however it's completely safe, quick, and the process utilizes simple muscle testing. Patients often report strong emotional discharge that brings deep peace after the procedure. No part of the Kousouli® Method uses psychiatric evaluation and is a totally drug free therapy. KNER® is in the 4th part, Reset, of the Kousouli® Method 4R Intervention System.

7.4 The 4R Kousouli® Method Intervention System

My experience with the different aspects of chiropractic care, clinical research, energy healing, clairvoyant meditation, hypnosis, and personal experiences in and out of the clinic both as a doctor and as a patient have helped me develop the 4R Kousouli® Method of Health. **The main goal of the Kousouli® Method is to treat the patient by addressing vital energy loss in 4 main arenas (spiritual, mental, emotional, and physical) utilizing the 'antenna' called the nervous system.** The nervous system allows us to interact with our internal and external environments and is the master communicator of our health. The Kousouli® Method 4R Intervention System gives patients a daily checklist and simple structure for making sure they are on point to "Rejuvenate the Body, Empower the Mind, and Free the Soul."

The following diagram has three main circles, two of which are cycle states of health. The first cycle reflects where most people are when they feel something is wrong or feel ill. Because of accumulated poor lifestyle habits and neglect over time, they feel lousy and seek out a healthcare provider to deal with the physical body. The first cycle (left) reflects the negative aspects of health. The center circle represents the **Kousouli® Method 4R Intervention System**. When one becomes proactive by utilizing the Kousouli® Method, they complete the 4 steps of ***Remove, Revive, Rebuild, and Reset.*** This is where change starts, and if maintained during a set care plan over time, favorable results will start to appear. The third circle (right) reflects the positive benefits of health after incorporating the Kousouli® Method. If maintained, the patient stays in this positive cycle until neglect over time pulls the process back to the negative cycle. **The success of the method is due to the focus on the *4R continuous processes*:**

1. ***Remove the* toxins**. Cautiously limit or remove (as much as possible) all drug use (prescription, over-the-counter, or recreational), alcohol consumption, caffeine, sodas, smoking, intestinal worms & parasites, heavy metal toxicity, allergens, electro-magnetic radiation, old scar tissue build-up, junk food and fast food, environmental and occupational ergonomic hazards.

2. ***Revive* the nervous system utilizing correct chiropractic care.** Chiropractic adjustments reduce spinal stress and open vital communication pathways from the brain to every cell, tissue, and organ in the body.

3. ***Rebuild* the body through whole food nutrition and exercise.** Proper hydration, nourishment, oxygenation, supplementation, exercise, stretching, and deep tissue re-organization of spinal muscle attachments.

4. ***Reset* your thoughts and programming.** Prayer, meditation, visualization, hypnotic suggestion, Kousouli Neural Emotive Reconditioning (KNER®), and proper

mind and body rest will ensure that the whole process is perpetuated within yourself, and you continue to reap the benefits for the rest of your life.

Going through the Kousouli® Method 4R intervention system will ensure you get the 5th 'R' too; ***Recovery***! My simple message is: Those with beautiful posture, flexibility, strength, unlimited energy, and youthful and healthy lives make daily healthy choices. Don't lie to yourself thinking that just going to the gym, eating a few days' worth of salads instead of meat, one day of yoga, or a week of Hollywood's latest detox craze will get you healthy. To stay in the positive cycle, without losing any progress by relapse, you *must* decide your health is a priority worth maintaining over the course of your life - not just for a week or a few months. The 4R system of the Kousouli® Method Intervention System now makes it much easier to keep yourself on track and move toward your health goals.

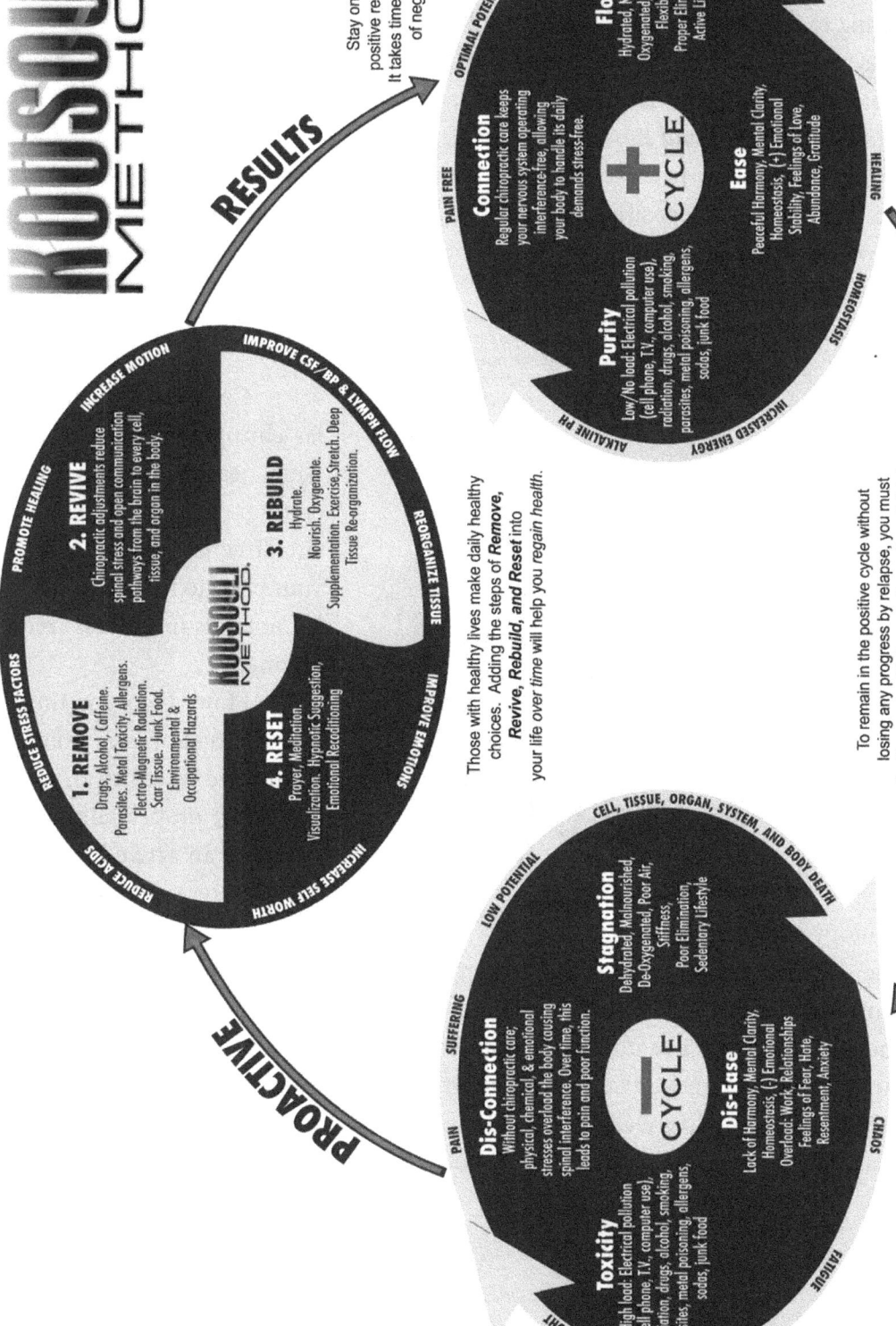

Neglecting to do all of the above 4 steps will bring you backwards into the negative cycle. Choose to be healthy by paying the price of health. The price is dedication and commitment to a new paradigm that maintains your health priorities. Adding the steps of **Remove, Revive, Rebuild, and Reset** into your life consistently will help you regain and maintain your healthy new perspective. I will summarize below the attributes that will help you in maintaining the positive cycle, and also explain the lifestyle events that will push you towards the negative cycle.

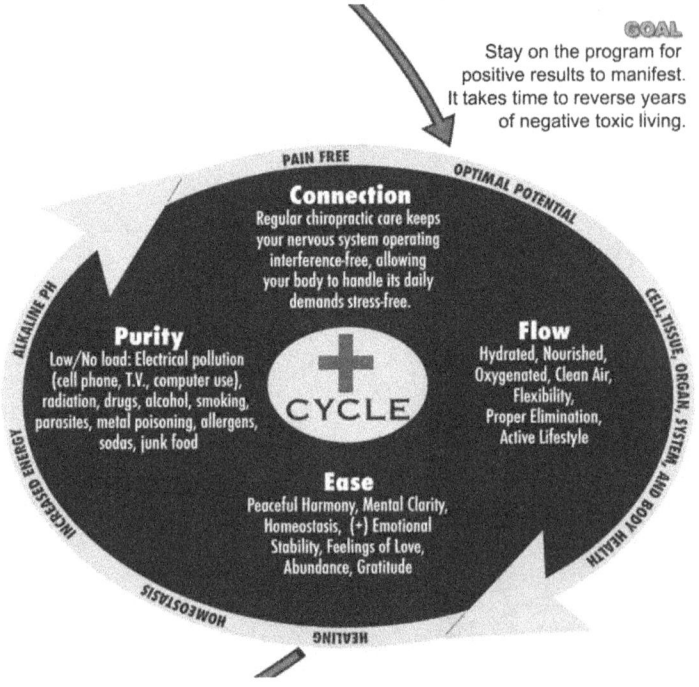

Staying in the Positive Cycle

- **Connection:** Regular chiropractic care keeps your nervous system operating in an interference-free fashion, allowing your body to handle its daily demands in a stress-free manner.
- **Flow:** Incorporating proper hydration, nourishment, oxygen, clean air, flexibility, proper elimination, and an active lifestyle will ensure a smooth flow of energy within your body.
- **Ease:** Having peaceful purpose, harmony, mental clarity, homeostasis, positive emotional stability, feelings of love, abundance, and gratitude for yourself and others will keep you in a positive frame of mind.
- **Purity:** Avoid or remove electrical pollution (cellular phone, televisions, and computers), radiation, drugs, alcohol, smoking, parasites, metal poisoning, allergens, sodas, caffeine overload, junk, or fast food.

The Kousouli® Method of Healing

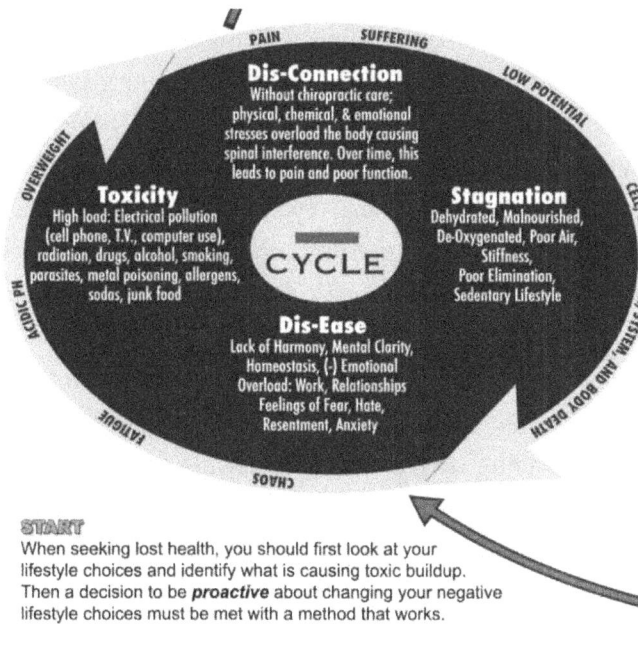

START
When seeking lost health, you should first look at your lifestyle choices and identify what is causing toxic buildup. Then a decision to be *proactive* about changing your negative lifestyle choices must be met with a method that works.

Reverting Back to the Negative Cycle through Neglect

- **Dis-connection:** Irregular, discontinuous, or complete lack of chiropractic care; physical, chemical, and emotional stresses all compound spinal overload. Over time, this miscommunication of brain-to-body leads to pain and poor function.

- **Stagnation:** Staying in a dehydrated condition, receiving improper nutrition, no or low supplementation, poor air or water quality, lymph flow backup, poor elimination, and a sedentary lifestyle are cardinal signs for bringing your health down.

- **Dis-Ease:** Lack of harmony, mental clarity, negative emotional stresses, work or relationship stress overload, feelings of fear, hate, resentment and anxiety all will contribute to disease conditions.

- **Toxicity:** High load of electro-magnetic pollution, radiation, drugs, alcohol, smoking, parasites, heavy metal poisoning, allergens, sodas, and junk food will result in an overall imbalance and a downslide of your health condition.

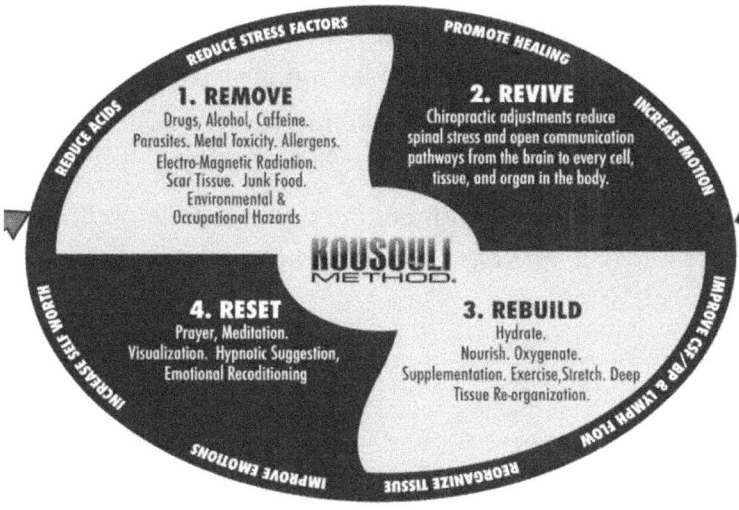

Those with healthy lives make daily healthy choices. Adding the steps of *Remove, Revive, Rebuild, and Reset* into your life *over time* will help you *regain health*.

It becomes apparent from the above points that most of your health is a matter of lifestyle choice; being able to regulate your temptations and not resorting to the lazier lower vibration path at every whim. Sometimes, taking the tougher route ultimately proves to be wiser, healthier, and perhaps easier in the long run. The very same conditions, when done properly, induce and maintain the positive cycle, and a slight imbalance in any aspect can tilt the whole balance towards the negative energy cycle. Consistency is key in maintaining a healthy condition, and the more consistent you are with your good habits and lifestyle choices the better you will be served by your body. This system is a great guide for allowing you the ability to keep yourself in check by referring to it often to ensure you are doing all 4 aspects adequately to maintain your homeostatic balance. It will help remind you if you've been skipping or neglecting yourself by smoking, eating junk food, forgetting to get your workout in, staying dehydrated, or missing your last chiropractic appointment, all of which would start leaning you towards the negative cycle.

The Kousouli® Method 4R Intervention System is continuously being adapted through clinical application and research. When correctly applied, it has shown successful symptom reduction or elimination of headaches, dizziness, fatigue/low energy, carpel tunnel, whiplash pains, muscle spasms, joint pains, neck pain, back pain, allergies, depression, hormonal imbalances, fibromyalgia, numbness, limb tingling, IBS, asthma, acid reflux/GERD, arthritis, insomnia, and toxicity - just to name a few. The Kousouli® Method through KNER® also takes into account the spiritual, mental, and emotional aspects of health, which usually manifest into the physical plane as pain and dis-ease. By accessing specific energy points and balancing these points from leaking, the individual can focus their energy on healing with quicker results.

This system's powerful technique of replenishing health naturally goes beyond the surface scope of this book and is taught privately to interested practitioners at live seminar events. Details can be found at www.KousouliMethod.com.

Spiritual	Mental	Emotional	Chakra	Physical			Function	Malfunction
				Spinal	Organs			
Trance mediumship, Knowingness, Higher self, Cosmic energy intake	Clarity, Pure awareness, Optimism/Pessimism, Imagination	Peace, Tranquility, Chaos, Blame, Arrogance, Dissatisfaction	Cranial Crown 7	Skull Bones, Cranial nerves	Brain, Pineal gland, CSF ventricles		Cognition, Critical thinking	Mental disorders, Head pain, Dizziness
Clairvoyance, Abstract intuition, Precognition, Inner voice	Trusting, Memory, Intellect, Reasoning, Ignorance	Fear, Pride, Inflexibility, Self conscious, Confusion, Envy, Humiliation	Cranio-Cervical 3rd Eye 6	Occiput, C1 Atlas, C2 Axis, C3-C7 Cervical & Brachial plexus	Brain, Cerebellum, Hypothalamus, Pituitary, Eyes, Ears, Nose, Throat		Brain-body communication, Hearing, Seeing, Smelling, Tasting, Chewing	Head & Neck pain, Dizziness, Eye, Ear, Nose, Throat issues, Migraines, Jaw pains, Sleep disorders
Clairaudience, Telepathy, Pragmatic intuition	Authority, Creative identity, Inner drive	Expressionless, Feeling Stuck, Sadness, Vulnerability, Disgust	Cervical Throat 5	C1-T1 Cervical & Brachial plexus	Thyroid, Vocal cords, Heart, Lungs, Neck & shoulders, Brachial plexus		Brain-body communication, Verbal communication, Hormone regulation	Neck pain, Sore throat, Arm & Shoulder pain, Stiffness, Hormonal disorders, Sleep disorders
Love Affinity	Self acceptance, Harmony, Equilibrium	Compassion, Love, Tenderness, Joy, Abundance, Heartache, Betrayal, Grief, Rejection, Hatred	Upper Thorax Heart 4	T1-T6 Sympathetic ganglion	Heart, Lungs, Thymus, Liver, Gallbladder		Circulation, Breathing	Chest pain, Breathing issues, Asthma, Heart circulation, Heartburn
Out of body experience, Life force energy distribution, Inner integration	Will Power, Egotism, Restlessness	Paranoia, Anger, Low self esteem, Resentment, Nervousness, Worry, Guilt, Anxiety, Jealousy, Regret	Lower Thorax Solar Plexus 3	T7-T12 Ileocecal valve, Celiac plexus, Pyloric valve	Kidneys, Diaphragm, Liver, Gallbladder, Spleen, Pancreas, Stomach, Adrenals, Large & Small intestine		Breathing, Detoxification, Elimination, Digestion, Assimilation	Kidney Stones, Liver, Pancreatic failure, Gall Stones, Gastric disorders, Sleep disorders, Allergies
Clairsentience	Sexuality, Emotional need, Relationships, Social ambition, Addiction	Enthusiasm, Inner conflict, Peeved off, Frozen will, Fear, Lust, Manipulative	Lumbo-Sacral Navel 2	L1-S1 Lumbar plexus, Celiac plexus, Sciatic nerve	Bladder, Sex organs, Prostate, Uterus, Large intestine, Appendix		Reproduction, Elimination	Low back pain, IBS, Allergies, Sciatica, Kidney & Urinary issues, Constipation
Survival, Material harmony	Safety, Security, Emotional, Physicality, Sense of Lack	Vulnerability, Neediness, Insecurity, Control issues, Obsession, Materialism, Distrust	Sacro-Pelvic Spinal Base 1	S1-S5 Sacral plexus, Sciatic nerve	Rectum, Anus, Colon, Bladder, Sex organs		Reproduction, Elimination	Menstrual pains, Cramping, Sterility, SI pain, Leg circulation, Knee pains, Numbness, Digestive disorders, Allergies
Psychometry, Healing, Telekinesis			Hands Palm center	Radial, Medial, Ulnar nerves			Creative manifestation, Energy transfer	Arthritis, Swelling, Gout, Inflammation, Cramping, Carpel tunnel
Grounding, Earth energy intake			Feet Foot arch	Tibial, Sural, Peroneal, Cutaneous, Plantar, Saphenous Nerves			Transportation, Physical manifestation	Arthritis, Swelling, Gout, Inflammation, Cramping, Tarsal tunnel

Note: Points will cross and may affect multiple chakra sites. This chart displays the most basic relationship between the spiritual, mental, emotional, and physical human planes.

KOUSOULI METHOD. Copyright 2004-2016. All Rights Reserved.

7.5 The Kousouli® Method and Acidosis

When people feel pain, are distressed or grieving, they are exhibiting manifestation of the negative cycle. A patient in less than optimum states is most likely starting, or already in, the process called the 'acid state.' You need to understand the basics of acidosis, as it is the root cause of all dis-ease afflicting us as humans. Our bodies work under a finely regulated homeostatic balance of acids and bases (a.k.a. alkalis) 24/7, 365 days a year. The body also produces its own neutralizing buffers to keep the overall acidity under control. By encouraging a proper whole food diet and removing toxic loads through the 'Remove' phase of care, the body is given a chance to come back to balance. The pH scale is measured from 0 to 14, with 7 being the neutral point. Substances that are below 7 are considered acidic and substances over 7 are considered alkaline or more basic (pH or "potential for hydrogen" is the given term to designate acidity or alkalinity). An internal environment like the body favors the alkaline side of the scale. Human saliva or urine levels in a slightly alkaline state are considered healthier, as dis-ease seems to favor the acid state. Let's take a look at why an over-accumulation of acids is not a good thing.

How Does Acidosis Affect Your Organs?

Organ	Effects of Acidosis
Colon	Acidosis can result in unwanted dead fecal material to get stuck in the colon and subsequently flushed back to the main bloodstream. Hence, ensuring good bowel elimination 2-3 times a day is imperative.
Heart	The vagus nerve, which innervates the heart, operates at alkaline pH. Acidosis alters heart rate, decreases heart muscle oxygenation, and causes slow wasting over time.
Stomach	Different manifestations of inefficient digestive capability are: inhibited appetite, belching, bloating, hiccups, regurgitation, vomiting, nausea, intestinal gas, flatulence, constipation, or diarrhea. May also cause hiatal hernia syndrome, which reduces hydrochloric acid levels in the stomach, in turn further impeding the digestive process.
Liver	Being the body's detoxifier, it absorbs acids and secretes out alkali ions. Acidosis significantly increases the load on the liver and if persistent can cause liver failure, which is a fatal condition.

Kidneys	They are one of the most vital organs responsible for maintaining the overall alkaline pH of the blood by constantly filtering out acidic waste products. Overworking the kidneys can result in kidney stone formation, a highly painful disorder.
Small Intestine	There is a lining in the small intestine, called the Peyer's Patches, which are normally involved in producing lymphocytes. An enzyme, 'chyle,' is secreted in generous amounts to maintain alkalinity and function of the patches; incremental acidosis significantly impedes Peyer's Patches functionality.
Pancreas	It has two important functions: regulate blood pH and sugar. An overall alkaline diet is thus important to let your pancreas do its job.
Lymphatic System	Lymphatic fluid carries nutrition and removes waste products from areas where blood cannot reach. It functions optimally at alkaline conditions. Acidosis slows the lymph system and all its functions.

Does Negative Energy Contribute to Acidosis?

Any kind of negative emotion can use up reserve energy, tax body function, increase free radicals, and create acidity. An increase in stress beyond normal amounts will lead to acidosis. Have you ever heard the saying "I am sick to my stomach"? Hearing phrases like "Your problems are getting the better of you" or "Your problems are eating away at your happiness" – these are emotional states, which make you highly prone to acidosis and set the stage for dis-ease. Oftentimes, it is the fear (of reprimand, rebuke, rejection, etc. from your peers) that sets you off on this phase of negative energy. So choose the company of positive people who only talk of good things and throw away the thoughts of fear and anger. Choose the path of love for both yourself, and others!

Tips YOU Can Adopt to Get Rid of Acidosis

1. **Chiropractor-Mediated Adjustments.** It is highly recommended that you get adjusted correctly by a chiropractor in the cervical and thoracic area to ensure that nerve supply to different pH-regulating organs is uninhibited. Spinal adjustments will also improve your respiration and oxygen intake, thus contributing to boost your alkalinity.
2. **Exercise.** If you are facing problems of heavy acidosis, DO NOT resort to a heavy exercise regimen, as that will further build up lactic acid in your system, causing more acidosis. Exercise breaks down tissue and sends toxins away from the muscles for

excretion. Moderate exercise with plenty of hydration, however, *will* benefit you. No exercise at all is a contributor to acidosis as well, so a sedentary lifestyle is not at all recommended.

3. **Air Quality.** Pollutants in the air means a lot of our bodies' energy goes to detoxifying the air we're breathing in. Limit your exposure to air pollution such as: enclosed crowded office buildings, dampness, musty or moldy air in the home or basement, synthetic furniture or carpet smells, air fresheners, garages, factories, chemical colognes and perfumes, etc. All the aforementioned are known causes of acidosis and can cause inflammation.
4. **Eat Your Greens.** Maintain a clean diet with very light meat and heavy greens.
5. **Drink Water, not Soda.** Keeping hydrated allows acids to flow out easier and maintains normal blood pH and viscosity. Phosphoric acid is in all sodas and causes havoc in your body. Instead load up on green drinks that contain chlorophyll.

7.6.1 The Kousouli® Method and Detoxification

Besides the skin, the liver and the kidneys are our most important detoxifying organs within the body. Kidneys filtrate out all acid and unnecessary ions, and the liver basically has the capability of tackling any kind of detoxification. If they become overworked, they will give out and you'll end up in renal (kidney) failure, liver cirrhosis, or liver failure. Detoxification is defined as the process that helps you get rid of the toxins, by either neutralizing them or transforming them to benign forms. Detoxification also incorporates removal of congestions and excess mucus. Having two to three regular bowel movements is an important aspect of maintaining great health. Constipation or diarrhea can both throw your electrolyte balance off track and make you feel sick. The colon can also accumulate toxins if improper bowel movements become a norm. Therefore, the first part of any effective corrective program is toxin removal through digestive tract cleansing. Colon cancer now occupies the second position among cancer-related deaths in the US. The colon is considered the body's 'sewage system,' and if not emptied correctly, it will accumulate toxic poisons that get absorbed into the bloodstream, creating dis-ease.

Every One Can Benefit From a Good Colon Cleansing Program

Proper colon detoxification programs prepare your body for optimal health by eradicating mucoid plaque. Colon hydrotherapy, psyllium, home enemas, and herbal colon cleansers that incorporate a combination of internal cleansing herbs are all part of an ideal detoxification program. Someone on a typical Western diet accumulates 8 meals of undigested food and waste within their colon at any given time. Someone living on a high fiber diet may accumulate only 2 or 3 meals between our bodies' natural expulsions of waste. Appropriate intestinal cleansing will help shed accumulated food debris.

Remember, if you are obese or have too much 'bad' cholesterol floating around, this can also generate free radicals that will function as toxins. In the Kousouli® Method, *Step 1 - Remove* - of the 4R system, a combo of lifestyle changes and a good diet regimen are highly recommended. After removing the already accumulated toxicity of the body in *Step 1 - Remove*, and opening the nervous system, *Step 2 - Revive* will help the glands, hormones, organs, stomach, intestines, rectum, and colon re-communicate with the brain and re-regulate the shedding of unhealthy weight. Then we support the body through proper diet and supplementation in *Step 3 - Rebuild*. In *Step 4 - Reset*, we address the emotional and subconscious reprogramming of possible thought-limiting factors or bad habits the patient is suffering from.

Detox with Caution

When performing a system detox, consider starting slowly. The body will go through withdrawal symptoms, especially if the patient is addicted to high glycemic carbohydrates, diet and caffeine drinks, smoking or drinking. A successful program leads to release of toxins, harmful bacteria, parasites, and yeast (Candida) overgrowth. This waste leaves the tissues and enters your blood system as it travels for neutralization and elimination. Therefore, patients will usually experience issues like: fever, nausea, headaches, chills, ulcers, skin rashes, thirst, increased urination, loss of appetite, eye pain, difficulty sleeping, extreme drowsiness and fatigue, diarrhea, muscle soreness, lack of motivation, and any already known problems usually become heightened briefly.

For example, a migraine or fatigue may become more intense than previously experienced, or a runny nose gets worse than before the detox. This detox side effect phenomenon is termed a 'healing crisis' and generally lasts for a 1 to 2 week period after starting a detox. Although it may not seem like it at first, this is a good thing as it means the body has begun cleaning up toxins and is beginning to repair and heal you. Though after this beginning detox phase, 'healing' is not yet returned. Healing occurs after the toxins have been dealt with and the body can start to rebuild in the healthier state.

We must remind ourselves of the many toxins we have come into contact with and multiply that by the number of weeks, months, or years our body has suffered. We must further understand that getting healthy will not result from a quick week's detox program. Therefore, as you go through your 'healing crisis,' expect to feel worse before you feel better as your body cleanses your 'house.' Follow your doctor's recommendations closely and take the detox seriously, so that you may give your body all the time it needs to regain its health. After a proper cleansing period while under continued care for your spinal health, you will notice that your body will start to respond by holding the spinal adjustment longer, and periods of pain will also start to minimize between visits. The key is to stay on the program and give it time to work for you as your body reprograms itself from the inside out.

7.6.2 The Kousouli® Method and Chelation Therapy

Chelation is the process by which a metal or mineral links to another substance, a mechanism by which most common substances perform their function in the body, like aspirin, antibiotics, vitamins, minerals and trace elements.

Intravenous chelation therapy is a non-invasive, safe, and effective methodology that reverses and slows the progression of atherosclerosis and other age-related and degenerative diseases. This therapy utilizes a small amino acid called ethylene diamine tetra acetic acid (commonly abbreviated EDTA), which links with harmful free metals in the body and excretes them out. On average, 85 percent of chelation patients that have the procedure improve significantly. It has been observed to be beneficial for heart attacks, leg pain, blocked arteries, stroke, diabetes, gangrene, and also cancer. It has also been considered as an alternative to bypass surgery, or angioplasty and stents. Starting in the 1950's, EDTA chelation therapy has been speculated as a treatment option for calcium associated with toughening of the arteries, with successful chelation therapies reported starting since 1955. It has also been used by the U.S. Navy for lead-mediated injuries. Rather than having invasive options for circulatory disorders such as coronary artery disease, or cerebral vascular disease, EDTA chelation therapy has been considered a better option in combination with a well-balanced diet and healthy lifestyle.

This outpatient procedure is mostly a painless treatment, with minimal discomfort and a normal lifestyle while doing infusion. With current advanced methods there is also the oral tablet, and now also an option of suppository chelation tabs which can be administered through the anal passage. Both of the administration methods are risk-free and non-toxic, when compared with other available drug treatment options. This method also has scored highly in terms of eliminating death rates generally caused by other conventional invasive therapy.

Although there has been substantial debate about the use of this treatment for coronary vascular disease, the progress rate is quite inspirational. Chelation therapy benefits have been widely known for decades in the holistic arena. Even though this promising therapy is gaining favor in specialty recovery clinics worldwide, chances are you won't hear about it as a viable artery cleansing option from your local hospital or traditional medical practitioner, since costs to perform more invasive and costly procedures are to their benefit.

7.6.3 The Kousouli® Method and Arthritis

Arthritis affects about 30 million Americans and has direct relationship to toxicity in diet and lifestyle. But through a combination of hematological detoxification (detoxifying your blood, lymph, and colon), boosting the immune system, dietary and moderate lifestyle changes, shifting weight off of misaligned degenerating joints, applying proper supplementation and hydration, the Kousouli® Method can help you significantly alleviate the pain and suffering associated with arthritis. See Chapter 11 for more information on dealing with arthritis.

7.6.4 The Kousouli® Method and Depression

Remember our discussion of Prozac earlier in the book? Depression has assumed the status of an endemic condition and has resulted in many suicides. We should never forget that our mental state is a direct reflection of internal biochemical status, our overall quality of life, and our thought process in general. Hence, 1) detoxifying yourself and fixing your biochemical status, 2) exercise programs to refocus yourself and divert attention from origins of negative energy, and 3) spine realignment to reduce overall stress - are the three facets utilized by the Kousouli® Method to get you into a more positive state for rehabilitation from depression. See Chapter 11 for more information on dealing with depression.

7.6.5 The Kousouli® Method and Scar Tissue Removal

The process of healing occurs through three separate phases during which a fibrous connective tissue or scar tissue is initially formed. During inflammation, prostaglandins act as master regulators, and activate the immune system along with trafficking of the immune mediators that help prevent infection. We also see an eradication of scar tissue during inflammation, which is a prelude for new, healthy tissue formation by cell proliferation. This is a longer step than the previous one and may take a couple of weeks for complete regeneration. By nature, scar tissue and healthy tissue can be differentiated in terms of elasticity and lubrication. An improper or hurried processing can cause weakened tissue formation, making it more prone to further injury. Since this can be disadvantageous for athletes, they strongly follow a multistep remodeling system carefully. Well-directed physical training helps develop stamina and endurance. Almost all physical activity-related exercises are beneficial while tissue remodeling.

What happens to the injured tissue? It contracts over time, as it is lacks elasticity. Excessive depositing of damaged tissue causes sensitivity to pain nerves due to stimulation. It also interferes with the circulation by blocking blood flow, and as a result, accumulation of toxins and other excretes causes different grades/degrees of complexity altogether. As a result, injured muscle becomes fibrous and confines movement and nutritious supply.

The hypersensitivity of pain nerves due to scar tissue deposits can be well identified during deep tissue massage or rolfing. We can identify scar tissue by simply determining its resistance to proper muscle tone and movement; healthy tissues behave differently, as they possess more elasticity and less resistance. For proper healing to occur in the spine and associated body parts, removal or breaking down and remodeling of improperly laid scar tissue by deep cross friction myofascial release is of utmost importance, as this helps oxygenate and improve blood flow to the stagnant area(s).

We Must Take Personal Responsibility

Within each of us lies both the problem as well as the solution for all of our various health problems as an individual, as well as a nation; acknowledging that is the first step to all wellness. It is important for the American healthcare system to rise from the delusional, lazy, or complacent state of self-denial and uncertainty in order to take greater responsibility and hold the utmost respect for both the mind and the body. Incorporating the aforementioned methods into our daily lives and routines can help solve many, if not all, of our current health issues.

Chapter 8:
The Kousouli® Method Spinal Stretches (KSS®)

"Lack of activity destroys the good condition of every human being, while movement and methodical physical exercise save it and preserve it."
~ Plato

8.1 Rejuvenate the Body, Empower the Mind, and Free the Soul

Unknowingly, many people are adding problems to their already over-stressed spines. Some well-known malpractices are: texting on a mobile device with necks flexed forward, carrying an over-sized heavy purse or backpack over one shoulder, long hours of slouching in a computer chair at work, holding the phone between a shoulder and tilted head, sleeping face down on an unsupported mattress or couch, placing a thick wallet in a back pocket, and wearing high heels all day without taking any breaks. These bad habits mold our spines forward into that unattractive hunched position (kyphosis), and can also eventually create large sideways back humps (scoliosis), causing us to shorten, disfigure, and look years older. Some even lose vital lung capacity from caved in chests, forward head postures, and tightened pectoral muscles, which leads to fatigued states of acidosis. We rarely get a chance to exercise truly correct posture, since very few chances throughout the day allow for the extension of our spinal column.

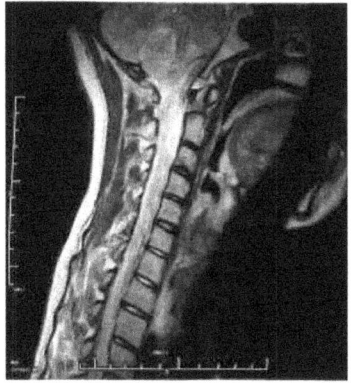

MRI SHOWS STRESSED TISSUES
IN THE CERVICAL SPINE

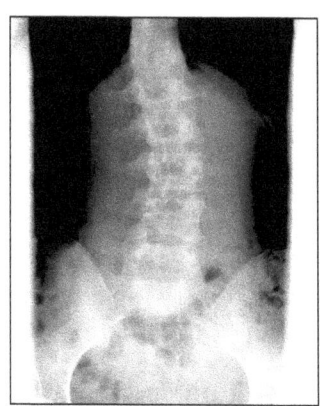

X-RAY SHOWING A
LUMBAR SCOLIOSIS

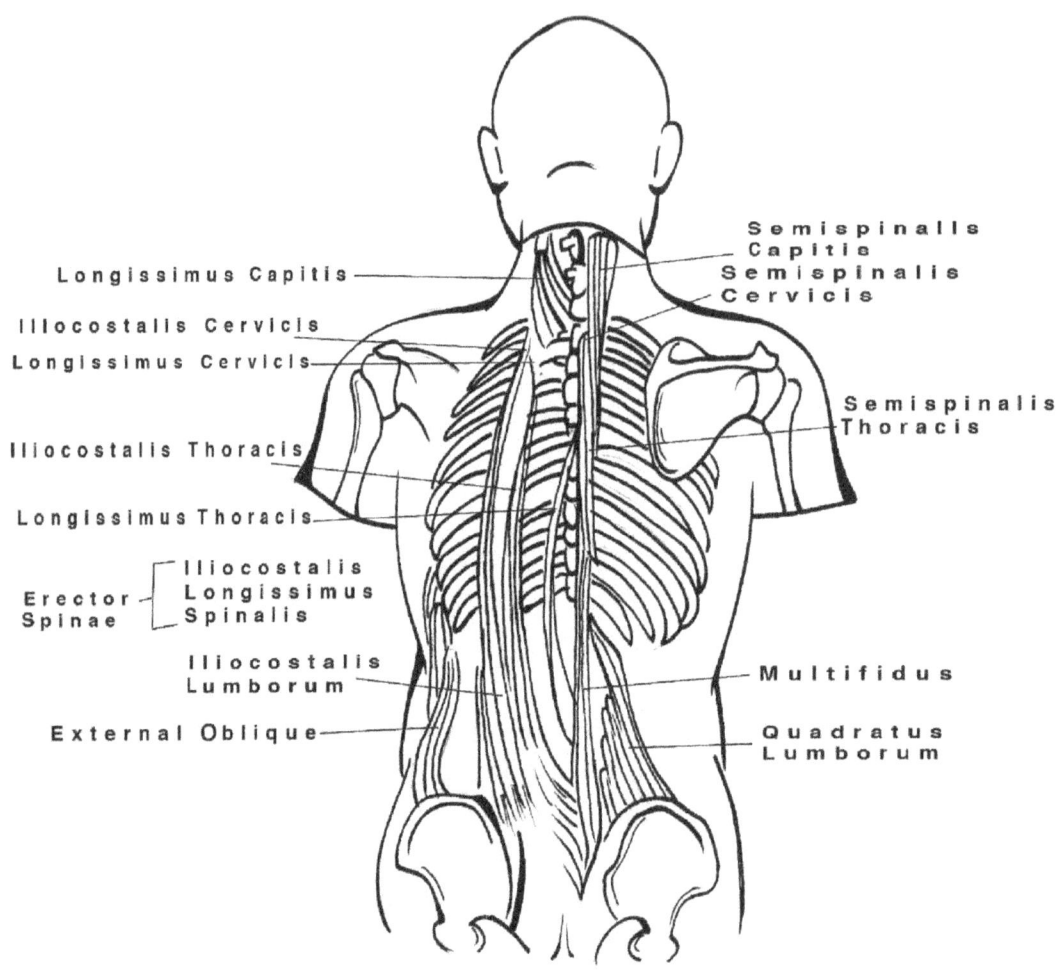

I decided to help patients improve their posture by developing nine simple and easy to remember stretches (Kousouli Spinal Stretches or KSS®) that can be incorporated into one's daily routine effortlessly for a more erect posture. These nine stretches strengthen the very muscles that encourage proper form - the erector spinae muscle group. They consist of the spinalis, longissimus, and iliocostalis muscles of the back. In addition, focus also centers on muscles of good head, neck, and shoulder posture: Semispinalis capitis, semispinalis cervicis, splenius capitis, splenius cervicis, levator scapulae, and rhombodeus major and minor.

Coupled with my fascination with mythology and the understanding of the human body over the years, I developed KSS® - an easy to remember, practical, and fun way to keep fit, stay positive, and move with energy and stamina throughout the day.

Kousouli Spinal Stretches (KSS®) Benefits:

- Strengthens erector spinae muscle groups; improves posture and overall physical appearance, helping you look and feel younger.
- Improves circulatory flow, cardiovascular fitness and health.
- Releases stored tensions (physiological reduction of stress).
- May help slow down osteoporosis when done regularly.
- Burns calories and may help with weight management.
- Release endorphins and enkephelins that block pain and help you feel good.
- Positive outlet for releasing emotionally stored stress; depression, frustration, anger, and anxiety.
- Increases oxygen to brain and breathing capacity for improved alertness, concentration, and mental ability.
- Increases muscular strength, endurance, and flexibility for improved body balance and coordination.

Precautions:

KSS® can be a magnificent workout program for all ages to bring more energy, stamina, and power into your life. Nevertheless, there are some safeguards that you should keep in mind when starting the program.

- Always consult your doctor before beginning any exercise or stretching program like KSS®.
- If you feel pain when performing any movements - stop immediately.
- Begin your KSS® gently - do not 'jump right in' forcefully. Give yourself time to adapt.
- If you have had a joint replacement or are just coming out of surgery, simply limit, restrict, or avoid major movements.
- KSS® movements and methods may be modified and adapted to suit an individual's age, needs, and abilities. Do the modified versions labeled 'M' if the original stretch is too difficult for you.
- A KSS® program for seniors or arthritis sufferers may be applied slowly, and modified gradually over a period of time, depending on skill level. Move your joints slowly through a full range of motion several times, to help enhance overall circulation, and decrease any stiffness. KSS® may be resumed once tenderness has diminished and your doctor allows you back to total activity.
- Rest painful, inflamed, or hot joints with a cold ice compress at 15-30 minute in-

tervals, and discontinue for the time being if pain occurs.
- Always breathe deeply down into your diaphragm (not chest), and allow unrestricted flow of your airway while doing KSS® movements.
- Be sure to use a pillow or soft mat for any joints (like the knees) that make constant contact with the ground during modified stretching.
- Practice good technique; do not overextend joints beyond the normal range of motion. Maintain good form and posture.
- Hydrate often throughout the day (A full glass of water per hour awake is recommended.) *See section 10.16 for recommended water requirements.*
- When learning the stretches, consult a more experienced KSS® user for proper form and execution, rather than learning the poses incorrectly.
- Follow your stretching with a cool-down period, including sustaining the end of the stretch to avoid tenderness or stiffness. If soreness or stiffness occurs despite performing a cool-down, reduce your movements and try the modified 'M' version of the stretch.

KSS® is powerful, quick, and easy to do. Just nine key stretches total; three easy to do stretches in the morning, three mid-day, and three in the evening. You may choose your favorites and make a personalized routine. Adding these stretches to your chiropractic care program and a clean diet, can help you gain the posture you deserve, encourage healthy circulation, and help oxygenate your entire body!

The following pages will detail the various stretches along with images for instruction. Each stretch can also be performed by persons with disability who are not able to stand, or have weak lower extremities. The modified versions of each stretch will be denoted by the letter 'M.' **Let's Get Started!**

(A.) HERMES STRETCH

Hermes was the flying messenger of the Gods, thus the pointed hands and fingers in this pose (to resemble flying). This is a recommended morning stretch. Start with one arm extended straight up over your shoulder and the knee bent towards your chest. Inhale deeply, and slightly extend your back as you hold the stretch for three seconds. Slowly switch the arms and legs as you exhale. Repeat the stretch on the opposite side. Modified Hermes is done by lying on your back. As you inhale and exhale from your diaphragm, visualize your body healing itself, sending messages more effectively from your body's control center (the brain).

(B.) POSEIDON STRETCH

Poseidon was the ruler and God of the sea. This stretch is designed to look like Poseidon as he shoots from the sea. This is a recommended morning stretch. Poseidon should be performed by starting in a crouched position. Inhale deeply from your diaphragm and rise up into a standing position with one leg back, as if emerging out of the ocean. Extend the spine and push the chest out. Keep your arms wide, and hold up your chin. Hold for three seconds, and then exhale as you come back down into a crouched position. Repeat the stretch with the opposite leg. Envision yourself victorious as you explode past any current tension, body pain, or health issue you may be facing.

(C.) APHRODITE/EROS STRETCH

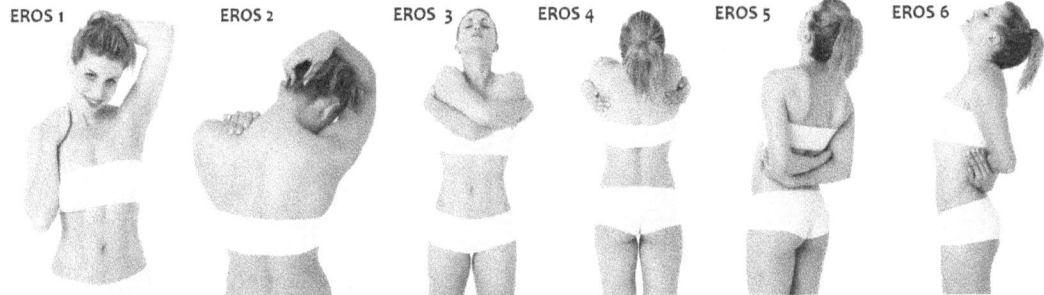

Aphrodite was the Goddess of love, beauty, and desire. This is a recommended morning stretch and can be performed in the shower while warm water washes over the back of the neck, shoulders, and upper back. Stand with your left hand on your trapezius and pull the shoulder muscles down and forward. Anchor your fingers from your right hand onto the left posterior inferior occipital ridge (bottom left edge of skull, see picture: Eros2). Gently pull your head forward, down, and to the right with the chin towards your right chest. Inhale and exhale feeling the stretch. Repeat on the opposite side (Eros 1). Next, perform a loving heart hug by wrapping your arms around your chest (Eros 3, 4) as you extend your head back. With a gentle squeeze, try to move your fingers as far back to your spine as possible. Next, wrap your arms around your low back for support. Extend your upper body back gently, feeling the stretch (Eros 5, 6). The modified version of this stretch can be done seated. Appreciate yourself and feel love for the healthy being that you wish to be.

D.) APOLLO STRETCH

Apollo was the God of music, healing, and archery. Thus, the archery style pose. This is a recommended mid-day stretch. Apollo should be performed in a standing position. Inhale deeply from your diaphragm, arch your spine, and push out your chest as you pull one arm and leg back. Put yourself into an archer position, and hold for a three second count. Exhale as you come back to starting position. Focus on the fluid motion of your body as tension builds upon extension of the back and arms. Repeat on the opposite side. Modify this stretch by kneeling or sitting with legs crossed. Imagine you reaching your target for a healthy, long life.

(E.) HEPHAESTUS STRETCH

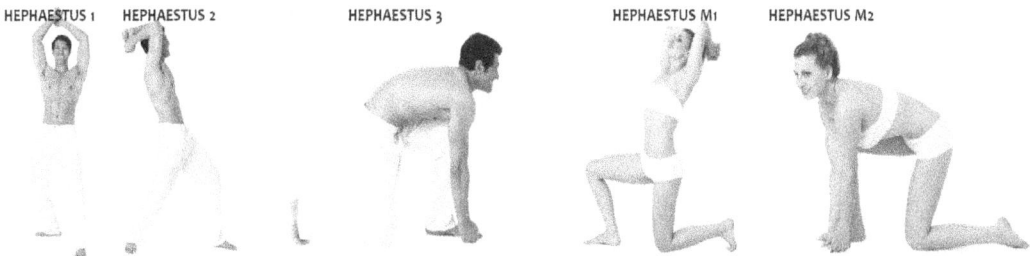

Hephaestus was the master blacksmith and craftsman of the Gods; God of fire and the forge. This is a recommended mid-day stretch. It is done by going from an extended standing position to a crouched forward pose, as if you were wielding a large axe or hammer to the ground. Inhale as you slowly extend a leg and stretch back, hold for three seconds, and then come down gently forward overhead, bending the knees as you exhale. Rotate slightly your upper body through the movement to isolate the abdominals. Go slow and do not overextend your back. Repeat the stretch on the opposite side. Modified version is done by kneeling or sitting with legs crossed. Imagine, with each extended movement of your arms, that your efforts to better yourself inside and out begin to manifest.

(F.) ATHENA STRETCH

Athena was thought as the wisest of all, and was the Goddess of warfare and reason. This is a recommended mid-day stretch. Stand with flexed biceps as if you are holding a large shield in each arm. Extend slightly your spine and inhale deeply. Turn your arms and upper torso to one side and bring up the opposite knee. Tighten your abdominal muscles and hold for three seconds. Exhale and repeat on the other side. As you breathe deep from your diaphragm, perceive yourself as an impenetrable fortress. Any negative energy (or dis-ease) that may be coming from the world around you simply bounces off.

(G.) ZEUS STRETCH

Zeus was Greek mythology's king of the Gods and ruler of Mount Olympus; the God of the sky and thunder. This is a recommended night stretch prior to ending your day. Zeus should be started with your body crouched and then slowly extend your arms up as you stand into a body X position. Inhale deeply as you slowly stretch to the sky pushing up on your toes. Feel the stretch as you hold for three seconds. Exhale slowly as you descend back into a crouched position. As you descend and exhale, cross your arms, as if throwing lightning bolts down to Earth from the heavens. Repeat. Envision throwing dis-ease and toxicity from your body, just as Zeus threw lightning bolts.

(H.) DIONYSUS STRETCH

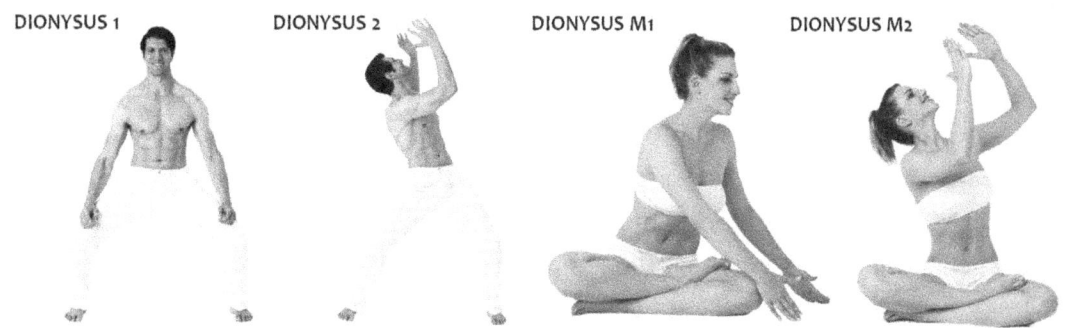

Dionysus was the God of enjoyment. He was often represented by wine, alcohol, parties, festivals, and merry occasions. This is a recommended night stretch. Dionysus should be performed while standing in a saddle stance. Slowly bring up both arms as if holding an oversized glass of wine. Inhale deeply from your diaphragm, and slowly extend your torso as you rotate to one side. Gently extend your neck and upper back as if you are drinking the wine. Hold for three seconds, and keep your core tight. Return to center as you exhale, and then repeat on the opposite side. Your meditation should focus on thoughts of a happy moment for celebration, either from the day's events, or something in the near future. You may also envision a goal you have set, and how happy you will feel when you complete it.

(I.) DEMETER STRETCH

Demeter was the Goddess of fertility, agriculture, harvest, nature, creativity, and the seasons. This is a recommended night stretch. Lie on your back and inhale as you squeeze your knees to your chest; this signifies fertility or pregnancy (new life). Hold for three seconds, and then exhale as you slowly extend your legs down; depicting the seasonal summer/winter cycles. At the completion, slightly arch your cervical (neck) and the lumbar area (low back). Repeat. The modified version is done with hands palms down under the low back or hips for support, and makes the stretch a little easier. With gratitude in your heart and mind, envision all the good that happened throughout your day. Replay any less than optimal events as more positive. As you drift off to sleep, plant in your mind good thoughts that will produce an even better tomorrow.

KSS® can become an integral part of a healthy lifestyle. Based on the discipline of 'visual meditation and diaphragmatic breathing during spinal motion,' KSS® is a significant form of exercise, self-discipline, and empowerment. If yoga or tai chi is intimidating, difficult for you, or you're short on time - you'll love KSS® because it feels good, is easy to remember, it will help your posture look great, and you'll want to keep doing it!

A daily KSS® routine yields many physical benefits. KSS® improves musculo-skeletal aches and pains by stretching out stiff muscles, tendons, and ligaments that affect the spine. As your posture improves, your organs will also work more efficiently, as less pressure is put on them from slouching forward. It helps your digestive system eliminate more efficiently, and improves your sense of core stability.

KSS® can help you achieve deeper sleep so you're more rested throughout the day. Patients report that they feel energized and focused in the morning. They feel inspired to get on with their day, and have more clarity after stimulating their circulation. While performing these spinal stretches, be sure to meditate while you move your body, and breathe deeply from the diaphragm. Encouraging movement of the spinal column's cerebrospinal fluid (CSF) pump, and getting more oxygen into the blood, is vital for an alkaline internal environment and quick recuperation.

KSS® may also help people mentally. Moving our body through space creates a sense of focus, and through exercising self-will you can become more aware of your spatial alignment. Patients have claimed KSS® to be help with depression, the after-effects of quitting smoking or alcohol, as well panic attacks and anxiety. The deep diaphragmatic breathing done in KSS® is very detoxifying and calming. KSS® is also a low impact form of exercise for those rehabilitating from surgery. Osteoporosis patients, or those with disability who cannot easily get to the gym, can handle the gentle movements involved.

8.2 Ergonomic Do's and Don'ts for the Home and Office

Sitting (Desk, Home, Office, etc.)

Avoid prolonged sitting, as the body demands movement. If you must sit for long periods of time, take a break, and get up to stretch your legs every twenty to forty minutes. When in a seated position, avoid looking down (neck flexion) for extended periods of time. Position your monitor as high as possible on your desk to encourage good neck and back posture. Your eye level should be angled upwards towards the computer screen or slightly higher than straight ahead, to reduce neck flexion. If you are working with a laptop, the laptop should be boosted up high, and not be lying on your lap as you work. Keep the keyboard in easy reach. Use wrist pad supports if you are typing for long hours to ward off pressure on the wrists, which could lead to carpel tunnel symptoms (finger numbness and tingling). Sit with your knees slightly higher than your hips. Roll a small bath towel (size equal to the circumference of your forearm), add two rubber bands (one on each end to make it firm), and place it at the small of your lower back if you do not have a lumbar support built into the chair. Don't slouch!

Driving

Position your seat forward enough where your knees are slightly higher than your hips. Push the seat forward to an upright position for back and neck support. Use the small rolled towel as mentioned above, and add it to the small of your lower back if your car does not have a built in lumbar support. If you are experiencing sciatica, this may be because you are spending long hours in a seated position daily. Invest in a memory foam seat cushion for your car. Be sure to wear your seatbelt, as this helps keep your shoulders back, and keeps you safe. While driving avoid resting one arm out the window as this encourages shoulder problems over time. Keep both hands on the wheel and remember - don't slouch!

Bending (moving, construction, etc.)

Do not bend from the waist forward, especially when your knees and legs are locked straight. Always bend with your knees while keeping your back straight;

don't rotate. Rotating the upper torso at the waist while bending over is a sure way to injure your lumbar disks, spasm your back, and miss months of work. Keep your back straight and allow your bodyweight to drop down with your legs (squat) allowing the legs to do all the heavy work, not your back muscles.

Lifting (moving, construction, etc.)

Avoid lifting any heavy objects by yourself. Get a friend to help you whenever possible to evenly distribute the weight. If you must lift, squat down (don't bend the back), and use your legs for power and support. Avoid lifting any objects above shoulder level, and avoid carrying heavy purses, luggage, or other objects on your shoulders. Use common sense and don't overload your body – it's not a forklift.

Standing (cashiers, concerts, church, etc.)

Standing perfectly still without moving is unnatural. Place your one foot slightly in front of the other foot, and slightly bend your knees to take off some pressure from your lower back. You may also place one foot on a raised footstool or phone book to help reduce the pressure in your lower back if your occupation demands standing for an extended period of time. Acquire a soft mat to stand on if you are going to be standing due to your work as a cashier, hostess, or bartender. Ergonomically correct workplaces make happier (and healthier) workers.

Telephone

While you talk, never laterally bend your neck to keep the phone balanced between your ear and shoulder. This causes unnatural neck stress, setting you up for headaches, neck and shoulder pain, arm numbness and tingling. Invest in a headphone set, and you will be glad you did.

Sleeping

Don't sleep on your stomach. Oxygen, blood, and nerve supply through the neck and arm (brachial plexus) gets cut off for hours when your neck is turned, leaving you waking up very groggy and with numb limbs. Limit sleeping on your side as there is less support of your neck and shoulders. Sleeping on your back with the knees bent is the best option for a good night's rest. Choose a firm, non-toxic, chemical free mattress and neck pillow set. Sleeping on the floor would be considered too firm. Sleeping on most couches is too soft. Find a happy medium that supports your spine but does not contort it. Speaking of sleep…

8.3 Sleeping Incorrectly Can Make You Look and Feel Older Than You Are

Sleep is often called the greatest medicine available to a patient. If you have read carefully, sleeplessness is one of the common features of any dis-ease. Sleep affords continuous rest that is required by the body to repair itself. Normally six to eight hours of uninterrupted sleep is recommended, but it is highly case-specific. Sleep duration normally decreases with age and babies tend to sleep a lot more than eight hours as their energy goes to cell growth. How fresh are you feeling when you wake up? Do you feel like you need to go back to bed immediately? Do you hit the snooze button on your alarm often? Are you feeling more tired than you think you should be? These are cardinal signs of a disturbed sleep pattern. An uninterrupted sleep pattern has four distinct cycles, the last of which is called the Rapid Eye Movement (REM) sleep. This is also the phase where you have dreams. Therefore, a good way to know whether you are completing your sleep cycle is to keep track of whether you are dreaming often. Sometimes, in patients who have disturbed sleep or insomnia, the cycle duration is way off and a person can go to REM sleep within half an hour of falling asleep. These people often sleep-talk and normally wake up more exhausted than before going to sleep. You may want to investigate your sleep patterns by conducting your own inexpensive sleep study. Purchase and set up a video camera that has night vision or low light filming capability. Go to bed, allowing the camera to record all through the night. Review the footage in the morning. Look for how long it took you to fall asleep (on average it takes most people seven minutes), how many hours you slept, how deep your breathing was, how much you tossed and turned, if you snore, if you maintain your sleeping position, if you dream, if you talk in your sleep or if you sleep walk. You will be amazed at the data you can attain in the course of a week. If you feel your sleep patterns are abnormal, you should discuss this with your doctor.

The most important thing that determines your sleep pattern is the relative positioning and alignment of your spine. If the spine is aligned in a stress-free orientation that allows flow of your blood, oxygen, and nerve impulses, then you will have better chances at well-defined sleep patterns and waking up refreshed.

- Choose a mattress that is firm yet can shape itself according to your body contours. Seek out 'chemical and toxin free' memory foam mattresses without the fire-retarding chemicals. They are only available with your doctor's prescription, so do your research prior to buying so you're not stuck inhaling toxins throughout the night.
- Try a lot of different mattress before deciding on the best one for yourself.
- If you are sharing a bed with your partner, it is important to determine mutual

compatibility as far as mattress choice is concerned. The goal is to find a mattress where one person won't get affected by the movement of the other during sleep.
- Choose your pillow properly. Neck pillows should be semi-firm. Not too hard and not too soft; the non-toxic memory foam option works to conform to each neck uniquely. Most pillows incorrectly raise your head position too high off the mattress, stressing your neck and head. The right-fitting pillow should be thinner/softer under the head and firmer/thicker under the neck. Orthopedic or cervical pillows should fit well no matter whether you sleep on your back or side. The back of your head and the top of your shoulders should be making contact with the mattress. The only part supported away from the mattress should be the neck. This helps ensure proper neck curvature is maintained and allows nerves, blood, and oxygen to flow properly during sleep. Be sure to point the chin up as a checkpoint in making sure you're in proper position. Any large pillows should be placed under your knees (not your head - see photos below) to take the pressure off of the low back. Some will need to use a large wedge pillow to bring their upper body to a 40-45 degree angle while using the above position. This will be especially true for those with acid reflux or digestive troubles where sleeping flat would cause distress at night.
- Do-It-Yourself Neck Pillow: Roll your own neck support if you do not have a non-toxic memory foam neck pillow, or need a quick temporary solution. Roll a small bathroom towel to the diameter equal to the circumference size of your forearm. Place two large rubber bands on each end to hold it in place. Place it under your neck for support. That's all you need!
- If you insist on sleeping on your side, keep your knees bent at a 45-degree angle and place the rolled towel or small pillow between your knees to relax the pelvis. The pillow you choose for your head should fit the space from the ear to the mattress without kinking your neck. Your neck should be perfectly aligned with the rest of your spine with your head tilted slightly back.
- For the ones who are used to sleeping on their stomachs, I recommend slowly training yourself each night to sleep either on your back or on your side. If you sleep on your stomach, you are getting less oxygen through the night (your chest is compressed). You are also sleeping with a kinked neck. Stomach sleepers often complain of numb limbs due to inefficient blood and nerve circulation to their appendages. This makes them feel tired even after a long sleep session. In summary, choose a pillow that will support your natural spinal contours and slowly train

yourself to sleep on your back as shown in the photos below, starting with small naps at first, and then whole night sessions. *For more information on dealing with insomnia or sleep supplementation, see section 10.15 and Chapter 11.*

Incorrect Neck Position

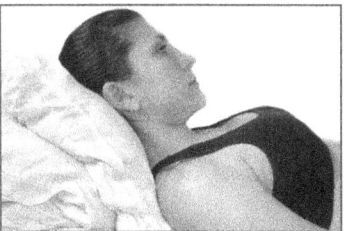 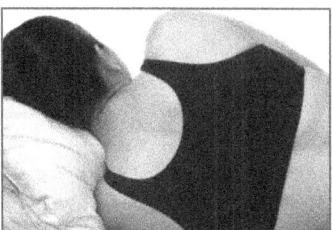 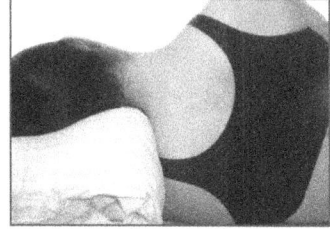

Correct Neck Position

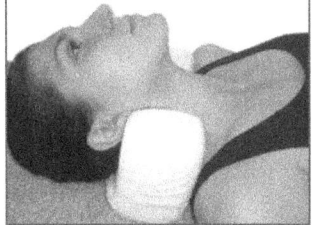  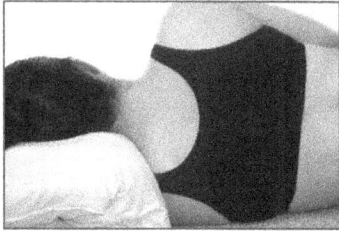

Correct Leg Position

Please keep in mind that regular bad posture while sleeping (or sitting), will nullify the efforts of your chiropractic treatments and destabalize muscles and ligaments from holding your spine in proper form. Help your chirporactor help you by adhering to correct body postures. You live in a world where the majority of your activities are done looking down (texting, reading, typing, etc.). Kyphotic (forward hunched) postures are made worse when you spend one-third of your life sleeping in improper positions.

The difference in the posture examples below is clear. The first two examples (kyphotic and swayback postures) show rounded shoulders, incorrect eye line, forward head flexion position, sagging upper thorax, and a depressed rib cage. The 'normal' example is the truly more attractive and healthy example. Notice the body symmetry where the shoulder is directly under the ear. The head is aligned over the thorax, which in turn is aligned perfectly over the hips. The difference in lifestyle quality and function is tremendous between a 65 year old with years of chiropractic care, proper diet, and exercise, opposed to a 45 year old without any chiropractic care, poor diet, and minimal exercise.

Kyphotic Posture

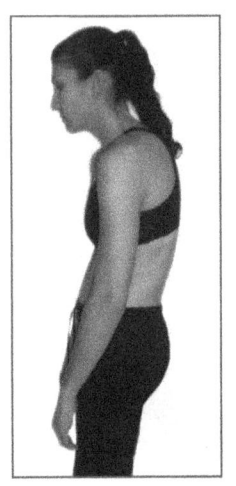

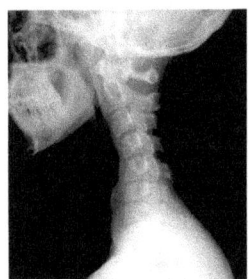

XRAY OF A REVERSED CERVICAL CURVE (KYPHOTIC)

Swayback Posture

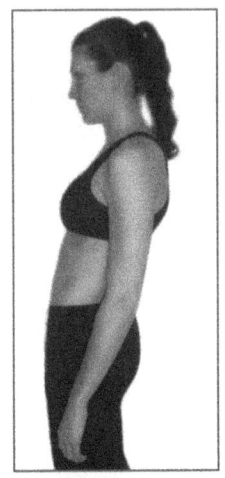

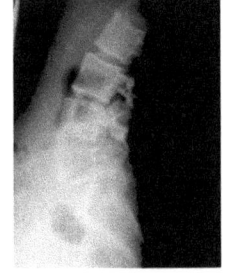

XRAY OF A HYPER-EXTENDED LOW BACK

Normal Posture

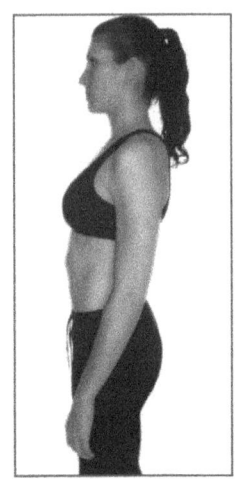

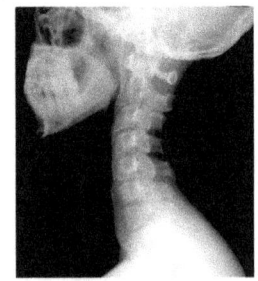

XRAY OF A NORMAL CERVICAL LORDOTIC CURVE

8.4 How Are Your Organs Affected by Bad Posture?

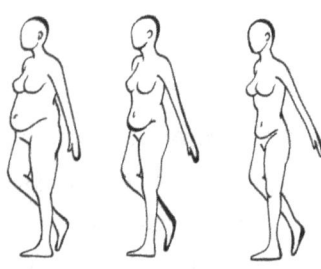

Incorrect posture disturbs proper weight distribution, putting unnecessary pressure on your organs and nerve impulses to and from the spine, causing sluggish operation over time. Constant pressure on the chest, for instance, will cause decreased and shallow diaphragmatic breathing. Overweight individuals with a large midsection tend to counterweight themselves into a swayback posture, as weight pushes down on vital organs like the uterus and ovaries. This alone may be responsible for many female organ malfunctions, including menstrual and reproductive issues. Overweight men experience horrible low back pains due to the large gut phenomenon, which is caused by slow-working intestinal systems. Let's take a closer look at the function of each organ and how bad posture may affect it.

Heart: Pumps oxygen-rich blood throughout your body and oxygen-poor blood to your lungs for oxygen uptake. Forward rotated shoulders and a caved in chest in the thoracic spine can depress the sternum (breastbone) down onto the heart, causing chest pains or angina.

Lungs: Oxygen passes from your alveoli into your blood. Air is forced in and out of your lungs by diaphragmatic movements, and other breathing muscles. In persons with depressed sternums or kyphotic thoracic cages, this can't happen as efficiently, causing less ability to breathe fully and deeply. Over time, this creates an acidic and sluggish internal environment. Improper posture could be putting undue pressure on the lungs, leading to acidosis.

Liver: The liver is located under the diaphragm on the right side of your body. A classic sign of liver damage is: yellow coloring of the eyes and skin, called jaundice. This can happen when backed up bilirubin, a red blood cell byproduct, builds up in the blood. Improper posture could be putting undue pressure on the liver causing improper function and stagnation.

Gallbladder: Located on the underside of the liver. The gallbladder contracts and squeezes bile (what the liver produces) into the small intestine. Gallstones form when cholesterol, a component of bile, abnormally crystallizes to form a stone-like material. Improper forward leaning (kyphotic thoracic spine) posture could be putting undue pressure on this organ causing improper function and stagnation.

Spleen: Located on the left side of the body, between the stomach and diaphragm. The spleen keeps the blood clean and helps defend against infection. Improper posture could be putting undue pressure on this organ, causing malfunction. Without a fully functioning spleen, you are more at risk for infections and diseases.

Pancreas: Located at the level of the small intestine and just behind the stomach. It is responsible for discharging hormones and digestive enzymes that govern blood sugar. It produces and discharges two hormones that regulate blood sugar; glucagon and insulin. Improper forward leaning (kyphotic thoracic spine) posture puts undue pressure on this organ causing distress, stagnation, and malfunction.

Stomach: A naturally acidic organ (1-4 pH), the stomach functions as a short-term food storage and mixing facility; food breakdown and mixing contents with juices secreted from the stomach's lining. Improper posture could be putting undue pressure on your stomach, causing a food breakdown malfunction.

Kidneys: Excess water found in blood and waste products end up being made into urine, playing a critical part in maintaining blood makeup. Every minute, one fourth of all our blood passes through our kidneys! Improper posture, scoliosis, or excessive trunk weight over time could strain or put pressure on your kidneys, leading to malfunction.

Bladder: Stretches the more liquid you consume. The average adult bladder can hold about a pint of fluid. If it over-stretches, the bladder's wall nerves send a signal to your brain telling you that you need to empty soon. Improper forward leaning (kyphotic thoracic spine) posture, in addition to an overweight mid-section, could put undue pressure on the bladder causing malfunction or a frequent need to urinate.

Small & Large Intestines: The intestines are tubular muscular structures that move along food for nutrient extraction through a contracting and relaxing process called peristalsis. Improper posture puts pressure on the gut, causing malfunction and stagnation of feces, keeping it from leaving the body, hardening further, and causing constipation.

An important structure joining the intestines is the Ileocecal valve. It is a valve positioned between the ileum (end part of the small intestine) and the cecum (beginning part of the large intestine). Its job is to allow the assimilated food to pass freely into the large intestine when operating normally. A condition called Ileocecal valve syndrome happens when the ileocecal valve, a one way valve, gets obstructed and waste materials push backwards into the small intestine. Poor posture and internal stagnation of improperly broken down food (e.g. seeds and nuts), puts pressure on this structure, causing a referral pain to the low back and abdomen. Ileocecal valve syndrome is a common condition that mimics low back pain, especially in overweight men and women. In many cases, soft tissue manipulation such as massage or rolfing provides relief from symptoms and revives proper intestinal function.

8.5 Staying the Course With Chiropractic Relief and Corrective Care Plans

Chiropractic therapy can be done for a short-term alleviation of suffering and pain (relief care), or it can iron out and stabilize the root cause of the spinal dis-ease, thus alleviating the pain and suffering for a longer term (corrective care). Corrective care is how supporting structures (ligaments, tendons, and muscles) get a chance to repair. This basic chart shows phases of care, along with a timetable and frequency of treatments. As one starts life healthy (optimized - top), but neglects their spinal health, they drop down the

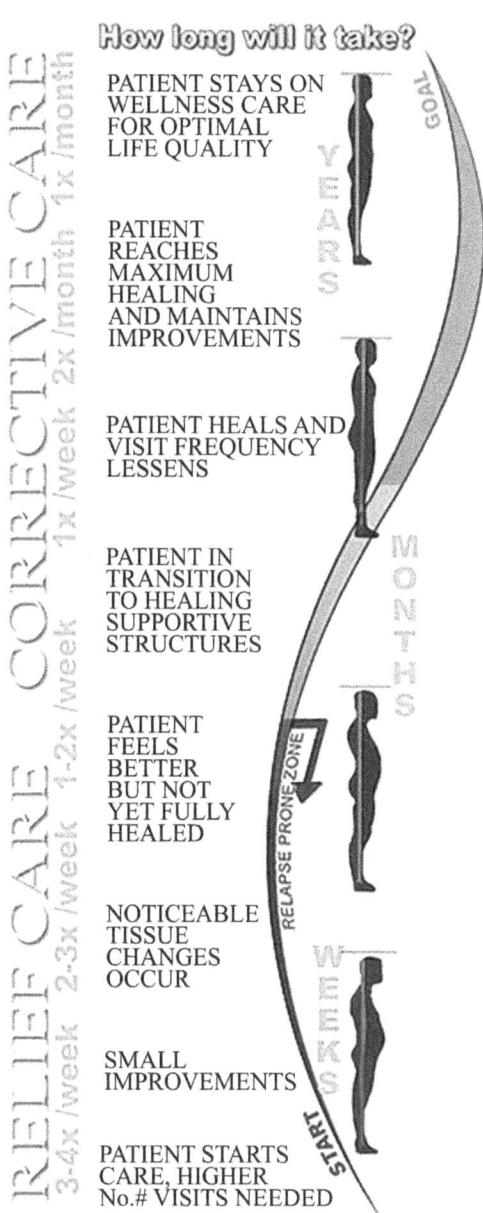

chart curve. Symptoms appear at the end of a dis-ease process and new patients start at the bottom of the chart (in pain and suffering - bottom). When symptoms and pains are evident, patients are forced to address the problem and look to move up the chart again towards optimization. However, before we can correct the problem, we must first address the immediate pains and symptoms that are being felt. The tricky thing is the 'relapse prone zone' that is depicted with an arrow down mid-way. If a patient does not commit to further their progress, they will fall victim to the faulty assumption that the injury or spinal issue has been completely healed since they feel no more pain, and so may lessen or stop care, only to relapse again. Actual healing starts to happen after the immediate symptoms and issue of pain is relieved; then the body lays down a supporting foundation with more time and energy dedicated in strengthening the tissues. Time and financial constraints can sometimes unfortunately force patients to choose a limited relief care program. Corrective care is always recommended over relief care, as it is more rational and provides a much more stable, long-term basis for healing. It's been proven that ligament and muscles that support the spine require longer healing times - long after even the pain and symptoms appear insignificant. That's how important regular non-stop care of the spine is; it's absolutely essential to ensuring the best possible outcome when the spine has completely healed. Of note, not everyone can reach complete correction or optimization. Sometimes a person's problem has reached a point where complete correction is impossible due to many limiting factors - most notably patient age and extent of damage through toxin accumulation. This is why early detection (by starting chiropractic care earlier in life) can save both your life and your lifestyle.

8.6 Corrective Care for Chronic Pain

Chronic pain is frequently resistant to conventional treatment. As recent research findings suggest, chronic pain may also result in structural alterations of the brain. Changes in function, chemical profile, or structure - also known as neuroplasticity - observed in the peripheral and cerebral nervous systems have been related to chronic pain. The etiology of chronic pain can be visceral, ischemic, nociceptive, neuropathic, or a combination of etiologies. Nociceptive pain (somatic / body or visceral / organ) is caused by stimulation of the nociceptors (pain receptors) located at nerve endings; arthritic pain is an example of nociceptic pain. Neuropathic pain involves pain impulses generated in the nerve, spinal cord, or brain, and is a consequence of injury to the central nervous system. Other chronic pain syndromes include chronic neck and back pain, headache, migraine, whiplash, rheumatoid arthritis, fibromyalgia, facial pain, pelvic pain, perineal pain, abdominal organ pain, irritable bowel syndrome, postsurgical pain syndrome, phantom limb pain, and chest pain syndromes. Some chronic pain disorders commonly found in older adults are spinal canal stenosis, osteoarthritis, degenerative joint disease, tumors and malignancy, post-stroke pain syndrome, post-herpetic neuralgia and diabetic peripheral neuropathy.

The Kousouli® Method reflects aspects of sound biomechanical therapy, spinal, neural, and emotional reconditioning, biofeedback, diet modification through whole food nutrition, and hypnosis as approaches to pain management. Hypnosis for chronic pain can be utilized to (a) reduce pain intensity and related suffering and (b) improve the self-management of pain. Hypnosis is a quintessential mind-body therapy. Hypnosis actually consists of multiple dimensions, such as altered states of consciousness, expectancy, and suggestibility to pain levels.

Dr. Elena Gabor, a medical Hypnotherapist, and author of *Home at the Tree of Life*, excellently defines hypnosis as, "A deep meditative state that helps shift the brain activity from the stress-prone areas to the calmer areas, leading to the release of happiness hormones, and, as a result, to good feelings… Basically, hypnosis is a natural state of the mind that favors healing." Hypnotic suggestions for deep relaxation are increased comfort, decreased pain, increased control over pain, and decreased aggravation by pain. Hypo-analgesic suggestions are most often followed by post-hypnotic suggestions for pain displacement, decreased pain or sensation alteration, and distraction.

8.7 Stress

On the surface, stress may not seem like a big deal because many of the physical reactions to stress are not immediately visible. Many people do not realize how critical it is to reduce overall levels of stress because they are unaware of the negative long-term impact stress can have on the body. There are enough studies now, though, that have shown stress does in fact kill.

The effects of constant levels of stress include negative reactions such as: a constant flood of hormones and chemicals, lower immune system function, interference with cholesterol levels, overworking the adrenal glands (which leads to craving unhealthy foods like flours, refined sugars, and sodium). Stress can also cause (I) impaired immunity, digestion, and detoxification; (II) parasympathetic and sympathetic nervous systems are over-stimulated; (III) pupils dilate and hence causes sleep deprivation; (IV) blood pressure increases; (V) glucose and cholesterol is released; (VI) bones are gradually demineralized; (VII) fatty acid metabolism is impaired, and inflammatory mediators are stimulated; (VIII) fat deposits occur, energy decreases, and mood fluctuations occur.

Hence, it is apparent that there is an excess of adverse effects of stress and negative energy regulation on the body. It is also thus impossible and irrational to target just one or two symptoms in the healing process, as the entire body will be affected when alternative treatments are implemented to reduce the risk of any particular condition. Decreasing stress levels and managing reactions to stress can be one of the most effective ways to improve health and decrease the risk of chronic diseases. This further outlines the great benefit of chiropractic care in general, and the Kousouli® Method in particular.

Now that you understand the negative impact that stress can have on health, it is important to look again at the steps taken in the Kousouli® Method in order to reduce the levels of stress in your life. We all experience stress on some level, and it is critical to keep those stress levels controlled in order to prevent chronic diseases. We have discussed that chemical reactions occur in response to stress, but it is also important to note other negative side effects that can occur as a result of stress. For example, it is common for a person experiencing high levels of stress to react with habits that are not healthy, which can result in their health declining even more. Some of these habits include smoking, drinking, or excessive eating.

This is a vicious cycle: the person feels stressed about something that is occurring so they drink, smoke, or overeat in order to escape and dull the pain. It may make them feel better for a moment, but these 'looping' poor habits will put more strain on the body, which results in declining health, leading to more stress. The loop then continues as it grows in momentum. The goal is to stop the pre-programmed loop and energy leak that is occurring both in the physical spine as well as the energy body. This is where the Kousouli® Method comes in.

8.8 Healthy Stress-Free Lifestyle Approach

The most essential aspect of reducing stress through mind-body techniques is to improve your overall health by not giving pain the power. In stress management, it is essential to address spiritual, mental, emotional, and physical issues in order to improve your level of wellness. Mental health is inherently connected to physical health, and one element cannot be treated without consideration for the other factor. Check each of the 4 steps of the Kousouli® Method 4R intervention system (Remove, Revive, Rebuild, Restart), and see that you adhere to them daily as a checklist for living a healthy life.

8.9 Biofeedback

We are all a living part of the universe and its rules. The universe has different energy bodies - very complex combinations form the Universal Energy Field (UEF). We humans are guided by this Human Energy Field (HEF), commonly known as an *aura*, which defines the spiritual, mental, emotional, and physical entity of every single individual. The Kousouli® Method deals directly with these aforementioned aspects. A trauma in the spiritual, mental, or emotional body can upset the balance and become a manifestation of a physical issue, and vice versa. Examples: A physical accident can cause someone to feel handicapped, and then emotional pain affects the mental field, with feelings of perceived limitation in abilities or worth. Emotional heartache due to loss of a loved one can cause severe depression, loneliness, or loss of purpose, which could eventually lead to cancer or organ death. Mental worrying can cause a stomach ulcer; High drug toxicity can overload the body's systems, producing lymph backup, mucus, ankle swelling, pains and aches. Holding your attention to the physical pain, you are not able to expand and experience manifesting or operating through the higher self, thus limiting the experience to the lower three chakras (our baser instincts). The spine binds the physical body through these unseen other energy bodies, and allows us healthy interaction and harmony between all our worlds.

The practice of biofeedback teaches a person to recognize physiological functions in order to correct the problems that are occurring. Biofeedback can be used to lessen pain and regain muscle strength. These changes occur as a result of behavior, emotions, and thought, and biofeedback is used to encourage physiological health improvements. One visual simple example of using biofeedback is taking a person's temperature, because the thermometer will provide feedback on what is occurring in the body. Once the information is obtained, specific steps and treatment techniques can be applied in order to correct the problem.

By providing biofeedback, the practitioner is in a 'coaching' position, helping the patient see the feedback that is received from their body, and helps set goals in order to improve the situation. Typically, a biofeedback treatment will teach the patient how to identify conditions that may trigger symptoms, as well as relaxation techniques to give them the ability to cope with certain events. These processes are important in the mind-body connection because they focus on the fact that thoughts, feelings, and behaviors have a very strong influence on physical conditions. Using biofeedback during a treatment program can help the patient see there is progress occurring, adding self-confidence and moving them faster towards the positive energy cycle. The patient needs to be increasingly aware of their daily reaction to triggers, in order to recognize which behavioral changes need to be taken. Relaxation exercises, whole food diet modification, exercise, and lifestyle changes need to be made, in addition to doctor-mediated intervention to improve health.

8.10 Energy Management

Many people make the mistake of focusing only on time management, the physical element of a busy schedule. However, by redirecting the focus to include time and energy management, a person can more successfully complete tasks and reduce stress at the same time. Consider this: When managing time, one's schedule often becomes more packed as additional commitments are squeezed into the day. Everyone has a limit of 24 hours to get everything done, and because of this, it is common for schedules to become stressed when trying to fit everything in. Often, this results in frantic attempts to keep up with everything, causing an increase in cortisol levels and energy depletion. However, changing your focus to energy management in addition to time management can be an effective way to manage your schedule and still get everything done - without causing damage to your health. It is important to start out by understanding that energy management is actually a cycle: Energy flows and when it is depleted, it is necessary to give yourself the rest and support needed to refill the reserves. If you push through a busy schedule when your energy is depleted, it causes a deficit in energy which has many negative results: higher levels of nutrient and vitamin depletion, acid production, frustration, exhaustion, confusion, irritability, and a lack of joy or enthusiasm. Keeping a good mind-body balance can help prevent an energy deficit, especially when you recognize that recovery time is needed if you are pushing too hard. It might even be a good idea to make time and go on that long overdue vacation.

Focusing on both energy and time management will help you use your energy only when needed, and then allow your energy reserves to recharge instead of going into an energy deficit. There will be times when focused engagement is needed on a specific prioritized task, and it is also important that you plan time for energy recovery once that particular task is completed. Keeping this balance will help to keep the stress levels down, which will in turn help to prevent dis-ease. It is also possible to increase the amount of energy that you have each day by using mind-body techniques that work out your energy 'muscle.' Stretching it a little bit at a time, followed by recovery, will help you to expand capacity, but it is important that recovery time is available.

It is important to take small breaks and step away to let your mind and body rest. In your non-working hours, use techniques such as hypnosis, meditation, deep tissue massage, the stretches in this book, and other alternative stress reduction activities. If you manage this type of a situation correctly, you can prevent dis-ease because the stress cycle is not constantly running. These mind-body techniques can help you keep your stress levels down, and still work efficiently and effectively.

Chapter 9:
Healing of the Emotional Subconscious and Unconscious Mind

"The doctor of the future will give no medicine, but will interest his patients in the care of the human frame, in diet, and in the cause and prevention of disease."
~ Thomas Edison

Auras are a phenomenon that can be seen using biofeedback.

I refer to the marvel called the human spinal cord as our 'super antenna,' since it's the communication not only between our brains, bodies, and their internal and external environments, but also as the receiver and transmitter between the earth realm and the spiritual realm.

Let's take a look at the seven main chakras often depicted in Eastern healing methods. The chakras affect the aura, which is believed to exist in and around the surface of the subtle body of living beings. Notice that in the Kousouli® Method master chart (Chapter 7), the chakras line up in order from the base of the spine to the crown top of the head, and are attributed to certain characteristics of health. Coincidence? I think not.

9.1 The Chakras

Chakra is a word that is derived from the Sanskrit word for 'wheel-like turning vortices,' and is a concept of traditional Indian medicine. The Indian and Chinese meridian systems describe a particular framework for the 'chi' or 'qi' that is circulated within the organs by various channels. These channels relate to the physical organs, giving them innate energy to maintain health. The chakras themselves are always changing; interweaving in color and in constant motion. The chakras reside over points of the spine as energy portals that interchange unseen spiritual information between our body, others' bodies, and our environment. The Kousouli® Method master chart (Chapter 7) shows the chakras, their positioning over the spine, and the relationship between the spiritual, mental, emotional, and physical aspects of health. When helping a patient find their way to better health, it is these that Kousouli® Method practitioners must fully investigate, in addition to lab results and imaging procedures, prior to administering treatment.

Muladhara: 1st Root Chakra (RED color) EARTH element

Root chakra at the base of the spine. It grounds us, and connects us to what is most important. Located at the base of our spine; the coccyx, tailbone. Relates to the primitive life force energy, natural survival needs, grounding, assertiveness, aggression, adventure, impulsiveness, lustful passion, raw attraction, the need for feeling secure, and vitality. There is also a connection to the color red and primitive feelings, such as anger. Red in this chakra also is related to the power hormone testosterone, temperature increase, heat, hemoglobin production, and cell growth. It is important to avoid wearing red if healing from cancer or any tumors; for red represents fast growth.

Svadhisthana: 2nd Sacral Chakra - Spleen or Splenic (ORANGE color) WATER element

Lower abdominal chakra. Located at the level of the genitals and reproductive systems, this chakra relates to primitive life, reproduction energy, raw emotions, primary interpersonal relationships, and emotional stability. Energy disharmony here can show up as a disturbance in the digestive and reproductive systems. Feelings of sexual or emotional repression may be linked to physical manifestations of diverticulitis, urinary trouble, fibroids, infertility, or cramping.

Manipura: 3rd Navel Chakra - Umbilical Solar Plexus (YELLOW color) FIRE element

Located at the navel under the breastbone, this chakra relates to power integration and life force management. Digestive system, pancreas, liver, stomach, adrenals, and the spleen connect here. It is the psychic energy battery, and storehouse for positive energy. This chakra links to the mind for processing negative feelings and is the area of your life force distribution. This is where your "gut reaction" comes from, and relates to your intuitive guidance and feeling in your truest desires and needs stem from this chakra being aligned.

Anahata: 4th Heart Chakra - Cardiac (GREEN color) AIR element

Located at the center of the chest, over the heart. By location, it separates the higher three chakras (5th, 6th, 7th) from the lower primitive three chakras (1st, 2nd, 3rd). Affects heart, lungs, upper chest, back, bronchial tubes, thymus, and immunity. This green chakra is the seat of higher emotions of true love, tenderness, compassion, honesty, and human con-

nection. Many spiritual teachers claim that all of humanity is "plugged in" to each other through this chakra. This chakra is key in developing and maintaining intimate relationships, as it both attracts and sustains them.

Vishuddha: 5th Throat Chakra - Laryngeal (BLUE color) ETHER element

Throat chakra. This is the source of your inner and outer voice, and location of your inner truth. In a relationship setting, this is the chakra that needs be in balance; be who you are and don't be afraid to express yourself. Front and back of the throat; relates to the power of thought through communication, speech, expression, and self-identification. Some health connections with this chakra are metabolic rate, thyroid gland, vocal cords, eyes, ears, nose, mouth, and neck. Repression of this chakra is commonly seen in those who tend to be shy or scared to "speak up" in public to express themselves. Repressing the 5th chakra can lead to upper respiratory weakness, sore throat and susceptibility to head colds.

Anja: 6th Brow Chakra - Frontal Chakra 3rd eye (DEEP INDIGO color)

Third eye chakra. This houses your intuition, reason and wisdom. Located between the eyebrows; relates to powers of mind and heightened self-awareness, psychic abilities, connection to physical and psychic eyes/vision. This energy is usually activated through a deeply focused and relaxed meditative state. For more information on how to open and develop your intuitive psychic abilities read the book, *BE A MASTER OF PSYCHIC ENERGY*.

Sahasrara: 7th Crown Chakra - Coronal (VIOLET color)

Crown chakra. This is where our bliss and our ability to connect spiritually stem from. Located on top of the head, designated for self-realization and enlightenment, knowingness; the seat of the soul. Associated also with perfection of mind, body, and spirit; connection to God, or The Source. The 7th chakra is usually depicted in religious iconography as a gold glowing disc or circle around the head. This energy is also usually activated through a deeply focused and relaxed meditative state.

9.2 The Importance of Color

Colors are used to reflect our personalities, moods, or subconscious states of being. Color vibrates on a specific level, depending on the shade, and can be used effectively help calm, sooth and heal. Consider the importance of colors in your choice of bed sheets, flowers, or clothing and fashion apparel.

RED	Love, passion, sexual desire and activity, fast / quick speed, masculinity, strength, and stimulation. Wear red or use red sheets in bedroom décor to encourage sexual exploration. **Light Red or Pink:** Softness, tenderness, romance, caring, femininity, and emotional love. Wear pink to encourage gentle lovemaking. **Dark Red:** Anger, rage, lust, war, internal conflict, stifled aggravation, and impulse. These are not the best characteristics to encourage restful healing; so avoid.
ORANGE	Warmth, cheer, openness, freedom, creativity, enthusiasm, expression, kindness, celebration, sensual enjoyment, and zest for life. Wear this color to exude your inner energy, or paint a room or wall in order to stimulate it. **Dark Orange:** Materialism, insensitivity, overindulgence. These are not the best characteristics to encourage restful healing; so avoid.
VIOLET INDIGO	Spirit, divinity, compassion, transformation, renewal, meditative, electric, calming, and purifying. This color encourages a spiritual connection during sex, so use it liberally in clothing, sheets, décor and Feng shui or bagua settings. **Dark Violet/Indigo:** Slow movement, trickery, lowered potential. These are not the best characteristics to encourage restful healing; so avoid.
WHITE	Purity, spiritual energy, balance, positivity, enlightenment, divine inspiration, innocence, simplicity, and oneness. This clean, crisp color promotes a positive and spiritual connection with your partner. **Foggy, Off-White, or Grey:** Deceitful, depressive, apathetic. While white is considered "heavenly," muddled shades mean unconscious energy usually related to religious control or dogma that interferes in healing and restful sleep.

BLACK	Mystery, stealth, secrets, death, and negativity. The void of life or light. Wearing black shields you from openness. Overuse of this color can unbalance the chakras and can breed hate, rage, seclusion, depression, stagnation, or fatigue. This is not an ideal color to wear for healing; so avoid.
GREEN	Inner peace, harmony, healing energy, monetary wealth, honesty, hope, nurturing, safety, and connection. This is a great color to promote a mutual connection and a realistic, grounded relationship. **Earthy Green:** denotes grounding, nature, and connecting to Mother Earth. Can be great for exuding your natural spirit.
YELLOW	Joy, exuberance, cheer, happiness, logic, and optimism. This is a great color for brightening up your living space and showing your inner positive energy. This is also a strong attracting color, so wear it often when you feel like telling the world how happy you are. **Golden Yellow:** Authority, abundance, social power and status, absolute self-confidence, sun energy, luxurious, feeling like a winner. Can help a lot in attracting a partner.
BROWN	Practicality, stability, grounding, earth, elemental, solidity in relationship, and having a "down to earth" personality. While many people don't associate brown with sex or love, it is a strong color for grounding with a longtime lover. **Dark Brown:** Similar to Black.
BLUE/ TURQUOISE	Healing, miracle energy, cleansing, awe, increased intuition and sensitivity, intellect, insights, invention, water and purity. This is a great color for a room, especially for relaxation purposes. Wear blue to exude a balanced emotional state, healing energy, and static mood. **Dark Blue/Turquoise:** Depression, heaviness, sadness, longing, or feeling stuck. Avoid these when you are feeling less than great, as they will affect your energies.

9.3 Epigenetic Changes in Healing

As a person moves through life, cells receive feedback from the environment, and they record the information to make changes in the epigenome (from epigenetics: the study of inherited changes in phenotype – appearance - or gene expression). This allows the cells in a person's body to respond to the outside influences and make changes as needed. The physical structure of the genome can actually be changed by the epigenome, making specific genes accessible or inaccessible.

Because our environment is constantly changing, it is necessary to make adjustments to the epigenome over time. The epigenome will always make adjustments in order to react to the different signals that it is receiving. But before that, it is important to know the environmental cues that can affect the epigenome, which includes things such as diet, stress, physical activity, social interactions, temperature, contact with chemicals and additives, constant exposure to alcohol, caffeine, negative thinking or negative people, and smoking habits to name a few. Essentially these factors also help decide whether you are in the negative or positive cycle of the Kousouli® Method.

These environmental (non-genetic) factors may cause genes to react differently, and over time, the epigenetic landscape gets altered. It is important to note that these alterations can occur in positive and negative ways. For example, if a person drastically changes their diet for the better, the epigenetic landscape can be changed, causing the cells to react in a more positive way because of its improvement in environment. On the other hand, if a person begins to eat higher levels of unhealthy foods, the epigenetics will change as the body is trying to adjust to the lack of nutrition as well as the influx of toxic, unhealthy ingredients.

The reason it is important to understand epigenetics is because the risk of any disease can be greatly reduced on a cellular level. A person simply needs to focus on their environmental factors in order to change the epigenetic landscape, which in turn can reduce their risk of illness. Many people do not realize how powerful this process can be. People often resign themselves to high-risk dis-ease, simply because it runs in their family, or they have made poor health choices in the past and do not see the benefit of changing their habits now. The damage has already been done, right? Wrong! The truth is that healthy habits can be introduced at any time, and positive changes will almost always result in a reduction of dis-ease once the decision or thought to move in a new direction is acted upon. In fact, these healthy changes often lead to a dramatic improvement in overall health; as well as a reduction of symptoms and risks associated with chronic diseases. A glorious example comes from identical twins. Even though they may have the same DNA makeup, it is common for them to experience different diseases in life, depending on the influence of their environment or lifestyle choices.

9.4 The Placebo Effect in Healing

The placebo effect is a process that involves providing the patient with a 'fake' treatment, which actually contains no medication. This treatment is generally prescribed in order to reinforce the patient's expectation to get well when a medication is administered. Studies have found that the placebo effect can be just as powerful, or even more effective, than the medical treatment given. It is good for a person to have a strong understanding of the placebo effect so that they understand more about the power of mind-body connection and healing.

For example, when a person is given a sugar pill, (a treatment containing no medication), their perception of treatment will cause a therapeutic effect, which means that the person will experience their condition improving. The brain is expecting the change to occur, so it will start the process to produce the healing elements that are needed within the body. The placebo effect proves that the brain plays a big role in the healing process. It is interesting to see that patients can actually be healed by the suggestion of medication if they believe the medication is positive for them. The mind is so powerful that the body works through the healing process, even if their medication is simply a sugar pill.

The human mind is very powerful, and physical symptoms or healing can develop based on suggestion alone - especially when it is coming from a person of authority. For example, an experiment was done where patients with specific allergies were told that they were going to have skin contact with the offending plant. Even though patients did not actually have an allergy to the plant (because a different species was used), over 80% of the subjects had a physical reaction: redness, itching, boils, etc. This example shows how effective the power of suggestion can be when the patients' bodies actually created the physical allergic reactions, even though they were not initially allergic to the plant that they came in contact with. Likewise, there are multitudes of researched instances demonstrating that the human body is able to heal itself if the patient believes that they are receiving a treatment that will help their condition. As a person understands that it is possible to get well without medication, it increases their faith in their own ability to find better success in alternative treatments; through a healthier mind-body connection. Patients with a good attitude will actually have a faster and improved healing response when they actively participate in the treatment. Health is deeply rooted in the belief system. A person's beliefs, thoughts, and expectations have a strong impact on brain functioning.

Understanding this phenomenon will empower them to make lifestyle and belief changes towards a positive attitude about their condition and life.

The Kousouli® Method enforces clear communication to create an environment of positive energy via the 4th step - *RESET,* which helps reprogram the subconscious mind for success. Remember that positive communication is more effective for healing than negative communication, whether it is from a doctor, family member, or friend. Surround yourself with loving people who will build you up with positive language. You can tell your family and friends that you are looking for positive verbal support, and ask them to help you in your communication also.

9.5 Hypnotherapy

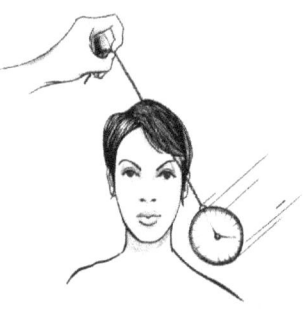

Questions concerning the relationship known as the mind-body problem have been of considerable interest to philosophers and scientists for centuries. At the center of the debate are two opposing philosophies: dualism versus monism. According to mind-body dualism, the mind and body are distinct mental and physical entities. The alternate view, monism, suggests the existence of a single entity (mental or physical). Proponents of the former case (mentalists) attribute all physical states to mental states; and advocates of the latter (physicalists) attribute all mental states to physical states. For instance, a mentalist might consider the mind as a spiritual substance and the body as a sensation of the mind. Conversely, a physicalist may attribute mental states to physical process within the brain. Within the discovery of previously unknown and unsuspected psychological, neurological, endocrinological, and immunological communication systems, a shift from reductionism towards holism is beginning to occur. The emergent mind-body relationship focuses on wellness and the physical, emotional, mental, and spiritual levels of development. The nature of the relationship between the mind and body gives us an option of identifying natural remedies for different dis-eases.

The Influence of Mind-Body Theory on Medicine

Eastern philosophy has long embraced the integration of mind and body. Acknowledgement of a relationship between mind and body has been integral to Chinese and Ayurvedic medicine for over two millennia. Prior to the emergence of the biomedical model, the Western philosophy of medicine was holistic. In many indigenous cultures, the practice of medicine continues to be holistically oriented. The whole person is treated, and the interconnections between mind, body, spirit, and environment are acknowledged. Energy therapies, herbs and natural remedies, massage, trance, and rituals are illustrative of treatment regimens found in holistic health practices. In fact, the Kousouli® Method is a well-rounded integrative mind-body treatment regimen that incorporates the holistic principle.

Myths or Truths about Hypnosis Exposed!

Hypnosis as a whole is one of the most misunderstood practices ever, thanks to propaganda and mistruths in society. Clinical hypnosis is safe when performed by a qualified practitioner whose intent is to help a patient heal their disruptive subconscious programming. I am going to help clear up some common misconceptions for you.

1. Dr. Kousouli, I saw a hypnotist make someone do odd things on stage; what is going on?

The type of hypnosis used in an office session is very different, in delivery style and intention, than the hypnosis done in front of a large crowd or stage. Clinical hypnotherapy promotes health and well-being, whereas stage hypnosis is done purely for entertainment value. In clinical hypnosis, you relax and focus on the sound of the hypnotist's voice while you are guided to remove stress, heal an addiction, toss a bad habit, or gain more self-confidence.

2. Can hypnosis be used for brain washing? Does the hypnotist control my brain and mind?

The hypnotist is actually a guide who helps you transcend the path to self-hypnosis. If you are unwilling to follow suggestions, unable to relax, or can't focus while the process is being conducted, there is no force that can hypnotize you. You still have free will, and it cannot be taken from you unless you give it over willingly.

3. Can hypnosis be used to enslave me?

Hypnosis can be used for positive intent as well as negative, but no one is permanently able to take your consciousness away from you. The intended process in a doctor's office is focused on helping you; teaching your mind to relax and let go of the negative stress or subconscious programs that no longer serve you. If you continuously watch negative television programming, your television acts as your hypnotist. The television programming will input negative thoughts (fears, violence, or other unacceptable behavior) into your mind over time because you allow it to, and by giving your focused attention to it.

When you use hypnosis for the right reasons regularly with a relaxed open mind, you can literally change your life for the better.

4. Do you forget everything that happened during a hypnosis session?

As I mentioned above, all that hypnosis does is teach your mind to relax and focus. If you do not remember anything from the session how in the world will your mind remember to utilize it when you need it? The body and mind always remember subconsciously; it is what we choose to recall consciously and what we retrieve from our stored memories that we use in our daily lives. You will not remember your session consciously if the hypnotist suggests you will not remember the session upon waking.

5. Can I lie while under hypnosis?

You will have all thinking capabilities active. In fact you'll be more focused and more active because your mind is freer to create. It is your choice to "create" the truth or lie, even though it is never advisable to lie. The suggestions you make or are given will be more real or true to you depending on what you feel the 'truth' is.

6. Isn't Hypnosis against the basic principle of Christianity?

Seventh Day Adventists and Christian Scientists have religious doctrines that speak against using hypnosis, but not because it goes against Christianity. Rather, it is for possible traditional and political reasons. All Christians practice meditation through a modified form of self-hypnosis, or what some religions like to refer to as *prayer*, which helps them relax the mind towards asking God for divine intervention.

7. I've heard Hypnosis is very common in our day-to-day lives; how so?

Hypnosis is a natural process and all of us have experienced a form of it at some point of our lives. Road hypnosis is common for those who drive often on highways and suddenly find themselves at their destination in little or no time at all, wondering how they got there so quickly. Prior to bed every night, the body goes through a shutting down cycle referred to as sleep hypnosis. Some spouses claim their significant other unknowingly talks in his or her sleep, but seems very awake. Unresponsive teenagers, staring at the television with solid focus while mom is telling them dinner is ready, are the effect of television covert (concealed) hypnosis. A usual trait among hypnosis episodes is that time seems to have gone by quickly, or that time simply does not exist at all. Everyone at some point in his or her life has been in a self-induced hypnotic state without even knowing it. Clinical hypnosis refocuses and targets its use for positive changes in one's life.

Chapter 10:
Nutrition/Diet, Rest, and Exercise - Keys to Success

"A wise man should consider that health is the greatest of human blessings, and learn how by his own thought to derive benefit from his illnesses."
~ Hippocrates

The goal of this nutrition and diet section is to help you understand why healthy eating is so important, and also to explain the reasons for planning a healthy diet. The Western diet has decreased in quality over the past 50 years, and it is known that the "standard American diet" (SAD) is causing poor health. There are many dis-eases and poor health conditions that can be linked directly to diet, including diabetes, heart disease, cancer, obesity, etc. In fact, between the years of 1980-82 and 1992-94, it is estimated that women in the United States experienced a 38% increase in body weight.

The soil of the United States is critically mineral deficient. In 1936, United States Senate Document #264 highlighted the problem of depleted soil borne micronutrient and trace minerals, concluding that the nation was coming into a mineral deficiency food crisis. That was over 80 years ago! The study concluded: "Countless human ills stem from the fact that the impoverished soil of America no longer provides plant foods, with the mineral elements essential to human nourishment and health!" Between 1940 and 1991, statistics for both the UK and the US Government show degeneration in trace minerals by 76% in fruit and vegetables, according to The Journal of Complimentary Medicine.

We have indeed become a nutrient deficient country. Although we believe we are eating a healthy, nutrient rich diet, this is not the case when compared to the same food amounts and values seventy years ago. Nutrient deficient people exhibit nutrient deficiencies, and get sick much more often. It's a vicious cycle, and it gets worse. It is a fact that people now are eating higher amounts of processed foods, and lower amounts of whole foods. Processed foods have been stripped of their nutrition and they are often filled with harmful ingredients such as herbicides, pesticides, fungicides, preservatives, artificial flavors and colors, unhealthy fats, high levels of sodium and high levels of sugar. In addition, there are countless other chemical ingredients that are added to these foods to preserve shelf life 'freshness' that can harm your health.

On the other hand, eating a diet full of fresh foods in their natural form is a great way to prevent disease, regain and maintain health. These foods are lower in calories, and higher in nutrition; they contain vitamins and minerals that will improve health and prevent disease. The varied Mediterranean diet has been linked to better health and disease prevention, and many doctors recommend this diet. Other diets low in meat consumption and high in greens or those that totally forgo animal meat are great options. When people make the change to a more natural way of eating, they find that their overall health always improves.

For those who choose the Mediterranean diet for example, they eat vegetables and fruits, legumes, nuts, cereals, fish, and minimal amounts of alcohol. This diet focuses on a healthy ratio of monounsaturated and saturated fats, which has been shown to help prevent disease. In order to keep a healthy balance of these fats, it is important to focus on eating the foods listed above, as well as avoiding foods with unhealthy fats such as heavy red meat, dairy, and certain types of vegetable oils.

Research has revealed that a healthy balance of monounsaturated and saturated fat consumption reduces cardiovascular disease risk by 14%, and eating nuts, seeds, fruits and vegetables can further help lower overall disease risk. Another study examined how a vegetarian, low-fat diet along with moderate exercise, stress management, and smoking cessation decreased the risk of disease. It is common for people to have a hard time understanding that this type of diet is good for health; especially because the standard American diet has become so different from what a healthy eating plan actually should be.

The usual American diet is rich in meat, dairy products, and mostly processed foods. Hence, changing to the aforementioned diet program might require some readjustment. Keep in mind that even moderate changes can make a big difference in overall health, and it is better to start making incremental changes in the right direction instead of staying in the rut of continuing to eat unhealthy foods. Set a goal to work your way into healthy habits every day, and identify areas in your eating plan that can be improved. The following steps are recommended for an easy transition into your new and healthy diet regimen.

- Introduce a lot of variation in what you are eating. Boredom is one thing, which normally makes adherence to a diet regimen very difficult. You start with lots of hope, stick to the strict diet regimen for a few days, get frustrated, and then eat so much junk food that you undo all the good you achieved through your hard work.

If you mix and match the healthy foods and give yourself lot of options on your menu, it will be that much easier for you to transition to your new diet, and then maintain it through your lifetime.
- Adequate amounts of protein and monounsaturated fatty acids in your diet are highly recommended, as you will get the correct nutrition and sense of satisfaction.
- Use various herbs and spices in your food as this will add taste to your food and make them interesting and enjoyable to eat.
- Eliminate any kinds of processed food products, specifically the ones that have artificial coloring and flavoring components. It is also recommended to stay away from frozen food items as they come with high amount of free radicals, which will compromise the alkalinity of your body. One big disadvantage of processed foods is that it makes your healthy food items tasteless and uninteresting; tempting you to cheat on your diet regimen.
- If you are feeling that you are not eating enough, include a lot of fruits and vegetables into your diet. They add roughage to your food content, which helps clear your bowel movements; thus enhancing natural colon cleansing. The additional advantage of fruits and vegetables is that they are always low in calorie content, but rich in nutritional value. Fruit should also be part of all your daily diet.
- Above all, knowing why you are changing your diet and appreciating the cause wholeheartedly will tremendously help you with adhering to the new regimen. Remember, you made the choice to switch because your old dietary habits made you unhealthy. Hence, even if at the start you do not feel good about yourself, overtime when you feel healthy you will really enjoy your life a lot more as your energy levels soar.

10.1 Nutrition

Chemists usually love defining food items based on their content of protein, carbohydrates, fats, vitamins and minerals. However, it is imperative to remember that once you ingest different components separately, they are not being utilized in a compartmentalized fashion within your body. A natural food item is a complex entity, built of individual components, and that is how the body recognizes it; making it very apparent that less processing is closer to our body's nature. Stick to unprocessed food items for all your diet requirements!

Practicality does not rule the society, however. Money does, and as a result 80% of all food items you see in the store are processed. You can basically label them as FAKE FOODS because they hardly offer any nutritional value. Why? Because for them to be digested and absorbed by the body, they depend on other food items you intake. For example, if you are eating a lot of protein but not enough fat, then you do not have enough metabolic energy to utilize the entire protein intake. Hence, completely avoid foods that come as 'empty calories' because that completely de-tracks your metabolism.

I call all processed convenience foods 'junk foods,' and highly suggest avoiding anything which has been artificially sweetened, inclusive of soft drinks, ice-creams, chocolates and candies, diet or normal pastries, and processed cereals. Do not worry – you will ultimately lose your cravings for these food items and will feel good about it! This will also ensure that you are eating a good amount of nutritional food to satisfy yourself. It is also highly recommended that you stay away from food items that you are allergic to. If you are a person who affords a wide variety of choices in your diet, then you can always find items that do not give you any allergic reactions. Typical allergic reactions from your body are: coughing, mucus or phlegm production, sneezing, difficulty breathing or swallowing, skin rashes, face swelling, watery eyes, and fever. These symptoms are commonly seen a few minutes after consuming processed dairy drinks or foods like milkshakes or cheesecake.

10.2 Myths and Truths of Genetic Engineering

A study conducted on genetically modified crops from Monsanto, the largest producer of GM crops in USA, showed that they each resulted in organ failure. Still, the Obama administration gave more funds to help in all kinds of agricultural GM crops. There has been increasing push in the last decade and a half to champion the use of genetically engineered (GE) food products. It started off as a fun exercise, and then caught the eye of opportunists who thought of the higher yield of returns on investments, but they're forgetting to think how they would be affected in the long term. We the public are the sacrificial rats of this GE experimental testing!

Myth #1: Genetic Engineering (GE) is a long practiced methodology. What people often confuse it with is selective breeding, where one never manipulates genes, as opposed to genetic engineered plants. Modern genetic engineering began in the early 1970's, and is now rapidly progressing. It is simply too soon to know how this will effect humans genetically in the coming decades.

Myth #2: Because they are resistant to insects and other contaminants, the use of pesticides and herbicides will significantly decrease. When people make such an assertion, they often forget that there is phenomena called evolution, and insects and pests might undergo mutation to circumvent the resistance. Additionally, such a notion inspires people to unbridled amounts of herbicides as they think their crop will not get affected. Cross-pollination can also happen between seeds of GE and non-GE plants and give rise to non-resistant or mutant varieties; the end result of which can be disastrous.

Myth #3: If you do not like it – do not eat it! When 80% of the food items sold are GE products, how can one refrain from eating them? In fact, there is no way to find them, as they never are mentioned on the food label as of yet. Passionate protestors are pushing for GMO labeling nation-wide, but have so far fallen short of their goal (thanks to tons of lobbyist money in Congress).

Myth #4: All GE food that hits stores has been tested and found to be safe. Even the persons who advocate for GE food products are not educated about acceptable testing methodologies. Long-term epidemiological research statistics are required to make such a conclusion. In fact, GE foods come with the risk of us developing resistances to antibiotics, since that is the gene always used to make these GE products.

Myth #5: GE foods are nutritionally enriched. The only way GE foods are better is in possibly ensuring higher yields, more resistance to herbicides, and increased shelf life. However, each one of these can actually modify the capacity for human digestion, causing many dis-eases and mutations, such as cancer.

Myth #6: GE foods vary from organically grown food products only in the modified traits. Due to random genetic integration methodology, it would be scientifically incorrect to make such an assertion. No one has ever done a whole genome sequencing of an organically grown fruit and its genetically modified version to compare the two.

Myth #7: GE food products are 'great for the farmer.' This is absolutely ridiculous, as GE seeds are far more expensive and the crops are less reliable. The overall profits also do not see any marked improvement. Awareness is increasing about the downside of having GE foods, further cutting down profit margins. Moreover, if you are growing GE crops you are in a contract of using a particular brand of herbicide, no matter how expensive it is, and also you cannot save any seed for your next crop season. Monsanto has also begun to sue people whose crops have been cross-pollinated with their GE seed, thus showing GE characteristics. Monsanto sues farmers over seed patents because of a natural phenomenon like crosspollination. Not very 'pro-farmer.'

Myth #8: GE is very specific. There is no way that one can precisely tell where a gene will integrate within the plant genome after being transduced using a virus. It is approximate at best, and often times wrong integration can cause a recombinant DNA technology catastrophe. Genetics Professor at Harvard University, Dr. Richard Lewotin, has mentioned while talking about GE that, "we have such a miserably poor understanding of how the organism develops from its DNA that I would be surprised if we don't get one rude shock after another."

Myth #9: Because we can make drought resistant GE crops, the world will never have scarcity of food, even if a famine strikes. Famine and drought have only a causal relationship, and famine will not decrease the buying and hoarding capacity of affluent groups or individuals. Moreover, GE crops have not shown consistent and convincingly more yields in comparison to non-GE products. Statistics show that the US produces enough GE corn and wheat crop to feed the world (and everyone in it), but instead uses that crop to feed the cattle that Americans eat. Even if there was enough GE crop, odds are it wouldn't be going to prevent/decrease famine.

Myth #10: Trust the word of scientists that make GE food products. Haven't we already seen enough of money-dictated research results in this book? How will trusting GE scientist be any different? The 1995 Nobel Laureate in Physics, Joseph Rotblat said, "My worry is that other advances in science may result in other means of mass destruction, maybe more readily available even than nuclear weapons. GE is quite a possible area, because of the dreadful developments that are taking place there."

GE foods are resistant to pathogens and pests. Seedless tomatoes and lemons were made, and even a potato and tomato were crossed to make a *Pomato*. What's next? A hybrid of all fruits and vegetables - no more cooking fun in the kitchen or tasting our favorite raw foods – we'll just eat the one super hybrid vegetable with no 'real' flavor. Ugh - How cataclysmically boring!

10.3 Know Your Greens

Dark green is usually considered the color of healing, in sync with the color of grass and plants. This signifies that all our healing secrets lie in Mother Nature. Even when you go under our enormous stretches of ocean, you find the single cell chlorella, the macro-algae kelp (also known as seaweed), and plenty of other greenery. Humans have long understood the benefits of a green-food based diet, and only in recent decades have we begun to move away from this innate knowledge.

Wheatgrass – Where it all Started

Thank Dr. Anne Wigmore every time you hear about Wheatgrass. She was diagnosed with cancer in the 1960's, and was advised a lower limb amputation to prolong her life. She refused the treatment strategy and withdrew from the medical field, relying on common grass extract to treat her wounds; she even ate grass. The rest is part of medical folklore…she was cured of cancer and she went forward and opened a clinic in Massachusetts to help others. Needless to say, she had no scarcity of patients; many of the patients were people the medical field could not help. Her clinic flourished to different parts of the continental US and even globally in India, Puerto Rico, and Australia. She made 'kitchen gardening' of wheatgrass famous. However, one down side was the yield and the special needs required for juicing the grass, in turn limiting its widespread use. Currently, wheatgrass comes in two flavors – the original 10-day-old indoor one and the 30-day-old outdoor grown form. The outdoor grown one is more heavily used and gives more favorable outcomes when used regularly.

Kamut and Barley Grass – Pals of Wheatgrass

We can call kamut and barley siblings because of comparable nutritional value to wheatgrass. Even though they have their own pros and cons, together they are a shining example of 'superfoods.' How to choose, then? Use your discretion, taste requirements, and price for which one you want to use regularly as a supplement. Durum or pasta wheat is a distant relative of the kamut grass family. It is a purebred grass and has never undergone any cross breeding. Thus, it falls under the very exclusive category of 'heirloom.' It is richer in protein, lipid, and mineral content to the wheat that we normally have daily.

In 1935, scientists from the University of Wisconsin did an experiment to study why milk sourced in the winter was distinctly poorer in nutrition to the milk created by summer cows when in the pastures. It was found that "the growth stimulating factor of grass was distinct from all the known vitamins." After testing the three grasses wheat, barley, and oats, it was found that barley grass had the most effect on the growth of the guinea pigs that the formula was tested on. After the seventh week, the guinea pigs were taken off the formula and given only mineralized milk. The scientists found that their growth stopped instantly, only to resume when the guinea pigs were given the barley grass formula again, showing clearly that grasses contain nutritional factors eminent in our health maintenance.

Barley grass juice, better known as "Green Magma" is a nutritional supplement that we get off our green sources. In fact, even in the above research, barley grass showed some of the most promising results. Barley grass is a 'super' source of proteins, minerals (contains 11 folds more calcium than cow milk, 4 folds more iron in comparison to spinach), vitamins (especially vitamins B1, B12 and C), enzymes, polysaccharides, and low molecular weight protein fragments or polypeptides.

Chlorophyll – It's All in the Leaves

The 1988 Nobel Prize in chemistry was awarded for the discovery of the chemical structure of chlorophyll. It is a green color pigment in plants, housed in organelles named chloroplasts, that makes plants appear green. They can use solar energy to synthesize food for the plants – something we intelligent human beings can never do. Hence, they occupy the #1 position in the food chain, and because they use carbon dioxide to make food and give off oxygen in the process, thus performing a critical role. It has long been known that chlorophyll can (I) inhibit bacterial growth, (II) prevent foul mouth odors, (III) inhibit growth of putrefactive bacteria in the gut, (IV) prevent gum disorders, and (V) expedite wound healing. Professor E. Bircher sums up chlorophyll as: "It increases the functions of the head, affects the vascular system, the intestines, the uterus, and the lungs. It raises basic nitrogen exchange and is therefore a tonic which, considering its stimulating properties, cannot be compared with any other." Chlorophyll can be likened to hemoglobin in your red blood cells, the protein that carries oxygen to different tissues of your body through your circulatory system. It has been used to successfully treat anemia in animal experiments.

Algae – The Water-Grown Wonder

All vegetables are not grown in the soil – there are hydrophytes, which are grown in water without any substratum, and there are others like algae, which grows in water wherever it finds bedrock. Nowadays, algae are part of vegetable farming. Not all are edible -- in fact most are not – but the select few that are edible come as huge nutritional boosters, easy to grow, and should be incorporated in our diet. Spirulina, chlorella, and blue-green algae are the currently approved ones for usage. If used alone, they are like green grasses (around 25% protein), but when used as a combo they have 70% protein. Chlorella grows best in Asian climates, whereas spirulina grows best in the arid desert weather of Southern

California and Hawaii. Since they occupy such a small place for growth, a minimal cultivation requirement, and easy harvesting and post-processing, they are perhaps the food solution for the future - nutritious, natural, and cheap. The only downside is digesting the cellulose present in their cell walls. Unlike herbivores, we do not make cellulose-digesting enzymes. Hence, efforts continue to get rid of the cell wall post-harvest.

Spirulina is often prescribed by naturopaths as an immune booster. Rich in anti-oxidants and phytonutrients, they hold much promise for the future. Given the abundance of phycocyanin, chlorophyll, sulfolipids, linoleic acid (essential fatty acid), glycolipids, beta-carotene and other carotenoids, spirulina has the power to repair and rejuvenate. I strongly recommend you incorporate it in your daily diet. Additionally, it has a rich supply of iron and vitamin B-12, perfect also for vegetarians.

10.4 Take Advantage of Light to Enlighten Your Life

You might have seen babies born prematurely then kept in chambers lighted with ultraviolet light. Such babies suffer from jaundice, and ultraviolet light helps in recovery by degrading the bilirubin and biliverdin, the two central substances involved in jaundice. Similarly, light can be used to heal you as an adult as well, and you should never underestimate the power of a little UV or Vitamin D.

Ultraviolet Light

UV light has been used in the healing process from the beginning of the twentieth century. The best thing is, such treatments have almost zero side effects, unlike conventional drugs. It essentially works by boosting and stimulating the immune system. The process involves treating a small volume of ejected blood to UV, and then re-injection of the same into the parent person. This is often termed as photoluminescence therapy. Your body has amino acids that are light sensitive. In fact, the way UV works is as an 'autogenous vaccine.' Photoluminescence also helps in (I) dilation of coronary arteries, (II) increased oxygenation, (III) prevention / reversal of thrombophlebitis, (IV) cure of paralytic gut, (V) restoration of autonomic nervous system, and (VI) significant alleviation of symptoms in asthma patients. There has been some indication that it can help in treating gout by eliminating uric acid. Some suggestions also exist for its use in diabetic patients. UV light is classically also used as a disinfectant in research labs and hospitals.

Medication will be largely ineffective whenever the normal mechanisms of a body are malfunctioning. Photoluminescence, or UV light therapy, has the potential to rapidly restore normal physiological body functions and increase the efficacy of medication in-

10.5 Should You Avoid the High Protein Diet?

A continuous trend, especially among athletes and bodybuilders, is resorting to high protein diets and shakes that help build muscles without contributing to obesity. Once we ingest proteins, they are broken down to their constituent amino acids (the building blocks of proteins), which are then absorbed into the body to help repair tissues after exercise. Our body normally does not synthesize all these amino acids; hence our food is the only source for them. Methionine is one of these essential amino acids. But too much of it is toxic, as it makes the body acidic to compensate the body leaches calcium from the bones, which will cause bone dis-eases. Remember, everything in moderation.

10.6 Healthy Plant and Meat Protein

One main hang-up that people often have with healthy eating plans lies in the fact that we should be avoiding dairy, meat, and other animal products. Many cultures have developed a strong opinion about eating red meat with every meal, and many people do not realize that doing so may be damaging to their health. The truth is that there are no nutrients in meats that cannot be accessed in plants. In fact, many plants are a better source of the nutrients, because they do not contain the unhealthy fats that are found in animal meat.

Studies are emerging that show that a higher level of meat consumption is directly correlated with certain diseases, such as cancer and heart disease. Following a mostly vegetarian diet will drastically reduce the risk of these diseases. At this point, many people are wondering where the protein source is in a vegetarian diet, and this question often emerges because people do not understand how plant food can provide protein. In fact, many plant foods are great sources of protein, and eating a variety of these foods can easily provide you with the protein that is needed to be healthy.

For example, leafy green vegetables are great sources of protein, with spinach calories actually containing 49% protein! Take a moment to think about the fact that animals like cows and chickens need protein to survive as well. Where do you think big cows get the protein that is needed to build their muscles? Their source of protein comes from the green grass that they eat all day long. There are other plant foods that contain protein, such as beans, nuts, and seeds, as well as numerous vegetables that provide the protein that is needed for healthy living. Be sure to eat a variety of these foods in order to get the different nutrition that each food type contains.

Also, keep in mind that wild caught, non-coastal fish can be a great source of protein, and should be eaten on a regular basis. Additionally, you can eat other sources of protein in very small portions, like lean meat, cheese, eggs, etc., once or twice a week.

Fish Frequency Eating Guide

Low Mercury (Enjoy 2-3x week)	Mid-Level (1x / week – 1x / month)	High Level (Avoid)
Mullet, Oyster, Catfish, Flounder, Herring, Anchovies, Pollock, Haddock, Hake, Pink / Sockeye Salmon, Tilapia, Whitefish, Cod, Calamari, Crab, Clams, Butterfish, Sardines, Trout, Carp, Crayfish, Squid, Scallops, Shrimp	Bluefish, Striped Bass, Sablefish / Black Cod, Monkfish, Chinook Salmon, Grouper, Mahi Mahi, Rockfish / Snapper, Croaker, Canned Tuna White Albacore, Halibut, Lobster, Farmed Mussels	Shark, Swordfish, Tuna Steak, Marlin, Ahi Tuna, King Mackerel, Bass, Orange Roughy, Tilefish

Fish provides us with healthy amounts of omega 3 fatty acids, and is considered healthier than land animal meat. However, pollutants such as polychlorinated biphenyls (PCBs), and mercury (toxin that damages the nervous system of humans) are dumped in our ocean waters, contaminating sea life and causing concern. When we eat contaminated fish, toxin levels build up and pose major neurotoxic effects on our nervous system health (especially to the elderly, pregnant women, and the unborn). Fish eaters should do regular heavy metal detoxification to be sure their toxin levels are safe. Some fish are consistently higher in mercury, but it varies from state to state. Check with your local seafood authority, department of health (DOH), or environmental protection agency (EPA) on what fish are safe to eat in your area.

10.7 Milk Does a Body What?

Advice against drinking cow milk comes from one of US's leading authority on childcare, Dr. Benjamin Spock, who refers to cow milk as 'cow's glue.' Bovine growth hormone, antibiotics, pesticides, chemicals, pus, and blood are in regular cow milk at your local grocery store. Research has unequivocally shown that drinking cow milk can cause migraines, bloating, indigestion, gas, asthma, anemia, prostate cancer, and serious allergies. Do you still want to drink cow milk? Consider this – even a calf does not drink cow milk except for a very short period after birth. So why do we need to drink it? We don't. It's called marketing. Clever marketing and massive lobby efforts by the dairy industry for decades has solidified their industry, and brainwashed millions of Americans into reaching for their product. Their efforts have worked so well that you can go right now to your local grocery store and stand at the refrigerated milk section for just a few minutes to witness the true 'mad cow' craze. I see countless people reaching for that cow glue without even thinking twice about its contents. Try telling any one of these people that they should be drinking almond or rice milk, found in the non-dairy section, and that it is a far healthier choice for them. They will look at you as if you're the crazy one.

10.8 Dining at Fast Food Restaurants – Should you Re-consider?

If ever you have the urge t0 feast on all those food items on big M's menu, then please do see Morgan Spurlock's documentary, 'Super-Size Me.' Eating and surviving only on fast food for a month, Morgan Spurlock candidly records all the physiological abnormality, inclusive of increasing weight, hypercholesterolemia, abnormal liver function, bloating, edema, and loss of libido that he faces after consuming various fast food items. So, the lesson is – stay away from junk and fast foods as much as possible! If you MUST sacrifice in the name of convenience, seek out the nutritional charts of the food items in the restaurant. If not displayed, ask the manager for a nutrition chart. They must supply the nutrition chart to the public when asked. Make your food selection from the nutritional information listed and not from the beautifully photographed – yet highly misleading --images placed in the menus.

10.9 Carbonated and Diet Sodas – Great Alternative Uses

Our bodies do not derive any valuable nutrition from carbonated sodas. Consuming sodas on a regular basis can set you up for long-term chronic dis-ease like diabetes and osteoporosis. Sodas are not totally useless however; here are some proactive uses around the house:
- Clean your toilet: Empty a cola can in the toilet and let the treatment last an hour. The phosphoric acid in the cola will purify your toilet rendering it clean and shiny!
- Use it to remove water spots from chrome bumpers.

- Use it to take off the corrosion on your car's battery terminals.
- To release a rusted bolt, dab a rag drenched in carbonated soda to the rusted bolt for a few minutes and it will loosen up.
- Add a can of non-caramel colored cola into your regular laundry cycle. The carbonated soda will help take the grease off your clothes.
- Use carbonated soda to clean the road haze on your windshield.
- Sodas are often used by hazard clean-up crews to remove bloodstains from roads after fatal accidents.

Consider all the above points. The pH of carbonated soda is 2.8, acidic enough to dissolve a T-bone from a steak in five days or an eggshell in two days. In fact, distributors have been using carbonated drinks to clean the engine of their trucks for over two decades now. I will leave the decision on YOU to decide whether to drink carbonated sugar sodas. Waiter, I'll have a lemon water, thanks.

10.10 Be a Mindful Eater

In addition to eating the right types of food, it is also important to focus on how and why you are eating the food. The process of mindful eating is an important part of reducing the risk of dis-ease, because it lowers stress levels, and improves digestion. Many of our modern food choices are based around speed, accessibility, and convenience. We are heavily influenced by advertisements, and tend to eat whatever food is easily available. Americans eat three to four times more than their European counterparts! The problem with reactive eating lies in the fact that we are unaware of the ways those foods can affect the body.

Taking it back to the basics, we need to focus on the fact that eating is a necessary part of life that provides our bodies with nutrition. The vitamins and minerals we get from food are essential to maintaining good health and preventing dis-ease. Unfortunately, many people forget this fact, and they fall into the pattern of eating to satisfy hunger and just fill their stomach, regardless of the type of foods they are consuming. Sometimes food is even eaten to comfort emotions or for entertainment. Food is very often eaten in a rushed state, as we hurry to work or our next important destination. Many people eat their meals quickly while doing something else at the same time. This habit of multi-tasking while eating actually causes the mind to register stress, putting pressure on the entire body. That daily stress pattern, over time, can cause chronic health problems.

There are actually various physical ways that stress can hamper digestion, and stress signals can be alleviated by multitasking while you are eating. Even a simple task such as reading or working at the computer can cause a "stress" signal to be sent, because the multitasking registers as stress in the brain. When the body initiates the reactions that occur when stress is present, digestion is essentially put on hold because the body needs those energy resources elsewhere. So, even though you are trying to save time by working at the computer and eating simultaneously, the body actually perceives the activity as stress, which inhibits digestion. This in turn reduces the effectiveness of eating!

When stress shuts down the digestive system, it reacts by decreasing the amount of digestive enzymes that are released, in addition to decreasing the amount of hydrochloric acid that helps to break down the food in your stomach. When stomach acids are limited, your body is unable to access the vitamins and minerals that are available in the foods that you are eating! Additionally, stress impairs the body's ability to metabolize fatty acids, which means that muscles may begin to break down. When the muscles are broken down, the body often reacts by replacing them with excess fluids and fat, leading to weight gain. To make matters worse, the stress reaction also releases extra glucose in order to provide the energy that is needed for the 'fight or flight' response. Because glucose is released, the pancreas needs to release insulin, and this reaction may actually cause the person to have additional cravings for high sugar foods.

It is common for many people to respond to stress by eating a poor diet, which exacerbates the problem because the necessary nutrients are not available in the empty calories that are being consumed. Eating healthy, nutrient-dense foods is essential during stressful times, simply because the body needs those nutrients to keep the organs functioning correctly. As you can see from the processes that have been described, mindful eating is very important in order to limit the stress reactions that can occur from multitasking while eating. It has been found that paying attention to our food is a critical part of the eating process. When a person takes the time to focus on their food while eating, they are more likely to reduce their portion sizes, enjoy the meal more, and have better digestion.

10.11 Eating According to You

Peter D'Adamo, a naturopathic physician, advocates a diet regimen based on your ABO blood group. This is based on the capacity of lectins within food items to react differently with various blood group antigens. He classifies blood Group A as agrarian or cultivator; the vegetarian types. Blood Group B is nomad; varied food types, Group O are hunters; the meat eaters, and Blood Group AB is enigma; the smaller meals and grain types. Each group has specific diet requirements based on its name. Of note, widespread clinical evidence is still ongoing for this type of diet regimen, but the observations on which it is based are sound and worth consideration.

Debbi Larkins, a Holistic Nutritionist and detoxification expert in Beverly Hills, also advises keeping a food journal to gain insight into your relationship with food and how it affects you. She further states, "Our body chemistry is unique in that there is no one perfect 'diet' for everyone. The key is to pay attention to what *your* body is telling you. If you learn to listen closely, your body will tell you what it needs and what it won't tolerate *every time.*"

10.12 Antioxidants, Diets, and Degenerative Diseases

Many people know that antioxidants are good for your health. In fact the word 'anti-oxidant' is often used in marketing to convince people to buy a product. Researchers are becoming more and more aware of why antioxidant nutrients are important for health, and they have discovered that these nutrients can be an essential part of disease prevention and treatment. Antioxidants can be found in specific types of foods, such as fruits and vegetables. The Merriam-Webster online dictionary describes the role of antioxidants in an easy to understand way: "An antioxidant is a substance (as beta-carotene or vitamin C), that inhibits oxidation or reactions promoted by oxygen, peroxides, or free radicals."

Why We Need Antioxidants

Antioxidants promote health and youthfulness by fighting and preventing dis-ease. They are basically your army of good nutrients fighting against the bad things that are happening, or could happen, in your body. One of the main functions of antioxidants is to clean up free radicals and prevent them from causing damage to your body. Here's how the process works:

Everybody experiences oxidation, which is a natural process that damages our cells over time. Oxidation causes wear-and-tear on the body, aging, illness, and degenerative diseases. Because this process is normal, most of the time the body is able to get rid of damaged cells and replenish again with healthy cells. But, if there are too many damaged cells from the oxidation process, the body might not be able to efficiently get rid of them, thus resulting in the cells becoming 'free radicals.' These free radicals can actually lead to molecular changes and cause damage to the healthy cells in the body. Researchers have found correlations between high levels of free radicals and chronic disease, such as heart disease and cancer.

Toxic substances can cause free radicals, and there are toxic substances all around us: pollution, pesticides, high amounts of alcohol, cigarette smoke, and even unhealthy foods, such as processed foods with additives and chemicals. These toxic substances and the normal process of oxidation actually start a chain reaction in the body, leading to dis-ease and a decrease in health. The free radicals begin to take over, and the functionality of the healthy cells decreases.

Set a goal to provide your body with the antioxidants that it needs, and you will be able to prevent dis-ease and support your health. Foods that are high in antioxidants actually prevent the chain reactions that are set off by the free radicals. Additionally, antioxidants can reverse damage that has already occurred, making antioxidants the perfect way to prevent and treat chronic dis-ease.

How Antioxidants Work

Antioxidants can be found in fresh, natural foods such as fruits, vegetables, nuts, seeds, etc. They can also be gained through supplements. However, many doctors suggest that eating an abundance of fresh fruits and vegetables every day is the best source for providing your body with rich antioxidants to prevent dis-ease and stay healthy. The body will break down various nutrients into a usable format, and those antioxidants will begin to work on a cellular level to neutralize and clean up free radicals. As these antioxidants work to clean up the free radicals, the body must get rid of both the used antioxidants as well as the free radicals. It is important that you are replenishing by eating fruits and vegetables on a daily basis as to avoid serious chronic dis-eases, such as heart disease and cancer.

Sources of Antioxidants

There are various sources of antioxidants, and it is important to eat a variety of these foods in order to ensure that you are getting all of the nutrient types that your body needs. These are some healthy foods that are high in antioxidants. Keep in mind that these are just examples and this list is not comprehensive because many types of whole, plant-based foods contain nutrients that promote health and prevent dis-ease.

- **Vitamin C Sources:** Strawberries, tomatoes, broccoli, leafy green vegetables, and any type of citrus fruits such as mandarins, tangerines, oranges, grapefruits, etc.
- **Vitamin E Sources:** Leafy green vegetables such as spinach, chard, collard greens, kale, etc. Also, wheat germ, almonds, walnuts, avocado, and many types of seeds.
- **Beta-Carotene Sources:** Any type of orange colored fruit or vegetable, includ-

ing squash, carrots, apricots, peppers, cantaloupe, pumpkin, sweet potatoes, etc. Additionally, leafy green vegetables provide beta-carotene, so eat lots of collard greens, romaine, spinach, kale, etc.
- **Sources of Selenium:** Selenium can be found in many whole grains and nuts, such as whole wheat bread, brown rice, oatmeal, brazil nuts, and walnuts.

These are a few of the important antioxidants that the body needs, but there are also other antioxidant nutrients that can be found in whole foods. Some of the other nutrients include zinc and flavonoids. Remember that each type of nutrient and antioxidant works in a different way, so it is critical that you are eating a variety of foods in order to get the whole range of antioxidants that your body needs to be healthy.

How to Provide Your Body With Antioxidants on a Daily Basis

Because there are various antioxidants found in different foods, it is essential that you eat a variety of fruits and vegetables, nuts and seeds, and whole grains in order to get all of the nutrition that is needed for optimal health. Following the food guidelines discussed in this book will help you to get the nutrition that is needed.

Fresh, organic raw fruits and vegetables are the best way to consume your antioxidants every day. There are various canned versions of many of these foods, and the heating and canning processes actually deplete the antioxidants that are available. Foods in their most natural form are the healthiest options.

Antioxidants in Superfoods

Over the past few years, there has been an increase in the companies and products that promote the consumption of superfoods to improve your health. These big businesses use the hot topic of superfoods to sell more products and make quite a bit of money. Popular superfoods are flaunted as the healthiest in the world, and they can be found in far-off countries, which means that they can be quite expensive to bring to the consumer. Do not be fooled by the marketing, because there is not one pill or potion that can give you the nutrition that you need to lose weight or improve your health. Many of these products make big claims. You need to remember that if something sounds too good to be true, then it probably is!

The truth is that yes, superfoods can be a great source of antioxidants for your body, but there are many superfoods that are easily accessible and quite a bit less expensive. Also, you need to consider the form of the product. For example, many of these companies are selling the superfoods in a juice format. The problem with these antioxidant juice supplements lies in the fact that the juices are highly processed and usually pasteurized, which decreases the overall nutritional value of the food. Like any other types of fruits and vegetables, superfoods should be eaten in the most natural form possible. It is always best to eat the raw version of the food instead of taking a supplement or drinking a juice that has lost some of its nutrition. Eating superfoods on a regular basis will provide you the nutrients that most American diets are missing, and there are many superfoods that are easily accessible. Here is a list of superfoods that are commonly found at the grocery store and can provide you with good sources of antioxidants:

- **Green Leafy Vegetables**

Green superfoods are known to have some of the highest levels of easily digestible nutrition. Green vegetables have antioxidants, protein, and phytochemicals, which promote health and protect you from dis-ease. Additionally, green vegetables contain chlorophyll, which increases the oxygen levels in the blood, helping your body thrive on a cellular level. Leafy green vegetables have been proven to reduce the risk of chronic diseases such as heart disease and cancer, and these foods are easily available at any grocery store. Some types of leafy green foods include spinach, kale, lettuce, broccoli, sprouts, mustard greens, chard, collard greens, and parsley. Additionally, there are other health foods that offer high levels of nutrition and antioxidants, including barley grass, wheat grass, and various types of algae.

- **Blueberries**

Many professionals agree that blueberries are a great source of nutrition. They provide you with phytoflavonoids and antioxidants, as well as vitamin C and potassium. Additionally, blueberries are a great anti-inflammatory food, and it has been discovered that eating blueberries on a regular basis can help to reduce the risk of cancer and heart disease.

- **Omega-3 Fish**

Omega-3 fatty acids are essential for reducing inflammation and preventing dis-ease. It is important to note that omega-3s are actually on the list of superfoods because of the strong effect that they have on a person's health. Omega-3s are found in cold-water fish, like mackerel, sardines, herring, and salmon. It is important to always buy wild caught (not farmed) fish, because they are a better source of clean nutrition. Other sources of omega-3s include walnuts and flax seeds.

- **Beans**

Because beans are loaded with fiber and nutrition, they are a great health food. Eating beans on a regular basis can help lower cholesterol levels and assist your body to get rid of waste (because of the fiber). Certain types of beans, such as soybeans, can provide the omega-3 fatty acids that help decrease inflammation.

- **Nuts**

Many people think that they should avoid eating nuts because they are higher in calories and fat, but the truth is that nuts are a great source of nutrition because they contain antioxidants, healthy fats, and high amounts of fiber. Add nuts like walnuts and chestnuts to other foods that you are eating, and they will help to improve your overall health. Just be sure to chew thoroughly and enjoy in moderation because they are high in calories. A small handful each day is plenty - about one to two ounces.

- **Quinoa**

Most grocery stores carry quinoa now, although this superfood is not as well-known as other foods on this list. Quinoa is a type of grain that is very high in protein as well as other nutrients, including selenium, vitamin E, and zinc.

10.13 Supplements and Vitamins

Supplements can be effective and useful, but they should be used in conjunction with a healthy eating plan. Some people do not want to take the time to seek out, clean, cook, and eat healthy foods, so they choose to purchase expensive antioxidant supplements to take instead. They choose to eat unhealthy, highly processed convenience foods and then take the supplements to fill the nutrition voids. This is clearly the wrong approach. Do not fool yourself into a false sense of security thinking that simply taking a supplement is sufficient. Taking supplements does not replace the need to follow a healthy diet on a daily basis. It is important to remember that the best sources of these nutrients are found in organically grown, pesticide and herbicide-free whole foods. For example, it is better to eat an orange in order to gain all of the nutrition that is available. Taking a vitamin C supplement is helpful, but not quite as effective.

There are many benefits to taking natural supplements, especially when these supplements are compared to taking drugs and medication. Taking vitamins and supplements can help improve health conditions, especially if the supplements are high quality products. As discussed earlier, drugs are often prescribed to treat specific symptoms without addressing the root of the problem, but certain types of supplements can be beneficial to treating the root of many dis-eases. Be sure to understand the condition first, as well as the supplements that can be taken in order to achieve the best results possible. Supplements often need to be taken in large doses on a regular basis in order to provide the health benefits that the person is looking for. If you are considering a supplement regimen, it is a good idea to talk with a professional about the correct dosages and possible side effects of each supplement.

10.14 Foods and Supplements That Reduce Inflammation for Faster Healing

We know that reducing inflammation can be an effective way to prevent or treat arthritis and other chronic conditions. Following an anti-inflammatory diet and supplementing correctly are great ways to reduce inflammation for quicker healing. Some of the best anti-inflammatory supplements are those that contain healthy fats, such as omega-3, flaxseed oil, or fish oil supplements. These supplements can be found in a liquid or capsule form, and you should be taking at least 2-3 grams per day. Other healthy anti-inflammatory oils include: rice bran oil, grape seed oil, olive oil, and walnut oil.

As with any supplement, it is important to check the quality of the product. Most high quality supplements can be found at a health food store; they often carry higher quality products than a general grocery store. Fish oil supplements are especially prone to contamination of heavy metals, so it is important to look for brands that have been certified pure. Cod, sardines, salmon, halibut, herring, striped bass, and snapper are excellent sources of protein that also reduce inflammation. One of the most potent anti-inflammatory supplement combinations is when docosahexaenoic acid (known as DHA, an omega-3 fatty acid) and eicosapentaenoic acid (known as EPA, another omega-3 fatty acid) are taken together. DHA and EPA are both found in fish oil, which is one of the reasons that fish oil supplements can be a great way to improve health. This combination works together to regulate brain chemicals and also manage damage repair in the body.

Other good anti-inflammatory supplements are those supplements that contain micronutrients, vitamins and minerals, and especially antioxidants. There are also herbs that have anti-inflammatory properties, and these can be taken as supplements. Some of the best anti-inflammatory herbs and seasonings that you can add to your meals include: ginger, basil, cloves, parsley, rosemary, cilantro, oregano, cinnamon, mint, turmeric and boswellia. Vegetables that help with lowering inflammation include: cauliflower, cabbage, chard, rhubarb, collards, sweet potato, green beans, broccoli, yams, Japanese pumpkin, spinach, fennel bulb and onion. Fruits that can help you heal faster include: avocado, apple, blackberries, blueberries, guava, black currants, mulberries, raspberries, kumquat, pomegranate, cherries, and pineapple.

Add powerful nuts, beans, and seeds that boost antioxidants and reduce inflammation to your plate; walnuts, almonds, hazelnuts, mung beans, lentils, flax seeds, sunflower seeds, split peas, pumpkin seeds, and soy beans. When healing or recovering from surgery, you will want to avoid foods that break down in the body and cause more inflammation such as: cow milk and dairy, processed and refined foods, potato, tomato, eggplant, frozen foods with trans fats, bell pepper, sugar, coffee, alcohol and red meat.

10.15 Supplements for Sleep

Some practitioners suggest that supplements can be taken in order to improve sleep. Having a good night's sleep each night will help reduce overall stress levels, which in turn will reduce the risk of chronic disease. Improved sleep can support the body in the healing process, because the body rebuilds and heals while you are resting. Sleep patterns can increase or decrease the inflammation in a person's body, and sleeping between seven to nine hours each night can help buffer the inflammatory effects in the body. Even though there are plenty of drugs on the market to help a person sleep, they often have undesirable side effects. Additionally, it is not a good idea to become dependent on a medication to sleep each night. Natural supplements are a far better alternative if you are having a hard time sleeping.

The following is a list of supplements that can be taken to reduce stress and improve sleeping patterns. Check with your doctor for dosage: L-Tryptophan, L-Theanine, GABA, B Vitamins - B2, B3, B6, B12, Magnesium, Choline Bitartrate, Inositol, Vinpocetine, Melatonin, Galantamine, 5-*hydroxytryptophan* (5-HTP), DMAE and Gingko-Biloba. *For more information on better sleep and dealing with insomnia, see section 8.3 and Chapter 11.*

10.16 More Water Please

No, water is not necessarily considered a supplement, but it is important to understand that water consumption needs to be a regular part of your daily habits. Many people are living in a constant state of dehydration, which causes unnecessary wear-and-tear on the body.

Some hard facts about dehydration are:

- 75% of the US population suffers from chronic dehydration!
- Interestingly, 37% of US citizens confuse their thirst as

hunger.
- Daytime fatigue is usually caused by dehydration; partial dehydration also slows down metabolic rate.
- Solving dehydration has been indicated to contribute in resolution of back and joint pain in up to 80% of patients.
- In a study conducted in the University of Washington, it was observed that a glass of water can tide over 'feeling hungry' episodes among dieters.

Your body is made up of 70% water, and all internal processes and reactions are dependent on good hydration. If you are not drinking enough water, it can put a strain on your major organs and hinder natural chemical processes. There are a few important benefits of drinking a lot of water, including:

- **Metabolism Optimization**

Drinking water helps the digestion process run smoothly. Water is necessary to flush out waste and toxins.

- **Nutrient Absorption**

Water also helps the digestive system to properly absorb the nutrients that are available in the food. Oxygen and nutrients are transported on a cellular level by water.

- **Body Temperature Regulation**

Body temperature is an important element of maintaining good health because many bodily functions depend on a correct body temperature. Water is a regulating factor to help maintain the right temperature in the body.

- **Blood Pressure Regulation**

One reason water is essential for heart health is because it helps to regulate blood pressure. Maintaining a healthy blood pressure level will reduce the risk of chronic heart disease.

- **Reduce Muscle Fatigue**

Muscles and joints need lubrication from water in order to prevent fatigue, cramps, aches, and pains. Remember that your heart is a muscle, and drinking water will help keep your organs and muscles in good working order. If you are thirsty, that is your body's last signal to you that you need water. You should always be hydrating yourself throughout the day so you never feel thirsty, have dry lips, skin or hands.

The mineral rich spring water found in nature is vastly different than city water. Tap and bottled water commonly has contaminants from the public water supply like fluoride, chlorine, heavy metals, and other impurities that find their way into your body. These impurities are acidic and toxic. Be sure that you are drinking purified water, and stick with water instead of drinking sodas, commercial fruit juices, etc., as you may not be sure on their source or processing. Invest in a reverse osmosis water purifier that can remove harmful materials and improve the taste of the tap water, making it healthy for consumption.

How Much Water to Drink?

There are many formulas for what and how you should drink. Water should not be served too cold or too hot, just regular room temperature. Some authorities claim you should drink at least half your body weight in ounces every day. So if you weigh 125 pounds, you need to drink a minimum of 62.5 ounces of purified water a day. Another good general rule is having one eight to twelve ounce glass of water for every hour you are awake. If active, add fifty percent to that total. For children, the glass amounts will be similar, though ounces are adjusted to size, height, and age. For example: An adult awake for twelve hours should drink twelve glasses of pure filtered water that day. If you work out, go hiking, or do strenuous activity that day, add fifty percent to make up for the increased activity levels (12 glasses +6 (50%) = 18 glasses that day). In the morning, you can activate your organs by drinking two glasses of water upon waking up, one glass prior to a meal (not during) to moisten and make ready your digestion, and one glass before bed to help moisten body processes while you rest. Doing so is believed to help avoid a heart attack or stroke while sleeping, by keeping up circulatory and heart hydration.

The ranges of water regulation are so vast that everyone can't fit into a mold or standard, so these are two general guidelines. Pick the one that works best for you. You may think that this is a lot of water to drink, but you may not realize how much water is needed to run your body functions. If levels drop past normal range, you get classic symptoms of dehydration; headaches, brain fog, dry skin, intestinal troubles, and muscle pains - just for starters.

10.17 Exercise

A significant factor in disease risk is the nature of a person's day-to-day activities. Our modern world of technological convenience has made us move less. As a result, the muscle wasting effects of a sedentary lifestyle are becoming more and more common. Several factors have contributed to a more sedentary lifestyle in our modern world:

- In previous eras, most people spent their day moving their bodies: working on

the farm, hunting, doing household work, etc. Now, many jobs involve sitting at a desk all day, without an opportunity to move around during work hours.
- Additionally, modern technology has made it possible for us to work less. We have machines to wash clothes, prepare food, do housework, etc.
- Much of our entertainment choices are sedentary activities: watching movies or television, playing video games, surfing the Internet, communicating by text messages, or watching sports events.

Because we are not as active throughout the day, it is important that each person takes some time to exercise in order to make sure that their muscles don't weaken or atrophy. It is good to include physical activities throughout the day whenever possible, because every little bit helps. Try aerobic exercise three times a week, twenty minutes a session. Exercise benefits the body in many ways and it improves overall health. Many people start exercising simply because they want to lose weight, but there are actually many other reasons that a person should exercise on a regular basis.

Benefits of regular exercise include:
- Lower risk of diabetes
- Lower high triglyceride levels / Increased HDL levels (good cholesterol)
- Reduced risk of various forms of cancer
- Builds healthy muscles, bones, and joints
- Lowered risk of stroke
- Decreased risk of obesity
- Lowered blood pressure
- Increased muscle strength and flexibility
- Combats osteoporosis
- Increased oxygen and alkalinity throughout the body
- Psychological improvements (reduction of depression, anxiety, etc.)

Chapter 11:
Natural Ways to Heal

"Water, air, and cleanliness are the chief articles in my pharmacopoeia."
~ Napoleon

11.1 Time to Take Charge of Your Health

Taking charge of their own health care, the ill-stricken are increasingly putting their trust and hard earned money back into the age-old wisdom of alternative holistic treatments that are less invasive, and in many cases, much more effective. Dissatisfaction with our present health care system is felt, not only by the individuals it is supposed to be serving, but also by health care professionals who do their best to work with the growing care-cutting methods imposed by insurance companies. If revolution promises change, we have to be the people who bring forth that change; change starts with each of us. Will you make the effort to change your lifestyle, so that it serves you in health and longevity? With the information in this chapter, I hope to help make this much easier for you and your loved ones. I wish you to be a seeker of information and research everything you are told. Come to your own truth and make informed decisions.

Disclaimer

Please note that information provided in this chapter should not be taken as complete personal medical or chiropractic advice or instruction. Although all efforts to print valid and updated information have been made, the author and publisher make no guarantees the print is free of errors or omissions. No diagnosis or treatment action(s) should be taken based solely on the contents of this book. All readers should consult their own appropriate health professionals for more information, instruction, dosage, and any other matter relating to their personal health and well-being.

Side effects may exist with natural herbs. Proper care is needed for correct administration and use. Everyone's situation is different. Do not mix supplements or herbs with medications you are already taking, without first checking with your primary health care provider(s) for your specific needs. Some herbs should not be taken by those with certain diseases, or by women who are pregnant or nursing. The following information is provided to you for educational purposes only, and as a general synopsis of possible options that should be discussed with your doctor(s). The information has not been evaluated or approved by the Food and Drug Administration for the treatment or cure of any disease, disorder, syndrome, or ailment mentioned herein. Reader uses information at their own risk.

11.2 Don't Forget Your Recommended* Daily Vitamins and Minerals

Vitamin/Mineral	Recommended Dose	Function	Most Popular Food Sources
Vitamin A	Men: 3,000 IU Women: 2,300 IU	Vision, growth, bone and red blood cell formation, reproduction, healthy immune and epithelial tissue	Fortified foods, foods high in beta carotene, liver
Vitamin D	9-50 years: 200 IU 51-70 years: 400 IU > 70 years: 600 IU Osteopenia or osteoporosis: 1,000 IU	Calcium metabolism and bone mineralization, possibly helps prevent cancer	Fish, fortified milk
Vitamin E	30-50 IU	Anticoagulant, antioxidant, heart disease, and cancer prevention	Nuts, vegetable oils, wheat germ
Vitamin K	M: 120 mcg W: 90 mcg	Blood clotting and bone mineralization	Dark green leafy vegetables
Vitamin C	M: 90 mg W: 75 mg smokers add 35 mg	Antioxidant, immunity, cancer prevention, increases iron absorption	Fruits and vegetables, citrus fruits, peppers
Thiamine (B_1)	M: 1.2 mg W: 0.9 mg	Energy metabolism, mood, nervous system	Oysters, whole grains, brown rice, legumes, pork, fortified foods
Riboflavin (B_2)	M: 1.3 mg W: 1.1 mg	Energy metabolism, antioxidant, possible migraine prevention	Dairy products, leafy greens, oysters
Niacin, Nicotinic acid (B_3)	M: 16 mg W: 14 mg	Energy metabolism, lowers LDL cholesterol and triglycerides, raises HDL cholesterol	Poultry, red meat, fish, legumes, nuts
Pantothenic Acid (B_5)	7-15mg	Used in the release of energy as well as the metabolism of fat, protein, and carbohydrates	Broccoli, squash, eggs, mushrooms, sunflower seeds, whole grains, bananas, corn
Pyridoxine (B_6)	M: 1.3-1.7 mg W: 1.3-1.5 mg	Helps PMS, protein metabolism, neurotransmitter synthesis (dopamine and serotonin), helps peripheral neuropathy, immunity	Meat, poultry, fish, nuts, potatoes, cereals, eggs, soybeans

Biotin, Vitamin H (B_7)	Babies: 4 mcg Child: 6-8 mcg Teen: 8-16 mcg Adult: 25+ mcg	Hair, skin and fingernail health, reduces fat, helps maintain good blood sugar and insulin levels	Egg yolk, soybeans, nuts, cereal, yeast, liver, kidney, cauliflower, bananas, mushrooms
Folate (B_9)	0.4 -.05 mg Pregnant or breast-feeding .05 -.08mg	Prevents (neural tube) birth defects, possible cancer prevention, cell division, lowers homocysteine	Oranges, legumes, broccoli, cauliflower leafy greens
Cobalamin (B_{12})	2.4 mcg	Cell division, amino acid metabolism, nervous system, mental function	Fish, shellfish, meat, fortified soy and rice milk, fermented soy products
Laetrile (B_{17})	Dosage varies; adult average is five to ten seeds a day is sufficient. Apx. 20mg of B17 is in an apricot seed.	Considered by many a strong anti-cancer vitamin, helps immunity.	Found in lima beans, peach, cherry and apricot seeds, macadamia nuts, grape seeds, black, blue, and straw berries, and bean sprouts
Calcium	1,000-1,200 mg	Muscle contraction and bone mineralization	Almond, rice and soy milk, dark green leafy vegetables, dairy products
Magnesium	M: 400 mg W: 320 mg	Bone mineralization, Needed in 300+ chemical reactions in our body	Green vegetables nuts, whole grains, legumes
Potassium	4,700 mg	Functions with sodium to maintain water balance	Bananas, plums, oranges, beets and raisins
Iron	M: 8 mg W: 18 mg	Makes energy in the mitochondria and hemoglobin which carries oxygen.	Breakfast cereals, meats, legumes, dark greens, tofu, spinach, kelp
Selenium	55 mcg	Antioxidant, cancer prevention, immunity, viral infection deterrent	Whole grains from selenium-rich soils, meat, poultry, dairy
Zinc	M: 11 mg W: 8 mg	Growth, antioxidant, immunity, wound healing, taste, prostate health and sperm production	Meat, , fish, poultry, oysters

*Daily recommended Intake (DRI). Actual needs vary per individual, ask your doctor.

11.3 Your Holistic Reference Guide – Take Control of your Health!

Ailment name	Western Medicine Approach	Alternative Medicine Approach	What you can do at home to take control?	How can Chiropractic Help?
HEADACHE (including migraine) There are various types of headache presentations, symptoms and reasons for them. Exertion / Activity related, Posttraumatic, Tension, Migraine with Aura, Migraine without Aura, Sinus / Cold related, Cervicogenic, Cluster, Aneurysm -related, Eyestrain - related, Fever – related, Hangover / Toxin / Drug related, TMJ related, Hypertension – related, Tumor – related, Menstrual / Hormonal – related, Temporal Arthritis, Prescription drug use side effect, Low blood sugar or Hunger related headache. Recent falls or injuries to the head, neck, or mid-back may be causing headaches and nausea from slow internal bleeding. **Headaches are not normal. If left unchecked, they could turn deadly.** **Be sure to see your doctor for proper diagnosis and management.**	*Ibuprofen* and other *Non-Steroidal Anti-Inflammatory Drugs (NSAIDs)*: Can cause gastric irritation, stomach ulcers, bleeding, belching, and dyspepsia; fatal if taken over long periods of time. *Acetylsalicylic Acid* (Aspirin): Laboratory version of willow bark. May cause blood thinning and gastric problems. *Acetaminophen* (Tylenol): Lowers the body's glutathione level (our natural internal detoxifier and super antioxidant). *Triptans (Eletriptan Hydrobromide, Almotriptan Malate; Relpax, Axert, Imitrex)*: Cause vasoconstriction relieving swelling, and block pain to the brainstem. *Dihydroergotamine*: An ergot alkaloid administered under the skin or through nasal mist. Effective for moderate to severe migraines; must be monitored by physician for side effects. *Magnetic Resonance Angiogram (MRA)*: Provides blood vessel data in head and neck that X-ray, ultrasound, and CT scan can't provide.	*Willow Bark (Salix Alba)*: Most effective natural pain reliever; controls inflammation quickly; active compound is salicylic acid. *Chamomile*: Herbal; anti-spasmodic and mild sedative; reduces spasm in head. *Skullcap*: A herbaceous perennial mint; used as anti-spasmodic and anti-inflammatory. *Hydroxytryptophan (5HTP)*: Increases serotonin levels and may decrease pain symptoms. *Multivitamin Complex* with **Vitamins A, C, D, B6, Magnesium, Potassium,** and **Calcium**: Help maintain vessel and smooth muscle tone. *Riboflavin (B2)*: Aids in preventing mitochondrial energy dysfunctions. *Butterbur (Petasites Hybridus root)*: Studies show promising results in reducing migraine symptoms. *Feverfew*: A perennial herb with leaves containing parthenolide, a pain reliever; not recommended for pregnant women. *Coenzyme Q10*: For proper energy production and cell function. *Omega 3 EPA/DHA*: Increases anti-inflammatory prostaglandins. *Capsaicin cream* and **nasal sprays**: Active component in Chile pepper applied topically or inhaled; controls pain.	Diet and lifestyle play a vital role in headache and migraine management. Minimize and remove the things you can control: drugs, nitrites, glutamate, aspartate, caffeine, sugar, wheat, dairy, toxic gum, alcohol, and smoking. Cut down on wine, cheese, and chocolates as these can trigger a migraine. Also avoid foods with MSG or Tyramine: found in any food that is spoiled, pickled, aged, smoked, fermented, or marinated. Treat yourself right! Don't stress about events out of your realm of control. Practice proper sleep hygiene with a cervical pillow (see chapter 8). Keep your sleep cycles regular (6-8 hrs. nightly), avoid overstressing yourself with deadlines, and take a much needed vacation. Drink 10-12 glasses of water daily, and always keep hydrated. Get checked for infestation of *Strongyloides*: A small threadworm picked up by pets; Over production of *Staphylococcus Aureus*, *Clostridia*, or the bacteria in your mouth (dental infection), bowels, or from urinary tract infections; Gas leaks in your home or work. Any of these can be the cause of your headaches.	There usually is a spinal connection / nerve interference issue involved in the upper neck. Chiropractic adjustments can drastically reduce the severity and length of an attack. **Ask your Chiropractor about Occiput, C1 – C7 adjustments, Craniosacral therapy and Suboccipital deep myofascial release technique in the suboccipital triangle** (where the skull meets the back of the neck). Daily neck stretching is helpful for blood flow. Do neck KSS™ exercises in Chapter 8. Correcting postural imbalances may help relieve the condition. Uneven feet, ankle, pelvic and shoulder instabilities eventually end up causing neck and head distress. TMJ, food allergies, metal toxicity, menses, oral contraception, hormonal spikes, candida overgrowth, drug / toxin withdrawal, and emotional stress may be associated in bringing on or aggravating the condition. *Seek out a certified Kousouli® Method practitioner to remove spinal stress and align your energy bodies.*

BE A MASTER® OF MAXIMUM HEALING © by Theodoros Kousouli D.C., CHt.

Ailment name	Western Medicine Approach	Alternative Medicine Approach	What you can do at home to take control?	How can Chiropractic Help?
CHRONIC FATIGUE SYNDROME CFS is a name given to a collection of symptoms when a definitive diagnosis cannot be found for severe fatigue; which is not relieved by a normal night's rest. Symptoms of this syndrome mimic the fatigue experienced with the flu and are categorized by persistent fatigue over 6 months that reduces one's productivity by 50% - after the presence of any other psychiatric and health disorders have been ruled out. CFS can mimic anemia, celiac disease, low thyroid levels, lupus, multiple sclerosis, and liver disease; it's most often seen in patients 20 to 45 years of age. **Also see Fibromyalgia section.** **Be sure to see your doctor for proper diagnosis and management.**	*Ibuprofen* and other *Non-Steroidal Anti-Inflammatory Drugs (NSAIDs)*: Can cause severe gastric irritation, stomach ulcers, bleeding, belching, and dyspepsia; can be fatal if misused or taken over long periods of time. *Acetylsalicylic Acid (Aspirin)*: Modified laboratory version of willow bark extract. Can cause blood thinning and gastric problems. *Trazodone (Desyrel, Oleptro, Dividose)*: A triazolopyridine derivative. Antidepressant for sleep and bipolar disorders, given also for CFS and depression. Dizziness, drowsiness, dry mouth, headache, nausea, fatigue, blurred vision, constipation, diarrhea, back pain, and libido loss are some common side effects. *Not surprising*: CFS patients experience extreme fatigue and body pains from drug side effects. The body uses all of its energy to fight off the toxic drug effects, leaving less energy for proper body regulation. Check with your doctors on slowly weaning off excess prescription drugs. You may want to co-manage your case with a doctor of naturopathy and a doctor of functional medicine.	*Oat Straw, Ginkgo Biloba,* and *Dandelion root*: Improve energy and vitality. *Siberian Ginseng (Eleutherococcus), Ginger,* and *Licorice root*: Strengthen adrenal glands, increase longevity, decrease fatigue and weakness. *Passionflower* and *Valerian root*: Calming and restful effect on the nervous system of CFS patients. *Goldenseal, Garlic,* and *St. John's Wort*: Bacteriostatic and antiviral functions that prevent disease and resulting fatigue. *CoQ10* and *L-Carnitine*: Necessary for energy production and cell function. Stimulates energy levels. *Malic Acid*: (In apple juice) Needed for sugar metabolism and energy production in muscle cells. *Glutathione Peroxidase (GPx)*: Antioxidant enzyme. Both found highly deficient in those diagnosed with CFS. *Probiotics; Acidophilus*: Fights candida infection and replaces friendly bacteria in the gut. *Vitamins A, C, D, E, Calcium, Manganese, Magnesium, Potassium, Selenium,* and *Zinc*: Necessary in cellular balance, immunity, and overall health. *Vitamin B Complex + Niacin (B3) + Pantothenic Acid (B5)*: Essential for increased cell energy, adrenal, and brain function.	Minimize and remove the things you can control: drugs, artificial flavorings, caffeine, toxic gum, drinking alcohol and smoking. CFS is directly related to food allergy, difficulty of nutrient uptake, and gastrointestinal health. Eat more fruits, dark leafy greens, and vegetables. Remove white sugar, gluten, wheat and dairy; especially cow's milk. Increase fiber intake. Minimize malnutrition and dehydration. Use a chlorine shower filter and switch to non-fluoride toothpaste. Keep your sleep cycles regular (6-8hrs nightly), choose an appropriate mattress, and cervical pillow. Consider using a magnetic mattress pad. Get 5-10 mins daily sun exposure, and spend more time outside in nature's fresh air, away from heavy EMF. Add an exercise program and the KSS™ stretches in Chapter 8 to your daily regimen; start out slowly, pace yourself, and build up. De-worm your pets. Those who handle pet feces may have been contaminated with parasites and toxins that have overloaded the body systems. Switch to a vegan or anti-inflammatory vegetarian diet. Use an alkaline Ph water conversion filter for home and travel use.	There usually is a spinal connection / nerve interference issue associated with the adrenal glands, as well as the gastrointestinal tract that needs to be addressed. **Ask your Chiropractor about adjusting the Occiput, C1 - C4; T5- T10 and L1-L5 spinal levels.** Chiropractic has helped many CFS patients thrive. ❦ Discuss with your dentist the removal of your amalgam fillings. Metal fillings have been linked as a possible cause of CFS. Talk to your holistic doctors about doing a kidney, liver, candida, and parasite cleanse. Look into chelation therapy for heavy metal cleansing, which could also be connected to a hypoactive thyroid condition. Research further the possible benefits of magnetic healing, blood electrification, 35% food grade hydrogen peroxide therapy, oxygen therapy, ozone therapy, and chlorine and fluoride removal from your water. *Seek out a certified Kousouli® Method practitioner to remove spinal stress and align your energy bodies.*

BE A MASTER® OF MAXIMUM HEALING © by Theodoros Kousouli D.C., CHt.

Ailment name	Western Medicine Approach	Alternative Medicine Approach	What you can do at home to take control?	How can Chiropractic Help?
FIBROMYALGIA Fibromyalgia (FMS): Also called fibromyositis, Chronic Pain Syndrome (CPS), or Chronic Fatigue Syndrome (CFS); means pain or inflammation of the muscle fibers. It is an "umbrella" diagnosis; meaning that when doctors do not know what you have, they must call it something, and fibromyalgia sometimes fits as a diagnosis when symptoms can't be fully classified. Some experts claim fibromyalgia is a condition of excess lactic acid buildup in the muscles; a metabolic dysfunction. Difficult cases of fibromyalgia should be looked at closely for streptococcus, staphylococcus, or clostridium infection from trichinella and ancylostoma worms. The cause could be from several aspects that are associated, including hookworm or ascaris infection. **Also see Chronic Fatigue Syndrome, CFS.** **Be sure to see your doctor for proper diagnosis and management.**	*Non-Steroidal Anti-Inflammatory Drugs (NSAIDs)*: Usually limited with low success rate. *Prescription Drugs: Acetominophen (Elavil), Tramadol (Ultram), Cyclobenzaprine (Flexeril, Amrix), Low-Dose* and *Tricyclic Antidepressants: Amitriptyline, (Tryptomer, Elavil); Cymbalta, Lyrica,* and *Guaifenesin.* All have side effects that can add to the existing problem: drowsiness, dizziness, muscle pain, dry mouth, constipation, difficulty concentrating, swollen arms or legs, fatigue, blurred vision, heartburn, and weight gain. *Not surprising:* Some patients report CFS and fibromyalgia symptoms after receiving a vaccination. Prior to giving your permission to be vaccinated, be sure to speak with your doctor about all the ingredients in the vaccine and get a list of expected side effects.	*St. John's Wort:* Most effective herb against depression; also shows promise with fibromyalgia patients. Must not be mixed with other drugs. *Ginger*: Anti-oxidant properties; can relieve muscle aches, tension, and decrease nausea, vomiting, and headaches. *Ginseng*: Recommended for anti-stress and energy boosting; recommended in extremely small amounts. *Turmeric*: Helps the body clear damaging toxins. The active compound is curcumin, a potent anti-inflammatory agent. Useful against muscle pain and swelling. *Hydroxytryptophan (5HTP):* Works by increasing levels of the neurotransmitter serotonin in the brain. May reduce the number of tender points. *Melatonin:* Taken prior to bedtime; may help improve energy during waking hours. *Oral Magnesium Malate (Malic Acid; found in apples, grapes),* and *Magnesium:* Help produce energy in the form of adenosine triphosphate (ATP). *Vitamin E:* Helps circulation and reduces muscle pain. *L-Theanine:* A helpful antioxidant found in black, green or white tea leaves.	Minimize and remove the things you can control: drugs, caffeine, alcohol smoking, and junk food. Hydrate with 10-12 glasses of water per day. Go on a sugar, gluten, and dairy free diet. Remove processed sugars, toxic gum, artificial flavors, colors, additives, and artificial sweeteners from your diet. A vegan diet may serve you best. Reduce stress. Get 5-10 minutes of sunlight daily. Consider a magnetic mattress pad, get 6-8 hours restful sleep, and practice good sleep hygiene. Daily exercise is helpful for blood flow to the muscles, improves joint motion and overall body strength. Add KSS™ stretches in chapter 8 to your daily routine and maintain a healthy lifestyle. Practice common sense hygiene; don't rub your eyes, bite your nails, or put fingers in your mouth. Use an alkaline Ph water conversion filter for home and travel use.	There usually is a spinal connection / nerve interference issue. **Ask your Chiropractor about adjusting Occiput, Atlas (C1), Axis (C2),** and other necessary vertebrae according to your x-ray and exam findings. Ask a qualified holistic nutritionist or naturopath about food allergy testing and diet modification. Speak to your veterinarian about testing and deworming your pets. Pet owners who handle feces may have been contaminated with parasites and toxins that have overloaded the body systems. Ask your doctors about cutting back prescribed drug dosages and checking for possible drug interactions. Consider holistic avenues; look into boosting glutathione levels, removing amalgam fillings, and doing kidney, liver, candida, parasite, chelation, and heavy metal cleansing. *Seek out a certified Kousouli® Method practitioner to remove spinal stress and align your energy bodies.*

BE A MASTER® OF MAXIMUM HEALING © by Theodoros Kousouli D.C., CHt.

Ailment name	Western Medicine Approach	Alternative Medicine Approach	What you can do at home to take control?	How can Chiropractic Help?
PAIN Inflammation is a natural process to injury and infection, as the body brings nutrients to heal the injured site. It's when the inflammation isn't controlled or stopped that there may be reason for concern. **INFLAMMATION** Any organ or tissue of the body, internal or external, can become inflamed, and the associated pain may be difficult to diagnose. If neglected, an internal bacterial infection or virus that lingers could become worse over time and can turn fatal. See your medical doctor for the proper tests and procedures to clear you from any immediate danger and stabilize you. Once stabilized, see your holistic primary care provider for treatment and maintenance of good health. **Also see Circulation, Swelling section.** **Be sure to see your doctor for proper diagnosis and management.**	*Ibuprofen* and other *Non-Steroidal Anti-Inflammatory Drugs (NSAIDs)*: Can cause severe gastric irritation, stomach ulcers, bleeding, belching, and dyspepsia; can be fatal if misused or taken over long periods of time. Ibuprofen and Naproxen have been linked to kidney cancer. *Acetylsalicylic Acid (Aspirin)*: (modified version of willow bark extract). Can cause blood thinning and gastric problems. *Oxycodone*: A strong and addictive opioid analgesic medication. *Codeine*: A narcotic analgesic painkiller used for mild to moderate pain relief. *Darvocet*: A strong narcotic analgesic painkiller for many types of pains. Addictive. *Morphine*: Blocks pain. Addictive and given only in serious cases.	*Willow Bark (Salix alba)*: Nature's aspirin; effective on fever, flu, joint, and body pains. *Feverfew*: A good pain reliever; not recommended for pregnant women. *Ashwagandha* a.k.a. *Indian Winter Cherry*: Reduces both pain and inflammation; used as liquid and powdered form in teas. *Ginger, Kava Kava root, Turmeric,* and *Licorice root*: Enhance muscle relaxation, reduce inflammation, relieve pain, decrease nausea, vomiting, and headaches. *Methylsulfonylmethane (MSM)*: Nourishes joints and reduces inflammation. *Potassium*: A natural powerful anti-pain agent found in bananas, beets, and citrus fruits. *Homeopathic Arnica*: Contains anti-inflammatory properties. *Capsaicin cream* and *nasal spray*: Helps migraines, arthritis, shingles, or neuropathy; active component of Chile pepper. *Bromelain*: Found naturally in pineapples, a proteolytic enzyme helpful in protein digestion with anti-inflammatory effects. *Omega-3, Fish Oil*: Strong anti-inflammatory effects for pain. *B Complex (B1, B6, B12)*: Proven to be effective in treating pain. *Dong Quai* a.k.a. *Angelica*: Known for improving pain symptoms in menopause, PMS, arthritic joints, and headaches.	Apply **RICE**. **R**est, **I**ce, **C**ompress, and **E**levate the area above heart level when possible. Minimize and remove the things you can control: drugs, caffeine, alcohol, smoking, junk food, and stressful worry. Cook with black currant and olive oils. Drink 10-12 glasses of water daily; keep hydrated. Drink mangosteen juice; has a high ORAC value (Oxygen radical absorption capacity). Helpful for swelling, joint aches and pains, cardiovascular system and blood sugar issues. Supports youthful cell and immune function. Helps prostaglandin and histamine levels for fighting inflammation. Drink liquid chlorophyll regularly as it helps strengthen your immunity, helps cell regeneration; lowers stomach pains, alkalizes and detoxifies blood and body. To relax from the mental aspects of chronic pain, look into hypnosis for pain management. Meditate more often. Get 6-8 hours restful sleep. Consider sleeping on a magnetic mattress pad. Switch to a vegan or anti-inflammatory vegetarian diet. Use an alkaline Ph water conversion filter for home and travel use.	Ensuring proper nerve flow to the inflamed or painful area is vital for quick healing. **Ask your Chiropractor about adjusting Occiput, C1, C2** and the associated spinal areas pertaining to your exam, x-rays, and condition. ❧ Ask your holistic nutritionist or naturopath about kidney, liver, candida, and parasite cleanses. Look into chelation therapy for heavy metal cleansing. Research further the possible benefits of magnetic healing, blood electrification, 35% food grade hydrogen peroxide therapy, oxygen therapy, and ozone therapy for alkalizing the body and general good health. *Seek out a certified Kousouli® Method practitioner to remove spinal stress and align your energy bodies.*

BE A MASTER® OF MAXIMUM HEALING © by Theodoros Kousouli D.C., CHt.

Ailment name	Western Medicine Approach	Alternative Medicine Approach	What you can do at home to take control?	How can Chiropractic Help?
CIRCULATION PROBLEMS **SWELLING** The circulatory system moves water, gases, nutrients, and wastes, to and from cells. When blood cannot move back easily to the heart, stagnation occurs; plaque and clots (fatty deposits) form along artery walls and harden. Blood flow constricts and increases pressure. Poor circulation leads to hypertension, heart attacks, kidney damage, stroke, varicose veins, swelling (edema), gangrene, amputation, tingling or cold in the hands and feet, shortness of breath, fatigue, stamina loss, white fingers or toes, migraine headaches, and dizziness upon standing. Circulation problems have also been linked to prescription drugs, birth control, and emotional life changing events, or traumas. Poor diet, lack of hydration, lack of exercise, and backup of toxins are all contributing factors. Symptoms and poor circulation are more severe in diseases like diabetes, Marfan's syndrome, Raynaud's disease, and in smokers who develop Buerger's disease. Also see Pain, Inflammation section. **Be sure to see your doctor for proper diagnosis and management.**	*Imaging:* Venous doppler ultrasound, blood, liver, cholesterol tests, and angiogram. *Anticoagulants (Blood Thinners):* Intravenously, subcutaneously or orally. Prevent clot formation and stroke by keeping the arteries clear of blockages. *Angioplasty* and *Stenting*; Open blocked or narrowed arteries caused by blood clot blockages. *Artery Bypass Surgeries:* Can effectively treat poor circulation by side-stepping blood pathways around blocked arteries.	*Black Cohosh:* Reduces blood pressure (do not take while pregnant). *Sodium Bicarbonate; Non-Aluminum Baking Soda* (not baking powder) mixed with ½ tablespoon *Raw Black Molasses:* Helps balance out blood Ph and delivers vital minerals and nutrients. *L-Carnitine:* Helps heart health by transporting long chain fatty acids. *Chlorophyll:* Wheat grass; daily smoothie shakes with plenty of green leafy vegetables help build a healthy circulatory system. *Omega-3, Fish Oil:* Strong anti-inflammatory effects for pain. *Coenzyme Q10:* Improves blood oxygenation. *Coenzyme A:* Needed for fatty acid synthesis and oxidation. *Vitamins A, C, E, D3, Vitamin B Complex, Para-Aminobenoic Acid (PABA), Thiamine (B1), Niacin (B3), Pyridoxine (B6), Cobalamine (B12), Folic Acid (B9),* and *Natural Vitamin E:* Improve blood flow. *Calcium, Magnesium, Potassium, Zinc:* May help reduce the risk of stroke. *Vinpocetine, Ginko BIliba,* and *Cayenne:* Increase blood circulation. *Butcher's Broom:* For poor circulation in the legs, pain, heaviness, leg cramps, and swelling.	Stop smoking. Avoid alcohol, caffeine, and sodas. Lower salt intake (use raw sea salt instead of white refined table salt). Maintain an alkaline saliva Ph over 7 by alkalinizing your diet and lifestyle. Drink 10-12 glasses of filtered water daily. Blockages in the arteries can stem from toxic water. Ozonate your water, and purify it with a water filtration system that removes lead, chlorine, and fluoride. Eat a high fiber diet, and avoid homogenized dairy products, trans fats, and hydrogenated oils. Make a vegetable super broth; boil together collards, swiss chard, Brussels sprouts, daikon radish, kale, mustard greens, cabbage, dandelion, baby choy sum, Napa cabbage, ginger, turmeric, anise, fennel seeds, garlic, leek, shitake mushroom, cilantro, kelp, watercress, and then bring to warm simmer. Drain and drink daily. Do not wear restrictive underwear, belts, or clothing. Get deep tissue massages regularly which help the circulatory and lymph systems flow. Sleep in comfortable room temperatures. Invest in a magnetic mattress pad. Install a chlorine shower filter. Only use natural makeup, antiperspirants, shampoos, body lotions, and non-fluoride toothpastes. Add an EMF blocker in your home and office environments. Add a daily exercise program and do the KSS™ stretches in Chapter 8.	Chiropractic care helps circulation by balancing the nerve signals to blood vessels. **Ask your Chiropractor about adjusting Occiput, C1 – C7, and the associated spinal areas pertaining to your exam, x-rays, and condition.** Talk to your naturopath or holistic nutritionist about kidney, liver, colon, gluten, candida, and parasite cleansing. Look into chelation therapy for heavy metal and arterial cleansing. Diabetics have poor fat metabolism, as well as poor sugar metabolism, so cholesterol builds in the bloodstream, and clogs the arteries in the extremities causing gangrene. *Seek out a certified Kousouli® Method practitioner to remove spinal stress and align your energy bodies.*

Ailment name	Western Medicine Approach	Alternative Medicine Approach	What you can do at home to take control?	How can Chiropractic Help?
RESPIRATORY ALLERGIES An allergy is a state of hypersensitivity with an exaggerated immunologic reaction to what otherwise would be a harmless substance. Respiratory allergies like hay fever are caused by a "trigger" called an antigen or allergen that proceeds to cause nose, sinus, eye, ear, throat, and airway tissue swelling and inflammation. **ASTHMA** Asthma is a chronic inflammatory disease of the respiratory airways, characterized by reversible airflow obstruction and periodic occurrence of bronchospasms. **COPD** Chronic Obstructive Pulmonary Disease (COPD) is a progressive and irreversible airway disorder connected to smoking. **Be sure to see your doctor for proper diagnosis and management.**	*Inhaled* or *Oral Corticosteroids* and *Antihistamines*: No remedial measures yet known for asthma; asthma nebulizer pump inhalers for transient comfort. Steroids cause a lot of water retention, weight gain, fluffy stature, and hypertension. Long term use leads to cataracts, diabetes, osteoporosis, chronic coughing, throat hoarseness, pancreatitis, yeast infections and muscle fatigue. *Albuterol:* Bronchodilator that relaxes muscles in the airways and helps increase air flow to the lungs. *COPD:* Involves chronic bronchitis and emphysema. It is preventable by not laboring the airway system. Medications will be needed to control lung inflammation, dilate closed bronchi, and reduce airway obstruction. Eventually portable supplemental oxygen tanks will be needed by the patient.	*Licorice root:* Allergy-calming properties reduce inflammation and restore normal breathing. *Ma Huang* or *Ephedra Sinica*: Herb used since 3000 BC. Ephedra Tea soothes asthma and high blood pressure stress. Do not take high dosage as it is very strong. Ask your doctor. *Ginkgo Biloba; Ashwagandha, Omega-3, Omega-6:* All have anti-inflammatory effects. *Haridra*: Used for inflammation and allergy in India. *Shirish Herb*: Removes accumulated toxins, and flushes out allergens. *Peppermint, Primrose,* and *Flaxseed Oil:* Anti-inflammatory. Check with your doctor prior to use. *Cayenne Pepper* or *Capsicum*: Has a stimulant, antispasmodic, and antiseptic action. *Mullein Oil* and *Eucalyptus*: Break up bronchial congestion. Potent expectorants. *Vitamins A, C, E, B Complex, Magnesium,* and *Calcium:* Necessary in cellular balance and overall lung health. *Stinging Nettle (Urtica Dioica):* Contains butyric acid and helps asthma, hay fever, and hives. *Vitamin D3:* Asthma patients tend to be deficient. Switch to a vegan or anti-inflammatory vegetarian diet. Use an alkaline Ph water conversion filter for home and travel use.	You must quit smoking to start healing. Minimize exposure to common triggers for allergic asthma including stress, abrupt cold temperature changes, dust mites, pollen, mold, and pet dander. Drink Chamomile tea. Helpful for general allergy and asthma. Drink plenty of fluids and keep yourself hydrated daily. Get your apartment or home's air and water tested by the city health department if there are any doubts on air quality. Check your home and work areas for mold, allergens or other aggravating factors. Consider a dehumidifier or air filtration system, and address musty smells and water leaks immediately. Air ozonation therapy for musty rooms may also help. Don't breathe the air while treating it, as it may irritate you further. Pets should not sleep in the same room as humans. This may spike allergies; especially with new pet owners. Switch to a vegan or anti- inflammatory vegetarian diet. Use an alkaline Ph water conversion filter for home and travel use.	There usually is a spinal connection / nerve interference issue associated with the sinuses, bronchus, and lungs: **Ask your Chiropractor about adjusting Occiput, C1, C2, C3, and T1 - T5 spinal areas.** ❦ Talk to your naturopath about doing a kidney, liver, candida, and parasite cleanse. Look into chelation therapy for heavy metal cleansing, which could be connected to long standing toxin overload in your system causing sensitivity to triggers. Ask a qualified holistic nutritionist about food and allergy testing. Remove processed foods, sugar, dairy, wheat, and artificial flavorings from your diet. Ask your doctor about starting an exercise regimen that you are comfortable with. Go slow, and increase your efforts over time to build lung capacity. *Seek out a certified Kousouli® Method practitioner to remove spinal stress and align your energy bodies.*

BE A MASTER® OF MAXIMUM HEALING © by Theodoros Kousouli D.C., CHt.

Ailment name	Western Medicine Approach	Alternative Medicine Approach	What you can do at home to take control?	How can Chiropractic Help?
DEPRESSION Depression is a mental and emotional state of feeling disconnected from normal states of events, or overpowering feelings of sadness, apathy, gloom, and hopelessness. Some say it is caused by chemical and energetic changes in the brain and spinal cord. Periods of sadness and anxiety are normal. However, it becomes pathologic when it interferes with important aspects of life such as school or work, keeping relationships, or the ability to function daily. More prevalent among females; may accompany other concomitant illnesses or be a byproduct of (illegal as well as legal) drug use. **Be sure to see your doctor for proper diagnosis and management.**	*Tricyclic Antidepressants (TCAs).* *Monoamine Oxidase Inhibitors (MAOIs).* Use caution; can cause dangerously high blood pressure when taken with certain foods. *Selective Serotonin (SSRIs) and Norepinephrine Reuptake Inhibitors (SNRIs).* All the above have similar side effects to Prosac and lead to more complications rather than solutions to relieve depression. Medication history is important to consider; especially length of time patient is on the drug, dosage taken, and interactions with other drugs. Many patients on depression drugs will at some point have suicidal thoughts and tendencies. Psychotherapy or cognitive-behavioral therapy may help improve drug outcome when used in combination.	*St. John's Wort:* Most effective herb against depression and is the best available option where depression is combined with exhaustion and tension. Must not be mixed with other drugs. *Noni (Morinda)* and *Schisandra:* Powerful natural antidepressants. *Ginkgo Biloba:* Recommended for brain stimulation. *Inositol:* A substance found in many foods (legumes), can help reduce anxiety. *Kava - Kava:* A good muscle relaxer; non-habit forming. *Lemon Balm:* Eliminates digestive disorders associated with depression. *Rhodiola Rosea:* Improves mood and readjusts serotonin and dopamine levels. *Vitamin B Complex: B3, B5, B6, B12, Vitamin C, Magnesium,* and *Folic Acid:* Strong anti-stress options for brain and nervous system. *Vitamin D3:* Depression patients tend to be deficient. *Omega 3 Fatty Acids EPA/DHA:* Increases anti-inflammatory prostaglandins. (Ex. Cod Liver Oil) *S-adenosylmethionine (SAMe):* Mood enhancer/Antidepressant. *Hydroxytryptophan (5HTP):* Increases serotonin levels and may decrease pain symptoms. *Siberian Ginseng:* Helps the body fight stress reaction.	Quit smoking. Smoking restricts blood flow in the body and you need oxygen to get to your cells. Go on a sugar, gluten, and dairy free diet. Remove processed sugars, artificial flavors, colors, additives, and artificial sweeteners from your diet. L-Tyrosine and L-Phenylalanine are amino acids which are precursors to neurotransmitters. These, as well as Glutathione (found in walnuts), should be in high supply in your diet. Hydrate well (10-12 glasses of filtered water daily), and get 6-8 hours restful sleep. De-stress yourself. Meditate, listen to soft music, eat healthy comfort fruits, do things that you enjoy, read a book, or spend time with a pet and other loved ones. Appreciate yourself and do nice things for 'you'. Try aromatherapy essential oils which sooth and relax the senses. Depressed individuals MUST get adequate exercise and sunlight daily. Both are proven natural remedies for depression. Daily stretching is helpful for blood flow to the brain. Add KSS™ exercises in Chapter 8 to your daily routine. Switch to a vegan or anti-inflammatory vegetarian diet. Use an alkaline Ph water conversion filter for home and travel use.	There usually is a spinal connection / nerve interference issue associated with the adrenal glands as well as the gastrointestinal tract that need to be addressed. **Ask your Chiropractor about adjusting the Occiput, C1 - C4; T5-T10 and L1-L5 spinal levels,** and incorporate a good aerobic exercise and diet program. ❦ Ask your doctors about cutting back prescribed drug dosages and checking possible other drug interactions. Depression is a very common side effect of oral contraception. Consider holistic avenues and look into kidney, liver, candida, parasite, and heavy metal cleansing (chelation therapy), due to possible dental filling toxicity. *Seek out a certified Kousouli® Method practitioner to remove spinal stress and align your energy bodies.*

BE A MASTER® OF MAXIMUM HEALING © by Theodoros Kousouli D.C., CHt.

Ailment name	Western Medicine Approach	Alternative Medicine Approach	What you can do at home to take control?	How can Chiropractic Help?
IRRITABLE BOWEL SYNDROME Allergy of the gut or Irritable Bowel Syndrome (IBS) is symptomized by abdominal pain, cramping, and major changes in bowel movements. It is different from Inflammatory Bowel Disease (IBD) in that the structure of the bowel in (IBS) is not changed. **BLOATING / GAS CONSTIPATION DIARRHEA** Gas is not made by the body. Gas is made by bacteria. Bloating is pressure from gas as food is broken down in the body. Foods, medications, artificial additives, family history, diet practices, high emotional distress, heavy metal toxicity, history of fever, parasites, and possibility of Shigellas, E. coli, Bacteroides Fragilis, or Salmonella infection should all be considered by your doctor. **Be sure to see your doctor for proper diagnosis and management.**	*Pain Killers* and *Anti-Spasmodic Medications:* Given for gut spasms and abdominal pain. Side effects include flatulence (gas), bloating, dry mouth, heartburn, and constipation. *Anti-Diarrheals, Anti-Constipation Agents, Laxatives for Constipation:* Glycerin suppositories, Magnesium Citrate, Milk of Magnesia or Senokot (Senna). *Antibiotics:* Worsen the situation by eliminating healthy intestinal bacterial flora. *Tricyclic Antidepressants:* Given for depression and sometimes used for abdominal pain. *Lab Testing:* Blood chemistry panel, complete blood count (CBC), thyroid testing, food allergy blood panel, and 24 hour stool sample collection for parasite testing. If over 50, get a colonoscopy to rule out colon cancer and inflammatory disease.	*Peppermint Oil:* Anti-spasmodic action; produces calm in the gastrointestinal tract. *Fennel:* Effective in treating bloating and gas. *Ginger:* Anti-spasmodic action; improves tone of intestinal muscles and prevents vomiting. *Chamomile:* Has anti-peptic, anti-inflammatory, anti-bacterial, anti-fungal, anti-spasmodic, and sedative properties. *Caraway:* Treats indigestion, colic, and nerve disorders. *Anise:* Can prevent fermentation and gas in the stomach. Anti-fungal and anti-spasmodic property. *Superoxide Dismutase (SOD):* Anti-free radial enzyme. *Digestive Enzymes* and *Probiotics:* Including *Saccharomyces Boulardii:* A non–pathogenic yeast. Increases healthy intestinal bifidobacteria, while decreasing numbers of disease-causing organisms. *Black Walnut Hull:* Kills bowel fungi and parasites. *L-glutamine:* Needed for healthy gut lining. **Vitamin C Powder:** Sprinkle over food or into drinks to help kill molds. *Spanish Black Radish:* Phytonutrient rich; provides systemic detoxification.	Drink at least 10-12 glasses of filtered water daily; it is important to keep hydrated if having diarrhea. Increase fiber supplementation. Dried blueberries, prunes, figs, probiotics, and Greek yogurt can help diarrhea cases. Bentonite clay, and psyllium husks help bulk up fiber content to improve your bowel movements. Avoid gas producing foods: cabbage, grapes, cauliflower, beer, red wine, onions, coffee, beans or nuts. Never hold in the need to defecate. Go at least 2-3x a day regularly. Use a squat stool under feet. Don't over-tighten belts. Switch to a gluten, wheat, and dairy free diet. Avoid antibiotics, sodas, red meats, and trigger foods with artificial colors, flavorings, or sweeteners. Taking 2 tablespoons of apple cider vinegar in 12 ounces of water 3 times a day can help digestion. Switch to a vegan or anti-inflammatory vegetarian diet. Use an alkaline Ph water conversion filter for home and travel use.	There usually is a spinal connection / nerve interference issue: **Ask your Chiropractor about adjusting Occiput, C1, C2, and T10-L5.** The celiac and lumbar plexuses flow nerve flow from the brain to the gut and regulate good function of the elimination systems. ❧ Ask a naturopath about food allergy testing, diet modification, and colonic cleansing. Remove all food allergens, check intestinal flora health, possible leaky gut syndrome, candida albicans (yeast syndrome) overgrowth, and celiac disease, (also known as gluten intolerance). Symptoms of celiac disease include diarrhea, weight loss, malnutrition, and nutrient deficiencies. Check for Patulin; a mold toxin that gets into our systems from badly bruised fruits. Patulin can weaken your intestinal integrity by spreading more bacteria. It can be killed with black walnut hull and a proper intestinal cleanse. *Seek out a certified Kousouli® Method practitioner to remove spinal stress and align your energy bodies.*

Ailment name	Western Medicine Approach	Alternative Medicine Approach	What you can do at home to take control?	How can Chiropractic Help?
HEARTBURN Heartburn is usually felt as a burning pain radiating into the chest or throat which becomes worse when you eat, bend over, or lie down. The tone of the lower esophageal sphincter (LES) decreases with age, hiatal hernia, calcium channel blockers, anticholinergic medications, caffeine, fatty eating, alcohol, and smoking. **G.E.R.D.** Gastroesophageal reflux disease (GERD) involves the stomach's juices (acids and digestive enzymes), flowing backwards into the esophagus (swallowing tube), and causing lining irritation. GERD is commonly seen in those with high emotional upset, grief, anxiety, and worry. **Be sure to see your doctor for proper diagnosis and management.**	*Over the Counter Antacids:* Tagamet, Zantac, etc. Aluminum based antacids have been linked to Alzheimer's. *Histamine 2 (H2 Blockers), Proton Pump Inhibitors*: Stop acid production in the stomach. Essentially what is in drugs such as Prilosec. May help reduce stomach acidity, but not inflammation of the esophagus itself. *Oral Suspension Medications:* Act as liquid antacids; **Sucralfate, (Carafate, Pepsigard)**; Liquid or tablet that provides short term relief. Act by forming a coating or barrier over ulcers through the esophagus, keeping away acids, and in turn allowing the healing process to set in. **Nissen Fundoplication** is used as a surgical remedy to treat GERD and hiatus hernia.	**Rosemary:** Contains variety of tonic chemicals that treat heartburn and indigestion. Tea preparation is the most effective way to utilize the herb. **Licorice root extract:** Helps restore the mucus lining of the inner stomach. **Aloe Vera:** Soothes the esophageal lining. **Marshmallow, Slippery Elm, Garlic, Saint John's Wort**: They alone are not completely effective, but can be used in combination with the before mentioned ones to get better outcome. **L-glutamine:** Very important for helping a leaky gut and supporting the gastrointestinal structures. **Calcium** and **Magnesium:** Essential for a healthy, normal functioning digestive system. Absorbs excess stomach acid in gastritis and acid reflux; helps stabilize Ph. **N-Acetyl Glucosamine:** Promotes communication between the cells; improving immunity and digestive health. **Rice Bran Oil (Gamma Oryzanol):** Stimulates the release of endorphins (pain-relieving substances made in the body). **Thyme:** Treats cough symptoms and irritated intestinal tracts.	Stop smoking, drinking alcohol, caffeine, and don't eat large spicy, heavy, fatty, or greasy meals. When eating take your time and chew thoroughly. Go to bed with a near empty stomach and eat smaller meals throughout the day. Drink at least ten glasses of water every day, but limit fluid during meals. Two tablespoons of non-aluminum baking soda or apple cider vinegar, mixed in a glass of water and taken after meals, may help ease burning sensations. Go on a sugar, gluten, and dairy free diet. Remove processed sugars, artificial flavors, colors, additives, and artificial sweeteners from your diet. A vegetarian or vegan diet may serve you best. Replace your refined white table salt with mineral rich sea salt. Add more fiber, digestive enzymes, and probiotics to your diet. Maintain correct sleep posture on your back, and on an incline. Keep your upper body 45 degrees elevated as to not allow stomach acids to back up into the esophagus while sleeping. Avoid tight belts or clothes. De-stress yourself from worries. Weight loss also helps to improve symptoms. Use an alkaline Ph water conversion filter for home and travel use.	There usually is a spinal connection / nerve interference issue: **Ask your Chiropractor about adjusting Occiput, C1, C2 and T2-T12.** If there is an associated hernia, a soft tissue manipulation may help with adjustment of the epigastric region. Ask a qualified holistic nutritionist or naturopath about food allergy testing and diet modification to support good health. Diet plays a large part in GERD symptoms. Remove all food allergens, check intestinal flora health, check for leaky gut syndrome, candida albicans (yeast syndrome) overgrowth, and celiac disease; also known as gluten intolerance. Recovery takes time once triggers are removed and lining begins to heal. Patience is needed. *Seek out a certified Kousouli® Method practitioner to remove spinal stress and align your energy bodies.*

BE A MASTER® OF MAXIMUM HEALING © by Theodoros Kousouli D.C., CHt.

Ailment name	Western Medicine Approach	Alternative Medicine Approach	What you can do at home to take control?	How can Chiropractic Help?
RHEUMATOID ARTHRITIS A chronic, progressive autoimmune disease causing connective tissue inflammation, mostly in synovial joints. May occur at any age, though more common in women. It usually starts gradually with pain and stiffness in one or more joints until swelling and heat is also felt. Muscle pain may accompany joint pain. **GOUT** Arthritic attack resulting from elevated levels of uric acid in the blood, and the deposition of urate crystals around the smaller finger and toe joints. When chronic, it results in deformity. It is usually seen with those who eat heavy seafood, wine, cheese, or red meat. **OSTEOARTHIRITIS DEGENERATIVE JOINT DISEASE (DJD)** Mechanical abnormalities that affect the articular cartilage and subchondral bone of joints. Mechanical, hereditary, developmental, or metabolic predisposition may be responsible for this disorder. **Be sure to see your doctor for proper diagnosis and management.**	Rheumatologists prescribe **NSAIDs, Disease-Modifying Antirheumatic Drugs (DMARDs), TNF-alpha Inhibitors, Immunosuppressant Narcotics,** and **Corticosteroids**: Offer temporary symptom reduction. Damaging to your joint health when used for long periods of time. **Etanercept Injection:** Used mostly for the treatment of adult and child rheumatoid arthritis. Some side effects include: hair loss, fever, chills, bleeding, excessive bruising, vision changes, weakness, leg swelling, depression, and vomiting. **Surgery:** Total Joint replacement, joint fusion, and tendon repair is done in severe cases.	***Dong Quai*** a.k.a. ***Angelica***: Contains 10 antispasmodic constituents, 12 anti-inflammatory elements, and 5 pain relieving compounds. ***Boswellia*** and ***Gotu Kola***: Potent anti-inflammatory herbs shown to help arthritis pain. ***Alfalfa, Feverfew, Hop plant, Rosemary, Oregano, Sesame seeds, Curcumin***: Have pain alleviating benefits. ***Glucosamine Sulfate*** and ***Chondroitin Sulfate***: Help stimulate the rebuilding of cartilage. ***Hyaluronic Acid***: Supports healthy joint cartilage. ***Horsetail*** and ***Ginger***: Decrease inflammation. Can be used as a compress, or in tea. ***Vitamin C, Iron, Mag Glycinate,*** and ***Alpha-ketoglutaric Acid***: For collagen production. ***Calcium, Magnesium, Zinc,*** ***Niacinamide, (Form of B3): Pyridoxine (B6)***: Relieve pain and reduce inflammation. ***Omega-3, Vitamin E***: Anti-inflammatory properties. ***Bromelain***: A proteolytic enzyme found in pineapples; helps in protein digestion. ***Devil's Claw***: Analgesic, anti-inflammatory; eases arthritis. ***New Zealand Green Lipped Mussel Extract***: Contains powerful Omega 3 Eicosatetraenoic Acid (ETA). Highly anti-inflammatory.	Cut all fried foods. Dandelion and yarrow tea is a good treatment for arthritis and rheumatism. Snack on celery or parsley daily; juice in tea. Follow the anti-inflammatory diet in chapter 10. Add the following to your daily regimen to help reduce inflammation: Use olive and coconut oils, flax seed oil, turmeric, cod liver oil, cinnamon powder and manuka honey mixed together. Drink organic red cherry juice to help bring down gout pain and inflammation. Drink chlorella, Spirulina; liquid chlorophyll. Helps balance blood Ph. Wrap painful joints with comfortable dressing overnight to keep warm. Gentle massage with warm olive or castor oil is very comforting. Lavender epsom salt baths, capsaicin cream and paraffin wax baths can help relieve the pains of arthritic joints. Switch to a vegan or anti- inflammatory vegetarian diet. Use an alkaline Ph water conversion filter for home and travel use.	There usually is a spinal connection / nerve interference issue: **Multiple sites are usually affected;** Ask your Chiropractor about joint supplementation. Chiropractic management is excellent in maintaining and restoring spinal joint function when in conjunction with proper bone nutrition. (Best results when caught early on X-ray). ❦ Diet modification is essential. Ask a qualified holistic nutritionist or naturopath about borax, boron deficiency, food allergy testing, and diet modification. Remove all food allergens, check intestinal flora health, check for possible leaky gut syndrome, candida albicans (yeast syndrome) overgrowth, and celiac disease; also known as gluten intolerance. Ask your doctors about cutting back prescribed drug dosages, and check possible drug interactions. *Seek out a certified Kousouli® Method practitioner to remove spinal stress and align your energy bodies.*

BE A MASTER® OF MAXIMUM HEALING © by Theodoros Kousouli D.C., CHt.

Ailment name	Western Medicine Approach	Alternative Medicine Approach	What you can do at home to take control?	How can Chiropractic Help?
INSOMNIA **SLEEP PROBLEMS** Insomnia is either a problem falling asleep, staying asleep for a long duration, or once sleeping you're getting up throughout the night for no reason. It can happen in spurts (episodic), last a few weeks (short-term), or be permanent (chronic). Improper sleep habits, stress, and too much nervous thinking are the major causes of insomnia. Improper sleeping habits begin at a young age when children learn to stay up late studying for exams or partying. This new lifestyle habit follows through to college and eventually into adult life. The natural sleeping rhythm and cycle is reprogrammed. **Be sure to see your doctor for proper diagnosis and management.**	*Over the Counter Sleeping Pills, Antihistamines, and Anti-Depressants*: *Diphenhydramine Citrate, Doxylamine, Diphenhydramine Hydrochloride*; are the active ingredient in over the counter sleep aids and mainly meant for treating allergic reactions by blocking the brain chemical histamine and suppressing the nervous system making you drowsy and sending you into pseudo-paralysis. The above are short term occasional fixes perhaps, but not at all a long term solution for people with insomnia. Headache, Irritability in the morning, blurred vision, dizziness, nausea, vomiting, dry mouth, dry nasal passages, constipation, and dependency are some of the side effects of use.	**Kava Kava:** Widely used for anxiety, menopausal symptoms, and insomnia due to its calming effect that brings clear thinking, sense of well-being, and relaxed muscles. **Valerian root:** Used as a sedative in herbal medicine for over 1,000 years. **Chamomile:** Perennial herb that is known as a mild sedative. **Lemon Balm, Sage Herb,** and **Valerian** teas are also known to help induce sleep. **Passion Flower:** Holds anti-depressant properties with tranquilizing effects. Affects central nervous system, and has an antispasmodic effect on smooth muscles. **Melatonin:** Natural hormone released by the pineal gland that is activated by darkness. Also found in high amounts in sour cherries. **Rooibos:** Tea from South African shrubs contains high level of antioxidants, flavonoids, phenolic acids, quercetin, and luteolin but lacks caffeine. Drink a cup right before going to sleep. Great for headaches, tension, and colic as well. *See section 10.15 for more helpful sleep supplements, and 8.3 for tips on sleep hygiene.*	Start a routine waking up at 7am and getting to bed by 10pm. Turn off any distractions and allow your body to drift to sleep. This will help reprogram your natural circadian rhythm. Create a playlist of relaxing music that helps put you to sleep or use hypnosis CDs. Practice proper sleep hygiene with a cervical pillow (see chapter 8). Keep your sleep cycles regular (6-8hrs nightly), avoid overstressing yourself with deadlines, and take a much needed vacation. Treat yourself right; don't take things to heart that are out of your control. Review your stress levels in the categories of personal, relationships, and work. Examine your connection with co-workers and loved ones for possible tension that could be carried over and preventing you sound sleep. You may want to limit exposure to these individuals or situations. Be hydrated well as you sleep. Void your bladder first, and drink 1 cup of water prior to bed. Clear your sleeping area from any electromagnetic frequency (EMF), as it may conflict with your body's natural biorhythms. Invest in a magnetic mattress pad as some say this improves chances for restful sleep.	There usually is a spinal connection / nerve interference issue: **Ask your Chiropractor about adjusting the Cranial bones, Occiput, C1 – C7 areas.** Chiropractic is well known for distressing the nervous system and allowing patients relaxing of their system. ❦ Dietary habits play a large role in the rest and recuperation of the body during sleep. Ask a qualified holistic nutritionist or naturopath about food allergy testing and diet modification. Remove all food allergens, check intestinal flora health, check for possible leaky gut syndrome, candida albicans (yeast syndrome) overgrowth, and celiac disease; also known as gluten intolerance. Ask your doctors about cutting back prescribed drug dosages, and check possible drug interactions. *Seek out a certified Kousouli® Method practitioner to remove spinal stress and align your energy bodies.*

Ailment name	Western Medicine Approach	Alternative Medicine Approach	What you can do at home to take control?	How can Chiropractic Help?
COMMON COLD / FLU, COUGH AND SORE THROAT The adenovirus, also known as the common cold virus is believed to actually be caused by the parasitic debris of tapeworm stages, E.coli, and mites. If you have mold toxins in your system, you are more susceptible to infection in the moist respiratory tract. Best to act upon the first signs of a sneeze or throat tickle. Colds are either bacterial or viral in nature and will thrive when your immune system is in a compromised state. Sneeze or cough into your bent elbow, not in your hands; this helps keep infections from spreading. Never "keep in" a sneeze as this could cause serious internal pressure problems in the head, eyes, and neck. **Be sure to see your doctor for proper diagnosis and management.**	*Over the Counter Drugs: Acetaminophen (Tylenol), Aspirin, Ibuprofen, Naproxen.* Many over the counter anti-cold and decongestants have side effects, and can cause stomach discomfort and liver damage. They focus on symptom relief and not on addressing, preventing the cause, or shortening duration of illness. If used often, they can actually make symptoms worse. *Flu Antivirals: Amantadine, Rimantadine, Oseltamivir, Zanamivir, Relenza.* Side effects include: nausea, vomiting, dizziness, runny or stuffy nose, cough, diarrhea, headache, and some behavioral changes like trouble sleeping and difficulty concentrating. *Ask your doctor about the ingredients; prior to taking a flu shot.*	*B Complex* with *Niacinamide (form of B3):* Detoxifies mycotoxins. *Zinc, Selenium, Colloidal Silver:* Powerful immune boosters. *Vitamin C* and *Vitamin D3:* Strengthen the immune system. *Grapefruit Seed Extract:* A wonderful anti-viral agent. *Astragalus:* Protects nasal passages from rhinoviruses, and boosts immune system. *Echinacea:* Reduce susceptibility to colds by stimulating immune system to speed recovery. *Black Elder Berries:* Contain flavonoids for immune boosting. *Fenugreek, Cat's Claw,* and *Chlorophyll:* All help boost immunity. *Garlic, Ginger,* and *Mullein (raw, boiled in hot water as tea):* Possesses anti-bacterial, anti-viral, and anti-parasitic properties; ginger gives great relief from a dry scratchy throat. Mullein relieves chest congestion. *Cinnamon Oil, Garlic,* and *Onion*: Highly appreciated for their anti-bacterial and anti-viral properties. *Cayenne Pepper* or *Capsicum Sprays:* Helpful in opening up nasal passages and naturally dealing with sinus pressure symptoms. *Mangosteen, Acai,* and *Noni Juice:* Strong immunity allies for beating flus and colds. *Homeopathic remedies; Gelsemium, Eupatorium Perfoliatum, Oscillococcinum, Influenzinum Nosode, Allium, Belladonna, Kali Bi,* and *Spongia:* helpful at the first signs of cold and flu symptoms. Ask your doctor for use.	Drink lemon or lime juice daily to boost your vitamin C reserves. Get away from the stagnant indoors and go outside to enjoy the fresh air. Wash your hands often; don't ever put them in your mouth, nose, or eyes. Keep yourself well hydrated. Avoid coffee, sugar, sodas, liquor, and smoking which increase dehydration. Avoid breads, crackers, or dried fruit in plastic which may have molded. Stop eating peanut butter, cheese, and breads at the first sign of a cold symptom. Alkalinize your diet (chapter 10). Have homemade chicken soup; never canned. Sleep right and sleep well (chapter 8). Infrared sauna, gua sha, cupping, and deep tissue massages help your body detoxify and stimulate the lymph system. For a scratchy throat, gargle hydrogen peroxide or mix warm water, sea salt, lemon juice, colloidal silver, raw manuka honey, and oregano and basil juice. Keep all animals away from bedding and mattresses as they cross contaminate your surroundings with parasites and bacteria. Switch to a vegan or anti-inflammatory vegetarian diet. Use an alkaline Ph water conversion filter for home and travel use.	There usually is a spinal connection / nerve interference issue with the sinuses, bronchus, and lungs: **Ask your Chiropractor about adjusting the Occiput, C1-C3, and T1 - T5 areas to help open head, neck, and lung pathways and boost immunity.** ⚜ Ask your doctor to assess your lymph glands for soreness under your jaw, and the front and back of your neck. Chronic re-occurring infections could be coming from problems in the mouth, gums, or teeth, and can be the cause of the symptoms. Ask your doctors about cutting back any prescribed drug dosages you may be taking and check possible other drug interactions or side effects. The toxic load may have weakened your immune system, thus causing your current cold/ flu symptoms. *Seek out a certified Kousouli® Method practitioner to remove spinal stress and align your energy bodies.*

BE A MASTER® OF MAXIMUM HEALING © by Theodoros Kousouli D.C., CHt.

Ailment name	Western Medicine Approach	Alternative Medicine Approach	What you can do at home to take control?	How can Chiropractic Help?
HYPERTENSION **HIGH BLOOD PRESSURE** High blood pressure or hypertension is a chronic condition where normal blood pressure is elevated. Untreated hypertension over long durations can be fatal. Hypertension can lead to heart failure, coronary heart disease, stroke, and kidney failure. Smoking, diet, obesity, genetic predispositions, improper life styles, and mycotoxic activity, (particularly T2 mold toxins; consumed through peas, nuts, rice, and beans) may all be factors to chronic high blood pressure and kidney disease. If you have a high systolic number, this could mean you have clogged arteries and possibly liver problems (atherosclerotic hypertension). If you have a high diastolic number it could be caused by liver and kidney problems (hepatic, portal, or renal hypertension). **Be sure to see your doctor for proper diagnosis and management.**	Medication forces body functions to change through chemical means without addressing lifestyle choices. Side effects usually follow. **Beta Blockers:** Erection problems, asthma symptoms, insomnia, cold hands and feet. **Diuretics:** Erection problems, frequent urination, leg cramping due to low potassium, foot pain from possible gout. **Angiotensin II receptor blockers (ARBs):** Dizziness. **Angiotensin Converting Enzyme (ACE) Inhibitors:** Skin rash, loss of taste, and dry cough that won't leave. **Calcium Channel Blockers (CCBs):** Dizziness, headache, odd palpitations, constipation, and swollen ankles. **Blood Vessel Dilators:** Headache, dizziness, swollen ankles, constipation, irregular heartbeats. **Vasodialators:** Eye swelling, headaches, fluid retention, joint pain and tachycardia. **Renin Inhibitors:** Rash, stomach pain, cough, heartburn. **Peripheral Adrenergic Inhibitors**: Erection problems, heartburn, stuffy nose, diarrhea, dizziness, lightheadedness, weakness when standing up suddenly from bed or chair.	***Chelation Therapy:*** Well known within alternative medicine for cleaning artery plaque, and improving the circulatory system. ***Ginseng*** and ***Pine Bark:*** Lowers high blood pressure, relaxes blood vessel muscles, and reduces cholesterol levels. ***Flax Seed Oil:*** Contains essential fatty acid that helps reduce "bad" LDL cholesterol. ***Bilberry Leaves:*** Help keep arteries flexible and strong; also help prevent forming of atherosclerotic plaques on arterial walls. ***Hawthorn Berries:*** Significantly supports heart and circulatory system. ***Dong Quai (Angelica):*** Helps make the resting periods between heartbeats longer. ***Grape Seed Extract:*** Dilates blood vessels, lowers cholesterol, and neutralizes free radicals in the bloodstream. Do not combine with vitamin C as it may increase blood pressure. ***Maitake*** and ***Reishi Mushroom:*** Help decrease blood pressure, and tones blood vessels. ***Garlic*** and ***Ginger:*** Contain antibiotic and anti-inflammatory properties. ***Noni Juice:*** Studies show when taken regularly, it lowers blood pressure and cholesterol levels.	Minimize and remove the things you can control: drugs, caffeine, alcohol smoking, and junk food. Eat a low-fat, fruit rich diet. Eliminate soda, fast food, processed sugars (use raw manuka honey or powdered stevia instead), white flour, trans-fats, high-fructose corn syrup, and beef. Reduce sodium. Cook with extra virgin olive oil and coconut oil. Treat yourself to relaxing spa massages, vacations and take breaks more often. Eliminate emotional stress. Remove negative people and situations from your life. Cut all exposure to negative news and television programs. Try sound therapy, hypnosis, and aromatherapy essential oils, which all sooth and relax the senses. Switch to a vegan or anti- inflammatory vegetarian diet. Use an alkaline Ph water conversion filter for home and travel use.	There usually is a spinal connection / nerve interference issue: **Ask your Chiropractor about adjusting the Occiput, C1, C2, and T1 - T5 areas.** Chiropractic research shows that realigning the atlas (C1) vertebrae in the neck decreases both systolic and diastolic numbers. ⚜ Ask your doctors about doing chelation therapy, and going on a liver and kidney cleanse. These steps alone may ease body system stress and strengthen organs, helping to normalize blood pressure. Ask a qualified holistic nutritionist or naturopath about diet modification, food allergen testing, intestinal flora health, leaky gut syndrome, candida albicans overgrowth, and celiac disease (gluten intolerance). Ask your doctors about cutting back prescribed drug dosages, and check possible drug interactions. *Seek out a certified Kousouli® Method practitioner to remove spinal stress and align your energy bodies.*

BE A MASTER® OF MAXIMUM HEALING © by Theodoros Kousouli D.C., CHt.

Ailment name	Western Medicine Approach	Alternative Medicine Approach	What you can do at home to take control?	How can Chiropractic Help?
GALL BLADDER STONES **CHOLELITHIASIS** Acute symptoms include right temporal headache, bloating, nausea, yellow skin or eyes, vomiting, and pain in the right side of the abdomen or back that lasts 15 minutes to several hours after eating a fatty meal. More common in females who are considered overweight, fertile and flatulent. A hard green deposit in the gallbladder forms as a result of a high cholesterol diet. Lodging of a gall stone can happen in the bile duct causing a block and sharp pain attack. Gas, belching, intolerance to fatty food, decrease in appetite, or nausea may be signs of a chronic issue. Diabetes, hyperparathyroidism, sickle cell or pancreatic disease, cirrhosis and Crohn's disease patients can be susceptible to frequent gall bladder attacks. **Be sure to see your doctor for proper diagnosis and management.**	Depending on their density and size, gallstones won't usually be seen on x-rays, but will be picked up by ultrasound. Clay colored stools, yellowing of the skin, or body chills warrant immediate referral for further testing. ***Pain Medications***: Prescribed when pain hits, but do nothing to get rid of the stones. ***Surgery***: Laparoscopic cholecystectomy is routinely the avenue for gallstone sufferers who do not change diet and lifestyle. A bile salt complex may be taken with meals for those who remove their gallbladder. Gall bladder removal is often an unnecessary but very lucrative procedure for hospitals in the US. Prior to considering surgery, all holistic methods of revitalizing the gallbladder through detoxification should be considered with the guidance of a qualified naturopath and doctor of functional medicine.	***Gallstone Flush***: Indians and Egyptians have been using this to cleanse for centuries. **Caution!!! First consult your doctor and research flushing risks thoroughly.** Take no other vitamins or medications while doing this flush. Do not eat food past 2pm; only drink water. Prepare by taking 4 tbsp. of epsom salts, adding 2/3 cup fresh squeezed grapefruit (or lemon) juice, ½ cup extra virgin olive oil (or walnut oil), 15 drops of black walnut (for killing parasites), and mix it all together. Allow to aerate for 20 minutes before drinking it all down. Drink mixture around ten p.m. that night on Friday or Saturday night so you can rest the next day. Lay on your right side and go to sleep; once you wake up you will probably have diarrhea. Gallstones will float in the toilet and will appear round and somewhat green in color. The film on top of the water is also gallstone elements that did not form into stones but is just as important to remove as the stones themselves. ***Manganese, Choline, Hydrangea root*** and ***Marshmallow root***: May improve bile duct flow and support digestive health. ***Licorice root*** and ***Fenugreek***: Contain antioxidants for the liver, and supports digestive health. ***Yellow Dock***: Blood purifier. Helps organs of detoxification and metabolism.	Minimize and remove the toxins you can control: drugs, caffeine, alcohol, smoking and junk food. Prevention is your best weapon. No deep-fried foods or dairy. Foods high in fat, especially cholesterol, should be stopped immediately; these contribute to formation of stones: red meat, margarine, hydrogenated oils, pork, sugar, cheese, sweets, radishes, cabbage, nuts, and turnips. Avoid black tea, sodas, and coffee. You may have carrots, beets, apricots, whole grains, gluten free pasta, wild caught fish, potatoes, turkey, fruits, and vegetables; especially grapes, pears, papayas, and avocados. Occasionally, before or after a meal, take a spoonful of apple cider vinegar to stimulate your gastrointestinal system. Attacks usually happen suddenly at night after a fatty meal. Hydrate often. Drinking plenty of water after meals may also help calm the pain.	There usually is a spinal connection / nerve interference issue: **Ask your Chiropractor about adjusting the Occiput, C1, C2, and T4-T7 areas** which control the nerve impulses to the liver and gallbladder. ❦ Upper back pain, dull ache between the shoulder blades, and right shoulder pain shooting through to the front or back of the chest, could mean you are having an allergic reaction to something you just ingested, or could be a gallstone stuck in a bile duct. Liver and gallbladder flushes improve digestion, allergies, shoulder, arm, back pain, improve energy and increase sense of well-being. Ask your doctors about cutting back prescribed drug dosages, and check for other possible drug interactions or side effects. Birth control pills increase the chances of gallstone formation. *Seek out a certified Kousouli® Method practitioner to remove spinal stress and align your energy bodies.*

BE A MASTER® OF MAXIMUM HEALING © by Theodoros Kousouli D.C., CHt.

Ailment name	Western Medicine Approach	Alternative Medicine Approach	What you can do at home to take control?	How can Chiropractic Help?
KIDNEY STONES **NEPHROLITHIASIS** Chronic dehydration, prescription and non-prescription drug use, junk food diets, and nutritional deficiencies can quickly lead to formation of kidney stones. Calcium oxalate, ammonium phosphate, uric acid, calcium phosphate, or cystine stones are common in the west due to pollution and toxins in unnatural food and drink. The major symptom of kidney stones is a slight back ache which then turns to severe excruciating flank (side) pain when a stone lodges in the ureter. Some women describe the pain level to be similar to child birth. Swift medical attention is needed for this condition. **Be sure to see your doctor for proper diagnosis and management.**	*Pain Medications*: Temporarily numb the pain; do nothing to get rid of the stones. *Alpha Blockers:* May help some pass stones out quicker. *Lithroscopic Surgery* 85% success rate though may need a second or third surgery. Recovery is usually slow. *Note:* All holistic methods of revitalizing the kidneys through detoxification should be considered with the guidance of a qualified naturopath as a preventative for those with low back and flank pain. Patients with kidney disease (different from kidney stones) experience: back pain, extreme fatigue, low urine output, and unusually clear urine and unexplained hyperkalemia (high potassium levels). They should be careful using any products with potassium, as well as see a doctor immediately upon first signs of urinary distress.	*Kidney Flush*: **Hydrangea root tincture** plus ***Raw Organic Apple Juice*** (the malic acid component helps dissolve the stones). The cleansing has to be done 3-4 times per day for 3 weeks. Research and consult your doctor before starting the program. ***Gravel root, Parsley, Bearberry (Uva Ursi), Marshmallow root, and Ginger root***: They can be used in addition to the above kidney cleanse formula to boost the cleansing effect. ***Pyridoxine (B6) and Magnesium Oxide:*** Help boost your kidney functions. ***Olive Oil and Lemon Juice:*** Used as an age old remedy for healthy kidney and liver. Mix 1/4 cup olive oil with 1/4 cup lemon juice and drink throughout the day. ***Chanca Piedra Herb***: Reduces inflammation, increases urination, lowers cholesterol, lowers blood pressure, breaks stones, and supports kidney and liver. ***Kava Kava:*** Helps relax the urethra and spasms from stones. Can be strong; use sparingly. ***Gogi Juice:*** Supports blood pressure, cholesterol, libido, liver, kidney, and cardiovascular health. ***Noni Juice:*** Known for its pain relieving, immune boosting, digestive support, antifungal, anti-parasitic, and antibacterial properties.	Prevention through full water hydration (10-12 glasses per day) is vital. Eliminate drinking sodas of any kind. Phosphoric acid in soda eats away the calcium in bone and acidifies your body. Eliminate refined table salt, sodium, and salty foods. Avoid processed foods. Try a vegetarian or vegan diet. Limit foods high in oxalate such as nuts, chocolate, and dark green vegetables. Do not eat high protein diets. Severely limit animal meat: pork, fish, beef, and even eggs. Increase your fiber intake to include oat bran, carrots, cabbage, and beans. Mix 4 tbsps. of apple cider vinegar in water, and drink twice a day to stimulate the urinary system and dissolve stones.	There usually is a spinal connection / nerve interference issue: **Ask your Chiropractor about adjusting the Occiput, C1, C2, and T6-T12** for neural flow to the kidney areas. ❦ Ask a qualified holistic nutritionist or naturopath about diet modification, heavy metal and food allergy testing, intestinal flora health, leaky gut syndrome, candida albicans overgrowth, and celiac disease (gluten intolerance). Craving salt or "salty" foods like potato chips could mean you need a kidney and adrenal gland cleanse. This could indicate there is a need for potassium chloride and sodium balance in the body. Polluted colon, kidneys, liver, or gallbladder may also be the cause of many elbow, wrist, hand, and joint pains. *Seek out a certified Kousouli® Method practitioner to remove spinal stress and align your energy bodies.*

BE A MASTER® OF MAXIMUM HEALING © by Theodoros Kousouli D.C., CHt.

Ailment name	Western Medicine Approach	Alternative Medicine Approach	What you can do at home to take control?	How can Chiropractic Help?
HERPES Herpes is a viral disease that affects the mucus membranes causing painful sores in the mouth and genital areas. It is caused by Herpes Simplex virus type 1 and type 2. Herpes is either oral or genital, and is spread through sexual or physical contamination. The primary outbreak lasts 10 to 14 days. There can be continual outbreaks over time, or dormancy of the virus. It is said that 1 in 10 people carry the virus for genital herpes, however many do not know it as symptoms can be mild, and the virus can lay dormant. Sexual contact, including kissing, should be avoided during an outbreak. The Herpes Zoster virus (also known as Shingles) is a reactivated infection of the chickenpox virus and usually appears along a dermatome. **Be sure to see your doctor for proper diagnosis and management.**	*Acyclovir*: Antiviral drug that slows the spreading and growth of the herpes virus. Overuse can result in renal toxicity; use caution. *Valtrex* and other synthetic forms of *Famciclovir*, and *Valacyclovir*: Cause headache, nausea, and vomiting; cannot prevent recurrence. *Note:* Even though according to Western medicine herpes is incurable, Eastern medicine claims it can be reversed when the body is detoxified, nourished, supplemented, and supported by whole foods. Also see Nerve Pain and Inflammation sections if you are experiencing herpes.	*Prunella Vulgaris*: A medicinal herb that treats herpes. *Oregano, Aloe Vera* **(Acemannan)**, *Raw Manuka Honey, and Olive Leaf Extract:* Antiviral properties with some successes. **35% Pure Food Grade Hydrogen Peroxide (H_2O_2):** Dilute with water; use doctor supervision. (Do not use over the counter drug store Hydrogen Peroxide. It is not the correct type.) *Dimethyl Sulfoxide (DMSO):* An all-natural substance derived from wood pulp that has high oxygen value. *L-Lysine:* Amino acid that stunts the virus activity. *Red Marine Algae:* Studies show red algae extracts have antiviral properties and are able to inhibit the herpes simplex and zoster viruses. **Black Elder Berry Botanical Extract:** Effective against HSV Type 1. Contains powerful flavonoids that stimulate pro-inflammatory cytokine production. *Juniper Berry, Bearberry (Uva Ursa), Licorice:* May also inhibit the herpes virus. *Reishi Mushroom:* Helps boost the immune system and acts as an antiviral. *Tea Tree Oil*: Has been sporadically used to control herpes.	Stay away from diet products and artificial sweeteners; eat a diet rich in L-lysine, and low in arginine. Lamb, chicken, brewer's yeast, cheese, sheep milk, fish, mung bean, chicken, beef, sprouts, many fruits, and vegetables are the best choices. Go on a sugar, gluten, and dairy free diet. Remove processed sugars and artificial flavors, colors, additives, and artificial sweeteners from your diet. Refined sugar often triggers herpes attacks, because refined sugar is a known immunosuppressant. Do not overstress yourself; doing so tends to allow outbreaks to occur more often. Stay warm and dry in colder environments, as cold also tends to stress the body into more outbreaks. Do not share drinking cups or other intimate items when there is an open, active sore.	There usually is a spinal connection / nerve interference issue: **Ask your Chiropractor about adjusting the Occiput, C1, C2, T1 – T6 and L1 - S2** to maintain strong immune system function and keep neural flow open to the reproductive glands. ❧ Consider holistic avenues and look also into kidney, liver, candida, parasite, and heavy metal cleansing. Ask a qualified holistic nutritionist about doing food allergy testing and diet modification. Ask your doctors about cutting back prescribed drug dosages and checking other possible drug interactions that may be taxing on your immune system. Keep a positive outlook in life, stay away from stress, eat a pure diet, and get regular exercise. Help your immune system by living clean, and removing the toxins that have overloaded the body systems. *Seek out a certified Kousouli® Method practitioner to remove spinal stress and align your energy bodies.*

BE A MASTER® OF MAXIMUM HEALING © by Theodoros Kousouli D.C., CHt.

Ailment name	Western Medicine Approach	Alternative Medicine Approach	What you can do at home to take control?	How can Chiropractic Help?
BENIGN PROSTATE HYPERPLASIA (BPH) **PROSTATITIS** The prostate is a male reproductive organ; responsible for generating the ejaculation fluid that carries sperm. Some prostate enlargement happens at a steady rate with age, and problems typically start after 35. However, abnormal enlargement causes extra pressure on the urethra, and hence causes urination and bladder problems. Signs of prostate dysfunction are: Frequent urination, smaller urine stream, foamy urine, (protein in urine, possible kidney disease), inability to fully empty bladder, pain upon intercourse or burning sensation during urination. **Be sure to see your doctor for proper diagnosis and management.**	*Finasteride (Proscar)*: Prescribed to shrink the enlarged prostate. However it does have many side effects which include erectile dysfunction (E.D.), decreased libido, abnormal ejaculation, orgasm failure, male breast enlargement, chronic fatigue, sleep disturbances, muscle atrophy, depression, memory and cognitive impairment, and low testosterone. Also prescribed for male patterned baldness. *Prostate Surgery*: Is never recommended unless absolutely necessary; massive procedural and post-operative hospital cost. Get a PSA test and rectal exam annually after age 50 as an early preventative screening.	*Seronoa Repens (Saw Palmetto Berries)*: Effective within a month with significantly fewer side effects than Proscar and 60% less cost; has been extensively used in Europe. *Pygeum (Pygeum Africanum)*: African herb; helpful like saw palmetto. *Beta Carotene:* The orange pigment found in carrots, oranges, and sweet potatoes; a secret weapon in the promotion of men's prostate health. *Selenium and Zinc:* Very important for prostate, sex, and general male health. *Lycopene:* Pigment found in watermelon, tomatoes, and shrimp. Known to stop the growth of prostate cells. *Bee Pollen:* Anti-oxidant used widely in Germany for prostate health. Caution: some may be allergic to it. *Red Raspberries:* Have vitamins C and K, plus Ellagic Acid, powerful dose of antioxidant protection. *Pumpkin Seeds:* Anti-inflammatory in nature. *Omega 3 EPA/DHA:* Increases anti-inflammatory prostaglandins, and is great for prostate health.	Stay away from sweet, starchy foods (like doughnuts and cake), and overtly seasoned foods; occasionally eat basil or use it to season your food; quit smoking and drinking coffee. Eat nutrient rich foods that lower your risk for prostate cancer: eggs, sesame seeds, onions, herring, sunflower seeds, wheat germ oil, oatmeal, zucchini, Brussels sprouts, broccoli, cabbage, kale, tomatoes, watermelon, papaya, and mushrooms. Eat plenty of fruits and raw vegetables. Get a full body massage twice a month to relax and give foot reflexology a try. The Achilles tendon and heel are points connected to the low back and prostate. Massage lightly for a few minutes a day. Sexual release through orgasm is healthy for the prostate gland; keeps it active, and healthy. Sexual hygiene is also equally important.	There usually is a spinal connection / nerve interference issue: **Ask your Chiropractor about adjusting the Occiput, C1, C2, and L1-S2** (innervate the associated area). ☘ Ask your doctors about doing chelation therapy and going on a liver and kidney cleanse for heavy metals; lead, nickel, and mercury can collect in organs. Look for Nickel and other heavy metals when testing. Overexposure to metals, some types of jewelry, and other things we come in contact within our environment could be the main issue. Ask a qualified holistic nutritionist or naturopath about diet modification, food allergy testing, intestinal flora health, leaky gut syndrome, candida albicans overgrowth, and celiac disease (gluten intolerance). Ask your doctors about cutting back prescribed drug dosages, and check for other possible drug interactions or side effects. *Seek out a certified Kousouli® Method practitioner to remove spinal stress and align your energy bodies.*

BE A MASTER® OF MAXIMUM HEALING © by Theodoros Kousouli D.C., CHt.

Ailment name	Western Medicine Approach	Alternative Medicine Approach	What you can do at home to take control?	How can Chiropractic Help?
PEPTIC ULCER Called a gastric ulcer if found in the stomach lining, or considered duodenal if it occurs in the first part of the small intestine. Excess acid production in the stomach; due to irregular food habits, and long durations of starvation. May cause upper abdominal and chest pain (that may wake you up), feeling of fullness, nausea, bloody stools, fatigue, or weight loss. **GASTRITIS** Gastritis is an inflammation of the stomach's mucosa lining. Ulcers go deeper and erode through the muscularis layer of the gastric or duodenal mucosa. **Be sure to see your doctor for proper diagnosis and management.**	Rule out carcinoma and H. Pylori infection. Surgery is needed when gastric ulcers perforate. This is a surgical emergency. **Upper Gastrointestinal Endoscopy with Barium Swallow** if no perforation is suspected. **Cimetidine (Tagamet):** Histamine receptor antagonist. **Omeprazole (Prilosec):** Proton pump inhibitor. Both used to treat ulcers and gastroesophageal reflux disease (GERD) by reducing stomach acid. Usually used in conjunction with **Antibiotics (Clarithromycin, Amoxicillin)** to treat gastric ulcer caused by infection with helicobacter pylori (H. pylori). **Histamine -2 Receptor Blockers (Zantac, Pepcid):** Over the counter oral antacids. Antacids rarely give permanent relief. Some of the side effects of antacids include: easy bruising, dizziness, joint and muscle pain, rashes, cough, trouble breathing, jaundice, nausea, irregular heartbeat, diarrhea, agitation, fever, or problems urinating. **Colloidal Bismuth Subcitrate:** Shows promise where histamine 2 receptor blockers may fail. **Sucralfate (Carafate):** Binds to ulcers and contains ulcer area.	**Banana, Wood Apple, Lime, Almond Milk, Drumstick, Fenugreek, and Cabbage:** All contain enzymes that help digestion and thus the mucosal lining of your stomach. **Vitamin A, C, E and K:** Provide faster healing. **Thiamine (B1) and Zinc:** Needed to produce acidic environment in stomach. **Probiotics, ex. Lactobacillus, and Digestive Enzyme Support:** Gives a positive gut environment and supports proper digestion. **Capsaicin:** Hot chili peppers actually act as an antacid and aid in the protective lining of the stomach. Use sparingly. **Licorice, Deglycyrrhizinated Licorice (DGL):** Reduces mucosal lining inflammation. **Aloe Vera Juice and Apple Cider Vinegar:** One or two tablespoons with water each meal may help ease the stomach. **Raw Onion and Garlic:** Helps inhibit the levels of Helicobacter pylori (H. Pylori) bacteria and parasites.	Stop drinking alcohol, coffee (caffeine), and quit smoking. No Non-steroidal anti-inflammatory drugs (NSAIDs), like aspirins or over the counter medications. Avoid eating refined white salt, spicy, greasy or fried foods, tomatoes, or drinking cow milk. No cured meats: sausage, bacon or ham. Do a high fiber diet. Consider switching to a raw diet which is rich in live enzymes. Do not overeat. Lower your protein intake and eat smaller meals which will make digestion easier on the stomach. Eat bananas (increases mucus in digestive tract) and raw manuka honey, garlic (keeps levels of *Helicobacter pylori* bacterium in check), cabbage (cabbage juice), carrots (carrot juice), squash, tofu, beans, spinach, cod, kale, apples, celery, raw cranberry juice, and coconut water. Do not drink water while eating your meals. Drink a small amount prior and after. Hydrate well throughout the day. Get stress management. High stress levels are usually related with stomach ulcers. Eating in a stressed state upsets acid levels in your stomach, making it harder to digest properly. Eat in a peaceful relaxed way, and chew thoroughly before swallowing.	There usually is a spinal connection / nerve interference issue: **Ask your Chiropractor about adjusting the Occiput, C1, T5-T10, especially T5-T7** (innervate the associated areas). The key to healing is improving both digestion and absorption through diet. 🌿 Ask a qualified holistic nutritionist or naturopath about doing food allergy testing and diet modification. Helicobacter Pylori (H. Pylori) bacteria may be the root cause and must be eliminated with antibiotics to allow gut healing. Ask your doctors about cutting back prescribed drug dosages, and check for other possible drug interactions that may be eroding your stomach lining. *Seek out a certified Kousouli® Method practitioner to remove spinal stress and align your energy bodies.*

BE A MASTER® OF MAXIMUM HEALING © by Theodoros Kousouli D.C., CHt.

Ailment name	Western Medicine Approach	Alternative Medicine Approach	What you can do at home to take control?	How can Chiropractic Help?
ATHEROSCLEROSIS Atherosclerosis is essentially hardening and loss in elasticity of the arteries caused by fat and cholesterol build up (plaque) in the lining of the blood vessels. Since the blood needs more pressure to flow through the decreased area, it results in hypertension, and ultimately chronic cardiac conditions result over time. When the coronary arteries narrow, the blood pressure increases; resulting in squeezing chest pain (angina), shortness of breath, or heart attack. Other symptoms of atherosclerosis are: aneurysm, (when a blood vessel wall balloons out, making it weaker, and likely to rupture) renal failure, weak heart, cold extremities, and hemorrhagic stroke, (when someone with high blood pressure has an atherosclerotic brain artery rupture). Atherosclerotic heart disease is associated with a sedentary Standard American Diet, (SAD) and is a leading cause of death in both males and females. It is a preventable (and in many cases reversible) disease. **Be sure to see your doctor for proper diagnosis and management.**	*Aspirin:* Reduces blood clotting, and maintains blood flow through narrowed arteries. *Beta Blockers:* Commonly used for coronary artery disease to lower demands on the heart and relieve chest pain. *Angiotensin Converting Enzyme (ACE) Inhibitors, Calcium Channel Blockers (CCBs), Diuretics* and *Angiotensin II Receptor Blockers (ARBs):* Lower blood pressure. *Cholesterol Medication, Statins; Atorvastatin (Lipitor):* Forces lowering of LDL (low-density lipoprotein) to reverse fatty buildup in arteries. Medication forces body function to change through chemical means without addressing the source: Lifestyle choices. Side effects: Heartburn, stuffy nose, diarrhea, dizziness, lightheadedness, weakness when standing up suddenly from bed or chair, headache, palpitations, constipation, swollen ankles, erection problems, insomnia, cold hands and feet, rash and loss of taste, dry cough that won't leave, frequent urination, leg cramping, and asthma symptoms. *Surgeries: Coronary Artery Bypass, Balloon Angioplasty, Carotid Artery Bypass, Femoral Artery Bypass, or Amputation.* Fatality and cost is mind boggling, often problems recur and surgery is repeated.	*Chelation Therapy*: Improves arterial blood flow; research shows post-therapy requirement of surgery falls by 50%. *Vitamins B3 (Niacin), B6, B12, C, E, Magnesium, Chromium, Carnitine, Folic Acid, Potassium, Selenium, Copper, Grape Seed Extract, Chinese Red Yeast Rice Extract, Alpha-Lipoic Acid, Alpha-Linolenic Acid, L-Lysine, L-Arginine,* and *Coenzyme Q10:* These nutrients are of value in the treatment of heart attack, angina, atherosclerosis, and congestive heart failure. *Garlic* and *Ginger:* Powerful anti-inflammatory properties. *Pure Noni Juice:* Studies show it lowers blood pressure and cholesterol. *Hawthorn Berries:* Significantly supports heart and circulatory system. *Omega 3 Fatty Acids (EPA / DHA):* Increases anti-inflammatory prostaglandins. Ex. Cod Liver Oil.	Stop smoking, drinking alcohol and coffee. Include in your diet large amounts of leafy greens rich in chlorophyll (such as barley or wheatgrass). Stop using homogenized cow milk (use almond milk instead), fluoridated products (ex. fluoride toothpaste), all processed sugars, trans-fats and animal fats, as these together are most known to contribute to causing atherosclerosis and heart disease; Eat non-GMO soy protein, artichoke, oat bran, tofu, almonds and cereal fiber. Hydrate well (10-12 glasses non-chlorinated pure water daily). Get stress management. Treat yourself to relaxing spa massages; take breaks and vacations more often. Avoid all emotional stress and negative people. Try sound therapy, hypnosis and aromatherapy to de-stress. Daily exercise is needed for better blood flow to the brain and all vital organs. Add KSS™ stretches in Chapter 8 to your daily routine. Breathe deeply. **Also read: Page 29 on cholesterol hype** Switch to a vegan or anti-inflammatory vegetarian diet. Avoid meat.	There usually is a spinal connection / nerve interference issue: **Ask your Chiropractor about adjusting the Occiput, C1, C2, T1-T5, especially T1-T3.** Chiropractic has shown positive effects in lowering blood pressure and removing spinal stress. ❦ Ask your doctors about chelation therapy as this has been proven excellent in cleansing the arteries. Also discuss cutting back prescribed drug dosages and trying holistic alternatives, but also check possible drug interactions. Ask a qualified holistic nutritionist or naturopath about doing food allergy testing and diet modification. Look into kidney, liver, candida, heavy metal, and parasite cleansing. Hire a personal trainer that works with your doctor's instruction to help you lose weight, and regain your fitness levels. *Seek out a certified Kousouli® Method practitioner to remove spinal stress and align your energy bodies.*

BE A MASTER® OF MAXIMUM HEALING © by Theodoros Kousouli D.C., CHt.

Ailment name	Western Medicine Approach	Alternative Medicine Approach	What you can do at home to take control?	How can Chiropractic Help?
MYOCARDIAL INFARCTION **HEART ATTACK** A heart attack happens when blood flow to a particular region of the heart is impeded for a long-enough period that the particular region of the heart dies from lack of nutrients (oxygen). Most heart attacks happen because a blood clot (from plaque formation as in atherosclerosis) blocks one of the coronary arteries which brings blood and oxygen to the heart. Hypertension, obesity, smoking, atherosclerosis, and a host of other factors can put you at a higher risk for heart attack incidence. Heart attacks and strokes are the leading causes of death in the United States. They usually occur without any warning. **Be sure to see your doctor for proper diagnosis and management.**	Medications are used to limit the size of the heart attack, reduce the work of the heart, treat complications, relieve anxiety, and chest pain. *Aspirin:* Reduces blood clotting and maintains blood flow through narrowed arteries. *Beta Blockers:* Commonly used for coronary artery disease to lower demands on the heart and relieve chest pain. *Angiotensin Converting Enzyme (ACE) Inhibitors, Calcium Channel Blockers (CCBs), Diuretics, and Angiotensin II Receptor Blockers (ARBs):* Lower blood pressure. *Cholesterol Medication:* Forces lowering of LDL (low-density lipoprotein) to reverse fatty buildup in arteries. Clot busting medication is usually followed by intravenous blood thinners (ex. Heparin) to prevent new clot formation. *Coronary Artery Bypass, Angioplasty Surgeries, Fibrinolytic (clot-busting) drugs such as Tissue Plasminogen Activator (TPA) or Streptokinase*: Expensive, and may give no overall guaranteed improvement in health. *Intravenous Nitroglycerin* is used to treat chest pains (angina). Relaxes the smooth muscle walls of blood vessels. Morphine or other pain relieving drugs may be used to treat chest discomfort from a heart attack.	*Chelation Therapy:* Improves arterial blood flow; removes plaque. *Intravenous Magnesium:* Has shown amazing results with much fewer side effects than drugs. *Vitamins B3 (Niacin), B6, B12, C, and E; Magnesium, Chromium, Carnitine, Folic Acid, Potassium, Selenium, Copper, Grape Seed Extract, Chinese Red Yeast Rice Extract, Alpha-Lipoic Acid, Alpha-Linolenic Acid, L-Arginine, Coenzyme Q10*: These nutrients are often of value in the treatment of heart attack, angina, atherosclerosis, and congestive heart failure. *Garlic* and *Ginger:* Lower cholesterol and triglyceride levels; anti-inflammatory properties. *Wheatgrass* and *Barley Grass*: Rich in magnesium; balances blood Ph. *Hawthorn (Crataegus Oxyancantha)*: Significantly supports heart and circulatory system. *Bilberry (Vaccinium Myrtillus):* Contains flavonoids, powerful antioxidants. *Capsaicin:* Believed to lower cholesterol, and lessen blood clotting.	If you feel you're having chest pain, sudden constriction, or associated pains in the left arm, jaw, head and neck: DO NOT WAIT, get someone to take you to the emergency room immediately! Heart attacks are medical emergencies and every minute after an attack counts! Immediate lifestyle and dietary changes are needed. Stop smoking, drinking alcohol and coffee. Include large amounts of fruits, vegetables, and leafy greens in your diet. Stop using homogenized cow milk (use almond milk instead), fluoridated products (ex. fluoride toothpaste), all processed sugars, trans-fats, and animal fats, as these together are most known to contribute to causing atherosclerosis and heart disease. Reduce emotional stress and negativity in life. Switch to a vegan or anti-inflammatory vegetarian diet. Avoid meat. Use an alkaline Ph water conversion filter for home and travel use.	There usually is a spinal connection / nerve interference issue. **After you have been stabilized and cleared from medical emergency, ask your Chiropractor about adjusting the Occiput, C1, C2, T1-T5, especially T1-T3.** Chiropractic has shown positive effects in lowering blood pressure and removing spinal stress. Ask your doctors about chelation therapy, as this has been proven excellent in cleansing the arteries. Ask a qualified holistic nutritionist or naturopath about doing food allergy testing and diet modification. Look into kidney, liver, candida, heavy metal, and parasite cleansing after you've stabilized and are in better health to do them. When given the okay from your doctors, hire a personal trainer that works with your doctors' instruction to help you regain your fitness levels, lose weight, and strengthen your cardiovascular system. *Seek out a certified Kousouli® Method practitioner to remove spinal stress and align your energy bodies.*

BE A MASTER® OF MAXIMUM HEALING © by Theodoros Kousouli D.C., CHt.

Ailment name	Western Medicine Approach	Alternative Medicine Approach	What you can do at home to take control?	How can Chiropractic Help?
EAR INFECTIONS ACUTE OTITIS MEDIA (AOM) Referred to as otitis media. Most common in children and young adults. Often caused in the middle ear because the eustachian tubes become clogged or infected. Causes include: bacteria and viruses, streptoccocus pneumoniae, haemophilis influenza, moraxella catarrhalis, sinus infections, oversized adenoids, excess mucus, saliva, allergies, or air irritants such as tobacco. Symptoms include ear pain, fever, feeling of fullness in the ear, irritability, hearing loss, vomiting, and diarrhea. **TINNITUS VERTIGO MENIERE'S DISEASE** A buzz, hissing noise of various noise levels, in one or both ears that pulses or stays continuous. May also include nausea, vomiting, dizziness, or spinning upon head movement. Bacterium Streptococcus pneumoniae detox, avoiding salicylate medications (aspirin, cough syrups, lozenges), and removal of toxic metals (lead, benzalkonium, beryllium, and zirconium) all seem to help. **Be sure to see your doctor for proper diagnosis and management.**	*Antibiotics; Amoxicillin.* Will help if the ear infection has been caused by bacteria. Useless if the cause is viral. Destroys all the required commensal organisms and can also cause stomach and gut flora disruption. *Over the Counter Medications:* Ibuprofen or acetaminophen helps relieve the pain. *Scopolamine Patches, Diazepam, Dimenhydrinate,* or *Chlordiazepoxide Medications:* For those suffering from vertigo symptoms. *Tympanostomy Tube Surgery*: Considered if AOM conditions persist. *Surgery* for Meniere's patients; Decompression of the endolymphatic sac may help. *Note:* Never give children or teenagers aspirin for flu symptoms, as it could lead to Reye's Syndrome, a very dangerous condition (brain swelling, enlarged liver, rash, vomiting, and fever).	*Garlic* and *Mullein drop supplement* in the affected ear: Usually gives complete pain relief in approximately 24 hours. *Colloidal Silver:* A few drops in the ear several times a day. Continue using after the infection has cleared to be sure. *B Complex Vitamins; B1, B2, Niacin(B3), B5, B6, Biotin (B7), Folate (B9), B12, C, E, Choline Bitartrate, Chromium, CoQ-10, Calcium, Inositol, Magnesium, Manganese, Lecithin, PABA, Thiamin* and *Zinc:* All support inner ear health. Mix and dilute with water 1 teaspoon of *Grape Seed Oil* (or sweet almond oil) with 3 drops of *German Chamomile*, plus 1 drop of *Tea Tree Oil*, and *Echinacea*: Use as soothing ear drops. *Xylitol:* Inhibits the growth of bacteria, Streptococcus pneumoniae, associated in ear infections. A sugar found in strawberries, plums, raspberries, and in some sugarless gums.	Stop all alcohol intake. Avoid allergenic foods; Limit the foods that produce mucus in the body and avoid dairy products. Stop all salt and caffeine intake. Stop eating processed sugars and restrict the use of antibiotics. Eating garlic, onions, and celery will help reduce mucus production. Drink 2 tablespoons of apple cider vinegar in 8 ounces of water twice a day. Avoid exposure to cold drafts or wind tunnels as this seems to activate attack episodes of tinnitus, vertigo, or ear symptoms. You must alkalize and detox the bloodstream to aid in limiting bacteria and virus growth. Add liquid chlorophyll and a variety of dark leafy greens to your diet. Water trapped in the ear from swimming in infected waters could lead to infections. Be sure to dry ears thoroughly after using pools or showering. Gentle earwax removal kits, are available at your local pharmacy; help clean your ears and restore function.	It is essential that anyone (baby to seniors) with an ear infection consider a chiropractic spinal checkup, in addition to medical care. There usually is a spinal connection / nerve interference issue. Particular areas of focus are the cranial bones, notably frontal, sphenoid, ethmoid, temporal, occipital, as well as the cervical vertebrae. **Ask your Chiropractor about adjusting the Occiput, C1, C2, and associated Cranial bones.** Your chiropractor will test your cranial nerves for proper function as well. Ask a qualified holistic nutritionist or naturopath about doing food allergy testing and diet modification. Look into kidney, liver, candida, heavy metal, and parasite cleansing. Bottle fed babies and children allergic to dust, molds, pollens, and foods may be more likely to develop an ear infection compared to breast fed babies. *Seek out a certified Kousouli® Method practitioner to remove spinal stress and align your energy bodies.*

Ailment name	Western Medicine Approach	Alternative Medicine Approach	What you can do at home to take control?	How can Chiropractic Help?
LUPUS (SLE) **Systemic Lupus Erythematosus** SLE is an autoimmune disease affecting 1.5 million Americans and characterized by acute and chronic inflammation of various body tissues; malar rash, discoid rash, photosensitivity, oral or nasopharyngeal ulcers, arthritic joints, blood, renal, and neurological disorders, serositis, antinuclear antibodies, nephritis, leukopenia, thrombopenia. The most prominent mark is the 'butterfly' shaped rash on the face. Mild to seriously life threatening. Attacks the organ systems of the body; mainly the skin, joints, nervous system, kidneys, and lungs. Destruction of the organ tissue is associated with fever, fatigue, vasculitis, and weight loss. Likely at 20-50 years old. Mostly in African Americans (2-3x more likely) and native Americans, Asians, and Hispanics. 90% affected are female. **Be sure to see your doctor for proper diagnosis and management.**	**Nonsteroidal Anti-Inflammatory Drugs (NSAIDs):** Acetylsalicylic Acid (Aspirin), Naproxen Sodium (Aleve), and Ibuprofen (Advil or Motrin): Pain and inflammation relief. *Isonizid, Methyldopa, Hydralazine, Procainamide Drugs:* Sulfonamide drugs and NSAID use may exacerbate the disease. *Anti-Malarial, Anti-rheumatic Drugs.* **Hydroxychloroquine (Plaquenil):** The most commonly prescribed antimalarial. Side effects of antimalarial drugs include vision problems and muscle weakness. *Corticosteroids:* Counter the inflammation but have serious long-term side effects: weight gain, easy bruising, osteoporosis (monitored by dexa scan), high blood pressure, diabetes, and increased risk of infections. *Cyclophosphamide:* A cancer medicine used in extreme cases of organ and life threatening situations. **Promising but needs more research:** Stem cell transplantation, anti-B cell antibodies, and intravenous immune globulin.	*Dehydroepiandrosterone (DHEA):* Delays SLE onset and reduces the severity of the disease. *Willow Bark (Salix Alba):* Known to ease muscle and joint pain associated with lupus, as well as act as an anti-inflammatory against affected joints. *Burdock root, Cat's Claw, Ginkgo Biloba, and Devil's Claw:* Help reduce inflammation. *Colloidal Silver:* A natural treatment for lupus symptoms that offers helpful antibacterial, antifungal, and antiarthritic properties. *Omega 3 Fatty Acids (EPA / DHA):* Increases anti-inflammatory prostaglandins. Ex. Cod Liver Oil. *Flax Seed:* The Linum Usitatissimum plant seed. Rich in alpha-linoleic acid. Improves kidney function by decreasing blood thickness, reducing cholesterol levels, and swelling. *Glutathione:* Body's natural antioxidant. High in walnuts.	Stop smoking and drinking alcohol. Avoid allergenic foods, caffeine, sodas and artificial sweeteners. Stop ingesting homogenized cow milk (use almond milk instead), processed sugars, trans-fats, wheat, dairy, and animal fats. Intake large amounts of leafy greens rich in chlorophyll (barley or wheatgrass). Studies show an increase in bone loss and fracture through osteoporosis in individuals with SLE, so eat foods rich in vitamin C, E, and D3; oranges, cod liver oil, salmon, dark green leafy vegetables such as broccoli, collards, and kale. Consume wild caught fish which is rich in omega-3 fatty acids. Hydrate well (10-12 glasses daily) and get 6-8 hours restful sleep. Add a light exercise program and the KSS™ stretches in Chapter 8 to your daily regimen. Love yourself, and remove emotionally stressful triggers from your life. Switch to a vegan or anti-inflammatory vegetarian diet. Use an alkaline Ph water conversion filter for home and travel use.	There usually is a spinal connection / nerve interference issue with this dis-ease: **Multiple spinal sites are usually affected;** Ask your Chiropractor about co-managing your case with a doctor of functional medicine. Chiropractic management is excellent in removing stress irritation and improving lifestyle when in conjunction with proper nutrition and exercise. ❧ Diet modification is essential. Ask a qualified holistic nutritionist or naturopath about food allergy testing and heavy metal detoxification. Check glutathione levels. Remove all food allergens, check intestinal flora health, check for possible leaky gut syndrome, candida albicans (yeast syndrome) overgrowth, and celiac disease; also known as gluten intolerance. Ask your doctors about cutting back prescribed drug dosages, and check for other possible drug interactions or side effects. *Seek out a certified Kousouli® Method practitioner to remove spinal stress and align your energy bodies.*

BE A MASTER® OF MAXIMUM HEALING © by Theodoros Kousouli D.C., CHt.

Ailment name	Western Medicine Approach	Alternative Medicine Approach	What you can do at home to take control?	How can Chiropractic Help?
ERECTILE DYSFUNCTION (E.D.) IMPOTENCE Inability in men, as they age, to sustain or acquire an erection with rigidity to perform sexual intercourse; usually because of lack of vital life energy (chi or pneuma) via blood and nerve flow to the groin region. **LOW LIBIDO (low sex drive)** Loss of sexual desire. Anti-depressants are serious libido killers. **INFERTILITY** Inability of either partner to contribute their sperm or egg for successful conception. Substance abuse, previous surgery, diabetes, neurological and vascular disease, age, medications, radiation, chemotherapy, emotional trauma, hormone imbalance, and obesity all play factors to stress that causes infertility or sexual dysfunction. Some European studies blame male infertility on environmental causes by estrogen-like chemicals in shampoos, pesticides, plastics, cosmetics and other products. **Be sure to see your doctor for proper diagnosis and management.**	*Psychotherapy Counseling, Medications (Phosphodiesterase (PDE) Type 5 Inhibitors), Vacuum Pump Devices and Surgery* are medical treatments for erectile dysfunction. Some blood pressure medications, antidepressants, sedatives, ulcer, allergy drugs and appetite suppressants make it difficult for a man to get a firm erection. *Vardenafil Hydrochloride (Levitra), Avanafil (Stendra), Sildenafil (Viagra) for E.D.:* Helps the blood flow issue, not the desire issue. Some side effects include: risk of erection for hours, diarrhea, dizziness, headache, seizure, heartburn, loss of vision, fainting, shortness of breath, stuffy nose, and muscle aches. Male and female hormone replacement therapy may be helpful in some cases. Ask your doctor about the risks vs. benefits.	*Horny Goat Weed:* For male erectile dysfunction and sexual dysfunction in women; increases nitric oxide levels relaxing smooth muscle so more blood flows to the penis or clitoris. *Gingko Biloba:* Relaxes smooth muscle and enhances blood flow in the penis or clitoris. *L-Arginine (Precursor to nitrate oxide)* and *Panax Ginseng:* Increase nitric oxide; both show promise in treating E.D. and are a holistic alternative to Viagra. Talk to your doctor. *Zinc:* Deficiency in men may be linked to erectile dysfunction. *Yohimbe:* Stimulates blood flow to the penis, helps increase libido, and decreases the period between ejaculations. *Dehydroepiandrosterone (DHEA):* Building block for sex hormones, and helps in cases of low testosterone. *Homeopathic Baryta Carbonica:* Helps premature ejaculation, erection dysfunction, builds libido, and gives prostate support. **MACA Powder (Peruvian Ginseng):** For female fertility, thyroid hormone and mood support, stamina, energy, sexual function, and better semen quality in men.	Stop smoking, alcohol, and caffeine use. These severely inhibit libido and sexual organ function. Proper nutrition is vital for energy and ability to have sex (see chapter 10). Consider working with a nutritionist or naturopath for allergy counseling and detox. Relax more. Stress kills libido because cortisol levels go up. Avoid wearing tight pants or constrictive underwear that hinders pelvic motion, sexual organ freedom, and blood flow; switch to boxer briefs. Bicyclists should limit time sitting on narrow bicycle seats or install wider ones. Exercise increases blood flow and testosterone. Increases dopamine levels for desire. Eat foods high in L-arginine found in meat, dairy, poultry, and fish. Hydrate well (10-12 glasses daily) and get 6-8 hours restful sleep. Add a light exercise program and the KSS™ stretches in chapter 8 to your daily regimen. **Note: Also see sexual health section, here in Chapter 11.**	There usually is a spinal connection / nerve interference issue: **Adjustment of the C1-C7; T9-L5; S2-S4 levels** opens nerve flow to the thyroid, adrenal, and sexual reproductive glands. **Ask your Chiropractor about Lumbar and Sacral adjustments** as well as possible **Pudendal Nerve Entrapment (PNE).** There have been many reported cases of previously frustrated couples who were unable to conceive, becoming pregnant after receiving chiropractic therapy which opens up lower spinal pathways to the reproductive glands. ❦ Detox for heavy metals which can disrupt body physiology, and cause sexual malfunction. Detox Zearalenone (ZEN, ZEA, RAL, F-2) mycotoxin: A mycoestrogen toxin produced by molds that grow on wet grains. It can contaminate grain, processed foods, meat, and dairy products if given to cattle as a growth enhancer; causing Infertility, cancer, lower immunity, thymus atrophy, and may increase breast cancer risk. *Seek out a certified Kousouli® Method practitioner to remove spinal stress and align your energy bodies.*

Ailment name	Western Medicine Approach	Alternative Medicine Approach	What you can do at home to take control?	How can Chiropractic Help?
LOW BACK PAIN FROM PREGNANCY Pains associated with the additional weight, stress, and hormonal changes of pregnancy. **PMS** PMS is not healthy and a sign that something in the diet or lifestyle needs balancing. **PERIOD PAIN DYSMENORRHEA** Painful cramping during menstruals. **FIBROIDS** Uterine leiomyomas, (benign tumors of the uterus due to estrogen dominance), are common and usually asymptomatic. They can cause bleeding and heavy menses, pregnancy complications, and abdominal pain. Xenoestrogens found in common synthetic materials, may contribute to causing fibroids. Pelvic pain may be indicative of other problems such as endometriosis, cancer, or ovarian cysts. **Be sure to see your doctor for proper diagnosis and management.**	*Testing:* Vaginal exam, full blood count, thyroid panel, ESR, urinalysis, (HCG) pregnancy test, STD test, Pap smear, pelvic ultrasound, pelvic MRI, laparoscopy, hysteroscopy, transvaginal ultrasound, peritoneal tap or culdocentesis, hysterosalpingography, sonohysterography, tumor markers such as CA 125, and alpha fetoprotein tests. *Non-Steroidal Anti-Inflammatory Drugs (NSAIDs):* Usually limited success rate, and only temporary relief. *Contraceptives; (Oral Birth Control Pill, Patch, Vaginal Ring, Injection, Hormone-Releasing Intrauterine Device, IUD):* Treatments for dysmenorrhea. PMS does not resolve by taking the birth control pill. Synthetic estrogens and progestins are carcinogenic; deplete the body of key nutrients, impair fertility, and destroy normal physiology. *Natural Progesterone Cream:* Helps balance out over activity of estrogen production. *Surgery (Laparoscopic Myomectomy):* Fibroid removal from uterus.	**MACA Powder, (Peruvian Ginseng):** Rich in amino acids, phytonutrients, vitamins, and minerals. Effective in reducing cramping and regulating menstrual cycle. *Magnesium:* Very important for women; helps stop muscle cramping. *Vitamin E, Omega 3+6, Essential Fatty Acids, Flax Seed, Fish Oil,* and *Primrose Oil:* Help lower inflammation. *Probiotics:* Healthy gut flora has a direct relation to helping serotonin production (drink kefir). *Milk Thistle:* Helps liver and pelvic circulation. *Chase Tree:* Supports ovarian function. *Dong Quai:* Helps menopause, cramps, lack of sexual desire, and PMS. Do not take if pregnant.	Stop smoking, drinking alcohol and coffee (caffeine). Avoid bottled water; do not eat food or drink water heated or stored in plastic. Hydrate well, as this is known to lessen the occurrence of cramps. Get more potassium (bananas). Avoid gluten, trans-fatty acids, salt, refined carbohydrates, synthetic estrogens, food preservatives, dairy and sugar; as sugar fuels inflammation. To help shrink fibroids and ease pelvic pain, eat broccoli, kale, bok choy, collard greens, brussels sprouts, cauliflower, spinach, spirulina, chlorella, blue-green algae, wheat grass, alfalfa, and barley grass as they neutralize xenoestrogens and lower blood dioxin levels. Blackstrap molasses, activated charcoal powder, apple cider vinegar, and aloe blended together may also help. Lack of protein can severely increase PMS symptoms. Vegans and vegetarians need more protein. Do not use products that contain DDT, PCBs or Dioxin; Change your laundry detergent to a non-toxic brand; don't use fabric softener, switch to non-toxic soaps, shampoos, deodorants, and makeup. Apply a hot water bottle over the abdominal area and massage the low back to help ease pain.	The center of gravity and weight bearing of the spine change through pregnancy. **Chiropractic adjustments to the Lumbar L1-L5 and Sacral S1- S5 spinal levels** open the nerve flow to the reproductive organs and improve mobility, function, and overall health. Mother and baby are connected by the most important nerves via umbilical cord. Women can alleviate a lot of the discomforts associated with pregnancy by being under the care of a Chiropractor to normalize nervous system stress. Delivery is also usually faster and more comfortable for the mother. ❦ Diet modification is essential to improve PMS, fibroid, or dysmenorrhea symptoms. Ask a qualified holistic nutritionist or naturopath about food allergy testing, liver, gallbladder, and heavy metal detoxification. Remove all food allergens, check for possible leaky gut syndrome, and candida albicans (yeast syndrome). *Seek out a certified Kousouli® Method practitioner to remove spinal stress and align your energy bodies.*

BE A MASTER® OF MAXIMUM HEALING © by Theodoros Kousouli D.C., CHt.

Ailment name	Western Medicine Approach	Alternative Medicine Approach	What you can do at home to take control?	How can Chiropractic Help?
MENOPAUSE A normal phenomenon for women at approximately 45-55 years of age. It can even start as early as the 30's or 40's, or may not occur until a woman reaches her 60s. Daughters usually follow the menopausal age of their mothers. First, a woman's ovaries stop producing eggs. Then her body produces less progesterone and estrogen. Increasing menstruation slows down and then stops. This usually happens over a few years span. Transition periods are many times symptom laden with irregular menses, heavy bleeding, vaginal dryness, hot flashes, cramping, chills, shivering, and sweating. Psychological distress, depression, anxiety, irritability, fatigue, and difficulty focusing are common. **Be sure to see your doctor for proper diagnosis and management.**	*Hormone Replacement Therapy (HRT):* Is very helpful and has high success rate. However, risks include a higher percent of breast cancer, heart disease, stroke, and endometrial cancer. Many patients decide to try managing their menopause naturally through holistic means if their symptoms are manageable. *Clonidine* and *Gabapentin (Anticonvulsants):* Lower blood pressure and give hot flash relief. *Anti-Resorptive Drugs; Biphosphonates:* For elderly patients with osteopenia and osteoporosis. *Ibandronate (Boniva), Alendronate (Fosamax)* and *Risedronate (Actonel):* Some doctors claim these help with bone loss, but holistic experts warn of leg fracture, stomach pain, trouble swallowing, muscle pain, and jaw osteonecrosis risk with their use.	*Dong Quai* a.k.a. *Angelica*: Helps women's lack of sexual desire, menopause symptoms, cramps, and PMS. Antispasmodic and anti-inflammatory. Do not take if pregnant or breast feeding. *Chaste Tree:* Improves mood and hormone fluctuation. *Black Cohosh, Lecithin Granules, Currant Seed Oil, Red Clover,* and *Primrose Oil:* Reduce hot flashes. *Coenzyme Q10, Coenzyme A:* Supports immunity, adrenal glands, boosts energy, and mental capacity. *Beta 1,3-D-glucan:* Immune and bone marrow stimulant. *Vitamin B Complex + B5, B6:* Improve circulation. **Vitamin C, Vitamin E, (d-alpha-tocopherol form):** Reduce hot flash attacks. **Vitamin D3:** Helps regulate calcium. **Potassium:** Nervous system protector and heart rhythm regulator. **Calcium** and **Magnesium:** Help relieve nervousness and irritability. **Boron** and **Silica:** Help calcium absorption. *L-Lysine* and *L-Arginine:* Help detox the liver. *L-Theanine:* Amino acid found in green tea; helps alpha brain waves so you are alert but not stressed. *St. John's Wort:* Helps with depression and anxiety. *MACA Powder* (Peruvian Ginseng): For female stamina, energy, and sexual function.	Stop smoking, drinking alcohol, and coffee (caffeine). As these can trigger hot flashes. Try chamomile tea; helps calm the body. Consider diet modification and eat more raw enzyme rich foods. Eliminate wheat and dairy, (especially cow milk). Get more chlorophyll. Eat more dark greens: kelp, broccoli, kale; Eat fish, but go off of all red meats. Keep a low fat diet and get more fiber. Sweeten foods with blackstrap molasses, manuka honey, or organic powdered stevia instead of commercial white refined sugar. Cut all salt, processed sugars, sodas, and artificial chemicals. Manage stress and relax more. Hydrate well (10-12 glasses daily) and get 6-8 hours restful sleep. Add a daily exercise program and the KSS™ stretches in Chapter 8 to your daily regimen. If sexually active and intercourse is painful due to vaginal dryness, lubricate the vagina with vitamin E oil or aloe vera gel.	Your chiropractor will pay close attention to signs of osteoporosis, as fractures tend to be more common after the onset of menopause. A Dexa scan and X-rays will help determine the extent of bone loss, and check if other techniques to adjust your vertebrae are needed. **Ask your Chiropractor about adjusting Occiput, C1 - C7, T12 - S2, and any other affected spinal levels** which may help de-stress and relax you. With proper diet through whole foods, sleep, exercise, chiropractic adjustments, supplementation, hydration, and a positive mental attitude, many of the unpleasant effects of menopause can be minimized or eliminated naturally. Ask a qualified holistic nutritionist or naturopath about food allergy testing, liver detoxification, and talk to your medical doctor about HR therapy benefits and side effects. *Seek out a certified Kousouli® Method practitioner to remove spinal stress and align your energy bodies.*

BE A MASTER® OF MAXIMUM HEALING © by Theodoros Kousouli D.C., CHt.

Ailment name	Western Medicine Approach	Alternative Medicine Approach	What you can do at home to take control?	How can Chiropractic Help?
HYPO AND HYPER THYROIDISM Hypo-thyroidism is insufficient production of thyroid hormone by the thyroid gland. Common symptoms include a basal temperature under 97.5 degrees, hair loss, weight gain, body pains, headaches, acne, fatigue, temperature intolerance, loss in libido, foggy thought, gout, hypercholesterolemia, dry skin, and depression. Hypothyroidism is mostly caused by Hashimoto's thyroiditis (inherited; enlarged thyroid goiter), lack of the thyroid gland, or a deficiency of hormones from either the hypothalamus (TRH) or the pituitary gland (TSH). Hyper-thyroidism is from an overactive thyroid gland, resulting in overproduction and excess of circulating free thyroid hormones: thyroxine (T4), triiodothyronine (T3), or both. Thyroid hormone functions as a stimulus to metabolism and is critical to normal function. In excess, it overstimulates metabolism and exacerbates the effect of the sympathetic nervous system. Symptoms include, bulging eyes, lid lag, diplopia, irritability, rapid heartbeat, sweating, weight changes, cold intolerance, palpitations, tremors, anxiety symptoms, diarrhea, menstrual issues, and weight loss. **Be sure to see your doctor for proper diagnosis and management.**	*Testing:* TFT (Thyroid Function Tests) Thyroid-Stimulating Hormone (TSH, thyrotropin), Thyroxine (T4), and Triiodothyronine (T3). Free T4 and Free T3, Reverse T3, Thyroid Antibodies, (Anti-TPO and TgAb), Anemia, Iron Labs (Ferritin, % Saturation, TIBC and Serum Iron), Saliva Adrenal Cortisol Levels, Vitamin Testing, B9, and B12, D3, Increased Alkaline Phosphatase, Ultrasound, and Surgical Biopsy of thyroid nodule masses. *Hormone Replacement Therapy (HRT):* Personalized to the individual. Helpful and good success rate though can have long term side effects. *Beta Blockers; Propranolol (Inderal):* Help with the tremors and heart palpitations associated with hypothyroidism. *Anti-Thyroid Drugs; Methimazole or Propylthiouracil:* Thyroid inhibitors used in the treatment of hyperthyroidism. *Levothyroxine, (Euthyrox, Levothroid, Levoxyl, Synthroid):* Only contains T4 and does not help all hypothyroid cases and may be less effective option than desiccated pig thyroid like **Armour Thyroid, Thyrolar,** and **Nature-Throid.**	*Vitamins A, B Complex, C, Zinc, Copper, Manganese, Molybdenum, L-Tyrosine, Iodine, Withania Somnifera (Ashwaganda),* and **Myrrh *(Commiphora Myrrha)*:** All important in proper thyroid health. *Quercetine:* A bioflavonoid; helps reduce inflammation. *Liquid Magnesium Chloride* and *Hyssop Tea (contains high Iodide, caution!):* Ask your doctor about risks. *L-Tyrosine, L-Tryptophan:* Increases plasma levels and helps your brain create serotonin to lift mood. *Lemon Balm* and *Bugleweed:* Help an overactive thyroid. *Coconut Oil* and *Potassium Iodide:* (as iodine tablets) Both benefit hypothyroidism. *Cayenne:* Helps improve blood circulation. *Turmeric (Curcumin), Ginger,* and *Boswella:* Help reduce inflammation.	Stop smoking, drinking alcohol, caffeinated tea, and coffee. Add more raw, enzyme rich foods to your diet. Eliminate wheat, gluten, white flour, sugar, fried and processed foods, artificial flavors, dairy (cow milk), red meat, and keep a low fat diet. Avoid soy products. Hypothyroid patients should not eat cabbage, mustard, radishes, peaches, pears, turnips, soybeans, cassava root, peanuts, millet, almond seeds, and pine nuts as these inhibit thyroid function. Hyperthyroid patients should avoid foods high in iodine such as salt, kelp, and seaweed. Avoid food and liquids radiated by microwaves. Use fluoride-free toothpaste. Use a chlorine filter for your shower and drinking water. Fluoride and chlorine compete with iodine uptake! Drink 10-12 glasses of water daily and get 6-8 hours restful sleep. Manage stress. Severe emotional or physical trauma (ex. car accidents, whiplash) may instigate thyroid issues. Add a daily exercise program and the KSS™ stretches in Chapter 8 to your daily regimen.	There usually is a spinal connection / nerve interference issue associated with the upper cervical neurology. **Adjustment of the Cranial Bones; Occiput, and C1 – C7 spinal levels may be needed.** Ask your Chiropractor about co-managing your case with a doctor of functional medicine or endocrinologist. ❦ Ask a qualified holistic nutritionist or naturopath about doing food allergy testing, liver, colon, candida, heavy metal and parasite cleansing. Heavy metal toxin overload could be causing mineral imbalances (cadmium and mercury are closely associated with low T4). Prescription drugs such as antidepressants, tricyclic and monoamine oxidase inhibitors, dopamine, lithium bromide, and adenosine inhibit thyroid function. Ask your doctors about cutting back prescribed drug dosages, and checking other possible drug interactions. Studies show Per-Fluorooctanoic Acid, used in non-stick pans (Teflon) and water-resistant fabrics may contribute to thyroid disease. *Seek out a certified Kousouli® Method practitioner to remove spinal stress and align your energy bodies.*

Ailment name	Western Medicine Approach	Alternative Medicine Approach	What you can do at home to take control?	How can Chiropractic Help?
UTI — URINARY TRACT INFECTION Women are more susceptible to UTI's than men. The short distance from the uterus to the anus can transport bacteria and cause problems such as burning upon urination. Sexual intercourse and contraceptive use (diaphragms, spermicides) can also instigate UTI. Uncircumcised men are also at risk due to possibility of bacterial infection. **YEAST INFECTION** Presents as a white discharge, that is thick, and often described as a cottage cheese appearance which results from a yeast overgrowth (fungus). Too many yeast cells are growing in the vagina overpowering *Lactobacillus acidophilus* which helps keep other organisms under control. Most yeast infections are caused by *Candida albicans* which causes itching, soreness, pain or burning when urinating or having sex. **Be sure to see your doctor for proper diagnosis and management.**	*Urine Culture* is the gold standard for diagnosing a UTI. Urine microscopic analysis, prostatic secretion analysis, and renal ultrasound may also be used. *Over the Counter (OTC)* medicines offer relief from the pain and discomfort of UTIs but they don't cure UTIs. *Intravenous* or *Oral Antibiotics (Penicillin and Cephalosporin)*: When prescribed should be taken even after symptoms disappear as to not get a reoccurrence of the UTI. *Antifungal* or *Anti-parasitic Medications* for the more rare infections. *(DMSO, Diflucan, Ketoconazole, Sporonox, Nystatin, Vitrex, and Aphetoricin).* For yeast infections, a vaginal exam and culture of the yeast is done, followed by treatment by anti-fungal creams, vaginal suppositories, or antifungal tablets.	*Turmeric*: Helps the body clear damaging toxins. *Oregano Oil* and *Odorless Garlic caps*: Strong bactericidal agents. Help inhibit infection. *Cranberry Extract*: Contains proanthocyanidins. Prevents E. coli from grabbing onto the walls of the urethra. *Echinacea* and *Goldenseal*: Together enhance immune function to fight early UTI. *Uva Ursi*: A herbal diuretic, astringent, and antiseptic with powerful healing effects for the kidney and bladder. *MACA Powder (Peruvian Ginseng)*: Rich in amino acids, phytonutrients, vitamins, and minerals. Effective in reducing cramping and regulating menstrual cycle. *Baking Soda* and *Chlorophyll Douche*: 3-4 tbsps. liquid chlorophyll plus 2 tbsps. baking soda in warm water twice a day. pH balances and deodorizes vaginal odor. *Vitamins A, B Complex, Biotin, C, D, E, Grape Seed Extract, Essiac* and *Basil Tea, Caprylic Acid*: All helpful for vaginal health.	Sexual intercourse usually increases the occurrence of infection. Drink plenty of water directly before and after sex. Wash area with water and dry thoroughly prior to sleeping. Keep hydrated throughout the next 24 hrs. to flush the system as dehydration seems to worsen UTI's. Men should also practice good hygiene as candida can be transmitted between people by direct contact. Urinating before and after intercourse helps cleanse the urethra from bacteria. Stop the intake of alcohol, cow milk, cheese, wheat, gluten, and sugar as these aggravate the condition. Eat fiber rich foods and organic yogurt high in acidophilus; take live probiotics. Always practice clean pelvic hygiene. Wear clean cotton underwear. Change pads or tampons often. Avoid tight-fitting clothing, such as panty hose, and tight-fitting jeans. After defecating, always wipe from front to back to avoid spreading bacteria from your anus to the vagina or urinary tract. Switch to a vegan or anti-inflammatory vegetarian diet. Use an alkaline Ph water conversion filter for home and travel use.	There usually is a spinal connection / nerve interference issue associated with the urinary and reproductive neurology. **Ask your Chiropractor about adjusting your Occiput, C1, C2, and T7 - S5.** (innervate the associated areas). ⚜ Toxic additives in soaps, bubble baths, perfumes, body oils, sprays, aromatic tampons or pads, condoms, spermicide, nonoxynol-9, or sex lubricants may also trigger or worsen yeast infections. Diet modification is essential to improve UTI or yeast infection symptoms. Ask a qualified holistic nutritionist or naturopath about food allergy testing, gallbladder, liver, and heavy metal cleansing. Remove all food allergens, check for celiac disease, possible leaky gut syndrome and candida albicans (yeast syndrome). Yeast infections that return may be from medication overuse or a sign of a more serious disease in those with weakened immune systems such as diabetes, leukemia, sexually transmitted diseases, or AIDS. *Seek out a certified Kousouli® Method practitioner to remove spinal stress and align your energy bodies.*

BE A MASTER® OF MAXIMUM HEALING © by Theodoros Kousouli D.C., CHt.

Ailment name	Western Medicine Approach	Alternative Medicine Approach	What you can do at home to take control?	How can Chiropractic Help?
HIGH CHOLESTROL Many doctors believe the high / low cholesterol scenario has been manipulated by pharmaceutical companies to confuse the public for profit. Cholesterol is needed for every cell structure, brain, and nerve activity; it's a vital component also for making sex hormones. Low Density Lipoproteins (LDL) transport cholesterol from the liver to the arteries. Since they deposit cholesterol to the arteries, they got a bad rep and have been termed "bad cholesterol", while the opposite, High-Density Lipoproteins (HDL's) transport cholesterol from the cells back to the liver from the blood; so they have been termed "good cholesterol". In reality, both are vital for life! High LDL naturally happens if one consumes too much of the wrong foods, and it will overburden the liver's ability to remove cholesterol from the body back to the liver, thus showing high LDL levels in the blood. **Be sure to see your doctor for proper management.**	***Statin Drugs*** such as ***Simvastatin (Zocor):*** Blocks the liver enzyme (HMG-CoA reductase) that is responsible for making cholesterol. **Serum Cholesterol** in the bloodstream including LDL and HDL. **LDL <200 mg/dl = safe, 200-239 borderline 240+ high risk** for heart disease. **Men normal HDL range = 45 to 50 mg/dl, Women normal HDL range = 50 to 60 mg/dl** A **HDL under 35 is considered high risk** for heart disease. As your HDL lowers, your risk increases. There are cholesterol self-testing kits available at your local pharmacy. You can check your cholesterol prior to consulting a doctor. **Caution:** Steroids, oral contraceptives, diuretics, and beta blockers can cause increases in cholesterol levels. Talk to your doctor if you are using any of these.	***Omega 3's*** and ***Fish Oil:*** Reduces artery inflammation and lowers cholesterol. ***Apple Pectin:*** Binds heavy metals and fats to lower cholesterol. ***Chinese Red Yeast Rice Extract:*** Cholesterol lowering properties. ***NOTE:*** Contains small amounts of natural HMG-CoA reductase inhibitors. Do not use with statin medications. ***L-Carnitine*** and ***Chromium Picolinate:*** May improve HDL-LDL levels. ***Niacin (B3):*** Helps HDL (good cholesterol) Though do not take if you have liver disease, gout, high blood pressure, or are sensitive to niacin (may produce a red skin flush). ***Coenzyme Q10:*** Lowers cholesterol and beneficial if you are taking statin drugs. ***Mangosteen Juice:*** For pain, inflammation, swelling, and infection reduction. ***Ginger:*** Absorbs and lowers cholesterol. ***Shiitake*** and ***Reishi Mushrooms:*** Lower cholesterol levels and help in many diseases. ***Inositol:*** Lowers cholesterol, preventing artery hardening. ***Vitamin B Complex, Vitamin C*** with ***Bioflavanoids, Calcium,*** ***Licorice root, Hawthorn Berry, Alfalfa Herb, Garlic Bulb, Capsicum Fruit, Butcher's Broom,*** and ***Fenugreek seeds:*** Help balance cholesterol levels.	Avoid animal fats and trans fat foods, hydrogenated fats like margarine, lard, and butter. Eat a high-fiber diet that is made of fruits, nuts, whole grains, and seeds. Do not consume pork products, fried foods, fast foods, processed cakes, creams, pies, candy, carbonated drinks, and white bread. Stop sugars and alcohol, as these make the liver produce cholesterol. Avoid drinking coffee as it has been linked to higher cholesterol levels as well. Oat bran, brown rice, bran, carrots, bananas, grapefruit, apples, vegetables, and fruits have no cholesterol; eat up! Add extra virgin olive oil to your salads; improves your HDL (good cholesterol) lowers LDL (bad cholesterol). Drink red wine; contains saponin and resveratrol. Add a daily exercise program and the KSS™ stretches in Chapter 8 to your daily regimen. **Also read: Page 29 on cholesterol hype**	There usually is a spinal connection / nerve interference issue associated with the liver neurology. **Ask your Chiropractor about adjusting Occiput, C1, C2, and T5-T10, especially T7** (innervate the associated areas). The nervous system is the master system of directing communication between the organ (the liver) and the brain through neural impulses. Keeping specific areas of the spine interference-free helps regulate better your body's healing energy. ❧ High cholesterol should be co-managed between your holistic health care provider and your doctor of functional medicine. Ask your doctors also about cleaning your arteries with chelation therapy and herbal liver cleanses. It may be possible to remove chemical drug intervention and rebalance your cholesterol levels to normal using natural methods along with a well thought out exercise and diet plan. *Seek out a certified Kousouli® Method practitioner to remove spinal stress and align your energy bodies.*

Ailment name	Western Medicine Approach	Alternative Medicine Approach	What you can do at home to take control?	How can Chiropractic Help?
GENERAL WELL BEING Pains and aches are not just "part of getting old". There are many older Americans leading active pain free lives today, despite aging. Healthy habits can slow down the deterioration and help you look and feel decades younger than your peer group. It takes disciplined lifestyle changes, that when implemented, will bring you towards a much more youthful and vibrant you. **ANTI - AGING** Indigenous people routinely live past 78. Many elders of native tribes across the world routinely live past 100 years old. When we are connected to the earth and away from stress, our bodies benefit. Research "blue zones" for more information on living past 100. **Be sure to see your doctor for proper diagnosis and management.**	Routine medical examinations help in prevention. Allows the patient to know if they are within normal ranges for their age, height, and weight. For problems to be found in medical tests or x-rays there already has to be an intrusion on a body system that makes tests show up as positive. Be proactive and prevent disease by caring for your health before emergencies strike. **Functional Medicine; Functional Medical Doctors:** Practitioners that take the 'whole patient' biochemistry into consideration rather than only the part. Co-managing with a holistically minded conservative doctor of functional medicine is important to set the body's natural path back to health. In emergency situations of immediate life or death, medical care should be sought out first. When stabilized, proper daily body maintenance for well-being is best in the hands of alternative medicine practitioners. The more radical choices of drugs and surgery should be considered as last resort.	*Chiropractic:* Number one non-drug natural therapy in the United States. Removes nerve interference. *Acupuncture:* Effects meridian system by opening up chi for body balance. *Naturopaths, Nutritionists, and Herbalists:* Advise whole food nutrition and herbs personalized to your own lifestyle demands. Important for natural alternatives to drugs. *Massage* and *Rolfer Therapists:* Remove scar tissue, improve muscle balance, and aid lymph flow. *Glutathione:* A tri peptide: glutamate, cysteine, and glycine. Most important antioxidant in our body. Boost it by eating cauliflower, Brussels sprouts, broccoli, cabbage, Bioactive non-whey protein, walnuts, taking B6, B12, folate, selenium, milk thistle, turmeric, alpha-lipholic acid (in Brewer's yeast, red meat) or using an acetylcysteine supplement. *Super Fruits: Noni Juice* for digestive health. *Mangosteen* for pain, inflammation, swelling and infection reduction. *Acai Juice* for cellular repair. *Gogi Juice* for liver, kidney, energy, and immune system. *Resveratrol:* In grapes and red wine. Contains anti-inflammatory, anti-cancer, anti-fungal, and anti-aging ingredients.	Stop disrespecting your body with toxic poisons like cigarettes, coffee, and alcohol. Get a daily dose of sun exposure. 10 to 15 minutes is all you need. Avoid overexposure or long periods in blistering sun. Consider working with a nutritionist or naturopath for allergy counseling and heavy metal detox. Eat raw foods rich in active enzymes. Remove all refined sugars, artificial sweeteners, colors, dyes, etc. from diet. Hydrate well (10-12 glasses of water a day) and get 6-8 hours restful sleep. Add a light exercise program to increase oxygen (alkalinity), encourage cardiovascular health and good blood flow. Add the KSS™ stretches in Chapter 8 to your daily regimen. Use powdered Vitamin C. Helps detoxify all molds, including aflotoxin in food. Sprinkle some on all foods prior to eating. Known to help stop infection to disease in its tracks. Stop using any products on your body that are unnatural; including detergents, soaps, colognes, perfumes, sun blocks, etc. **A daily salt scrub and coconut (or olive oil) applied lightly prior to bedtime, helps slow aging of the face.** Switch to a vegan or anti-inflammatory vegetarian diet. Use an alkaline Ph water conversion filter for home and travel use.	Chiropractic has proven safe and effective in removing stress interference and maintaining life sustaining nerve communication from the brain to the body. It helps promote general health and well-being no matter what age, and is a non-intrusive therapy to the body. Chiropractic research studies continue to validate impressive results in improving the life quality of many conditions; not just relief of neck and back pain. ✦ Liver and colon cleansing is imperative for a healthy mind and body. Keep your digestion and elimination in top shape! Adults should have at least two healthy bowel movements a day. Putrid undigested rotting food, heavy metals, parasites, trapped chemicals, and more can hide in the large intestine. A toxic constipated colon is found in all sick people, and ages the body quickly. *Seek out a certified Kousouli® Method practitioner to remove spinal stress and align your energy bodies.*

Ailment name	Western Medicine Approach	Alternative Medicine Approach	What you can do at home to take control?	How can Chiropractic Help?
OSTEOPENIA Osteopenia is a reduction of bone mineral density and the early form of osteoporosis. Countries like the US and Canada tend to have higher rates of osteoporosis. Contrary to popular belief, consuming only high amounts of calcium does not build bones. Strong bones need proper calcium mineralization which depends on Vitamin D3, Vitamin K2, essential minerals, fatty acids, plant-based magnesium and silica, as well as animal forms of saturated fat, and the long-chain omega-3 fatty acids EPA & DHA. **OSTEOPOROSIS** A metabolic disease of progressive bone matrix and cortex thinning, that usually results in hip and vertebral fractures because of bone fragility. Usually seen with post-menopausal females and aging population who do not get adequate D3 and Vitamin K, exercise, or outdoor sunshine. Also can be caused by hyperparathyroidism, hyperthyroidism, diabetes, kidney disease, hepatic problems, malignancy, pancreatic problems, absorption issues, medication overdose (corticosteroid use), heparin and aluminum containing antacids. Six times more likely to be seen in females than males. **Be sure to see your doctor for proper diagnosis and management.**	*Dexa Scan, X-rays, Ultrasonography:* Usual tests for osteoporosis diagnosis. Other lab tests also checked: Comprehensive metabolic panel, thyroid stimulating hormone, complete blood count, serum proteins, 25-hydroxy vitamin D, electrophoresis, urine calcium, and calcium phosphate test. *(ERT) Estrogen Replacement Therapy; Estrogen:* Helps with bone resorption rate. Risky, must be monitored as it may increase risk of breast cancer, cardiac problems, and strokes. *Testosterone Therapy:* Could be beneficial for men; however must monitor PSA levels. *Bisphosphanates: Alendronate (Fosamax):* Some doctors claim these help with bone loss, but holistic experts warn of leg fracture, stomach pain, trouble swallowing, muscle pain, and jaw osteonecrosis risk with their use. *Raloxifene:* Inhibits bone resorption. *Teriparatide:* Stimulates bone formation. *Calcitonin:* Increases bone density.	*Vitamin D3* and *Vitamin K2:* For bone protein formation. Vital for strong bones. *Selenium* and *Boron:* Improves calcium absorption. *Copper:* aids in bone formation. *Coral Calcium, Magnesium, Silica* and *Phosphorus:* Help bone strength. Avoid too much phosphorus (moves calcium from bones into blood). *Methylsulfonylmethane (MSM):* A natural bioavailable form of sulfur; an essential trace mineral which nourishes joints and reduces inflammation. *Omega 3 Fatty Acids (EPA / DHA):* Increases anti-inflammatory prostaglandins. Fish oils like cod liver oil in combination with primrose oil and calcium, may increase bone density and slow bone loss rate. *Vitamin A* and *E:* Provide faster healing. *Multivitamin B Complex including B6, B 12, Folic Acid, and Choline:* All helpful. *Soy Isoflavanoids:* Estrogen may help encourage bone mass. *Alfalfa, Yucca, Dandelion root,* and *Black Cohosh*: Help build stronger bones.	Lifestyle modification is imperative. Immediately stop smoking, alcohol, caffeine, and eliminate sodas of any kind. The phosphoric acid in sodas eats away calcium and speeds up bone loss. Eat foods high in sulfur: asparagus, bok choy, broccoli, garlic, and tofu. Vitamin K; found in kale, dandelion greens, collards, spinach, and turnips. Cucumbers, celery, bell peppers, horsetail, nettles, oat straw and alfalfa contain silica which is good for bones. Sea vegetables such as kelp and sea algae like chlorella are also fantastic sources of bone-building nutrients. Pink salts and Himalayan sea salt have ideal mineral ratios for building bone. Remove commercialized white table salt. Non-commercial raw cheese is possibly the best bone building, cardio-protective food you could consume. Great source of magnesium is raw organic cacao. Work and live in an area where you have sunlight coming in. Get daily sun exposure to activate vitamin D in your body. As little as 5 to 10 minutes a day suffices. Do weight bearing exercises three times a week. 20 minutes or more each session is all you need. Add a daily exercise program and the KSS™ stretches in Chapter 8 to your daily regimen.	Chiropractors focus on disease prevention and inhibition of disease progression. Osteoporosis could result in thoracic fractures causing an overly pronounced forward curvature (a kyphosis) called a dowager's hump. In cases where bone fragility is suspect, the doctor will use gentle low-force or modified maneuvers to safely align your spine. ❦ Co-manage your case with a doctor of functional medicine, and a qualified holistic nutritionist. Osteoporosis is both preventable and treatable. *Seek out a certified Kousouli® Method practitioner to remove spinal stress and align your energy bodies.*

Ailment name	Western Medicine Approach	Alternative Medicine Approach	What you can do at home to take control?	How can Chiropractic Help?
NEURALGIA (Nerve Pain) Pain that is felt anywhere along the path of a nerve. Pain or loss of function is a normal signal in reaction to stress overload. When nerve pathways become hindered or blocked, symptoms (paresthesias) occur: lack of feeling, increased sensation, numbness, burning, tingling, electric shock, stabbing, or pins-and-needles sensations. Pain may be mild or extreme, and be given a diagnosis such as Shingles, Bell's Palsy (motor neuron lesion of facial 7th cranial nerve), Carpel Tunnel (median nerve pressure), Sciatica (pain along the sciatic nerve down the back of the pelvis and thigh), Brachial plexus (neck, shoulder and arm), or Lumbar plexus (low back) radiculitis. Your body tells you that something is wrong and makes you pay attention. Complications of neuralgia can be serious. Permanent disability, paralysis, or chronic pain results if untreated. Diabetic neuropathy if not traumatic and gradual, could be stemming from underlying vascular disease such as diabetes, stroke, transient ischemic attack, or multiple sclerosis. **Be sure to see your doctor for proper diagnosis and management.**	***Non-Steroidal Anti-Inflammatory Drugs (NSAIDs); Aspirin, Ibuprofen, Topical Nerve Blocks* and *Local Anesthetics:*** Aim to block or numb nerve pain temporarily. ***Corticosteroids; Prednisolone, Prednisone,* or *Dexamethasone.*** For pain; use short-term as long term use has side effects. ***Analgesics; Codeine; Fentanyl (Duragesic, Actiq), Oxycodone (OxyContin). Antiviral Medications:*** Reduce the recurrence of post-herpetic neuralgia. ***Antidepressants: Tricyclic Antidepressants (TCAs) Amitriptyline (Elatrol):*** Side effects include dizziness, constipation, dry mouth, blurry vision, sexual dysfunction, weight gain, and drowsiness. ***Anticonvulsants; Gabapentin (Neurontin), Carbamazepine (Tegretol).*** ***Morphine:*** Addictive opiate. Blocks pain fast for serious pain cases. ***Nerve Conduction Velocity*** and ***Electromyography (EMG):*** Help detect nerve signal strength and activity. ***Magnetic Resonance Imaging (MRI), Computed Tomography (CT)* with *Myelogram:*** For spinal cord compression or stenosis diagnosis. ***Surgery*** is done for extreme carpal tunnel, trigeminal neuralgia, or chronic nerve pains.	***Vitamin B Complex* with *Niacinamide* (form of *B3*):** Pain reliever. ***Pyridoxine (B6):*** Reduces inflammation. ***Folic Acid (B9), Cobalamin (B12):*** Aid in immune system function and maintain nerve cell health. ***Vitamin C, E,* and *Gamma-Linolenic Acid (GLA):*** Help repair nerve damage. ***Choline* and *Inositol:*** Aid in the transmission of nerve impulses. ***Capsaicin Cream:*** For migraines, arthritis, shingles, or neuropathy; active component in chile pepper. ***Chamomile Tea:*** Anti-inflammatory relaxing tea. ***Boswellia* and *Gotu Kola:*** Potent anti-inflammatory herbs shown to help pain. ***Willow Bark (Salix Alba):*** Most effective natural pain reliever; controls inflammation; active compound is salicylic acid. ***Kava Kava root, Turmeric, St. John's Wort,* and *Devil's Claw:*** Alleviate nerve pain and inflammation. ***Alpha Lipoic Acid (ALA):*** Helps treat peripheral nerve damage and helps control blood sugar. ***Licorice root, Arnica,* and *Bromelain:*** Contain powerful anti-inflammatory properties. ***L-AcetylCarnitine:*** Alleviates pain and aids nerve fiber regeneration.	Damage to nerves can take much time to heal. Cold or hot packs can help control pain. No coffee or alcohol. Meditation, massage, rest, pure nutrition, hydration, toxin removal, and sleep are all very important. For carpal tunnel; when typing, support wrists with gel cushions or use a wrist brace. A transcutaneous electrical nerve stimulation unit (TENS) can temporarily relieve pain. Men; avoid tight belts which disrupt lower body nerve flow, and do not sit on your wallet (in the back pocket) as this leads to low back and sciatic pain. Add a daily exercise program and the KSS™ stretches in Chapter 8 to your daily regimen; helps you maintain fluid motion of the (CSF) cerebrospinal fluid and stimulates mechano-receptors, blocking nociceptic pain signals.	Chiropractic is excellent for care of nerve imbalances utilizing the skeletal and surrounding muscular system to rebalance and structurally align the human frame; naturally helps **Thoracic Outlet Syndrome (TOS)**, **Brachial plexus** (traction trauma), **Sciatica, Carpel Tunnel,** or **Lumbar Plexus neuralgias**. For **Bell's Palsy**, your Chiropractor will look to the facial nerve path and stylomastoid foramen. Chiropractic adjustment of the **Cranial Bones, Occiput, C1,** and **C2** usually bring relief through improved nerve flow. In many cases, the cause of neuralgia is unknown, however it may be caused by pressure on nerves by nearby bones, ligaments, blood vessels, or tumors, trauma, surgery medications (such as paclitaxel, cisplatin, or vincristine), porphyria, chronic renal insufficiency, chemical irritation, diabetes, infections, Lyme disease, Syphilis, Herpes Zoster (shingles), and HIV. *Seek out a certified Kousouli® Method practitioner to remove spinal stress and align your energy bodies.*

Ailment name	Western Medicine Approach	Alternative Medicine Approach	What you can do at home to take control?	How can Chiropractic Help?
ADHD / ADD Attention Deficit Hyperactivity Disorder (ADHD) or Attention Deficit Disorder (ADD) is a disorder that usually appears in early childhood prior to age 7 and is more frequently seen in males. Characteristics of ADHD / ADD are: Poor impulse control, disorganization, inattention, inability to focus, poor ability to complete tasks or pay attention to details. **AUTISM** Autism may be caused by gene mutation, and environmental factors influencing early brain development. Characteristics of autism are verbal and nonverbal communication difficulties in social interaction, and repetitive behaviors. **Be sure to see your doctor for proper diagnosis and management.**	***Stimulants; Methylphenidate (Ritalin):*** Similar to morphine or cocaine in its effects. ***Dextroamphetamine (Adderall):*** Increases catecholamine release from presynaptic neurons. Some side effects include: insomnia, headache, irritability, lowered appetite, high blood pressure, suicidal thoughts, nervous system disturbances, and uneven heartbeats. ***Dopamine Reuptake Inhibitors; Bupropion (Wellbutrin):*** Block the action of the dopamine transporter; used in treating mood disorders like ADHD. ***Selective Serotonin Reuptake Inhibitors (SSRIs); Fluoxetine (Prozac):*** Antidepressants that treat OCD, anxiety, and autism.	***Omega 3 Fatty Acids (EPA / DHA):*** Increases anti-inflammatory prostaglandins (ex. Cod Liver Oil). ***GAMA and Zinc:*** Help in regulation of Dopamine, GABA, and Serotonin. ***Calcium and Magnesium:*** Give a calming effect to the body. ***CoQ10:*** Supports adrenal glands and improves brain function. ***Ginko Biloba:*** Protects brain by removing free radicals. ***Lipoic Acid (Thiotic Acid), Phosphatidylserine, N-acetyl-cysteine, Choline*** and ***Inositol:*** Help improve brain function. ***Taurine:*** Immune regulator. ***S-adenosylmethionine (SAMe):*** Mood enhancer and antidepressant. Helps relieve stress. ***Vitamin B Complex*** with ***Niacin (B3):*** Supports brain health. Avoid niacin in cases of gout or very high blood pressure. ***Vitamins C and E:*** Antioxidants. ***Acetylcholine:*** Helps attention and memory improve. ***Chromium:*** Helps maintain stable blood sugar. ***Methylsulfonyl-Methane (MSM):*** Helps body build new cells and remove toxins. ***Grape Seed Extract:*** Antioxidant. Neutralizes free radicals in the bloodstream. Do not take with vitamin C. ***Liquid Zeolite:*** Safe, natural detoxifier formed from volcanic lava and ocean water; helps neutralize heavy metal toxins.	The "brain chemical imbalance" concept given to patients is false. There are no tests to prove a chemical imbalance. Removing toxic pollutants, food allergies, and impurities are the key to improvement. However, parents must act quickly and be merciless in administering lifestyle and diet cleansing once the child is diagnosed. Many experts point to heavy metal mercury poisoning from vaccines (thimerosal) or dental amalgams as the main contributing factor. Family dynamics and emotional support also play important roles in therapy. A raw clean diet is essential for recovery: Go gluten and casein free (GF/CF Diet), wheat free, dairy free. Avoid shellfish with high mercury levels. Do not eat out of canned foods, any fried foods, lunch meats, or other processed foods. Eat citrus fruits and foods rich in iron, walnuts, vegetables leafy greens, Brewer's yeast, and brown rice. No fast food. Do not consume any of these food additives or ingredients: GMO's, artificial flavorings or sweeteners, Aspartame (NutraSweet), Butylated Hydroxyanisole (BHA), Acesulfame Potassium, Butylated Hydroxytoluene (BHT), Blue1, Blue 2, Green3, Red 3, Red 40, Yellow 5, Yellow 6, Casein - Sodium Caseinate, High-Fructose Corn Syrup, Olestra (Olean), Potassium Bromate, Propyl Gallate, Partially Hydrogenated Oil, Saccharin, Sodium Nitrate, Sodium Nitrite, or MSG. Switch to a vegan or anti-inflammatory vegetarian diet.	Proper brain to body nerve flow is crucial. Research indicates life quality improvement, lessening of nerve stress and symptoms with upper cervical chiropractic techniques. **Ask your Chiropractor about Upper Cervical Adjustments, Occiput, Atlas C1, and Axis C2 to C7.** ❦ Ask a qualified holistic nutritionist or naturopath about food allergy testing and diet modification. Do a liver, kidney, and heavy metal detox (Test for mercury, thallium and lead poisoning); commonly found in autistic children. Check for parasites: Ascarius worm infestation from pets; hookworm, strongyloids, trichinellas; can enter the brain. Check for leaky gut syndrome, candida albicans (yeast syndrome) overgrowth and celiac disease (also known as gluten intolerance). *Seek out a certified Kousouli® Method practitioner to remove spinal stress and align your energy bodies.*

BE A MASTER® OF MAXIMUM HEALING © by Theodoros Kousouli D.C., CHt.

Ailment name	Western Medicine Approach	Alternative Medicine Approach	What you can do at home to take control?	How can Chiropractic Help?
SCOLIOSIS Idiopathic scoliosis is a condition of an unknown cause that makes the spine curve in an abnormal sideways "S" or "C" shaped curve. Congenital scoliosis is caused by a failure of the vertebrae to form normally, and is present from birth. Neuromuscular scoliosis is from a neuromuscular condition such as myopathy, cerebral palsy, or spina bifida. Scoliosis can also form after osteoporotic vertebral fracture or spinal cord trauma. Scoliosis is a progressive lifetime neuromusculoskeletal disease most common in adolescent girls. The disease can be psychologically detrimental, with visible disfigurement and pain. Scoliosis should be co-managed between your Chiropractor and Orthopedist. All natural options and holistic treatment programs should be exhausted before deciding on surgery. There are surgical and non-surgical bracing options that may help. **Be sure to see your doctor for proper diagnosis and management.**	*Bracing:* Hard brace and flexible options; usually very awkward and uncomfortable for patients. Should be tried prior to surgery. *Surgery:* Bones may be intentionally fused, and stainless steel rods are screwed permanently under the skin next to the spine leading to vastly decreased range of motion. Surgery can be complex and may need several steps to get the desired results. Complications after surgery, lack of structural integrity, osteoarthritis, and degenerative joint disease may accelerate. Periodic scoliosis screenings done by grade schools or youth groups may help catch the problem early prior to further disfiguration, and allow enough time for conservative treatment, further monitoring, bracing, and stretching. Abnormal spinal curves over 40 degrees may require more aggressive measures (average pre-operative scoliosis is about 62-72 degrees). Abnormal curvatures, between 20 and 40 degrees, should be sent for orthopedic evaluation and possible bracing, though is still within the conservative management range to utilize conservative chiropractic care.	Non-surgical techniques of *Chiropractic Spinal Biophysics.* A specialization within chiropractic care dealing with mirror-image posture correction, and body symmetry. CBP Chiropractic has seen amazing results with treating scoliosis and is well researched and documented in making changes in spinal curvature. Scoliosis patients should seek out this care first. *Rolfing* and *Deep Tissue Spinal Massage:* Release scar tissue of tightly associated ligaments, tendons, and musculature to aid lymph function, support the framework, and increase range of motion. *Acupuncture:* Helps movement of innate energy / Qi and related curvature pain. Add a *Daily Exercise Program* and the *KSS™ Stretches* in Chapter 8 to your daily regimen. See *Neuralgia, Nerve Pain section* for relief from pain associated with side effects of scoliosis. See *Osteoporosis section* for nutrition tips to build strong bones.	Periodic scoliosis screenings as a child grows is important. Parents can take immediate action. Check your child. With shirt off and their shorts lowered from waist to mid buttock level, stand four feet in back of your child and ask them to slowly bend forward from a standing position to a forward flexed position, until their hands touch the floor. Have them slowly come back up. Repeat the procedure viewing the spine from the front and the side. Any rib humping or sideway distortion away from the body midline, should be examined by your Chiropractor. Teens or adults with scoliosis should maintain chiropractic care throughout their lifetime, not only to slow down progression, but to also benefit from increased flexibility and overall well-being. Always use both shoulder straps with backpacks. Posture pumps, stretches, traction devices, hang bars, or inversion tables suggested by your doctor may help in aiding your therapy.	Serious neurological and pathological causes must first be ruled out, and congenital anomalies assessed. **Curves less than 20 and up to 40 degrees may be kept from worsening, or improved, with proper chiropractic care.** Specific spinal adjustments; cervical and lumbar lordosis restoration, (must be addressed) neuromuscular re-education; isometric exercises; proprioceptive rehabilitation, ligament / muscle rehabilitation, and vibration therapy, are utilized by CBP practitioners. Care is based on freeing up needed movement in tight segments, leveling the pelvis and sacrum, and providing strict exercise regimens. Stretching the muscles on the concave side of the curve, and strengthening muscles on the convex side of the curve, should be a daily routine. Patient must be vigilant in maintaining good postural habits as doctor monitors progression of curvature. *Seek out a certified Kousouli® Method practitioner to remove spinal stress and align your energy bodies.*

Ailment name	Western Medicine Approach	Alternative Medicine Approach	What you can do at home to take control?	How can Chiropractic Help?
MULTIPLE SCLEROSIS An autoimmune patchy demyelination (scarring of the myelin sheath covering in the white matter of the central nervous system; brain, optic nerve, and spinal cord. When the myelin is lost, the neurons cannot conduct electrical signals, thus creating miscommunication between nerve endings. About 35,000 are affected in the U.S. yearly. Mostly affects individuals of Western European decent living in temperate zones. Patient is usually under 55 and presents with numbness, tingling, dizziness, diplopia, urinary sphincter issues (urgency or hesitancy), or weakness that resolves over a few days with similar events happening in the past. May be symptom free for years with the event re-occurring. **Be sure to see your doctor for proper diagnosis and management.**	*Lab Tests: Brain* and *Spinal MRI* will show multifocal areas of patchy demyelination as white matter lesions and M.S. plaques. Blood results will show mild lymphocytosis. Rule out lupus, ischemia, Epstein Bar virus, and chlamydia pneumonia as symptoms could be similar to M.S. *Lumbar Puncture* a.k.a. *Spinal Tap:* Attains cerebral spinal fluid (CSF); the fluid that surrounds the brain and spinal cord for diagnosis. Positive diagnosis of the CSF will show a high protein content, Immunoglobin G, and oligoclonal bands in the CSF. *Corticosteroids:* For acute attacks of M.S. to calm down flare-ups. Prednisolone or prednisone, dexamethasone. Using long term has serious side effects. *Interferon* or *Glatiramer Acetate Immunosuppresants*: Long term use leads to increased risk of malignancy and infection. *Benzodiazepines; Tizanidine (Zanaflex):* Helps reduce spasms.	*Vitamin A, Vitamin B Complex* with *Pyridoxine (B6), Cobalamin (B12), Vitamin E, C* with *Bioflavanoids, Vitamin D3, Selenium, Gamma – Linolenic Acid (GLA), Primrose Oil, Omega-3 Essential Fatty Acid Complex,* and *FlaxSeed Oil:* Promote immune system function and maintain nerve cell health. *Omega 3* and *6 Fatty Acids (EPA / DHA):* Increases anti-inflammatory prostaglandins. Ex. Cod Liver Oil. *Coenzyme Q12:* Strengthens immune system and improves oxygenation for cells. *Methylsulfonyl-Methane (MSM):* Helps body build new cells and remove toxins. *Garlic:* Excellent sulfur source for nerve health. *L-glycine:* Supports myelin sheaths. *Free-Form Amino Acid Complex:* Helps nutrients for brain function get absorbed. *Cannabis:* THC (tetrahydrocannabinol), an active ingredient in marijuana reported to help ease muscle spasms in some people with MS. *Liquid Zeolite:* Safe, natural detoxifier formed from volcanic lava and ocean water; helps neutralize heavy metal toxins.	Many experts point to long term heavy metal poisoning from vaccines or dental amalgam fillings as a possible root cause. Chronic emotional stress and malnutrition are believed to play a big role in development of the disease. Remove all dairy and gluten. No junk or fast food; Do not consume food additives, artificial flavorings, colors, or sweeteners, Ex. Aspartame (found in NutraSweet) and MSG; Eat a diet low in saturated fats (< 10 grams / day) and high in polyunsaturated fatty acids using metabolic enzymes to help supply nutrients for oligodendrocytes. Consider purchasing a magnetic mattress pad, remove all metal in dental work, and look into fluoride water removal systems for your home. Smoking increases risk; stop smoking. Stressful living exacerbates M.S. symptoms. Practice daily meditation and relax the mind. Add a daily exercise program and the KSS™ stretches in Chapter 8 to your daily regimen. Switch to a vegan or anti-inflammatory vegetarian diet. Use an alkaline Ph water conversion filter for home and travel use.	Proper brain to body nerve flow is crucial. Research indicates life quality improvement, lessening of nerve stress and symptoms with upper cervical chiropractic techniques. **Ask your Chiropractor about Cranial Adjustments, Occiput, Atlas C1, and Axis C2.** Co-manage your case with a neurologist and / or doctor of functional medicine. ⚜ Talk to your holistic nutritionist or naturopath about doing kidney, liver, gallbladder, colon, candida, and parasite cleanses; Look into chelation therapy for heavy metal cleansing, (which could be connected to symptoms mimicking or contributing to MS). Research further the possible benefits of magnetic healing, blood electrification, 35% food grade hydrogen peroxide therapy, oxygen, and ozone therapy. *Seek out a certified Kousouli® Method practitioner to remove spinal stress and align your energy bodies.*

Ailment name	Western Medicine Approach	Alternative Medicine Approach	What you can do at home to take control?	How can Chiropractic Help?
DIABETES **Type I Diabetes**, Insulin Dependent-Diabetes Mellitus [IDDM] is thought to be an autoimmune disease characterized by failure of insulin production. Some claim parasites, viruses, mold or fungus cause major metabolic disturbances that lead to diabetes. **Type II Diabetes**, Non-Insulin Dependent Diabetes Mellitus [NIDDM] or Age-Onset Diabetes is more common, and due to a decrease capacity of utilizing the body's insulin. Symptoms include increased thirst, urination, hunger, weight loss, fatigue, blurry vision, and slow healing infections. Obesity and high blood cholesterol are the two most important causative factors for Type II Diabetes. A third type, or **Gestational Diabetes**, is sometimes seen in pregnant women. Many people who have been considered diabetic have resolved their dis-ease naturally, and you can also; if you take serious control of your diet and lifestyle choices. **Be sure to see your doctor for proper diagnosis and management.**	*Lab Tests: Oral Glucose Tolerance Test (OGTT)* (>200/mg/dL), *Fasting Glucose Test* (>126/mg/dL), and the *A1C Test* (6.5% or higher). Blood glucose monitoring is done with a glucometer and managed through prescription drugs or synthetic insulin. *Type 1 diabetics* require insulin injections or insulin pumps. *Type 2 diabetics* use drugs to bring blood sugar levels back to normal. *Acarbose (Precose), Glimepiride (Amaryl), Glipizide (Glucotrol), or Sitagliptin (Januvia).* *Tricyclic Antidepressants; Amitriptyline (Vanatrip):* May affect neurotransmitters in the brain to ease associated depression and relieve painful diabetic neuropathy. *See Neuralgia, Nerve Pain section for more pain relief options.*	*Alpha Lipoic Acid:* Helps control blood sugar and treat peripheral nerve damage. *Pyroxidoxine Alpha-Ketoglutarate (PAK-B6):* Improves glucose tolerance. *Biotin (B7):* Reduces pains associated with diabetic neuropathy and improves glucose tolerance. *Chromium Picolinate:* Known to improve glucose tolerance. *Cinnamon Oil, Garlic, and Onion:* Stabilizes blood sugar levels for Type 2 diabetes, while providing immunity and circulation support. *Inositol:* Deficient in diabetics; assists with fat metabolism. *L-Carnitine:* Helps mobilize fats. *L-Glutamine:* Helps reduce sugar cravings. *Taurine:* Aids in insulin release. *Asian Ginseng:* Increases insulin receptors and production of insulin. *Magnesium:* Improves insulin production. *Coenzyme Q10:* Helps the body through carbohydrate metabolism. *Aloe Vera Juice:* Helps lower blood sugar levels. *Neem Leaves, Bittermelon, and Fenugreek seeds:* May increase the number of insulin receptors in red blood cells. *Gingko Biloba:* Helps circulation. *Betaine Hydrochloride* with *Pepsin:* Helps diabetics digest protein and absorb minerals; diabetics usually do not make enough stomach acid. *Capsaicin:* For migraines, arthritis, shingles, or neuropathy; active component in chile pepper. *Nigella Sativa (Black Seed a.k.a. Black Cumin):* Use in food as an oil to strengthen the immune system.	Stop drinking all liquor and stop smoking. Cut back on caffeinated coffee and tea. Proper diet is crucial for diabetes patients. Diabetics have poor fat metabolism as well as poor sugar metabolism. Take digestive enzymes; drink 1 tbsp. raw apple cider vinegar with meal. No processed foods. Stop consuming white flour products (increases risk of diabetes), trans fats, hydrogenated oils, white sugar (replace sugar use with small amounts of manuka honey). Get plenty of fiber. Avoid artificial sweeteners; they're polluted with wood alcohol (methanol). Try a Vegan diet. Include olive oil, figs, cinnamon, avocados, and apples in your diet. Add a daily exercise program and the KSS™ stretches in Chapter 8 to your daily regimen. Avoid meat heavy diet.	Proper brain to pancreas nerve flow is crucial. Research indicates life quality improvement, lessening of stress and symptoms with chiropractic techniques. **Ask your Chiropractor about Cranial Adjustments, Occiput, Atlas C1, Axis C2; and T7 to T9.** Your Chiropractor can co-manage your care with your functional medical doctor or endocrinologist. ❦ Your optometrist can check your eyes and screen for neuropathy, as signs of diabetes may also be found in a routine eye exam. Diabetics should get checked for parasites and mold toxins. Parasites disrupt, or utilize, the body's insulin causing symptoms. A common pancreatic fluke parasite, Eurytrema pancreaticum (harbors the HA virus), the fluke of beef and dairy cattle, usually finds its way into the human pancreas. Parasite eggs can be seen in blood, semen, breast milk, or any organ. Eurytrema will not settle and multiply in our pancreas without the presence of wood alcohol (methanol). The mycotoxin Kojic Acid mold (found in coffee and potato skins) has also been found to be toxic to the pancreas. *Seek out a certified Kousouli® Method practitioner to remove spinal stress and align your energy bodies.*

Ailment name	Western Medicine Approach	Alternative Medicine Approach	What you can do at home to take control?	How can Chiropractic Help?
OBESITY Obesity is caused by abnormal fat, or adipose tissue deposition in the body. It is mostly caused by a sedentary lifestyle and bad dietary habits. Obesity may also be a symptom of other underlying disease conditions like thyroid problems or type II Diabetes. Be cautious of quick fix products. Patients should be interested in making long term lifestyle changes. The goal to controlling and reversing obesity will require a team of support (doctors, a counselor, nutritionist, and physical trainer). **Be sure to see your doctor for proper diagnosis and management.**	*Prescription Drugs:* For weight control; however, when medication is stopped, the weight returns. *Orlistat (Xenical):* Blocks digestion and absorption of fat. Side effects include: Frequent oily bowel movements, urgency, and gas. *Phentermine, (Suprenza, Adipex-P), Phentermine-topiramate (Qsymia):* Side effects include: Hand and foot tingling, insomnia, dizziness, dry mouth, constipation, increased heart rate, suicidal thoughts, problems with memory or comprehension, sleep disorders, and changes to vision. *Lorcaserin (Belviq):* Affects chemicals in your brain that decrease your appetite and make you feel full. *Surgery:* *Gastrointestinal Bypass:* Risky and invasive; yet effective. *Laparoscopic Adjustable Gastric Banding (LAGB):* Less invasive, most popular. *Gastric Sleeve:* Some of the stomach is removed, creating a smaller pocket for food. *Biliopancreatic Diversion* with *Duodenal Switch:* Most of the stomach is surgically removed; greater risk of vitamin deficiency and malnutrition.	*Detoxification, Colon Cleansing:* Removes toxic debris. Bowel obstruction is one of the most common reasons for obesity, constipation, intestinal scaring, and stagnation in the 18-25 feet of intestinal tract. *Green Coffee Bean Extract:* Contains chlorogenic acid, which inhibits the release of glucose and increases the metabolic liver process to help shed pounds. *Garcinia Cambogia Extract, Conjugated Linoleic Acid (CLA), Chromium Picolinate, Glucomannan, Guarana, Guar Gum, Ginseng, Hydroxycitric Acid (HCA), Beta Glucan, and Mango Seed Fiber:* Shown significant promise in addressing weight loss. *Bitter Orange:* Used in treating constipation, indigestion, heartburn, and promotes weight loss. *Fucoxanthin:* Fat burning carotenoid found in wakame and red seaweed. *Dehydroepiandrosterone (DHEA):* Steroid hormone; may help body fat reduction. *Chitosan:* Disrupts lipid uptake and blocks body's response to hunger. *Hoodia Gordonii:* Popular natural weight loss herb from South African succulent plant; used for centuries to suppress appetite. *Oolong* and *Green Tea* are favorites among dieters. Recommended Reading: **BE A MASTER® OF SELF IMAGE** for more helpful tips on improving self esteem and body image.	A strict and intelligent detox, diet, and regular exercise program is required to burn fat cells and keep away obesity. Keep active! Join a gym, do aerobic exercise programs, and add the KSS™ workout in chapter 8 to your daily regimen. Stop all greasy, fatty, fried junk foods, alcohol, smoking, wheat, dairy, refined sugar, and artificial flavor intake immediately! Avoid antibiotic use which kills normal intestinal flora and upsets intestinal health. Supplement with probiotics (lactobacillus acidophilus), hydrate well, use digestive enzymes, drink raw apple cider vinegar, eat dark green vegetables, drink liquid chlorophyll, eat dulse flakes, mung beans, adzuki beans, broccoli, kale, cauliflower, spirulina, tofu, ginger, laminaria (kelp), sargassum seaweed, use psyllium, flaxseed, red pepper (capsaicin), triphala, and cinnamon in your diet. Eat for energy; do not eat emotionally by feeling guilty or shameful. Do daily abdominal self-massage (clockwise motion) to encourage peristaltic movement of food through intestines. Also consider Rolfing, a deep organ massage technique for breaking up adhesions; improves organ function and intestinal flow. Try hypnosis for weight loss and sugar detox.	There is usually a spinal connection or nerve interference issue with the digestive and intestinal systems. **Ask your Chiropractor about adjusting Occiput, C1, C2 and the associated gastrointestinal spinal areas and T5-S5 / coccygeal n.** pertaining to your condition for stimulation of the stomach, liver, small and large intestines, rectum, and colon. A congested liver, gallbladder, and large intestine are almost always compromised in obesity. See a holistic nutritionist and doctor of functional medicine for toxic heavy metal removal (could be connected to a thyroid condition). Check for leaky gut syndrome, candida albicans (yeast syndrome) overgrowth, and celiac disease (gluten intolerance). Do a liver, gallbladder, colon, and parasite cleanse which may lead to weight loss; this along with chiropractic care will lessen stress on your spine and joints. Remove all nonprescription and prescription drugs if possible, and look into the benefits of removing chlorine and fluoride from your water. *Seek out a certified Kousouli® Method practitioner to remove spinal stress and align your energy bodies.*

Ailment name	Western Medicine Approach	Alternative Medicine Approach	What you can do at home to take control?	How can Chiropractic Help?
CANCER When abnormal (malignant), cells in the body grow uncontrollably. Lymphoma (cancer of the lymph system), Leukemia (blood tissues), Sarcoma (muscle tissue), or Carcinoma; cancer affecting organs, glands, skin, and mucus membranes. Cancer is considered a disconnect of the body (diet and toxicity), mind (stress), and/or spirit (purpose). Re-connecting to your joy and happiness, letting go of anger, resentment, hate, or feelings of stress, changes the cell environment and adds to a positive spirit that allows cancer reversal. Treatment varies in type, location, cause, depth, and duration. **Be sure to see your doctor for proper diagnosis and management.**	*Surgery, Chemotherapy, Radiation Therapy,* and occasionally even *Amputation* of the affected area or organ. There is no single or standard test for cancer, only screenings that catch progressed cancer. Colonoscopy for colon cancer, mammography for breast cancer, (women should get preventative and safer thermography instead of mammography), PSA for prostate cancer, and the Pap smear for cervical cancer detection. When patients are told that there are no more cancer cells in their bodies after treatment, it does not mean they are 100% cancer-free. It only means the tests are unable to detect the cancer cells. Chemotherapy and ionizing radiation are proven to cause cancer or make cancer worse. These methods also harm healthy tissues. Being diagnosed with cancer indicates the patient has multiple nutritional deficiencies due to environment, lifestyle, or diet. Measures to starve only cancer cells, and build healthy cells should occur along with hyperthermia treatments.	Research the following popular natural anti-cancer treatments: *Inositol Hexaphosphate or Phytic Acid (IP6)* in beans, wheat bran, corn, brown rice, cereal grains, sesame seeds, and other high fiber foods. *Flor-Essence Tea, Essiac Tea, Mung Bean Tea* (without sugar); *Intravenous Vitamin C, Laetrile Injectable Shots* also known as *Vitamin B17, Amigdalina B-17* found in the kernels of apricots, peaches, and almonds; *35% 'Food Grade' Hydrogen Peroxide Therapy, Cannabis oil, Electronic Blood Purification, UV, Magnetic Mattress Pads, Oxygen, and Ozone Therapy.* *Organic Coffee Enemas:* Detoxifies liver, unloads toxins from the body. *Castor Oil:* Massage into the skin; relieves arthritis, gallbladder and liver congestion, inflammation, and pain associated with cancer. *Brown Sesame Butter:* Reported to be effective for treating leukemia. *Glutathione:* Most important antioxidant in our body. Naturally found in walnuts. *Alkaline Drink Mix:* ½ tablespoon *Sodium Bicarbonate, Non-Aluminum Baking Soda* (not powder) mixed with 2 tablespoons fresh lemon juice and 12 ounces purified water daily helps alkalize the blood and body.	Vaccines, processed and genetically modified food, chemicals in our air, food, and water, chlorine, fluoride, prescription drugs, pesticides, herbicides; all cause cancer. Immediately stop anything that taxes the body's cleanup systems: cigarettes, alcohol, and products with toxic chemicals: detergents, soaps, colognes, perfumes, and fluoridated toothpaste. Cut out dairy, sugar, and artificial sweeteners. Substitute with a little manuka honey or black molasses if you must. Use full spectrum mineral sea salt, not bleached white table salt. Instead of drinking cow milk (has hormones, antibiotics, and produces mucus) try unsweetened rice milk or almond milk. Follow a raw food diet. Don't eat pork or red meats (create an acidic environment that cancer thrives on). Change your diet to 80% fresh vegetables or pure juice (eat live enzymes), whole grains, fruits, nuts, and seeds. Do not use any products containing propyl alcohol. Avoid bread in plastics, crackers, dried fruits, and tea bags which may have mold. Do not eat mold-fermented cheeses or peanut butter (contain carcinogenic mold aflotoxin). Cancer cannot live in an alkaline or well oxygenated environment. Alkalize the body, bringing pH up for healing. Drink 12 glasses minimum reverse osmosis ionic water daily, and invest in a chloride and fluoride home removal system, a magnetic mattress pad, and electromagnetic frequency (EMF) blockers. Switch to a vegan or anti-inflammatory vegetarian diet. Avoid meat.	Gentle chiropractic care de-stresses the nervous system and provides cancer patients an active lifestyle. **Ask your Chiropractor about adjusting Occiput, C1, C2** and the associated spinal areas pertaining to your condition. Co-manage with your oncologist, doctor of functional medicine, nutritionist, naturopath or other holistic provider. Talk to your doctors about doing kidney, liver, colon, candida, and parasite cleansing. Do chelation therapy for heavy metal cleansing (ex. cadmium and mercury), which could be a contributing cause of the cancer. Look into aflotoxin toxicity; Zearalenone (ZEN, ZEA, RAL, and F-2): A mold mycoestrogen toxin that grows in wet grains. Can contaminate grain, processed foods, meat, dairy products, and may increase breast cancer risk. *Seek out a certified Kousouli® Method practitioner to remove spinal stress and align your energy bodies.*

Ailment name	Western Medicine Approach	Alternative Medicine Approach	What you can do at home to take control?	How can Chiropractic Help?
PARKINSON'S DISEASE A progressive disorder of the central nervous system (usually age 45 to 65), due to degeneration of the nigrostriatal system (substantia nigra), which signals the basal ganglia (putamen and caudate nucleus) to secrete dopamine. Lack of dopamine (affecting its imbalance with acetylcholine) allows the basal ganglia to send constant excitatory signals to the corticospinal motor control system. Parkinson's is evaluated by doctor observation, patient's subjective description of symptoms, and using the Unified Parkinson's Disease Rating Scale (UPDRS). Symptoms include rigidity, bradykinesia, tremor, and unilateral walking difficulty. Also associated: memory loss, slurred speech, depression, loss of motivation, illegible handwriting, difficulty rising from a chair, fatigue, insomnia, spinal pain, and weight loss. **Be sure to see your doctor for proper diagnosis and management.**	*Imaging:* CT Scan, MRI, and laboratory tests taken to rule out Huntington's disease, cerebrovascular disease, mass lesions, hydrocephalus, or Wilson's disease. *Carbidopa* and *Levodopa; Levodopa, L-Dopa (Sinemet):* Most effective medication for Parkinson's. Side effects of drop in blood pressure, fainting, and nausea may occur. *Dopamine Agonists; Pramipexole (Mirapex)* and *Ropinirole (Requip):* mimic dopamine effects in the brain. Side effects: skin molting, edema, confusion, blurred vision, insomnia, compulsive behavior (hypersexual, gambling, and eating) hallucinations, swelling, sleepiness, and anxiety. *MAO-B Inhibitors; Selegiline (Eldepryl, Zelapar)* and *Rasagiline (Azilect):* Impedes breakdown of dopamine. *Catecholamine – O– Methyl Tranferase (COMT) Inhibitors; Entacapone (Comtan):* Slows down dopamine breakdown (overuse causes liver toxicity). *Prescription Anticholinergic Drugs:* Block acetylcholine or restore dopamine with levodopa. *Amantadine:* Psycho-stimulant treatment for dyskinesias. *Methylene Blue:* Antimicrobial drug that may possibly slow the progression of Alzheimer's and Parkinson's disease. *Posteroventral Pallidotomy:* Surgery of the globus pallidus. *Bilateral Fetal Nigral Transplantation:* Electrical stimulation of the subthalamic nucleus.	*Botanical Mucuna Pruriens:* Tropical herb used in India for centuries, and a natural source of dopamine. *Vitamins C* with *Bioflavanoids, E,* and *Coenzyme Q10:* Helps preserve dopaminergic neurons from toxins. *Vitamin D3:* Deficient in those with Parkinson's. *Belladonna:* Helps rigidity, tremor, and sweating symptoms. *Curcumin (derived from Turmeric):* Has strong antioxidant properties. *Gingko Biloba:* Has antioxidant properties that help improve memory. *Omega 3 (EPA / DHA), Fish Oils:* Improves brain health. *Slippery Elm* and *American Saffron Tea:* Intestines and urinary cleansers. *N-Acetyl-Cysteine:* Antioxidant that may help regenerate glutathione. *Atomidine:* Liquid iodine preparation that is believed to improve glandular function.	Stop smoking, alcohol, caffeine, and soda drinks. Stop all dairy; (tetrahydroisoquinolines in dairy products may be potential cause of Parkinson's disease). Start a low fat alkaline diet. Meals must be full of fiber and you must hydrate well. Eat many calories from whole grains (barley, oat, bran, brown rice) fruits, and drink vegetable juices. Have high protein meals only in the evenings. Increase calcium in diet. If elimination is sluggish, a few colonics may help. Some research suggests eating antioxidant high flavonoid berries such as strawberries, blueberries, black currants, and blackberries, as well as drinking red wine and tea, could help protect against Parkinson's disease. Keep an active lifestyle that includes lots of exercise. Add the KSS™ stretches in Chapter 8 to your daily regimen. Switch to a vegan or anti-inflammatory vegetarian diet. Use an alkaline Ph water conversion filter for home and travel use.	Proper nerve flow in the body is always helpful, especially in cases of Parkinson's disease. Research indicates life quality improvement and lessening of stress symptoms, with use of upper cervical chiropractic techniques. **Ask your Chiropractor about adjusting Occiput (Cranio-Sacral), C1 – C7,** and any other affected spinal levels from exam and x-ray. Co-manage your case with a doctor of functional medicine, endocrinologist, physical and occupational speech therapists, and a qualified holistic nutritionist or naturopath. Pesticide exposure has been linked to Parkinson's. Two chemicals that hinder mitochondrial function, and cell health, are rotenone and paraquat. Ask your doctors about doing oral or intravenous chelation therapy, 35% food grade hydrogen peroxide therapy, oxygen therapy; candida, liver, and gallbladder cleanses to get the body in a healthier condition for focused healing. *Seek out a certified Kousouli® Method practitioner to remove spinal stress and align your energy bodies.*

BE A MASTER® OF MAXIMUM HEALING © by Theodoros Kousouli D.C., CHt.

Ailment name	Western Medicine Approach	Alternative Medicine Approach	What you can do at home to take control?	How can Chiropractic Help?
HAIR, SKIN, AND NAIL HEALTH One of the skin's functions is to remove toxins through sweat. If the liver and kidney's toxin removal systems are overwhelmed, the skin takes over. Acne is usually thought to be because of dirty skin, though more likely due to overactive oil glands, and poor skin nutrition. Acne and skin pigmentations are the most treated skin abnormalities. The radiance or lack of luster, in our outward appearances, could be a manifestation of what is occurring within our gut. Hair, skin, and nail health, have direct correlation to diet and emotional well-being. **Be sure to see your doctor for proper diagnosis and management.**	Drugs and procedures used in dermatology include: ***Over the counter lotions, creams, pills, glucocorticoids, retinoids, antibiotics, surgery, and cytotoxic drugs*** are all available for a variety of conditions. Hormonal changes, birth control use, pregnancy, childbirth, menopause, thyroid problems, or elevated levels of testosterone, along with medications, can cause many of the problems seen with slow hair growth, hair loss, or thinning, skin eruptions, and nail discolorations. **Ask your physician if your medications could be the culprit of your symptoms, and review the list of side effects.**	***Natural Vitamin E and A:*** Increase oxygen uptake and improve circulation to the skin and scalp. In avocados, olive oil, nuts, and seeds. ***B Vitamins*** are vitally important for hair growth. Get a good intake of ***Niacin (B3), B5, B6, Biotin, Inositol, Silica, Iron, Magnesium, Zinc and Sulfur:*** These may prevent hair loss and keep your hair from graying prematurely. ***Vitamin C:*** Eat lots of citrus fruits; kiwis, pineapples, strawberries, and green peppers. ***Vitiligo patients*** may be deficient in ***Zinc, Copper, Folic Acid (B9),*** and ***Cobalamin (B12).*** ***Fish Oil Omega 3 (EPA / DHA)*:** Increases anti-inflammatory prostaglandins. ***Manuka Honey:*** Heals scars, acne, pimples, etc. Eat and apply to skin. ***Methylsulfonyl-Methane (MSM):*** Helps body build new cells and remove toxins. Helpful in eczema. ***Castor Oil:*** Massage into the skin. May relieve fungal and bacterial infection, arthritis, keratosis, ringworm, sebaceous cysts, warts, itching, inflammation, and pain. ***Non-GMO Soy Milk:*** Some studies show that when the body breaks down soy products, it blocks the hormone DHT, a form of testosterone that has been linked to prostate cancer and hair loss. ***Habanero Chili, Turmeric and Cumin:*** Prevalent in the diets of societies with healthy hair, skin, and nails. ***Saw Palmetto, Pygeum Bark, Pumpkin Seed Oil, Procyanidin B-2, Emu Oil, Proanthocyanidins (in Grape Seeds) Capsaicin, Ginkgo Biloba,*** and ***Inositol*** may improve overall health and slow down DHT production; which is said to be the reason for hair loss.	Stop smoking. Smoking causes your capillaries to contract so less blood can get through to your hair follicles. Less blood means fewer nutrients to hair, nails and skin. A diet high in carbonated drinks, alcohol, animal fat, sugar, and caffeine intake impedes healthy hair, nail, and skin growth. Gluten, dairy, and yeast-free diets reverse many of the autoimmune skin issues. Get plenty of protein from fish, eggs, tofu, yogurt, whole grain cereals, dark green leafy vegetables, raisins, and eggs. Drink green tea for its powerful anti-oxidant properties. Hydrate well (10-12 glasses daily) and get 6-8 hours restful sleep. Learn to manage emotional stress effectively. A little fresh coconut paste combed into the hair and scalp helps to nourish it, and gives your hair the shine that pops. Oily hair? You may be eating too many spicy foods. Dull hair? That means you need more protein in your diet. Massage your body and scalp regularly. Only use certified organic oils, body soaps, shampoos, and conditioners. Switch to a vegan or anti-inflammatory vegetarian diet. Use an alkaline Ph water conversion filter for home and travel use.	Your skin is the largest organ innervated by your nervous system. Proper nerve flow is essential in allowing optimal brain body function. **Ask your Chiropractor about adjusting Occiput, C1 – C7,** and any other affected spinal levels according to your exam and x-rays. Ask your doctors about heavy metal detox, chelation therapy; oxygen therapy; candida, liver, gallbladder, colon cleanses; and if you can eliminate any unnecessarily prescribed or over the counter drugs. Autoimmune issues like vitiligo, have been linked to gluten sensitivity, and celiac disease; which causes malabsorption or deficiency of vital nutrients, B5, vitamin B12, folic acid, vitamin C, copper, and zinc. Intestinal mal-absorption leads to less than optimal skin tone, melanin, nail strength, and hair luster. Consider nutritional consultation with a naturopath or holistic nutritionist. *Seek out a certified Kousouli® Method practitioner to remove spinal stress and align your energy bodies.*

Ailment name	Western Medicine Approach	Alternative Medicine Approach	What you can do at home to take control?	How can Chiropractic Help?
ALZHEIMER'S Alzheimer's is the most common type of dementia. It is a disease of the brain characterized by pathological accumulation of senile plaques in the cerebral cortex and subcortical grey matter; usually starting after age 40. Alzheimer's may result from a deficiency in neurotransmitters used by nerves in the brain to communicate with one another. Symptoms include: difficulty completing common tasks, or solving problems, difficulty making easy decisions, confusion with time and place, difficulties in speaking, or remembering words, loss of memory that disrupts daily living, misplacing things with inability to retrace steps, difficulty judging distance or spacial dimensions, poor judgment, personality and mood changes, and seclusion from work, home, or social environment. Believed to be progressive and irreversible. It is important that this disease be caught and treated early. **Be sure to see your doctor for proper diagnosis and management.**	*Prescription Drugs; Cholinesterase Inhibitors, Donepezil (Aricept), Tacrine (Cognex):* Treat Alzheimer's symptoms in early to moderate stages. Treats Alzheimer's cognitive symptoms; memory loss, confusion, language, judgment, and problems with thinking and reasoning. Reported side effects include: nausea, vomiting, loss of appetite, headache, confusion, dizziness, possible liver damage, and drugs could interact with other medication causing fatality. A drug called **Etanercept** is showing some promise for helping Alzheimer's patients, though it is usually used to treat rheumatoid arthritis in adults and children. Side effects include: hair loss, fever, chills, bleeding, excessive bruising, vision changes, weakness, leg swelling, depression, and vomiting.	**B Complex Vitamins; especially Niacinamide, Niacin (B3), Pyridoxine (B6), *Folic Acid (B9)* and *Cobalamin (B12)*:** May slow the onset of Alzheimer's. Niacinamide should be taken only under doctor supervision if you have allergies, angina, ulcers, gallbladder disease, gout, kidney or liver disease, low blood pressure, or anticipate surgery. *Germanium, Vitamin C (Sodium Ascorbate), Grape Seed Polyphenols, and Turmeric:* Help brain neuron health by preventing and reducing amyloid plaque from collecting. *Omega Fatty 3 Acids and Vitamin E:* Known to help protect brain cells and body tissues from chemical wear and tear. *Thiotic Acid (Alpha-Lipoic acid):* Powerful antioxidant. *Acetyl-L-Carnitine:* Reduces free radical formation, thus improving brain function. *Ginko Biloba:* Increases blood flow to the brain. *Apple Pectin:* Helps detoxify blood. *Choline Bitartrate:* Raises levels of acetylcholine. *Selenium and Zinc:* Provide brain and cell protection. *Boron:* Helps brain memory and function. *Qian Ceng Ta, (Huperzia Serata or Chinese Clubmoss):* May increase memory retention, clear thinking, and improve learning by inhibiting acetylcholinesterase.	Nutrition is a major factor in brain and nerve transmission. Diet modification is essential. Remove all food allergens. Add more fiber to your diet. Avoid fried foods, cow milk, artificial colors and ingredients, vegetable oils (including margarine), reduce trans and saturated fats, keep a low plasma cholesterol, and eliminate smoking and alcohol consumption. Remove dental amalgam fillings. Metal toxicity, specifically aluminum buildup, is seen often with Alzheimer's patients. Eliminate all intake of aluminum from food, drink, and use. This includes pots, aluminum foil, and commercial products; such as soaps and shampoos. Also avoid excess iron or copper, which may contribute to memory and mental fog when in high amounts. Some antacids have aluminum in them; do not use! Discontinue eating out of canned containers or canned goods. Eliminate any beverages containing solvent pollutants such as Toluene or Xylene. Participate in stimulating hand eye activities, (ex. sports) read often, and remain social. Maintain a healthy weight, exercise regularly, and add the KSS™ stretches in Chapter 8 to your daily regimen. Switch to a vegan or anti-inflammatory vegetarian diet. Use an alkaline Ph water conversion filter for home and travel use.	Proper nerve and blood flow is essential in brain-body communication. Chiropractic can offer Alzheimer's patients a sense of wellbeing and relaxation while removing stress. **Ask your Chiropractor about adjusting Occiput, C1, C2 – C7, and any other affected spinal levels according to your exam and x-rays.** ❦ Ask a qualified holistic nutritionist or naturopath about food allergy testing and chelation therapy to remove toxic metals (ex. mercury, aluminum), from the body. Hair and urine analysis can help rule out heavy metal toxicity. Test for parasitic flatworm fluke: Fasciolopsis buski; ingested from undercooked meat and often found in those with cancer, Chron's disease, HIV, and Alzheimer's. Ask your doctors to check medication side effects, and other possible drug or herbal contraindications. *Seek out a certified Kousouli® Method practitioner to remove spinal stress and align your energy bodies.*

Ailment name	Western Medicine Approach	Alternative Medicine Approach	What you can do at home to take control?	How can Chiropractic Help?
HIV The human immunodeficiency virus is believed to be transmitted through direct contact of a mucous membrane or the bloodstream by a bodily fluid containing HIV, such as preseminal fluid, semen, vaginal fluid, blood, rectal (anal) mucous, and breast milk. **AIDS** Acquired immune deficiency syndrome (AIDS), is an immune disease believed to be caused by HIV. When the thymus cannot create sufficient T cells, immunity lowers. A common link among HIV/AIDS patients is emotional trauma and disastrous lifestyle habits that lower immunity: little sleep, massive drug (amyl nitrite) use, and unhealthy multi-sexual relations. Many scientists, patients and holistic doctors agree HIV and AIDS are curable. **Be sure to see your doctor for proper diagnosis and management.**	*Testing; ELISA, CD4, Western Blot. Prescription Drugs; Nucleoside Reverse Transcriptase Inhibitors (NRTIs), Abacavir (Ziagen),* and the combination drugs *Emtricitabine and Tenofovir (Truvada), Lamivudine and Zidovudine (Combivir):* NRTIs are faulty types of building blocks that HIV requires to make copies of itself. *Non-Nucleoside Reverse Transcriptase Inhibitors (NNRTIs); Efavirenz (Sustiva), Nevirapine (Viramune):* Help prevent virus reproduction. *Protease Inhibitors (PIs); Atazanavir (Reyataz), and Fosamprenavir (Lexiva):* Disable protease, required by HIV to create copies of itself. *Entry or Fusion Inhibitors; Enfuvirtide (Fuzeon), and Maraviroc (Selzentry):* Block HIV's entry into CD4 cells. *Integrase Inhibitors; Raltegravir (Isentress):* Disables integrase, the protein HIV utilizes to insert its genetic material into CD4 cells.	**Vitamins B Complex;** *especially Riboflavin (B2), Niacinamide, Niacin (B3), Pyridoxine (B6), Folic Acid (B9), Cobalamin (B12), and Amygdalin/Laetrile (B17):* Support neurology and immunity *Selenium* and *Zinc:* Immune protection. *Apple Pectin* and *Thiotic Acid (Alpha-Lipoic Acid):* Powerful blood antioxidant detoxifiers. *Acetyl-L-Carnitine:* Reduces free radial formation thus improving brain function. *N-Acetyl-Cysteine* in the order of 2000 mg/ day replenishes **Glutathione,** the most important antioxidant in our body (naturally found in walnuts). *Omega Fatty 3 Acids* and *Vitamin E:* Help protect cells and body tissues from chemical wear and tear. *Chlorophyll:* Wakunaga, kelp, wheat grass, and green leafy vegetables build a healthy circulatory system. *Aloe Vera, St. Johns Wort, Cat's Claw, Echinacea, Licorice, Ginseng, Cayenne,* and *Turmeric:* Antiseptic; antioxidant power. *Alkaline Drink Mix:* ½ tablespoon **Sodium Bicarbonate;** Non-Aluminum Baking Soda (not powder) mixed with 2 tablespoons fresh lemon juice and 12 ounces purified water daily helps alkalize the blood. *Biofield Therapies: Reiki, Qi Gong:* Believed to affect the energy fields surrounding and penetrating the human body, to improve energy flow and your health. *Hydrotherapy*: To restore health. Saunas, sitz baths, steam baths, foot baths, cold sheet treatment cold and hot water compresses.	Whole food nutrition is a major life or death factor for the HIV/AIDS patient and should be taken very seriously for recovery. Work closely with a qualified holistic nutritionist or naturopath to build immunity through maximum nutritional value. No smoking or drinking alcohol. Avoid GMOs and fried foods. Eliminate all benzene products and products containing solvent pollutants such as toluene isopropyl alcohol, methanol, or xylene. Remove dental mercury fillings. Remove greasy foods, cow milk, trans and saturated fats. Eat salads as part of your diet and add olive leaf, basil, onion, and garlic (strong antivirals). Drink chamomile tea: (eases digestion), cardamom tea (helps relieve diarrhea), and calendula tea (helps heal infections of the upper digestive tract). Cook with or add cinnamon oil to your tea (strong antiviral). Physical, emotional, spiritual, psychic healing is needed. You must re-evaluate your surroundings for positive input and remove all negativity of self-hate. Humor, funny movies, and inspirational audiotapes are helpful mind-body techniques. **Also read section 5.5**	Research suggests HIV/AIDS patients can live a higher quality of life and promote immune boosting of CD4 counts by utilizing Chiropractic. **Ask your Chiropractor about adjusting Occiput, C1, C2 – C7,** and any other affected spinal levels for your case. ⚜ Ask your doctors about oral or intravenous chelation therapy; heavy metal detoxification (EDTA), to remove toxins from the body. Also test for pesticide exposure and parasitic flatworm fluke infection: Fasciolopsis buski; ingested from undercooked meat and is found in the thymus of those with HIV and AIDS. Research further the benefits of Oleander and cesium chloride protocols, chlorine dioxide, 35% food grade hydrogen peroxide, cold sheet treatment, magnetic therapy, electromedicine (Bob Beck and Rife machines), and Ge-132 (germanium sesquioxide). *Seek out a certified Kousouli® Method practitioner to remove spinal stress and align your energy bodies.*

BE A MASTER® OF MAXIMUM HEALING © by Theodoros Kousouli D.C., CHt.

Ailment name	Western Medicine Approach	Alternative Medicine Approach	What you can do at home to take control?	How can Chiropractic Help?
SEXUAL HEALTH Sexual health can be maintained by any range of sexual unity that builds positive and respectful relationships, is safe, pleasurable and abuse-free. Stress, low testosterone or thyroid issues in men as well as unbalanced serotonin, norepinephrine, and dopamine levels in pre-menopausal women can lower sexual urges. Aphrodisiacs are foods or herbs that are used to improve libido or sexual pleasure in the expression of the sexual act. **WARNING:** Use of natural herbs or pharmaceutical drugs to rev up sexual performance should not be taken by anyone with known heart or circulatory issues due to life threatening side effects like stroke or heart attack. **Be sure to see your doctor for proper diagnosis and management.**	***Sildenafil: (Viagra)*** Increases blood flow to the penis to counter erectile dysfunction. (E.D.) Side effects include nausea, back pain, nasal congestion, headache, face neck and chest flushing, stomach pain, inability to differentiate between blue and green colors, indigestion, muscle pain and tenderness **Flibanserin : (Addyi)** is the controversial female version of 'Viagra' pill for hypoactive sexual desire disorder or (HSDD). It works by inhibiting release of serotonin and increasing the release of dopamine. Side effects include low blood pressure if used with alcohol, fatigue, dry mouth, nausea, (syncope) a partial or complete loss of consciousness and depression.	***Horny Goat Weed*** and ***Gingko Biloba:*** Relax smooth muscle and enhances blood flow in the penis or clitoris. ***Kava Kava:*** Helps relax muscles and blood vessels. Can be strong; use sparingly. ***L-Arginine*** *(Precursor to nitrate oxide)* and ***Panax Ginseng:*** Increase nitric oxide; both show promise in treating E.D. and are a holistic alternative to Viagra. Ask your doctor for dosage. ***MACA: (Peruvian Ginseng):*** For female fertility and better semen quality in men. ***Zinc:*** Deficiency in men may be linked to erectile dysfunction. ***Yohimbe:*** Stimulates blood flow to the penis, helps increase libido, and decreases the period between ejaculations. ***Dehydroepiandrosterone (DHEA):*** Building block for sex hormones, and helps in cases of low testosterone. ***Baryta Carbonica:*** Helps premature ejaculation, erection dysfunction, builds libido, and gives prostate support. ***Tongkat Ali root:*** A native root of Malaysia and Asia considered a natural aphrodisiac. ***Mucuna herb*** and ***Rhodiola:*** Stimulates mood by relaxing stress factors allowing sexual receptiveness. ***Tribulus terrestris:*** Increases orgasm, sex organ lubrication, and arousal / mood. Ashwagandha, Muira Puama, ***Catuaba Bark, Schizandra,*** and ***Oatstraw:*** Increase libido.	Recommended book reading: ***BE A MASTER® OF SEX ENERGY*** for helpful mind-body chi techniques that heighten orgasm and build the bond between you and your lover. Whole food nutrition is a major factor in sexual vigor and performance. Don't have sex immediately after dinner. Choose light organic raw foods one hour or two prior to engaging in sex. Avoid oily, fried or heavy protein foods that could bloat or fatigue you. Dark chocolate, oysters, asparagus, raw honey, cinnamon, and some coffees are believed to possess aphrodisiac properties while deer antler, pine pollen and orchic (bull testicles) are more 'exotic' examples. Safety and hygiene is very important when practicing sexual acts. Be sure to use protection (condoms, dental dams, etc.) and clean your body properly prior to and after sex.	Mobility and performance is improved when utilizing Chiropractic. Sex is mediated by spinal reflex. When there is a problem mechanically, there usually is a spinal connection / nerve interference issue: **Adjustment of the C1-C7; T9-L5; S2- S4 levels** opens nerve flow to the thyroid, adrenal, and sexual reproductive glands. **Ask your Chiropractor about Lumbar and Sacral adjustments** as well as possible **Pudendal Nerve Entrapment (PNE).** ⚜ Consult a holistic nutritionist and detox your body for heavy metals and prescription drugs which can disrupt body physiology, and cause sexual malfunction. Consult a certified sex or couples therapist which allows you and your partner to fully express your thoughts and feelings without judgment. *Seek out a certified Kousouli® Method practitioner to remove spinal stress and align your energy bodies.*

BE A MASTER® OF MAXIMUM HEALING © by Theodoros Kousouli D.C., CHt.

Chapter 12:
Conclusion

"The truth is incontrovertible, malice may attack it, ignorance may deride it, but in the end; there it is."
~ Winston Churchill

Any treatment that intimidates the prevailing institution's influence and power, especially when the treatment is extremely effective and inexpensive, will always be fought by the 'old energy' status quo establishment. Cures, remedies, and inventions have long been discovered and shared only among the most influential and elite, then hidden from sight. In America, controlling a dis-ease is far more profitable than curing it. There is no argument against a definite need for pharmaceutical drugs, or the fact that they have helped prolong or enhance our lives in some cases. What is being discussed here is the misuse, abuse, and overuse through a carefully orchestrated mass application of chemical agents for monetary gain - at the peril of humanity's well-being. This remains the greatest detriment of our lifetime. An old outdated 'drug for everything' system continues to thrive, only because its beneficiaries have fought hard and dirty for its survival. We should not blame them for wanting survival of their drug machine, as all business enterprises have the right to compete and exist in the marketplace. However, it is up to each and every one of us to take personal responsibility and awaken to all our health options so we may choose wisely which systems ultimately allow us real health.

Healthy lifestyle choices improve all aspects of our lives, including the mind-body connection. I truly believe that the health and condition of our nervous system, and spinal column, the antenna that transmits our personal power, will function best when maintained with the utmost care through chiropractic and proper nutrition. There is also overwhelming proof that the mind is a powerful source of healing. Maintaining a positive mindset and belief system will help make a huge difference in your quality of life through dis-ease prevention. Our current unhealthy habits are failing us; creating a vicious cycle of poor health through high levels of stress, unhealthy eating, sedentary living, and many other limiting factors.

And the old energy medical system is still covering and controlling these problems by using pharmaceutical therapies that offer either temporary symptom relief, or decreased risk through continued dependency; but this complacent approach allows patients to remain passive in their own care. Unfortunately, diseases often progress if lifestyle changes are not initiated and held to. Fortunately, many in medicine are realizing that the progression of diseases can be halted when natural therapies are used in combination with traditional medicine and common sense. Implementing chiropractic, diet, and lifestyle changes, while maintaining better daily habits, as well as the proper use of medication (when absolutely necessary), can be an effective way to improve health and prevent disease. Combined treatment plans focus on overall health and wellness, with emphasis on what the patient needs.

12.1 Setting Yourself Up For Success

If you want to change your daily habits, you must create a plan right now – no more procrastination. Every moment that goes by, you could be helping (instead of hurting) your body's chances for full recuperation.

1) Make a list of habits and lifestyle factors that you would like to change, and then rank them in the order that you would like to work on them.

2) Take action! It doesn't matter which approach you take; the important thing is that you are taking action steps immediately. Don't overanalyze the changes that you want to make. Simply pick one and start working on them.

3) Write your goals down and tape a copy of your goals to the wall, or the bathroom mirror where you will see them every day. Read your goals out loud on a daily basis to remember why you want to stay committed.

4) Use the Kousouli® Method 4R intervention system as a checklist of the steps you are doing, or need to improve upon, as you move towards the positive cycle of health.

5) Get a buddy, an accountability partner or another like-minded person to partner with you. Communicate on a regular basis to keep each other motivated while you both pursue your goals. Stay positive and avoid negative thinkers.

12.2 Start Making Changes

It is better to implement incremental changes as soon as possible to reverse any health damage that has occurred, as well as reduce the risk of more dis-ease. Start now, be proactive, be diligent, stay strong – and get results! Remember that a mind-body approach is the best way to improve health, so you should be implementing various aforementioned techniques; meditate to reduce stress levels, increase exercise frequency, hydration, and improve whole food nutrition and eating habits. It is my belief that all parties involved must always work together for the benefit of the patient's highest interest. Working closely with a qualified chiropractor, functional medicine practitioner, and holistic nutritionist can be one of the best ways to implement these changes in your life, because they have experience and knowledge that can catapult your path to success. The most important aspect of your treatment plan is that you have belief and hope that you can receive your healing. Without this first and crucial step, there is nothing that can be done for you. Rest assured that alternative treatments for diseases are very effective (especially when applied early along with proper conservative medical care), and countless people have experienced positive results by implementing these changes in their lives.

12.3 Keep an Open Mind, Use Common Sense and Do Your Own Research

You don't have to take my word; be your own detective and do your own research. Keep in mind that each person is unique, so it is important that you consider your personal situation to determine the best treatment plan with your doctors. A combination of alternative treatments is usually the most effective method to treat health issues, so choose a few methods to implement in your life with a willingness to make changes and adjustments as needed as your health changes over time. Be sure all your doctors are collaboratively looking after your best interest, and are knowledgeable about current alternative holistic methods or new procedures in functional medicine. If your medical doctor is ignorant of holistic methods of treating chronic diseases, or says to you there is "only this one way," don't be afraid to find another doctor who is more holistically minded. You are free to get second and third opinions; this is YOUR body and life. Let no physician with an ego take away your hope by telling you that you have X amount of time to live, or that you are stuck with a certain diagnosis the rest of your life. Just because someone wears a white lab coat and delivers a diagnosis doesn't make them God. Amass your own research, talk to other patients who beat the disease and challenge the statistics. Doctors are all human, and all humans can - and will - make mistakes.

May my patients and readers enjoy a very long, joyful and high function life, sustained with vigor and great health. Natural healing has been working for all life forms, throughout the millennia, and will continue to do so. The ultimate question is *what*, and *who*, do you *believe*? **Do you put more faith and belief in a man-made pill, or do you put your faith and belief in the power that animates both you and the living world?**

The choice is yours. It always is.

In love and health,

Theodoros Kousouli D.C., CHt.

About the Author

A holistic health care advisor, teacher, speaker, mentor and author who is featured on major networks, Theodoros Kousouli D.C., CHt., is Los Angeles' premier holistic metaphysical energy healer. He is recognized and trusted for effective quick drug-free results, and his remarkable natural, pain-free, holistic healing system, the Kousouli® Method, focuses on getting patients to their top performance levels by unblocking pathways using the body's own repair mechanisms.

His desire to help others stems from his personal journey recovering from semi-paralysis and major heart surgeries, and includes everything he's learned about the optimum wellness techniques that define his practice.

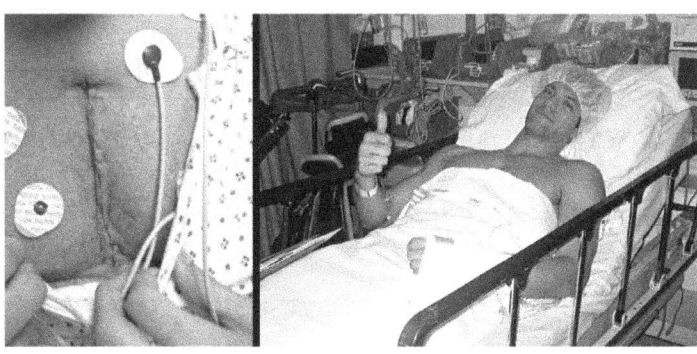

Dr. Theo Kousouli is the author of seven previous books, including *BE A MASTER® of PSYCHIC ENERGY* and *BE A MASTER® of SEX ENERGY*. (www.BeAMaster.com). A personal coach and advisor to entertainers, business leaders, energy healers, and spiritual seekers of all varieties, Dr. Kousouli holds seminars teaching people how to tap into their inner healing and higher level abilities through the use of their nervous systems. Visit www.KousouliMethod.com for more information on developing your intuition and personal power to live a more purpose-filled, meaningful, and healthy life. Dr. Kousouli is the ideal speaker for your next event.

To Schedule Dr. Theo Kousouli To Speak At Your Event:
www.DrKousouli.com

Be a Master® of Maximum Healing

Life Changing Products · Books · Seminars · Empowerment Audios · Get on the Newsletter!
Connect with Dr. Kousouli, www.DrKousouli.com and on all Social Media Platforms
@DrKousouli #DrKousouli #KousouliMethod

You Will Also Enjoy Dr. Kousouli's Other Published Works Available Now from Major Retailers:

BE A MASTER® OF PSYCHIC ENERGY
Your Key to Truly Mastering Your Personal Power
- Uncover and Amplify Your Hidden Psychic Abilities to Change Your Life!

BE A MASTER® OF SEX ENERGY
Hypnotize Your Partner for Love and Great Sex
- Build a Stronger Bond with Your Lover(s) Using Subconscious Science!

BE A MASTER® OF SUCCESS
Dr.Kousouli's 33 Master Secrets to Achieving Your Dreams
- Solid Success Principles You can Apply Right Now to Empower Your Life!

BE A MASTER® OF SELF IMAGE
Dr.Kousouli's 33 Master Secrets to Living Healthier, Happier and Hotter
- Simple Holistic Tips & Tricks for More Weight Loss and Body Benefit to You!

BE A MASTER® OF SELF LOVE
Dr.Kousouli's 33 Master Secrets to Loving Your Extraordinary Life
- Overcome Bullying, Abuse, Depression and Build Massive Self-Esteem & Self-Love!

BE A MASTER® OF YOUR REALITY
Authentically Manifest Your Desires
- Use the Law of Attraction to Radically Transform Your Life!

If you would like to share your story of how Dr. Kousouli's books, audios or seminars have impacted your life for the better, we would love to hear from you! (Messages are screened by staff and forwarded when appropriate.)

For A Free Gift from Dr. Theo Kousouli visit www.FreeGiftFromDrTheo.com

References

Abramson, J. (2004). Overdo$ed America: the broken promise of American medicine. New York, NY: Harpers Collins.

Accidental death from prescription drugs. (n.d.). *Alternative Medicine Magazine*, Issue #25. Retrieved from www.lightparty.com/Health/healingregeneration/html/accidentaldeathprescription.html

Adams, M. (2004, August 19). Elderly patients regularly prescribed dangerous medications with severe side effects. Retrieved from http://www.naturalnews.com/002032.html

Adams, M. (2005, June 23). What the American Medical Association hopes you never learn About its true history. Retrieved from http://www.naturalnews.com/008845.html

Adams, M. (2006, April 17). Study shows the public is turning to alternative medicine and away From dangerous prescription drugs. Retrieved from Http://www.naturalnews.com/019352_alternative_medicine_dangerous_drugs.html#ixzz1

Adams, M. (2008, June 5). Mercury fillings shattered! FDA, ADA conspiracy to poison children with toxic mercury fillings exposed in groundbreaking lawsuit. Http://www.naturalnews.com/023367_mercury_FDA_the.html#ixzz1pt5hr0cw

After the gold rush. (2009, December 9). *The Economist*. Retrieved from www.oecd.org/document/16/0,3343,en_2649_34631_2085200_1_1_1_1,00.html

Alesina, A., Di Tella, R. & MacCulloch, R. (2004). Inequality and happiness: are Europeans and Americans different? *Journal of Public Economics*, 88, 2009–2042.

Anick, D..J., & Ives, J. A. (2007). The silica hypothesis for homeopathy: physical chemistry. Homeopathy, 96 (3), 189-95.

Arguelles, J. Earth Ascending: An illustrated treatise on the law governing whole systems. Boulder, CO: Shambhala.

Arno, P.S., & Fiden, K. (1993) *Against the odds*. New York, NY: Harper Collins Press.

Aurobindo, S. (2006). *The mind of light*. New York, NY: E.P. Dutton.

Bach, E., & Wheeler, E. J. (1998). The Bach flower remedies. New Canaan, CT: Keats Publishing.

BackTalk Systems (2007). Cause & Effect [Poster].

Badgley, L. (1987). *Healing AIDS naturally healing.* Foster City, CA: Energy Press.

Bailey, H., & Robinson, M. (1993). Vitamin E: Your key to a healthy heart. New York, NY: Arco.

Balch, P. (2006). *A prescription for natural healing.* (3rd ed.). Garden City Park, NY: Avery Barbault, A., &

Bartlett, H. (Producer), & Bartlett, H. (Director). (1973). Jonathan Livingston Seagull [Motion picture]. United States: Paramount Pictures.

Baum, M., & Ernst, E. (2009). Should we maintain an open mind about homeopathy? American Journal of Medicine, 122, 973-974.

Bellhouse, E. (1980). *Measureless healing.* Somerset, England: Castle Combe.

Bent, S., & Ko, R. (2004). Commonly used herbal medicines in the United States: a review. American Journal of Medicine, 116 (7), 478-485.

Big Chart of Vitamins and Minerals [A chart listing vitamins and minerals needed by the human body]. The Body: The Complete HIV/AIDS Resource. Retrieved from http://www.thebody.com/content/art46419.html.

Bock, R. (1975). *Vitamin E: Key to youthful longevity.* New York, NY: Arco.

Book, R. A. (2009). Medicare administrative costs are higher, not lower, than for private insurance. Retrieved from http://www.heritage.org/research/reports/2009/06/medicare-administrative-costs-are-higher-not-lower-than-for-private-insurance

Breakthrough discovery! Iron mountain mine catalyst breaks down pesticide, herbicide, & fungicide residues in soil. (n.d.). Retrieved from http://www.ironmountainmine.com/ARMAN_part4.htm

Brody, J.E. (1999, March 9). Herbal remedies tied to pregnancy risks. New York Times. Retrieved from http://www.nytimes.com/1999/03/09/health/herbal-remedies-tied-to-pregnancy-risks.html

Brody, J.E. (1999, February 9). Americans gamble on herbs as medicine. New York Times. Retrieved from http://www.nytimes.com/1999/02/09/health/americans-gamble-on-herbs-as-medicine.html?pagewanted=all&src=pm.

Brunner, E. &, Marmot, M. (1999). Social organization, stress, and health in social determinants of health. M. Marmot & R. G. Wilkinson (Eds.). Oxford, UK: Oxford University Press.

Buericke, W. (2010). The twelve tissue remedies of Schuessler. New Delhi, India: B. Jain Publishers.

Buffum, H.E., Lovering, A.T., & Warren, I. (1905). The household physician: A twentieth Century medic. Boston, MA: Woodruff Publishing.

Burr. H. (1972). *Blueprint for immortality*, London, England: Neville Spearman.

Burstyn, B.S. (2003, July 16). Conventional medicine far riskier than supplements. New Zealand Herald. Retrieved from http://www.nzherald.co.nz/health/news/article.cfm?c_id=204&objectid=3507510

Calabrese, E. J., & Baldwin, L. A. (2002, July 1). Applications of hormesis in toxicology, risk assessment and chemotherapeutics. Trends in Pharmacological Sciences, 23, 331-337. doi:10.1016/S0165-6147(02)02034-5.

Calabrese, E. (2004). Hormesis: a revolution in toxicology, risk assessment and medicine. EMBO, 5, S37-S40. doi:10.1038/sj.embor.7400222.

Campbell, J. (1991). *The power of myth*. New York, NY: Doubleday.

Campbell, T. C. (n.d.). *The China study*. Retrieved from http://www.thechinastudy.com/

Cantwell, A.R. (1984). *AIDS: The mystery and the solution*. Los Angeles, CA: Aries Rising Press.

Carey, K. (1986). *The starseed transmission*. Kansas City, MO: Uni-Sun. The care of patients with severe chronic illness. (2006). Dartmouth Atlas of Health Care. Hanover, NH: Center for Health Policy and Clinical Practice.

Carter, J. (1992). *Racketeering in Medicine: The Suppression of Alternatives*. Hampton Roads, Norfolk, VA, 1992. ISBN: 978-1878901323

Case, P. F. (2006). The Tarot: A key to the wisdom of the ages. Richmond, VA: Macoy Publishing.

Case, P. F. (1933). *The true and invisible Rosicrucian Order*. New York, NY: Samuel Weiser.

Celebrex side effects. (n.d.) . Retrieved from http://celebrexlawsuit.lawinfo.com/celebrex-resources.html

Chaitow, L. & Martin, S. (1988) *A world without AIDS: The controversial Holistic health plan*. London, England: Thorsons Publishing Group.

Chaitow, L., Strohecker, J., & Goldberg, B. (1994). You don't have to die: Unraveling the AIDS myth. London, England: Future Medicine Publishing.

Chang, S. (1995). *The complete book of acupuncture*. Millbrae, CA: Celestial Arts.

Charlton, J.E. (ed.). (2005). Core curriculum for professional education in pain. Seattle, WA.: IASP Press.

Cheraskin, E. (1973). New hope for incurable diseases. New York, NY: Arco Publishing.

Cheraskin, E., & Ringsdorf, W. (1976). *Psycho-Dietetics* New York, NY: Stein and Day.

Cherkin, D., & MacCornack, F. (1989). Patient evaluations of low back pain care from family physicians and chiropractors. Western Journal of Medicine, 150, 351-355.

Chiropractic. (n.d.). Retrieved from http://www.tuquiropracticopr.com/index.php?p=77349

Chopra, D. (1990). *Quantum healing*. New York, NY: Bantam Books.

Christensen, C., & Bower, J. (1996). Customer power, strategic investment, and the failure of leading firms. Strategic Management Journal, 17, 197-218.

Clark, H., & Clark, R. (1993). *The cure for HIV and AIDS*. Chula Vista, CA: New Century Press.

Clark, H. (1995). *The cure for all diseases*. Chula Vista. CA: New Century Press.

Classical Cupping. (2013). *History*. Retrieved from http://classicalcupping.com/history.html

Clifford, L. (2000, October 30). Tyrannosaurus Rx. *Fortune*. Retrieved from http://money.cnn.com/magazines/fortune/fortune_archive/2000/10/30/290643/index.htm

Coates, B. (2010) Aloe vera, silent healer. Worthing, UK: Ava Publishers.

Collipp, P.J., Goldzier, S., Weiss, N., Soleymani, Y., & Snyder, R. (1975). Pyridoxine treatment of childhood bronchial asthma [Abstract]. Annals of Allergy, 35, 93-97.

Cook, C. (2011, February 23). Control over your food: Why Monsanto's GM seeds are undemocratic. *Christian Science Monitor*. Retrieved from http://www.csmonitor.com/Commentary/Opinion/2011/0223/Control-over-your-food-Why-Monsanto-s-GM-seeds-are-undemocratic

Corish, J. L, (1938). Health knowledge: A thorough and concise knowledge of the prevention, Causes, and treatments of disease, simplified for home use. New York: Medical Book Distributors. Corrective care: Getting to the root of the problem. (n.d.). Retrieved from http://www.woudsmachiropractic.com/corrective-CARE.aspx

Cranton, E. (2012). Chelation therapy: New hope for victims of cardiovascular and age- associated diseases. Retrieved from http://www.drcranton.com/newhope.htm.

Culpepper, N. (2010). *Culpepper's complete herbal*. London: W. Foulsham and Company.

Davidson, J., Gadde, K.M., & Fairbank, J. A. (2002). Effect of Hypericum perforatum (St. John's wort) in major depressive disorder: a randomized controlled trial. Journal of the American Medical Association, 287 (14), 1807-1814.

Davis, A., & Rawls, W. (1996). Magnetism and its effect on the living system. Hicksville, NY: Exposition Press.

References

Day, Dr. L. (1991). *AIDS: What the government isn't telling.* Palm Desert, CA: Rockford Press.

Day, L. (2006, January 24). How one wicked nation can kill billions around the world—with one Lie! Retrieved from: http://www.goodnewsaboutgod.com/studies/birdflu.htm

Deaton, A. (2003). Health, inequality, and economic development. Journal of Economic Literature, 41, 113–158.

Demangeat, J., Gries, P., Poitevin, B., Droesbeke, J., Zahaf, T., Maton, F., Pierart, C., & Muller, R.N. (2004). Low-field nmr water proton longitudinal relaxation in ultrahighly diluted aqueous solutions of silica-lactose prepared in glass material for pharmaceutical use. Applied Magnetic Resonance, 26, 465-481.

Dextreit, R., & Abehsera, M. (1993). Our earth, our cure. New York, NY: Swan House Publishing.

Diamond, J. (1989). *Your body doesn't lie.* New York, NY: Warner Communications.

Di Cyan, E. (1978). *Vitamin E and aging.* New Canaan, CT: Pyramid Publication.

Douglas, N., & Slinger, P. (1982). *Sexual secrets.* New York, NY: Destiny Books.

Doyle, J. (2011). Returns to local-area health care spending: evidence from health shocks to patients far from home. American Economic Journal: Applied Economics, 3(3): 221-43.

Drugs and medicines. (n.d.) Retrieved from http://www.healthsquare.com/drugmain.htm

Duff, P. (2002). Professionalism in medicine: An A-Z primer. Obstetrics and Gynecology, 99(6), 1127-1128.

Duffy, W. (1986). *Sugar blues.* Greenwich, CT: Fawcett.

Duke, J. A. (1993). Medicinal plants and the pharmaceutical industry. J. Janick & J. E. Simon (eds.). New York, NY: Wiley.

Ebrall, P.S. (1992) Mechanical Low-Back Pain: A comparison of medical and chiropractic management within the Victorian workcare scheme. Chiropractic Journal of Australia 22(2), 47-53.

Editorial staff. (1994, March 11). Stroke after chiropractic neck manipulation a 'small but significant risk,' says American Heart Association. *Dynamic Chiropractic. 12*, (6). Retrieved from http://www.dynamicchiropractic.com/mpacms/dc/article.php?Id=41126

Eisenberg, D.M., & Keseler, R. C.(1993). Unconventional medicine in the United States. The New England Journal of Medicine, 328, 246-352.

Eisenberg, D., Davis, R., Ettner, S., Appel, S., Wilkey, S., Van Rompay, M., & Kessler, R. (1998).

Trends in alternative medicine use in the United States, 1990-1997. Journal of the American Medical Association, 280(18), 1569-1575.

Elia, V., & Niccoli, M. (1999) Thermodynamics of extremely diluted aqueous solutions. Annals of the New York Academy of Sciences, 879, 241-248.

Ellsworth, P. (2011). *Direct healing*. North Hollywood, CA: Newcastle Publishing Company.

Finney, D. (n.d.). Methods of healing. Retrieved from http://www.greatdreams.com/healing-Methods.htm

Fishman, M., Herland, R. (Producers), & Haines, F. (Director). (1974). Steppenwotf [Motion picture]. Switzerland: D/R Films.

Fligstein, N. (1990). The transformation of corporate control. Cambridge, MA: Harvard University Press.

Forey, B., Hamling, J., Lee, P., & Wald, H. (Eds.). (2002). International smoking statistics: A collection of historical data from 30 economically developed countries. London: Oxford University Press.

Fox, E. (1931). *The golden key*. Marina del Rey, CA: DeVorss and Company.

Fox, M. (1988). *The coming of the cosmic Christ*. San. Francisco, CA: Harper & Row.

Fried, S. (1998). Chapter one. Bitter pills. Retrieved July 14, 2012 from Http://www.stephenfried.com/bitter-pills/bitterpillsbook_chp1.html

Friedlander, S., & Muzaffereddin, A.S. (1993). Ninety-nine names of Allah. New York, NY: Harper.

Gaby, A. (February/March 1993). NIH and alternative medicine, Reprinted from Townsend letter for doctors. Retrieved from http://www.lightparty.com/Health/NIH.html.

Gach, M. (1981). Acu-yoga, designed to relieve stress and tension. Tokyo, Japan: Japan Publications.

Gerson, M. (1977). A cancer therapy: Results of fifty cases. Los Angeles, CA: Cancer Book House.

Goddard, N. (1941). *Your faith is your future*. Marina del Rey, CA: DeVorss and Company.

Goldsmith, J. (1947). *The infinite way*. Marina del Rey, CA: DeVorss and Company.

Goldstein. K., & Gazelle, E. (2010, March 18). Monsanto's GMO corn linked to organ failure, Study reveals. Retrieved from: http://www.huffingtonpost.com/2010/01/12/monsantos-Gmo-corn-linked_n_420365.html

Goldstein, M. S. (2002). The emerging socioeconomic and political support for alternative medicine in the United States. *The Annals of the American Academy of Political and Social Science, 583*(1), 44-63.

Grabowski, H.G., & Vernon, J. M. (1992). Brand loyalty, entry, and price competition in pharmaceuticals after the 1984 Drug Act. Journal of Law & Economics, 35, 331- 350.

Gray, R. (1991). *Colon health handbook.* Berkeley, CA: Rockridge Publishing Company.

Greener, M. (2001). *A healthy business.* London, England: Informa Publishing.

Griggs, B. (1981). The green pharmacy: The history and evolution of western herbal medicine. Manchester: Healing Arts Press.

Grof, S. (1985). Beyond the brain: Birth, death and transcendence in psychotherapy. New York, NY SUNY Press.

Guimond, S., & Massrieh, W. (2012). Intricate correlation between body posture, personality trait and incidence of body pain: A cross-referential study report. PLOS ONE. 7. doi:10.1371/journal.pone.0037450.

Hacker, J. S. (2008). The case for public plan choice in national health reform. Retrieved from http://institute.ourfuture.org/report/2008125116/case-public-plan-choice-national-health-reform

Haught, J. (1983). *The American Experience of Max Gerson: Censured for Curing Cancer.* Station Hill, 1983. ISBN: 0882681095

Heffern, R. (1976). *Complete book of ginseng*, Millbrae, CA: Celestial Arts.

Hewlett-Parson, J. (1977) Herbs, health, and healing, Wellingborough, England: Thorsons Publishers.

Hilts, P. J. (2003). Protecting America's health: The FDA, business, and one hundred years of Regulation. New York, NY: Alfred A. Knopf.

Hoffer, A., & Osmand, M. (1992). How to live with schizophrenia. New York, NY: Universe Books.

Holmes, E. (1988). *Words that heal today.* Dodd, Mead & Company: New York, NY.

Hoppenfeld, S. (1977). *Orthopaedic neurology.* Philadelphia, PA: J.B. Lippincott.

Horowitz, L. (1996). Emerging viruses: AIDS & ebola: Nature, accident, or genocide? Rockport MA: Tetrahedron

How blood type determines your health. (2012) Excerpted from *Alternative Medicine Digest.* Retrieved from http://www.dadamo.com/program.htm

How do emotions affect my health? (n.d.). Retrieved from http://www.kinesiologyhealthpractice.com.au/page/how_does_emotions_affect_our_life.html

How to fit a cervical pillow. (n.d.). Retrieved from http://www.backdesigns.com/how-to-fit-a-cervical-pillow-w146.aspx

Ichazo, O. (1977). Arica psycho-calisthenics: The Arica Institute's original program of exercise and meditation. New York, NY: Simon and Schuster.

Issels, J. (1999). *Cancer: A second opinion.* Kent, England: Modder and Stroughton.

Jacka, J. (1996). The complete A to Z of common ailments and their natural remedies. Slough, England: Foulsham.

Jaffe, D. (1986). *Healing from within.* New York, NY: Alfred Knopf.

James, W. (1990). Immunization: The reality behind the myth. (2nd ed.). Santa Barbara, CA: Praeger.

Jarrett, R. H. (1928). *It works.* Marina del Rey, CA: devorss and Company.

Jarvis, C. J. (1997). *Arthritis and folk medicine.* New York, NY: Galahad Books

Jarvis, K. B., & Philips, R. B. (1991). Cost per case comparison of back injury claims of chiropractic versus medical management for conditions with identical diagnostic codes. Journal of Occupational Medicine, 33(8), 847-852.

Jayne, D. (1883). *Dr. Jayne's medical almanac.* Philadelphia, PA: Dr. D. Jayne & Sons.

Jensen, B. (1973). *Health magic through chlorophyll.* Solana Beach, CA: Jensen Books.

Kavasch, E.B., & Baar, K. (1999). *American Indian healing arts: herbs, rituals, and remedies for every season of life.* New York, NY: Bantam Books.

Kent, J. T. (1965). *Lectures on homeopathic materia medica,* Calcutta, India: Sett Dey and Co.

Kervan, C. L., & Abehsera, M. (1989). Biological transmutations. New York, NY: Swan House Publishing.

Kleijnen, J., & Knipschild, P. (1991, February 9) Clinical trials of homoeopathy. British Medical Journal, 302, 316-323.

Kloss, J. (1975). *Back to Eden.* Santa Barbara, CA: Woodbridge Press.

Koes, B. W., & Bouter, L. M. (1992). Randomized clinical trial of manipulative therapy and physiotherapy for persistent back and neck complaints. British Medical Journal, 304, 601-605.

Kurtz, G. (Producer), & Lucas, G. (Director). (1977). Star Wars [Motion picture]. United States: Twentieth Century Fox.

References

Lam, M. (n.d.) Blood type diet. Retrieved from http://www.drlam.com/blood_type_diet/

Lansbury, E. (Producer), & Greene, D. (Director). (1973). Godspell, Columbia Pictures [Motion picture]. United States: Columbia Pictures.

Lauite, R., & Passebeirg, A. (1979). Aromatherapy: The use of plant essence in healing. Wellingborough, England: Thronsons Publishers.

Lauritsen, J. (1992, June 15). AIDS criticism in Europe. New York Native. Retrieved from http://www.virusmyth.com/aids/hiv/jleurope.htm

Lauritson, J. (1993). The AIDS war: Propoganda, profiteering, and genocide from the medical-industrial complex. New York, NY: Aesculapius Press.

Law, D. (1974). *A guide to alternative medicine*, New York, NY: Doubleday.

Lawinfo. (n.d.). Celebrex side effects. Retrieved from Http://celebrexlawsuit.lawinfo.com/celebrex-resources.html

Lea, T.S. & Bond, F. B. (1979). The Apostolic Gnosis. Northhamptonshire, England: Thorson Publishers Ltd.

Levi. (2012). The aquarian gospel of Jesus the Christ. Marina del Rey, CA: DeVorss and Company.

Levy, B. (1996). *Common herbs for natural health*. New York, NY: Schocken Books.

The Light Party. (2000, Jan). 13 myths of genetic engineering. Retrieved from http://www.lightparty.com/Health/13mythsge.html

The Light Party. (1996). *The XI International Conference on HIV/AIDS*. Retrieved from http://www.lightparty.com/Health/AIDS-WholisticPerspective.html

Livingston, V. (1972). *Cancer: A new breakthrough*. New York, NY: E. P. Dalton.

Lovell, D., Perugia, L. (Producers) & Zeffirelli, F. (Director). (1972). Father Sun, Sister Moon [Motion picture]. United States: Paramount Pictures.

Lucas, R. (1986). *Secrets of the Chinese herbalists*. Englewood Cliffs, NJ: Prentice Hall.

Ludtke, R., & Rutten A. (2008, October). The conclusions on the effectiveness of homeopathy highly depend on the set of analysed trials. Journal of Clinical Epidemiology. doi: 10.1016/j.jclinepi.2008.06/015.

Lust, J. (2001). *The herb book*. New York, NY: Bantam Books.

Mann, J. (1980). *Secrets of life extension*. Berkeley, CA: And/Or Press.

McCaffrey, A.M., Pugh, G. F., & O'Connor, B. B. (2007). Understanding patient preference for integrative medical care: results from patient focus groups. Journal of General Internal Medicine, 22(11), 1500-5.

McDougall, J., & McDougall. (1983). *The McDugall Plan.* Piscataway, NJ: New Century.

McGregor, H.E. (2004, Dec 10) Squeeze in a yoga class while you wait for your prescription; Natural pharmacies offer herbalist, naturopaths, and more to a public eager for alternative therapies. Los Angeles Times, part F.

Mendelsohn, R. S. (1990). How to raise a healthy child…in spite of your doctor. New York, NY: Ballantine Books.

Meyerowitz, S. (1997). Green health foods in a bottle. Retrieved from http://lightparty.com/Health/greenfoods.html

Miscall, S. (n.d.). Scott Miscall. Retrieved from http://EzineArticles.com/?expert=Scott_Miscall

Miscall, S. (2009, June 3). The scientific evidence of mineral deficiency in food. Retrieved from: http://www.thefreelibrary.com/The+Scientific+Evidence+of+Mineral+Deficiency+in+-Food-a01073958478

Murray C., & Waters, K. (2002). Illuminations from the Bhagavad Gita. New York, NY: Harper and Row.

National Bureau of Economic Research. (2009). Low life expectancy in the United States: Is the health care system at fault? Cambridge, MA: Preston & Ho.

Netter, F. H. (1986). CIBA collection of medical illustration (Vol 1, nervous system). Summit, NJ: CIBA

Nissen, T. (n.d.) Environmental toxicity: An alternative way of assessing heavy metals. Retrieved from http://www.gwarehouse.com.au/articles/heavy-metals-Disease/environmental-toxicity-alternative-way-assessing-heavy-metals-dr-thoma

Odent, M. (1994). *Birth reborn.* New York, NY: Pantheon Books.

Ogle, K. A., & Bullock, J. D. (1980). Children with allergic rhinitis and/or bronchial asthma treated with elimination diet: a five-year follow-up. Annals of Allergy, 44, 273.

Oppenheimer, G.M. (1992). The making of a chronic disease. Berkeley, CA: University of California Press.

Organization for Economic Co-operation and Development (OECD). (2008). OECD health data 2008: How does the United States compare? Paris.

Ott, J. (2000). Health and Light: The extraordinary study that shows how light affects your Health and emotional well being. New York, NY: Simon & Schuster.

Papus. (2000). *The Qabalah*. New York, NY: Samuel Weiser.

Passwater, R. (1991). *The new super-nutrition*. New York, NY: Pocket Books.

Patton, C. (1990) *Inventing AIDS*. New York, NY: Routledge Books.

Perle. S. (2010, April 17). Science, sometimes - stroke and chiropractic. Retrieved from: Http://smperle.blogspot.com/2010/04/science-sometimes-stroke-and.html

Pierce, J. C. (2002). *The crack in the cosmic egg*. New York, NY: Washington Square Press.

Pike, D. K. (1976). Cosmic unfoldment: The individualizing process as mirrored in the life of Jesus. San Diego, CA: L.P. Publications.

Poison. (n.d.). Retrieved from http://www.chimachine4u.com/poison.html

Prabhavananda, S. (1980). The Sermon on the Mount According to Vedanta. New York, NY: New American Library.

Prabhavanada, S. (2002). *The Upanishads: Breath of the eternal*. New York, NY: Signet.

Prasad, R. (2007, November) Homoeopathy booming in India. *Lancet, 370*, 1679-80.

Preston, S., & Wang, H. (2006). Changing sex differentials in mortality in the United States: The role of cohort smoking patterns. Demography, 43, 413–34.

Pringle, P. (2003, Feb 21). Not-so corner drugstore. *Los Angeles Times*, p. 1

Project Health. (2006). Retrieved from: http://www.lightparty.com/Health/PROJHEAL.html

Randi, J. (2009, December 15). AGW revisited. Retrieved from: Http://www.randi.org/site/index.php/swift-blog/805-agw-revisited.html

Rappoport, J. (1988). *AIDS inc.: Scandal of the century*. Foster City, CA: Human Energy Press.

Russel, P. (2010). *The brain book*. New York, NY: E. P. Dutton.

Restak, R. (1982). *The brain: The last frontier*. New York, NY: Warner Books.

Rau, H. (1976) *Healing with herbs*. New York, NY: Arco Publishers.

Ravnvskov, U. (2009). The cholesterol hoax. Retrieved from Http://www.knowthelies.com/node/3489

Rawson, P. (1973). Tao, the Eastern philosophy of time and change. New York, NY: Avon Books.

Reinersten, M. (1978). High school astrology: A basic manual of occult science. New York, NY: Union Press.

Rose, J. (2002) *Herbs and things*. New York, NY: Grosset and Dunlap.

Rowe, A. H., & Young, E. J. (1959). bronchial asthma due to food allergy alone in ninety-five patients. Journal of the American Medical Association, 169, 1158.

Rutten, A., & Stolper, C. F. (2008, October). The 2005 meta-analysis of homeopathy: The importance of post-publication data. Homeopathy. doi:10.1016/j.homp.2008.09/008.

Samuels, M. (1974). *The well body book*. New York, NY: Random House.

Sekhon, J.S. (2010). *Statistics and Health Care Reform in the United States.* Retrieved from http://sekhon.berkeley.edu/papers/SignificanceSekhon.pdf

Selye, M. (1978). *The stress of life*. New York, NY: McGraw-Hill Books.

Shealy, C.N. (1975). *Occult medicine can save your life*. New York, NY: Dial/Delacourte.

Shealy, C. N. & Myss, C. M. (1988). *AIDS: Passageway to transformation*. New York, NY: Stillpoint Publishing.

Shealy, C.N. (1990). *90 days to self health*. New York, NY: Bantam Books.

Shute, W. (1980). Dr. Wilfred E. Shute's complete…updated Vitamin E book. New Carman, CT: Keats Publishing.

Siegel, B. (1990). *Love, medicine & miracles*. New York, NY: Harper Perennial.

Sloan, F.A., & Hsieh, C.R. (Eds.). (2007). The Pharmaceutical sector in health care in pharmaceutical innovation: Incentives, competition, and cost-benefit analysis in international perspective, New York, NY: Cambridge University Press.

Souza, T. A. (2008). Differential diagnosis and management for the chiropractor. Gaithersburg Maryland: Aspen Publishing.

Soyka, F. (1991). *The ion effect*. New York, NY: Bantam Books.

Spearman, N. (1975). Gold of a thousand mornings, London, England: Spearman.

Stano, M. (1993). A comparison of health care costs for chiropractic and medical patients. Journal of Manipulative and Physiological Therapeutics, 16(5), 291-299.

Stone, I. (1974). The healing factor: Vitamin C against disease. New York, NY: Grosset and Dunlap.

Straus, R.A. (2000). *Strategic self-hypnosis*. Englewood Cliffs, NJ: Prentice Hall.

Strobel Technologies. (2006). Supple-pedic. [Advertisement]. Retrieved from: Http://www.prescriptionbeds.com

Szekely, E. B. (1977). The Essene Jesus: A revaluation from the Dead Sea scrolls. San Diego, CA: Academy Books.

Szekely, E. B. (1981a). The Essene gospel of peace: Books 1-4. San Diego, CA: Academy Books.

Szekeley, E. B. (1981b). Guide to the Eessene way of biogenic living. San Diego, CA: Academy Books.

Temin, P. (1980). Taking your medicine: Drug regulation in the United States. Cambridge, MA: Harvard University Press.

Terrett, A. (1987). Vascular accidents from cervical spine manipulation: a report on 107 cases. Journal of the Australian Chiropractors' Association, 17(1), 15-23.

Terrett, A., & Leynhans, G.J. (1992). Complications from manipulations of the low back. Journal of the Australian Chiropractors' Association, 4, 129-140.

Tompkins, P., & Bird, C. (1989). *The secret life of plants*. New York, NY: Avon Books.

Troward, T. (1915). The creative process in the individual. New York, NY: Dodd, Mead & Company

Ullman, Dana. (2010, August 10). The case for homeopathic medicine: Consider the historical And scientific evidence. Retrieved from: Www.naturalnews.com/029419_homeopathic_medicine_evidence.html#ixzz1ppi9ka5z

United States Department of Agriculture (USDA) Food & Nutrition Center, http://www.nal.usda.gov/

Vickers A., & Smith, C. (2006). Homoeopathic oscillococcinum for preventing and treating influenza and influenza-like syndromes. Cochrane Database of Systematic Reviews, 3. doe: 10.1002/14651858.CD001957.pub3.

Vitamin and mineral supplement fact sheets. (n.d.). Retrieved from http://ods.od.nih.gov/factsheets/list-VitaminsMinerals/

Vitamins and supplements lifestyle guide. (2012). [Table: RDAs and ULs for Vitamins and Minerals]. Retrieved from http://www.webmd.com/vitamins-and-supplements/lifestyle-guide-11/vitamins-minerals-how-much-should-you-take?page=2

Walker, M. (1993). *Dirty Medicine: Science, Big Business and the Assault on Health Care*. Slingshot Press, London, 1993. ISBN: 0951964607

Walker, N. W. (1995). Colon health: The key to vibrant life. Phoenix, AZ: O'Sullivan, Woodside and Company.

Weinberger, S. (1990) Healing within: The complete colon health guide. Larkspur, CA: Colon Health Center.

Weishan, M. 1999. The new traditional garden: a practical guide to creating and restoring authentic American gardens for homes of all ages. Ballantine Publishing Group, New York.

Weissman, J. S., & Bigby, J. A. (2009). Massachusetts health care reform—near-universal coverage at what cost? New England Journal of Medicine, 361, 2012–5.

White, J. (1981). *Jump for joy.* La Jolla, CA: University of California, San Diego Press.

Whitelaw, W.A. (2002). *Proceedings of the 11th annual history of medicine day.* University of Calgary Press. Retrieved from http://www.ucalgary.ca/uofc/Others/HOM/Dayspapers2002.pdf

Whittle, T. G., & Wieland, R. (n.d.). The story behind Prozac…the killer drug. Retrieved from: Http://www.pnc.com.au/~cafmr/newsl/prozac.html

Wilhelm, R., Baynes, C., Wilhelm, H., & Jung, C.G. (1967). The I-Ching: The book of changes. Princeton NJ: Princeton University Press.

Williams, R., & Kalita, D. (1977). Physician's handbook on orthomolecular medicine. New York, NY: Keats Publishing Company.

Williams, R. (1981). *Nutrition against disease.* New York, NY: Bantam Books.

Willner, R. E. (1994). *Deadly deception.* Boca Raton, FL: Peltic Publishing.

Wilson, D. (2010, March 31). Pfizer gives details on payments to doctors. The New York Times. Retrieved from: http://www.nytimes.com/2010/04/01/business/01payments.html?Pagewanted=print

Woolhandler, S., Campbell, T., & Himmelstein, D.U. (2003). Costs of health care administration in the United States and Canada. New England Journal of Medicine, 349, 768–75.

Yates, R.G., & Lamping, D. L, (1988). Effects of chiropractic treatment on blood pressure and anxiety: a randomized, controlled trial. Journal of Manipulative and Physiological Therapeutics, 11(6): 484-488.

Younkin, P. (2010). *A Healthy Business: The evolution of the U.S. market for prescription drugs.* UC Berkeley: Sociology. Retrieved from: http://escholarship.org/uc/item/7zx4c61f

www.ingramcontent.com/pod-product-compliance
Lightning Source LLC
Chambersburg PA
CBHW080536170426
43195CB00016B/2576